MW01633014

THE FATHER'S WILL

The Father's Will

Christ's Crucifixion and the Goodness of God

NICHOLAS E. LOMBARDO, O.P.

OXFORD
UNIVERSITY PRESS

Great Clarendon Street, Oxford, OX2 6DP,
United Kingdom

Oxford University Press is a department of the University of Oxford. It furthers the University's objective of excellence in research, scholarship, and education by publishing worldwide. Oxford is a registered trade mark of Oxford University Press in the UK and in certain other countries

First Edition published in 2013

Impression: 3

Published in the United States of America by Oxford University Press
198 Madison Avenue, New York, NY 10016, United States of America

British Library Cataloguing in Publication Data
Data available

Library of Congress Control Number: 2013938310

ISBN 978–0–19–968858–6

Printed in Great Britain by
Clays Ltd, St Ives plc

To my father, Gaetano Lombardo

Christ's passion, like a key, has opened for us the understanding of sacred scripture.

—Stephen Langton, *Commentary on Micah*

Jonah is a type of Christ. The ship is the synagogue of the Jews; the captain is Moses; the sailors are the prophets; the sea is the suffering that we all must undergo; the lot is the will of the Father, according to which Christ was thrown into the sea of sufferings and entered the belly of the great sea monster of death. There he remained for three days.

—Hesychius of Jerusalem, *Commentary on the Minor Prophets*

Preface

When Christians hear the story of Jesus in the garden of Gethsemane, asking for his cup to pass from him, but then surrendering to the Father's will, they often think of their own lives, and their own suffering. They know instinctively that the Father's will for Jesus sheds light on the Father's will for them. They know that Jesus' suffering illuminates their suffering, and that the reason Jesus takes up his cross somehow relates to the reason they must take up theirs. Accordingly, theologies of redemption do not simply offer solutions to a theological puzzle. They answer numerous existential questions. Of these, the question that matters most is fairly simple: is God the Father with me as I take up my cross, or is he orchestrating my crucifixion? This book works towards a theology of redemption that can safeguard the goodness of God against any appearance of divine injustice, and thus affirm that God the Father is always with us, always on our side.

The best way forward, this book argues, lies in the recovery of the ancient theological category of ransom. According to the early Christians, Christ's crucifixion was a ransom that liberated us from the powers of evil, sin, and death. The theological category of ransom has long since been eclipsed, but it is the preferred category of the New Testament for interpreting the specific event of the crucifixion; it also lies at the etymological origins of the word "redemption" (in Latin, the word for ransom is *redemptio*). The category of ransom has many advantages. It frames the drama of salvation as a straightforward story of good triumphing over evil and death. It makes the goodness of God more evident. It also makes it easier to see God the Father as the author of our salvation, rather than a stern judge who must be placated. And since the category of ransom traces back to Jesus' saying in the Gospels about giving his life "as a ransom for many" (Mark 10:45; Matt 20:28), it has great claim to interpret the crucifixion in the way Jesus himself interpreted it.

By approaching the crucifixion from the perspective of the Father's will, this book also addresses the place of God the Father in Christian theology and culture. Many theologies of redemption inadvertently put God the Father in a negative light. These theologies make it more difficult to relate to him as Jesus relates to him in the Gospels. They also contribute to the ambivalence that some Christians feel about addressing God as Father. This book offers a corrective to such theologies. It takes as its point of departure Jesus' words to Philip: "He who has seen me has seen the Father" (John 14:9). There is no mercy visible in the Son that was not present first in the Father, and any theology that would give the slightest impression otherwise must be rejected—charitably, but firmly. What is at stake is nothing less than being able to hear the Father's words at Jesus' baptism spoken also to us, as they in fact are, through our baptism: "You are my beloved Son; with you I am well pleased" (Mark 1:11).

* * *

This book is the fruit of many conversations, and it is a privilege and a pleasure to offer my thanks and appreciation to all those who through their words and support have helped bring it to completion. Above all, I would like to thank Janet Martin Soskice, under whose supervision this book began as a doctoral thesis at the University of Cambridge, for her encouragement, insight, and guidance. I would also like to thank John Proctor, who supervised my work on the initial drafts of the scripture chapters with great generosity, and David Ford and Karen Kilby, my examiners, for their comments and suggestions. I am also grateful to the Dominican community of Blackfriars, Cambridge, for their warm welcome, and for making my stay in England thoroughly enjoyable.

Along the way many read drafts or portions of the manuscript, and I would like to express my great appreciation to all those who shared with me their comments, criticisms, and suggestions. While the flaws of this book remain entirely my own, their generosity has spared both my readers and myself from many errors, and their thoughtful comments significantly inspired and clarified my thinking. I am particularly grateful to Nicholas Ingham, O.P., for his detailed comments on the manuscript at multiple stages. I am also very grateful to Margaret Atkins, O.S.A., Amanda Perreau-Saussine Ezcurra (who sadly died last year), Kevin Flannery, S.J., Fergus Kerr, O.P., William Mattison, Francesca Aran Murphy, Benedict Viviano, O.P., Bruce Williams, O.P., and an anonymous reader for Oxford University Press.

Many others read various sections and chapters, and for their comments, suggestions, and questions I would also like to thank Rosemary Boyle, Clement Burns, O.P., Romanus Cessario, O.P., Mark Clark, Sarah Coakley, Barnabas Davis, O.P., Philip Devine, Hugh Vincent Dyer, O.P., Gilles Emery, O.P., Boniface Endorf, O.P., John Ford, C.S.C., Ky Heinze, Andrew Hofer, O.P., Aidan Nichols, O.P., Brian Kennedy, Matthew Levering, William Loewe, Peter Martens, Michele Ransil, C.D.P., Stephen Ryan, O.P., Eleonore Stump, Catherine Tkacz, Robert Sokolowski, Justin Taylor, S.M., Tarmo Toom, Joseph Vnuk, O.P., Susan Wessel, Thomas Joseph White, O.P., and Celia Wolf-Devine. Parts of this manuscript were presented in papers and lectures, and I am grateful for the questions and comments received afterward. Special thanks are also owed to Michele Ransil, C.D.P., for her exceptional (and exceptionally speedy) proofreading, and the late Louis Bataillon, O.P., who, immediately after hearing me describe the topic of my research, shared with me the quotation from Stephen Langton that serves as the first of its epigraphs.

As mentioned above, this book is the fruit of many conversations. In a special way, it is the fruit of conversations with my father. What I have learned from him has made everything else possible. This book is dedicated to him with gratitude and admiration.

Nicholas E. Lombardo, O.P.
The Catholic University of America
Washington, D.C.
May 2013

Contents

Introduction 1

Part I. Philosophical Prolegomena

1. Intending and Willing 21
2. Moral Value and Moral Obligation 42
3. Double Effect Reasoning 61
4. The Ethics of Self-Sacrifice 74
5. God's Will, Moral Evil, and the Crucifying of Christ 80

Part II. New Testament Evidence

6. Jesus' Attitude Toward His Death 95
7. The Crucifixion in God's Plan of Salvation 132

Part III. Theological Evaluation

8. Anselm and *Cur Deus homo* 145
9. Abelard's Response to Anselm 168
10. The Devil's Ransom Revisited 181

Epilogue 240

Bibliography 243
Index 259

Introduction

"You are not a God who takes pleasure in evil," the fifth psalm proclaims, and for two millennia Christians have prayed these words with utter confidence. And yet Christians also believe that the crucifixion of an innocent man happened according to God's will. The implicit tension between these theological convictions is not easily resolved. On the one hand, it seems impossible to imagine a good God approving moral evil, even in the slightest degree. On the other hand, Christians have always seen the cross of Christ at the center of God's plan of salvation. Together these two intuitions give rise to a theological difficulty: the problem of God's will and Christ's crucifixion. Through a combination of philosophical analysis, scriptural exegesis, and theological evaluation, this study aims to define the problem and work towards a solution.

THE PROBLEM OF GOD'S WILL AND CHRIST'S CRUCIFIXION

The problem of God's will and Christ's crucifixion crystallizes in Jesus' prayer in the garden of Gethsemane. In the garden of Gethsemane the night before his crucifixion, Jesus asks his Father to take away the cup of his suffering, but then says, "not my will, but yours, be done" (Luke 22:42). Shortly afterward Judas arrives, and his arrival reveals something important about the Father's will. Nonetheless, much remains obscure. The sheer fact of Christ's crucifixion shows only that God was not willing to spare his Son. It does not shed any light on the positive content of the Father's will, nor does it explain why God did not intervene.

The words of Jesus elsewhere in the Gospels offer only limited assistance in making sense of God's intentions. Although Jesus repeatedly predicts his crucifixion and repeatedly affirms its necessity, he does not offer any straightforward explanation for either its necessity or its salvific efficacy. The other books of the New Testament make up for his reticence with an abundance of theological commentary, but the sheer variety of their metaphors and explanations, and their occasional obscurity, make them difficult to interpret. Consequently, while Christians have always maintained that Christ's crucifixion plays a crucial role in God's plan of salvation, and that it happens according to God's will, no consensus exists about its exact function in the overcoming of sin and death. The ecumenical councils of the first millennia make many doctrinal affirmations about the person of Christ, but, remarkably, they say nothing about the precise way his crucifixion accomplishes humanity's redemption.

Nevertheless, while theologians rarely focus explicitly on the problem of God's will and Christ's crucifixion, the place of Christ's crucifixion in God's plan of salvation has been a perennial source of wonder and even disquiet. Since God redeems us through the crucifixion, does this mean God condones his Son's crucifixion, or even secretly orchestrates it? Fascination with the role of Judas may be the most common way these questions have surfaced among Christians. On the one hand, Judas' betrayal of his Master is reprehensible; on the other hand, Christ's crucifixion, and therefore humanity's redemption, happens through Judas' betrayal. In what sense, then, did Judas not do what God wanted him to do? Was his betrayal a "happy fault," and has he been unfairly reviled? The recently discovered Gospel of Judas, a gnostic gospel from the second century, indicates that these questions—although absent from the New Testament—surfaced very early in Christian history. The Gospel of Judas presents Judas in a positive light as the apostle with the most insight into Jesus. Among other things, it recounts a secret conversation between Judas and Jesus, in which Jesus seems to signal his approval of Judas' coming betrayal.[1] While this gnostic gospel does not represent mainstream Christianity,[2] and in fact was roundly condemned by Irenaeus for its positive portrayal of Judas,[3] its sheer existence at such an early date demonstrates how easily the Gospel narratives give rise to questions about the role of Judas in God's plan of salvation. These questions continue to fascinate. For example, while pointedly refusing to minimize Judas' guilt, Karl Barth maintains that in his act of

[1] Partly due to some missing text in the sole extant manuscript, scholars disagree about the proper interpretation and translation of the Gospel of Judas, and especially about its portrayal of Judas. Most see the portrayal as positive, but others disagree. The reading of the Gospel of Judas given here—which sees its portrayal of Judas as strikingly positive—follows the National Geographic translation in Rodolphe Kasser and Gregor Wurst, eds., *The Gospel of Judas, Critical Edition* (Washington, DC: National Geographic Society, 2007). For a critique of the National Geographic translation, which argues that the Gospel of Judas in fact contains a strongly negative portrayal of Judas, see April D. DeConick, *The Thirteenth Apostle: What the Gospel of Judas Really Says*, Rev. ed. (London: Continuum, 2009).

[2] For an appraisal of the Gospel of Judas and its relation to mainstream early Christianity, see Simon Gathercole, *The Gospel of Judas: Rewriting Early Christianity* (Oxford: Oxford University Press, 2007).

[3] Irenaeus, *Adversus haereses*, 1.31.1.

betrayal Judas is a privileged agent of God's will. "In one sense," he writes, "Judas is the most important figure in the New Testament apart from Jesus. For he, and he alone of the apostles, was actively at work in this decisive situation, in the accomplishment of what was God's will and what became the content of his Gospel."[4]

In a less explicit manner, questions about God's will and Christ's crucifixion also surface in speculation about what we might call the "mechanics" of redemption, that is, the precise causal process by which the crucifixion brings about humanity's redemption. The New Testament strongly affirms the crucifixion's salvific efficacy, but it does not fully explain it. Consequently, to greater or lesser degree, theologians have always been interested in clarifying the mechanics of redemption. In the course of their speculation, they often address the problem of God's apparent injustice to his Son, and thus, obliquely, the problem of God's will and Christ's crucifixion. In recent decades, theologians have been giving renewed attention to the mechanics of redemption. This renewed attention has awakened profound disagreements about the theology of redemption. While many theologians defend the received interpretations of their respective theological traditions, others have challenged them, and still others have offered new and innovative proposals.[5] Among Catholic authors, the scapegoat theory of René Girard, a French literary theorist, has been particularly influential, especially through its reception among theologians such as Raymond Schwager.[6] According to Girard, by willingly accepting his death on the cross, Jesus disrupted a sociological mechanism for achieving internal cohesion at the expense of scapegoated victims, and thus paved the way for authentic social harmony. While Girard's theory has not found anything approaching universal acceptance, no other recent proposal by a Catholic author has generated as much interest among Catholics and Protestants alike. The soteriology of Edward Schillebeeckx, a Flemish Dominican theologian, has also been influential. Emphasizing that God only permits "negativity," Schillebeeckx rejects as blasphemous the claim "that God himself required the death of Jesus as compensation for what *we* make of our history," and argues instead that "we are not redeemed *thanks to*

[4] Karl Barth, *Church Dogmatics*, trans. G. W. Bromiley et al., vol. II/2 (Edinburgh: T & T Clark, 1957), 502.

[5] For an overview of major themes in contemporary theology of the redemption, see Stephen T. Davis, Daniel Kendall, and Gerald O'Collins, eds., *The Redemption: An Interdisciplinary Symposium on Christ the Redeemer* (Oxford: Oxford University Press, 2004).

[6] See René Girard, *The Scapegoat* (Baltimore: John Hopkins University Press, 1986); René Girard, *Things Hidden Since the Foundation of the World* (Stanford: Stanford University Press, 1987); René Girard, *I See Satan Fall Like Lightning*, trans. James G. Williams (Maryknoll, NY: Orbis Books, 2001); Raymund Schwager, *Must There Be Scapegoats? Violence and Redemption in the Bible*, trans. Maria L. Assad (San Francisco: Harper and Row, 1987); Raymund Schwager, *Jesus in the Drama of Salvation: Toward a Biblical Doctrine of Redemption*, trans. James G. Williams and Paul Haddon (New York: Crossroad, 1999).

the death of Jesus but *despite* it."[7] His approach to the crucifixion has appealed especially to those looking to stress God's solidarity with the suffering. Among Protestant authors, theological controversy centers on penal substitution, a theory of redemption developed by early Protestant reformers, in which Jesus endures the Father's just punishment in our place. Some criticize the theory; others defend it; but this particular theory of redemption, because of its historical importance to Protestant theology, has assumed a central place in contemporary theological discussion.[8] Evangelical theologians are among its strongest defenders,[9] and feminist theologians have been particularly outspoken in their criticism.[10] While some general trends can be identified along confessional lines, the battle lines are not however clearly drawn, and the conversation is remarkably ecumenical. Protestant, Catholic, and Orthodox theologians frequently draw on each other's work, sometimes precisely in order to argue against the competing views of their own coreligionists. The lack of consensus about the mechanics of redemption, even among coreligionists, and the widespread interest in the radically new theory of René Girard, point to pervasive, "ecumenical" dissatisfaction with received theories of redemption. And since this dissatisfaction often stems from inadequate solutions to the problem of God's apparent injustice to his Son, it also implies pervasive dissatisfaction with received interpretations of God's will and Christ's crucifixion.

The problem of God's will and Christ's crucifixion also surfaces in hypothetical, counterfactual questions about the inevitability of the Incarnation. These questions first emerged during the Middle Ages in the wake of Anselm's theory of redemption, and they continue to be a locus of theological speculation.[11] Alexander of Hales, Albert the Great, John Duns Scotus, and the bulk of

[7] Edward Schillebeeckx, *Christ*, trans. John Bowden (New York: Crossroad Publishing Company, 1980), 728–9. In my reflections on God's will and Christ's crucifixion, Schillebeeckx's emphatic distancing of God from moral evil, especially in the last phrase of this quotation, proved particularly stimulating. Nonetheless, for reasons that should become clear as this study progresses, I find the phrase problematic in some important respects.

[8] See, for example, Derek Tidball, David Hilborn, and Justin Thacker, eds., *The Atonement Debate: Papers from the London Symposium on the Theology of Atonement* (Grand Rapids, MI: Zondervan, 2008). See also Mark D. Baker and Joel B. Green, *Recovering the Scandal of the Cross: Atonement in New Testament and Contemporary Contexts* (Downer's Grove, IL: InterVarsity Press, 2011.

[9] See, for example, Steve Jeffrey, Mike Ovey, and Andrew Sach, *Pierced for Our Transgressions: Rediscovering the Glory of Penal Subsitution* (Nottingham: InterVarsity Press, 2007).

[10] See, for example, Joanne Carlson Brown and Carole R. Bohn, eds., *Christianity, Patriarchy and Abuse: A Feminist Critique* (New York: Pilgrim Press, 1989); Mary Grey, *Redeeming the Dream: Feminism, Redemption and Christian Tradition* (London: S.P.C.K., 1990); Arnfridur Gudmundsdottir, *Meeting God on the Cross: Feminist Christologies and the Theology of the Cross* (New York: Oxford).

[11] With the exception of one or two patristic authors, Rupert of Deutz (1075–1129) was the first theologian to argue that God would have become man even if we had not sinned. After Rupert, who was writing shortly after Anselm, interest in hypothetical questions about the inevitability of the Incarnation became widespread. See Georges Florovsky, "Cur Deus Homo?

the Franciscan tradition maintained that God would have become man even if we had not sinned. Bonaventure, Thomas Aquinas, and the bulk of the Dominican tradition maintained that the Incarnation is intrinsically ordered to our redemption, or at least that sacred scripture gives no reason to think otherwise. Each position has its strengths. The Franciscan position more easily avoids the problem of God's apparent injustice because the crucifixion becomes a side effect of the Incarnation, rather than its principal objective. The Dominican position avoids committing itself to counterfactual theories, and it harmonizes better with sacred scripture's silence on the supposed inevitability of the Incarnation. For the purposes of this study, however, the theological differences between the Franciscan and Dominican positions are less striking than their common interest in these questions—which relate so closely to the problem of God's will and Christ's crucifixion.

These questions about Judas, the mechanics of redemption, and the inevitability of the Incarnation each witness in their own way to the perennial fascination surrounding the problem of God's will and Christ's crucifixion. These questions, though, do not address the problem explicitly. Likewise, historically, most theological reflection has also stopped short of engaging it directly. This study seeks to address the lacuna. It engages the problem of God's will and Christ's crucifixion directly and explicitly. It does not, however, offer a definitive solution; that would require a comprehensive theology of redemption, something well beyond its scope. Rather, this study provides tools for thinking about the problem with more precision and for judging proposed solutions. Then, by applying these tools to three influential interpretations of the crucifixion, it makes some suggestions for moving the question forward. It argues especially for the recovery of certain patristic approaches to the crucifixion. In the process, it aims to illuminate other issues in the theology of redemption.

GOD'S WILL AND THE FATHER'S WILL

Before proceeding, we must address some Trinitarian and Christological issues that complicate the problem of God's will and Christ's crucifixion.

The Motive for the Incarnation," in *Collected Works* (1976), 163–70; Donald Goergen, "Albert the Great and Thomas Aquinas on the Motive of the Incarnation," *The Thomist* 44 (1980): 523n3; Ilia Delio, "Revisiting the Franciscan Doctrine of Christ," *Theological Studies* 64 (2003): 3–23; Daniel P. Horan, "How Original Was Scotus on the Incarnation? Reconsidering the History of the Absolute Predestination of Christ in Light of Robert Grosseteste," *The Heythrop Journal* 52 (2011): 374–91.

The timing of their sudden popularity indicates that these hypothetical questions emerged in response to Anselm's theory of redemption. The timing may also indicate an undercurrent of dissatisfaction with Anselm's theory. It suggests that even theologians who embraced Anselm's approach to redemption recognized that his theory created new problems and raised new questions.

When Jesus prays in the garden of Gethsemane, he addresses his Father, not his God, and he accepts his Father's will, not God's will. This important detail raises some thorny questions. Can we speak interchangeably of the Father's will and God's will? That is, does the undivided Trinity have one divine will? And if so, in what sense can God the Son will something different from God the Father, as he appears to do in the garden of Gethsemane? Depending on how we answer these questions, focusing on God's will rather than the Father's will might yield significantly different results—a possibility that would have serious methodological implications for this study.

Over the course of several centuries, patristic theologians worked out answers to these questions, eventually achieving a consensus which continues to enjoy widespread (though not universal) support. The first part of the puzzle was resolved relatively quickly. From early on, orthodox patristic authors, both eastern and western, resoundingly affirmed that Father, Son, and Holy Spirit share one divine will.[12] "They are one in their one will," Ephrem writes, "but two in their two names."[13] In his *Fourth Theological Oration*, Gregory of Nazianzus explains that Father and Son have one will, just as they have one Godhead.[14] Likewise, Gregory of Nyssa maintains that the Father and Son share one will because they have one common nature.[15] In the West, Augustine takes a similar line. In the *De Trinitate*, he writes, "Father and Son have but one will and are indivisible in their working."[16] The patristic consensus is echoed by the Second Council of Constantinople. Although it does not mention the divine will explicitly, the Council of Constantinople nonetheless claims that Father, Son, and Holy Spirit have "one power and authority."[17]

The second part of the puzzle, the question of how the Son could will something different from his Father, took longer to resolve. After concluding that Father and Son share one divine will, patristic authors struggled to explain the apparent conflict of wills between Christ and his Father in the Gethsemane

[12] On the unity of the divine will in patristic theology, see Lewis Ayres, *Nicaea and its Legacy: An Approach to Fourth-Century Trinitarian Theology* (Oxford: Oxford University Press, 2004), esp. 235, 45, 89–96, 358; Demetrios Bathrellos, *The Byzantine Christ: Person, Nature, and Will in the Christology of Saint Maximus the Confessor* (Oxford: Oxford University Press, 2004), 140–7. For a study of the patristic doctrine of divine simplicity that undergirds this doctrinal understanding, see Andrew Radde-Gallwitz, *Basil of Caesarea, Gregory of Nyssa, and the Transformation of Divine Simplicity* (Oxford: Oxford University Press, 2009), esp. 154–69, 212–18.

[13] Ephrem, *Sermons on Faith*, 2 (CSCO 212–13), as translated in Ayres, *Nicaea and its Legacy*, 235.

[14] Gregory of Nazianzus, *Theological Orations*, 30.12.

[15] Gregory of Nyssa, *Against Apollinarius*, 31–2.

[16] *De Trinitate*, 2.9 in Augustine, *The Trinity*, ed. John E. Rotelle, trans. Edmund Hill (Hyde Park, NY: New City Press, 1991), 103. Augustine repeats this point in *De Trinitate* 4.12: "Father and Son are one not only by equality of substance but also by identity of will" (161). See also *De Trinitate*, 4.30, 13.15, 15.12.

[17] Second Council of Constantinople, in Norman P. Tanner, ed. *Decrees of the Ecumenical Councils*, 2 vols. (Washington, DC: Georgetown University Press, 1990), 114.

prayer. At first, in order to safeguard Christ's divinity, orthodox patristic authors downplayed the significance of Christ's human will, without denying its existence, and emphasized his divine will.[18] For example, Gregory of Nyssa attributes Christ's reluctance to his human will and his obedience to his divine will—thus passing over the question of whether Christ also obeys his Father with his human will.[19]

Then, in the seventh century, controversy erupted, forcing a more satisfactory resolution. Seeking to reconcile Christians who had rejected the Council of Chalcedon, the Byzantine emperor and the patriarch of Constantinople started to promote the idea that there was only one will in Christ, namely, his divine will. The anti-Chalcedonians had rejected Chalcedon on the grounds that it jeopardized the unity of Christ's person, thus undermining his divinity. Consequently, the emperor and the patriarch welcomed this monothelite teaching as a concession to their concerns. Others, however, immediately rejected it as an unorthodox innovation. They argued to the contrary that Christ possessed a human will in addition to his divine will. Maximus the Confessor became their principal spokesperson.

In articulating the dyothelite position, Maximus achieved a synthesis and terminological precision that had eluded earlier patristic authors.[20] He affirms, first, that Christ has a human will with its own proper dynamism and teleology, as the necessary consequence of being fully human. Therefore, Maximus argues, when Christ defers to his Father's will during the Gethsemane prayer, he does so not only with a divine will, but also with a human will acting from its own inner dynamism. Yet Maximus also maintains that Christ's human will is moved by Christ's divine person, and indeed by his divine will. By this delicate balancing act, Maximus sought to affirm the fullness of Christ's humanity without undercutting the unity of his divine person.[21] Although Maximus died in exile for his defense of dyothelite Christology, his theological synthesis was implicitly endorsed by the Third Council of Constantinople (680–681) soon after his death. The Council states:

> And we proclaim equally two natural volitions or wills in him and two principles of action which undergo no division, no change, no partition, no confusion, in

[18] For an overview of early patristic interpretation of the Gethsemane prayer, see Bathrellos, *The Byzantine Christ*, 140–7.

[19] Gregory of Nyssa, *Against Apollinarius*, 31–2.

[20] Maximus the Confessor, *Opusc.* 6, in Maximus the Confessor, *On the Cosmic Mystery of Jesus Christ*, trans. Paul M. Blowers and Robert Louis Wilken (Crestwood, NY: St. Vladimir's Press, 2003), 173–6; *Opusc. 7, 3* in Andrew Louth, *Maximus the Confessor* (London: Routledge, 1996), 180–98.

[21] This summary of Maximus' dyothelite Christology relies on Bathrellos, *The Byzantine Christ*, 99–174. For a discussion of Maximus' terminological distinctions regarding the concept of will, see John D. Madden, "The Authenticity of Early Definitions of Will (*Thelesis*)," in *Maximus Confessor*, ed. Felix Heinzer and Christoph Schonborn (Fribourg: Éditions Universitaires Fribourg Suisse, 1982), 61–79; Bathrellos, *The Byzantine Christ*, 117–29.

> accordance with the teaching of the holy fathers. And the two natural wills not in opposition, as the impious heretics said, far from it, but his human will following, and not resisting or struggling, rather in fact subject to his divine and all powerful will.[22]

Since this Council, dyothelite Christology has been doctrinally normative for most Christians and mostly uncontroversial. In hindsight, it has seemed obvious to most theologians that Christ could not be fully human if he lacked a human will or anything else proper to human nature.

This study takes as normative the Trinitarian and Christological doctrine worked out by patristic theologians and the early ecumenical councils. It presumes that the three Persons of the Trinity share one undivided will, just as they are one undivided substance. God's will does not differ from the Father's will, or the Son's will, or the Holy Spirit's will; there is only one divine will. Likewise, this study presumes that Jesus' prayer in the garden of Gethsemane does not express a tension between the Son's divine will and the Father's divine will, but only a tension between Christ's human will and the divine will shared equally by Father, Son, and Holy Spirit. Consequently, this study regards the problem of God's will and Christ's crucifixion as substantially identical to the problem of the Father's will and Christ's crucifixion. As far as this study is concerned, these two problems concern precisely the same theological difficulty and they do not require two separate investigations, let alone two different methodological approaches.

While this study takes the patristic consensus as normative, it remains alert to the possibility of alternative Trinitarian theologies, even among theologians who strive for conformity with the ecumenical councils. When necessary, therefore, the study draws attention to instances where God's will does not seem entirely interchangeable with the Father's will, or where God the Father's will differs from the divine will of the Son. Since the classical consensus is presumed, such instances are necessarily judged problematic.

OVERVIEW AND METHOD

In tackling the problem of God's will and Christ's crucifixion, this study confronts a number of interlocking questions and puzzles. Many seem simple—such as the question of what it means to say that God never wills moral evil—but actually are far from straightforward. They often require considerable background work to address adequately, sometimes in the domain of multiple disciplines. Their complexity and interconnectedness

[22] Third Council of Constantinople, in Tanner, ed. *Ecumenical Councils*, 128.

make it difficult to know where to begin. Many individual questions seem far removed from the problem of God's will and Christ's crucifixion, and yet they must be answered before any satisfactory solution can be proposed.

Among the various possible approaches to the problem of Gods' will and Christ's crucifixion, this study works from the ground up. It starts with basic philosophical and exegetical issues, and then gradually applies the results of these investigations to the problem of God's will and Christ's crucifixion. This methodology has significant advantages. By building in an orderly way toward a conclusion, it makes the argument more efficient and avoids redundancy and unnecessary repetition. This approach has limitations, however. It makes the full relevance of the earlier sections difficult to appreciate until the argument has run its course.

Before starting, therefore, it is helpful to look at this study's argument in reverse. Doing so makes it easier to appreciate where the argument is going from the beginning. Above all, the preliminary philosophical and exegetical investigations arise from observations about different theories of redemption. In some interpretations of the crucifixion, God seems to want the crucifixion to happen in a strong sense, as with Anselm's theory of redemption, in which Christ's crucifixion enables the Son to make satisfaction for the sins of humanity. In other interpretations, however, God seems to want the crucifixion to happen only in a qualified sense, as with Abelard's theory of redemption, in which Christ submits to his crucifixion in order to reveal God's love and inspire charity in Christian believers. Then there are still other interpretations where God does not will the crucifixion for its own sake, and yet allows men to crucify his Son as part of a strategy of deliberate provocation, so that he can overcome the power of evil and death. Examples include the interpretation of patristic authors variously known as the devil's ransom theory or the devil's rights theory and, arguably, theories of redemption that take their inspiration from René Girard.

While these observations capture something important about different theological interpretations of the crucifixion and their respective approaches to the problem of God's will and Christ's crucifixion, they remain little more than vague intuitions. They lack clarity and precision. What does it mean to say that God wants something to happen in a strong sense, or that he does not will something for its own sake? These expressions convey important intuitions, and at first glance their meaning seems transparent and obvious. But when we probe what these expressions mean, and especially when we try to use them to classify different theories of redemption, they become slippery and elusive. Before we can talk about what it means for God to want or will something to happen, we have to figure out what it means for anyone to want or will something to happen.

Likewise, Christians have a strong intuition that we can rule out any theory of redemption that would imply that God wills moral evil. But does this intuition have any practical implications? For those who think that moral value depends solely on God's will, no theological narrative could be ruled out as incompatible with God's will, because any human action that God willed would be morally good, by the very fact that God willed it. Likewise, for those who subscribe to consequentialist ethical theories, which determine the moral value of human actions from their effects, no human action that brought about the salvation of the world, no matter how unsavory, could ever be considered morally evil. And even assuming that moral value does not depend solely on God's will and that we reject consequentialist ethics, many human actions are downright difficult to evaluate, and thus difficult to rule out as incompatible with God's non-willing of moral evil.

Consequently, to rule out redemption theories for implying divine willing of moral evil, we must first address some fundamental questions about moral value. First of all, to defend the very possibility of ruling out such theories, we must show that moral value does not depend *solely* on either God's will or an action's consequences. Otherwise, redemption theories could never be judged to imply divine willing of moral evil, even in principle, and there would be no point in proceeding further. Then, we need principles for evaluating complex human actions and determining whether they involve moral evil. Many theological narratives of the crucifixion tell a story where it is difficult to say whether Christ commits an act of heroic self-sacrifice or something that approaches outright suicide. Therefore, we need tools to sort out when an action which terminates in the agent's death involves suicide, and thus moral evil, and when an action which terminates in the agent's death instead constitutes an act of heroic self-sacrifice. With these tools in hand, we will be in a position to distinguish between different narratives of Christ's crucifixion. It will allow us to rule out theological scenarios where Christ commits suicide, and it will also enable us to defend theological scenarios where Christ knowingly brings about his own death in an act of heroic self-sacrifice, without actually committing suicide.

It should be emphasized that this approach to ruling out theological narratives focuses entirely on human actions. Except for God the Son's actions in the flesh, which according to Council of Chalcedon are truly human actions, this approach does not consider divine actions. It rules out theological scenarios where Christ commits morally evil actions, or where God implicitly wills the moral evil of those crucifying Christ, but it does not try to evaluate divine actions. Ruling out God wanting a murderer to kill his victim is one thing; ruling out God hurling a lightning bolt at an innocent person is another. While we have solid grounds for judging human actions as evil and therefore incompatible with God's goodness, our grounds for making similar judgments about hypothetical divine actions are much shakier. The very possibility of describing divine actions in moral terms is disputed.[23] Having said that, there

[23] Brian Davies, for example, argues that it is category mistake to talk about God's goodness as though it involves moral goodness. See Brian Davies, "The Problem of Evil," in *The Philosophy of*

are strong reasons to think we can make moral judgments about hypothetical divine actions, and, say, rule out as incompatible with God's goodness the idea that God would ever create an intelligent being merely to torture it. This question, however, lies beyond the scope of this study; the problem of God's will and Christ crucifixion can be addressed without resolving it one way or the other.

Taken together, philosophical analysis of divine willing, moral value, and self-sacrifice lays important groundwork. It provides tools for ruling out theological interpretations of Christ's crucifixion as incompatible with God's goodness. It does not, however, suffice to resolve the problem in any definitive sense. It can only exclude tentative solutions as philosophically inadequate and logically incoherent. It cannot provide the basis for any positive proposal. For a positive proposal, we must turn to God's self-revelation in history, and thus move from philosophical prolegomena to the New Testament evidence.

Historical reconstruction of Christ's attitude toward his death is particularly important for the problem of God's will and Christ's crucifixion. Obviously Christ ended up crucified, but what were Christ's aims? In broad logical terms, how did his death relate to his intentions? And to what extent can we draw any firm conclusions from the historical evidence at our disposal? Since what Christ intended relates closely to what God willed, the answers to these questions lay down important parameters for any adequate solution to the problem of God's will and Christ's crucifixion. The New Testament, and especially the Gospels, constitutes the most significant source of historical information for determining what actually happened. Consequently, in order to work toward a positive proposal, and not simply exclude inadequate solutions, we need to examine the New Testament evidence and see what we can conclude about Christ's historical attitude toward his death.

For Christians, however, sacred scripture does not simply provide historical information; it also interprets Christ's crucifixion authoritatively. It thus reveals something about the positive content of God's will. Nevertheless, because sacred scripture itself requires interpretation, central topics such as redemption can be endlessly controversial and contentious. When it comes to mining sacred scripture for insights into the problem of God's will and Christ's crucifixion, it is therefore better and more efficient to focus on topics that are relatively simple and noncontroversial—such as what, in very broad terms, the New Testament says about the crucifixion in God's plan of salvation. By limiting the scope of our investigations, we can draw important conclusions from sacred scripture about God's will without getting bogged down in interminable exegesis. These conclusions can then

Religion: A Guide to the Subject, ed. Brian Davies (Washington, DC: Georgetown University Press, 1998), 177–82; Brian Davies, *The Reality of God and the Problem of Evil* (London: Continuum, 2006), 84–111, 251–5.

be used to make judgments about proposed solutions to the problem of God's will and Christ's crucifixion.

Having laid the groundwork with this philosophical analysis and these historical and exegetical investigations, we can return to theological interpretations of the crucifixion and judge their relative success or failure. Here, though, we face a dilemma. There have been countless theories of redemption and countless interpretations of the crucifixion. We cannot possibly consider them all, so which ones should we choose? We could evaluate "generic" theological interpretations, abstracted from particular interpretations. This approach, however, would be cumbersome and only moderately helpful. For such analysis to be useful, we would need to show that each generic interpretation accurately captured the main thrust of actual theological positions. Such a task would be difficult and time consuming, and our conclusions would inevitably provoke disagreement. Therefore, rather than evaluating generic interpretations of the crucifixion, it is much more helpful to focus on actual interpretations, and especially those interpretations widely regarded as paradigmatic and historically influential.

It is fortunately easy to identify which theological interpretations to evaluate. Especially since Gustaf Aulén's *Christus Victor* solidified the typology, scholars have long focused on three interpretations of the crucifixion: Anselm's, Abelard's, and the patristic approach often described as the devil's ransom theory, the devil's rights theory, or the *Christus Victor* theory. (Many scholars make distinctions among these various patristic interpretations, as though they constitute distinct interpretations of the crucifixion. For reasons that will be explained later, patristic authors should instead be seen as theologizing about the crucifixion within a single interpretative framework.) While few contemporary theologians would endorse any of them as completely satisfactory, these three interpretations are widely seen to represent the chief theological options available, and they are often either defended or attacked as surrogates for contemporary theories of redemption. Consequently, their evaluation has many contemporary applications; it is not simply an exercise in historical theology.

This study, therefore, focuses on these three interpretations, and especially their implied solutions to the problem of God's will and Christ's crucifixion. It does not, however, attempt to evaluate each of these interpretations comprehensively. Instead, it considers two very narrow questions: do the interpretations avoid implying that God wills moral evil, and do they align with the results of our historical and exegetical investigations? A negative answer to either question indicates that an interpretation falls short, but it does not invalidate everything else about it. Likewise, two positive answers indicate that an interpretation provides a satisfactory solution to the problem of God's will and Christ's crucifixion, but they do not guarantee its adequacy in every other respect.

In the end, this study concludes that Anselm's and Abelard's interpretations each fall short—Anselm's because it implies divine willing of moral evil and Abelard's because it cannot account for the salvific necessity of Christ's crucifixion (repeatedly affirmed by the New Testament)—but that the devil's ransom interpretation succeeds. It also draws out the negative implications of Anselm's and Abelard's errors and highlights the positive advantages of the devil's ransom interpretation. It does not, however, condemn every aspect of Anselm and Abelard's theories, nor does it lift up every aspect of the devil's ransom interpretation for emulation. While Anselm and Abelard's theories fall short, there is much that is compelling about them; they would not have influenced Western theology for so long otherwise. Likewise, the devil's ransom interpretation requires clarification, correction, and development. These considerations, however, lie beyond the scope of this study.

OUTLINE OF THE ARGUMENT

The argument of this study approaches the problem of God's will and Christ's crucifixion in three parts. Part I provides a grammar for talking about divine willing and moral evil, and then establishes principles for ruling out proposed solutions as philosophically unacceptable. Part II identifies necessary features of any adequate solution through historical-critical exegesis of the New Testament. Part III, building on the results of the first two parts, evaluates three influential interpretations of the crucifixion and their implied solutions to the problem of God's will and Christ's crucifixion.

Part I: Philosophical Prolegomena

Part I provides philosophical foundations for the rest of the study. It discusses intending, willing, and moral evil, and then it clarifies the problem of God's will and Christ's crucifixion by process of elimination. Through this *via negativa*, it offers philosophical prolegomena for ruling out interpretations of the crucifixion that compromise divine goodness. As a secondary objective, it also highlights the philosophical acceptability of interpretations that seem to involve God's willing of moral evil but in fact do not. Over the course of five chapters, Part I provides accounts of intention, moral value, and double effect reasoning, applies them to the ethics of self-sacrifice, and then draws some conclusions about God's will and Christ's crucifixion. It does not argue positively for any particular theological narrative of the crucifixion. It simply seeks to rule out certain kinds of theological narratives as logically inconsistent—and, therefore, philosophically untenable.

Chapters 1 and 2 discuss intending, willing, and moral value, thus laying foundations for evaluating human action and clarifying what it means to talk about divine willing. Then, in light of the conclusions of the first two chapters, Chapter 3 offers an account of double effect reasoning, a form of moral analysis that justifies actions on the grounds that their positive effects are intended, while their negative effects are not. Chapter 4 applies the discussion of double effect reasoning to the ethics of self-sacrifice. It seeks to formulate clear principles for distinguishing between suicide and self-sacrifice, so that theories of redemption that imply suicide can be more decisively excluded, and those that involve only self-sacrifice—even in situations where it appears like suicide—can be more decisively shown to be philosophically acceptable.

Chapter 5 applies the preceding analyses to God's will and Christ's crucifixion. First, it justifies ruling out theological narratives on purely philosophical grounds. It argues that creation contains within itself the structure of moral value. Since creation obviously manifests God's will, God cannot contradict the structure of moral value implicit in creation without contradicting himself. Therefore, it concludes, any theological narrative of the crucifixion that contradicts ordinary human morality can be ruled out as incompatible with God's will, in advance of any special revelation from God. Second, the chapter provides principles for judging when theological narratives imply divine willing of moral evil, and therefore must be ruled out. Finally, it considers theological narratives that seem to imply divine willing of moral evil, but in fact do not, and shows why they should be considered philosophically acceptable.

Part II: New Testament Evidence

Part II looks to God's self-revelation in Jesus Christ for insight into God's will. It examines the New Testament evidence and clarifies its implications for God's intentions in sending his Son. Unlike the first part, this *via positiva* does not proceed by process of elimination; through sacred scripture, it claims direct access to the positive content of God's will. Nonetheless, because sacred scripture offers such a surplus of meaning, and because its interpretation is so contested on questions surrounding Christ's crucifixion, the scope of the investigation is kept extremely narrow. The study focuses on a few, relatively noncontroversial topics: namely, Jesus' historical attitude toward his death, conceived in strictly logical terms, and New Testament affirmations about God's will and the necessity of the crucifixion. Scriptural exegesis can demonstrate much more about the positive content of God's will, but, for the purposes of this study, these areas of investigation suffice. Expanding the investigation's scope to any significant degree would multiply exponentially the work required, and it would make its conclusions less sturdy and less persuasive. By trying to cover more ground, it would inevitably leave more room for error and disagreement.

Part II consists of two chapters. Chapter 6 investigates Christ's historical attitude toward his death. By historical-critical analysis of the Gospels, this chapter seeks to determine whether Christ knew that he was going to be killed and, if so, whether he saw his death as somehow advancing his objectives. The chapter scrutinizes individual Gospel texts relating to this question and shows that a highly consistent portrayal of Christ's attitude toward his death pervades the Gospels. Based on the consistency of this portrayal, the chapter argues that, if we grant the Gospels any historical credibility, we must conclude that Jesus of Nazareth did in fact expect to be killed and saw his future death as somehow advancing his objectives. This conclusion provides a powerful tool for evaluating theological narratives of the crucifixion in subsequent chapters.

Chapter 7 examines what the New Testament reveals about the role of the crucifixion in God's plan of salvation, and especially its salvific necessity. Besides considering explicit references to God's will and Christ's crucifixion, it also looks at descriptions of God's intentions in sending his Son and handing him over to be crucified. The chapter concludes that the New Testament consistently portrays Christ's crucifixion as somehow necessary for God's plan of salvation, and somehow encompassed by God's will and God's intentions, even while simultaneously distancing God from the evil actions of those who crucify his Son.

Part III, Theological Evaluation

Part III evaluates three theological interpretations of the crucifixion. Drawing on the conclusions of the *via negativa* and the *via positiva*, this third and final part considers the theories of Anselm and Abelard, and then the devil's ransom interpretation against which both Anselm and Abelard are reacting. It concludes that the interpretations of Anselm and Abelard each fail for different reasons, but that the devil's ransom interpretation harmonizes with the New Testament evidence and successfully avoids any implication that God wills moral evil. It further argues that, once we appreciate its use of metaphor and its soteriological emphasis on the resurrection, the devil's ransom interpretation offers an attractive approach to the crucifixion.

Part III assigns one chapter to each interpretation. Chapter 8 evaluates Anselm's argument in *Cur Deus Homo*, focusing on three particularly relevant chapters. It argues that his interpretation harmonizes with the scriptural evidence but, despite his evident sensitivity to the problem of God's will and Christ's crucifixion, Anselm cannot avoid implying that God wills moral evil. Chapter 9 turns to Abelard's interpretation of the crucifixion, which he developed in response to Anselm, giving particular attention to Abelard's

Commentary on Romans. It concludes that Abelard avoids implying that God wills moral evil but cannot account for the scriptural evidence.

Finally, Chapter 10 considers the devil's ransom interpretation. After discussing the New Testament origins of this interpretation and its emergence among patristic authors, this chapter gives an overview of its major themes: the devil's rights, the deception of the devil, and Christ's descent to the dead. It also discusses the widespread use of Jonah imagery and shows how patristic authors took Jesus' saying about the sign of Jonah as a hermeneutical key to understanding the salvific significance of his crucifixion. After some discussion of metaphor, it argues that, contrary to Anselm's characterization and the default contemporary reading, patristic talk about the devil's rights and the devil's ransom should not be taken literally. Patristic authors are speaking metaphorically. They are describing how God allows evil to overreach in the crucifixion and then conquers sin and death in the resurrection. The devil does not have any legal rights over humanity, nor is any ransom paid to the devil. Strictly speaking, the existence of a devil is extraneous to the essential structure of the devil's ransom interpretation. Patristic authors certainly follow the New Testament in affirming that a demonic being helped bring about Christ's crucifixion, but the logic of their interpretation would hold together just as well if Christ's crucifixion instead had purely human causes. After this overview, the chapter gives a close reading of Gregory of Nyssa's *Catechetical Oration*, a famous instance of the devil's ransom interpretation. It shows that literal readings overlook evidence of metaphor and miss Gregory's emphasis on the resurrection and the sacraments.

Chapter 10 concludes that the devil's ransom interpretation provides an adequate solution to the problem of God's will and Christ's crucifixion. It coheres with the scriptural evidence and avoids implying divine willing of moral evil. Moreover, the chapter argues, the devil's ransom interpretation does not imply a mythological understanding of redemption. To the contrary, when properly understood, it opens up theological perspectives that are deeply attractive. Centuries of polemical distortion may have relegated the devil's ransom interpretation to the status of a historical curiosity, but it deserves serious and sympathetic attention by contemporary theologians.

Note to the Reader

This study is constructed as a continuous argument, and it builds gradually to a rehabilitation of the devil's ransom interpretation. Each chapter constitutes a separate lemma in the argument. The complexity of their subject matter varies, and consequently so does their length, but each chapter is crucial to the argument's success. Nonetheless, the argument does not need to persuade at every step to succeed in its primary objectives. The theological rehabilitation of the devil's ransom interpretation given in the final chapter can stand on its own merits, at least to some degree, as can the critiques of Anselm and Abelard. Consequently, depending on their interests, some readers may want to skip the earlier chapters and turn directly to the third part and its theological evaluations of Anselm, Abelard, and the devil's ransom interpretation.

Having said that, the argument's soundness still depends on each lemma. Each chapter depends on the one that precedes it. The reason that the latter chapters can stand on their own is not because they do not presuppose the earlier chapters, but because most readers will already have implicit answers to the questions those chapters discuss. And if the readers' implicit answers are sufficiently close to ones presumed by the final chapters, readers can skip over the earlier chapters, or even disagree with their analysis, and yet still find the argument's conclusions persuasive.

Nonetheless, the argument cannot dispense with the earlier chapters, nor can it replace them by simply summarizing the positions that would safeguard the argument's conclusions. There are a few reasons. First, any discussion of the problem of God's will and Christ's crucifixion necessarily relies on answers to philosophical and exegetical questions *about which there is no established consensus*. Unless we address these questions explicitly, our answers remain unexamined, and even the importance of the questions remains obscure. This study's proposals may or may not succeed, but regardless, in order to define the problem of God's will and Christ's crucifixion and work toward a solution, *something like them* must be provided. Second, the topics covered by the earlier chapters are complex and confusing. It is difficult even to summarize the various possible positions. Consequently, it ends up being more efficient to argue for a position rather than simply listing the different options. Third, terminological ambiguity accounts for much of the confusion surrounding the problem of God's will and Christ's crucifixion. The earlier chapters provide a grammar for talking about the problem and evaluating potential solutions. Whatever its strengths or weaknesses, this grammar provides a framework for theological conversation. Fourth, the purpose of this study is not simply to propose a solution to the problem of God's will and Christ's crucifixion; it also aims to define the problem with precision and provide tools for the analysis of potential solutions. The earlier chapters play a crucial role in achieving these objectives.

It should be emphasized that this study does not argue for a comprehensive solution to the problem of God's will and Christ's crucifixion. Such a solution would require an all-embracing theology of redemption and considerable engagement with contemporary theology, both of which lie outside the scope of this study. Rather, this study evaluates three theological positions on very narrow grounds, and then argues that the devil's ransom interpretation provides a solution that is both adequate and attractive. The relevance of these conclusions to other theologies of redemption, whether historical or contemporary, is left for the reader to judge.

Part I

Philosophical Prolegomena

1

Intending and Willing

The notions of intending and willing are firmly established in ordinary language. They also play a major role in philosophical discourse, especially in ethical matters. Their precise meaning is nonetheless disputed, and a lot hangs on how we understand them. For example, we intuitively distinguish between what we intend to cause, and what we cause without intending. It is one thing to run over the neighbor's dog by accident; it is quite another to do so intentionally. Either way, the dog is run over, but whether we intended to run over the dog makes a crucial difference. But where exactly should we draw the line between what we intend to cause and what we cause without intending? In many cases the answer is not obvious. Do surgeons intend to cause bodily harm to their patients when they make incisions to perform some helpful surgery? By their very nature, incisions involve bodily harm—the cutting of skin and other tissue—but since surgeons make incisions only in order to bring about bodily healing, we would hesitate to say that they intend to cause bodily harm. Tricky cases such as this one highlight the need for greater clarity about intending. They also highlight the need for greater clarity about willing, since willing is closely connected to intending.

This chapter, therefore, aims to clarify the nature of intending and willing. It considers the phenomenology of human action and the grammar of intention, and then provides principles for analyzing intending and willing in concrete human actions. Through this investigation this chapter accomplishes two objectives. First, it lays the groundwork for the moral evaluation of human action, and especially double effect reasoning. Second, it clarifies what it means to will something, and thus makes it possible to talk with more precision about divine willing and the problem of God's will and Christ's crucifixion.[1]

[1] The account of intending and willing given here grew out of my engagement with the vast and growing literature on double effect reasoning (which will be discussed in Chapter 3) and with the writings of Aristotle, Thomas Aquinas, Ludwig Wittgenstein, and (especially) Elizabeth Anscombe. Nonetheless, because the issues surrounding intention are so confused and confusing, this account deliberately eschews working within any established philosophical tradition. As far as possible, it tries to think things through fresh. In this way, it hopes to build on the existing

THE ONTOLOGY OF INTENTION

We do not regard all human action as having a moral quality. Human action, that is, action that has its origins in a human agent, whether mental, physical or both, is not the same thing as moral action, that is, action for which we may be praised or blamed. Human action must fulfill certain criteria in order to constitute moral action. Above all, human action must spring from free and rational choice in order to qualify as moral action. Everyone perceives this distinction between human action and moral action. Even those who deny the reliability of this perception—say, because they think that free will is an illusion—do not deny its force.

We praise or blame agents only for actions that they knowingly choose to perform. For human action to fall within the sphere of moral action, and for it to be susceptible to praise or blame in any ordinary sense, it must include some element of rational engagement. For example, our arm might twitch while we are asleep. This arm twitching is a human action, since it originates in a human agent, but we do not consider it a moral action. If the arm twitching knocks over a candle and starts a fire, we might be faulted for sleeping too close to the candle, but not for the twitching of our arm. Consequently, when freedom is diminished or absent we moderate our evaluation accordingly. For example, in the case of an addiction or an instinctive reaction to sudden stimuli, we judge defective actions leniently. Since interior freedom is lacking, we regard the agent's moral responsibility as reduced or, in some cases, obviated entirely. Likewise, when good actions are performed out of external compulsion we praise them less because they were not chosen in freedom.

Ignorance and misunderstanding can also influence our judgments about human action. When someone loses a wallet containing stolen money, and we find it and return it, unless we knew that the money was stolen we do not become accomplices to theft. Sophocles' *Oedipus* provides a vivid literary example of the exculpatory effects of ignorance and misunderstanding. Although Oedipus kills his father and marries his mother, he does not know that they are his parents, and so Sophocles presents his actions as more tragic than reprehensible. We are judged according to our knowledge of

literature while avoiding the exegetical controversies proper to particular traditions. Readers should therefore note that its use of terminology is often *sui generis*.

For some of the sources that I found most helpful in thinking through the issues, see Thomas Cavanaugh, *Double-Effect Reasoning: Doing Good and Avoiding Evil* (Oxford: Oxford University Press, 2006); Aristotle, *Nicomachean Ethics*, trans. Roger Crisp (Cambridge: Cambridge University Press, 2000), III.1–5; Thomas Aquinas, *Summa theologiae*, ed. Thomas Gilby, Latin and English ed., 61 vols. (New York and London: McGraw-Hill and Eyre and Spottiswoode, 1964–80), I–II 1–21, II–II 64.7; Ludwig Wittgenstein, *Philosophical Investigations*, trans. G. E. M. Anscombe, 3rd ed. (Oxford: Blackwell, 2001); G. E. M. Anscombe, *Intention*, 2nd ed. (Oxford: Blackwell, 1963).

what we are doing, not according to the full truth of what we are doing. So when we think we are acting inappropriately, but in fact are not, our ignorance does not absolve our guilt. For example, in *The Marriage of Figaro*, when the Count's wife disguises herself as a maid and the Count tries to seduce her, we do not see the Count as blameless.[2]

When we evaluate human action, we do not consider merely what agents are doing at one particular moment in time; we also weigh their aims and objectives. For example, we usually praise those who give money for disaster relief. If we find that their motives are not entirely honorable, however, we might alter our evaluation of their actions. If we discover that friends have given money primarily to impress influential people and only secondarily to relieve the disaster victims, our regard for their generosity diminishes. If we discover that they gave the money as a bribe to secure a political appointment, our praise might dry up entirely.

In this brief survey of our intuitions about action and intention, we have seen that our evaluations of human action turn on something irreducibly subjective: the agent's subjective vantage point. Since we praise or blame agents only for actions that they choose to perform, and only according to their knowledge of what they are choosing, moral evaluation must consider each action from the agent's perspective. We must consider the intention with which the agent acts. Or, to say the same thing in a different way, we must consider what the agent intends in performing some action. When an agent intends nothing—when there is no intention—moral evaluation does not apply; the action may be a human action, but it is not a moral action.

The actions considered in this brief survey have been "dramatic." In one way or another, they are limit cases, and they put the significance of intention in stark relief. Most of the time, however, the significance of intention is not so obvious, and we do not advert explicitly to agents' intentions when considering their actions; there is no need. Our analysis of human action inevitably depends on some implicit notion of intending, but only rarely are we self-consciously aware of this dependence. Like radioactive dye, these limit cases help us to spot the presence of intention in other human actions, so that we can see it even in mundane actions (such as walking down the street to buy milk) that we do not ordinarily praise or blame. They make it clear that intention is integral to any account of human action. Considering, however, that it takes the radioactive dye of "dramatic" actions even to spot intention, getting at the precise nature of intention is necessarily difficult.

One way to shed light on intention is to approach the question by indirection. Just as the radioactive dye of "dramatic" actions helps us to spot intention in mundane actions, so too intention-free actions can help us clarify the nature

[2] This example is taken from Stephen A. Long, *The Teleological Grammar of the Moral Act* (Naples, FL: Sapientia Press, 2007), 14.

of intention. By comparing intentional actions with intention-free actions, the essential characteristics of intention become more obvious. In his *Philosophical Investigations*, Ludwig Wittgenstein takes just this sort of indirect approach to the problem of intention:

> When "I raise my arm", my arm goes up. And the problem arises: what is left over if I subtract the fact that my arm goes up from the fact that I raise my arm?[3]

Wittgenstein's question suggests that something is "left over" when we subtract bodily movement from intentional action. By doing so, it forces us to recognize that intentional action is not identical with bodily movement. If they were identical, nothing would be left over when we subtracted one from the other. Instead, something is left over: our intending and our causing. Consequently, we must regard intention as a constituent element of intentional action. The single intentional action of "raising my arm" includes both physical movement and the intending of that movement. So, paradoxically, although intention directs action, it is also subsumed by it. The sum total of physical and mental activity associated with any intentional action includes the agent's intending of that action. Intention directs certain aspects of an intentional action—the raising of my arm, for example—without forfeiting its status as ontologically constitutive of the same intentional action. Wittgenstein's indirect approach to intention is effective precisely because intention does not exist apart from action. By getting at the question of intention indirectly, through a process of comparison, this indirect approach avoids tainting our analysis with seductive misconceptions about intentions somehow existing apart from the actions they inform.

Clarifying the ontology of intention is crucial, because we can be tempted to think of intention as separable from action, as though the same action can be informed by different intentions. For example, we might not be able to tell the difference between someone being friendly out of genuine hospitality, and the same person being friendly as part of a confidence scheme. Because the two actions look identical from the outside, we are tempted to say that the two actions *are* identical, and that only the agent's intentions are different. But the two actions cannot be identical, because intention is a constituent element of each action's ontology. Since the two actions differ in a crucial element of their ontology, the actions must be different. The sum total of any agent's psychic and material activity includes the agent's intending and, therefore, varies when the agent's intending varies. Intention gives shape to human action without standing apart from it.

We are also tempted to distinguish between our present actions and our future aims, as though they are two separate things. For example, if a novice

[3] Wittgenstein, *Philosophical Investigations*, §621.

chess player and a grandmaster make the same opening move, we are tempted to say that their actions are identical and only their intentions are different. The trouble is that our present actions include within themselves all of our aiming toward future objectives. When the grandmaster moves a piece, he does not simply intend to move the piece to a particular square; he also intends to set up his next ten moves. The novice has no such intention; he is thinking only about his current move. Since intentions are constitutive elements of intentional actions, and since the intentions of the two chess players differ, their actions cannot be identical. Their different intentions make their identical opening moves different kinds of actions. When it comes to intention, thinking in temporal categories such as present and future can be deeply misleading. It can give us the illusion that our future aims differ ontologically from our immediate intentions. In fact, our future aims are just as much a form of intending as our immediate intentions, and therefore just as ontologically constituent of our actions.

There is a valid distinction between what we intend for an action to accomplish in the present, and what we intend for that action to accomplish in the future. Nonetheless, we cannot separate what we are doing in the present from what we are aiming to accomplish, because what we are doing *includes* our aiming. Our present actions include our future aims. For example, suppose we are walking down the street to buy some toothpaste. As we walk down the street, our immediate intentions (e.g., to put one foot in front of the other, to walk south toward the store, etc.) and our future aims (e.g., to buy toothpaste, to keep our teeth healthy, to avoid trips to the dentist, etc.) simultaneously inform our present actions.[4] We cannot define our present actions without reference to our future aims. If someone asks us what we are doing, we can certainly say, "We are walking to the store," and it would be true. But we cannot truthfully say, "We are walking to the store, and that is all we are doing," because we are also buying toothpaste, keeping our teeth healthy, and trying to avoid trips to the dentist.

Although we cannot distinguish our present actions from our future aims, we can distinguish the physical movements of our bodies from our intentions.[5] We can talk about the physical movements of our bodies as we walk down the street, considering them from a purely material perspective, and distinguish these physical phenomena from the intentions informing them. When we do so, however, we need to be very careful. When we talk about the physical movements of our bodies, we almost inevitably smuggle in some reference to our intentions. For example, our tendency is to describe

[4] This point became clear to me while reflecting on Anscombe's suggestion that the various uses of the word "intention" are not equivocal. See Anscombe, *Intention*, §1.

[5] Aquinas, for example, seems to be getting at the same sort of distinction when he contrasts the external act with the internal act of the will. See *ST* I–II 18.6.

the physical movements of our bodies in this scenario as "walking down the street." By using this phrase, we are not simply saying that our bodies and limbs are moving in a certain way. We are also implicitly affirming that we *intend* to move our bodies and limbs in this way, and we *intend* to move our bodies in a certain direction (i.e., down the street). The very idea of walking implies an agent who does the walking, and so when we describe our actions as "walking down the street," we have smuggled in a reference to our intentions. And as soon as any reference to intention, no matter how slight, enters our language, we are no longer talking about the physical movements of bodies; we are now talking about intentional actions. So, while we can indeed distinguish our physical movements from our intentions, we have to be careful not to describe them in a way that implies intentionality. Otherwise we can lull ourselves into thinking that we can separate our present actions from our future aims.

THE LOGIC OF INTENTION

After these preliminary reflections, we can turn to the question of how to distinguish between what we intend and what we do *not* intend in performing some action. The upper limit of what we might be intending is easy to specify. There is no aspect or effect of an action that we cannot imagine intending, at least in theory.[6] For example, when we kick a soccer ball into a goal, there are many aspects and effects of our action. Our leg moves; air molecules are displaced; the ball moves forward at a certain trajectory and velocity; a goal is credited to our team; etc. We can imagine intending any of them. Likewise, for any given action, nothing less than the sum total of all its aspects and effects, in every physical and mental dimension, supplies the maximum extension of our intending. So that is the upper limit. But how do we go about specifying what we actually intend in our actions? And when, if ever, does intending a particular aspect or effect imply the intending of other aspects or effects?

Answering these questions is not a matter of a priori analysis; it is a matter of describing how we talk about intention in ordinary language. The fact is, whether we like it or not, we talk about intention in certain ways.

[6] There is a difference in connotation between *aspects* of an action and *effects* of an action. When we talk about aspects, we are usually referring to constitutive characteristics of the action. When we talk about effects, we are usually referring to something ontologically distinct, and chronologically subsequent, from the action. Nonetheless, the words are often used more or less interchangeably. In the absence of a compelling alternative, this study follows these ambiguous linguistic conventions: that is, it tends to use these two words in ways that respect their typical connotations, but without being slavish about it.

The philosophical task here is not to decide how we *should* talk about intention, but rather to thematize how we *already* talk about intention. Most of the time, when we talk about intention, we have little doubt that we are using the word appropriately. But sometimes, when considering limit cases, our intuitions conflict with each other and we hesitate. These limit cases can seem to stretch our concept of intention beyond the breaking point. They can make it seem that we cannot answer such questions, at least not in any consistent and meaningful way. Yet the strength and consistency of our intuitions about intention suggest that they are governed by some internal logic. By looking at the grammar of intention—that is, by looking at the syntactical structure that undergirds ordinary language allusions to intention—we should be able to articulate this inner logic. And having worked out the logic of intention, it should always be possible, at least in theory, to distinguish between what we intend to cause and what we cause without intending, even in the tricky cases.

Clearly, intention requires knowledge: for us to intend a particular aspect of an action, we must be aware of that aspect when we perform the action. For example, a postman delivers a package that, unknown to him, contains a bomb. We would not say that he intends to deliver a bomb, even though, as a matter of fact, he does deliver a bomb. He intends to deliver a sealed package, not a bomb, and thus fulfill his job as a postal worker.

Intention also implies desire. Knowledge is not enough. Simply being aware of some aspect or effect of an action does not mean that we intend it. We must also in some sense desire it. Desire is so central to intention that we often use the verb "to want" to talk about what we intend. For example, we might say, "Jane is running because she wants to make it home for dinner," and thus describe what Jane intends with the language of desire rather than the language of intention. In fact, when talking about intention, we usually talk more frequently about what we *want* to accomplish than what we *intend* to accomplish. Typically, we use the language of intention in two contexts: when talking about future plans (e.g., "He is saving up money because he intends to go to night school"), and when talking about obscure or hidden intentions, (e.g., "She did not intend to be insulting; she was just trying to be funny"). Otherwise, we describe intentions by referring to wants and desires.

Nonintended Effects

When we see others performing actions, we do not typically assume that they intend every aspect of their actions. For an aspect of an action to be intended, it must be foreseen and specifically desired by the agent. Otherwise it does not fall within the scope of the agent's intending. For example, on the way to a doctor's appointment, we stop to help someone stranded by the side of the road. We know that we will be late as a result, but we would not say that we intended to be late; what we intended was to assist the stranded motorist.

Some have argued that we necessarily intend every foreseen effect of our actions.[7] If we foresee an effect of our actions, we must also intend it. This position, however, is difficult to square with ordinary language, and it now attracts few adherents. In ordinary language, we assume that we can be fully aware of certain effects of our actions without intending them. For example, if Lisa plans to visit Paris at a time when she knows that François Hollande will be in Paris, it does not follow that Lisa intends to be in Paris at the same time as President Hollande.[8] She could have made her travel plans for reasons entirely unrelated to President Hollande's presence in Paris. After her return, it would not make sense to ask her: "Had you intended to visit Paris?" Obviously she had, by the fact of her trip. But it would make sense to ask her: "Had you intended to visit Paris while President Hollande was there?" It would not be obvious that she had, and in fact our default assumption would be that Lisa had not arranged her travel plans around President Hollande's schedule. In ordinary language, we assume that Lisa can intend to visit Paris and yet *not* intend many foreseen effects of visiting Paris.

Nonetheless, intending foreseen effects can sometimes imply intending other foreseen effects. When what we intend by definition implies other effects, then we must necessarily intend those other effects, too. For example, we cannot intend to win a hockey game without also intending to score at least one goal. Hockey games are won by scoring goals, and so by definition wanting to win a hockey game implies wanting to score at least one goal. Once we understand the meaning of the terms, the conclusion follows by logical necessity.

Ontological necessity, however, is not enough to imply transitivity of intention. For example, on a hot summer's day, Bill wants to mow the lawn. He foresees that, due to the heat, mowing the lawn will cause him to perspire. But he goes ahead and mows the lawn anyway, and he ends up perspiring.

[7] See, for example, Henry Sidgwick, *The Methods of Ethics*, 7th ed. (Indianapolis: Hackett, 1981), 202. For a critique of Sidgwick's understanding of intention, see G. E. M. Anscombe, "Modern Moral Philosophy," *Philosophy* 33 (1958): 11–12. For an excellent summary of the arguments for why foresight does not necessarily imply intention, see Mark Aulisio, "On the Importance of the Intention/Foresight Distinction," *American Catholic Philosophical Quarterly* 70 (1996): 191–2. For a fuller treatment of his argument, see Mark Aulisio, "In Defense of the Intention/Foresight Distinction" *American Philosophical Quarterly* 32 (1995): 341–54.

[8] This example is taken from Roderick Chisholm (with slight modification), who uses it to defend the opposite view. See Roderick M. Chisholm, "The Structure of Intention," *Journal of Philosophy* 67 (1970): 636–7. The problems with Chisholm's position—a position which he seems to put forward only tentatively—are demonstrated in a response by George Pitcher, "'In Intending' and Side Effects," *Journal of Philosophy* 67 (1970): 659–68. Later Castañeda defends Chisholm on this point against Pitcher: see Hector-Neri Castañeda, "Intentions and the Structure of Intending," *Journal of Philosophy* 68 (1971): 456–7.

Clearly, Bill knowingly caused himself to perspire, but we would not say that Bill intended this outcome. Although it was *ontologically* implied by his intentions, it was not *logically* implied by his intentions. Wanting to mow the lawn does not by definition imply wanting to cause oneself to perspire. Consequently, there is no transitivity of intention. The perspiration was an effect foreseen but not intended.

Given that we can foresee aspects and effects of our actions without intending them, what is the most clear and precise way of talking about these aspects and effects? It seems best to call these effects non-intentional, or nonintended.[9] We might be tempted to call these effects unintentional or unintended, but that would be misleading. If we are visiting a foreign country, and our hosts pull us aside and tell us that what we have just done has offensive connotations in their culture, we might say, "I'm sorry, any offense was entirely unintended." We had not realized the implications of what we were doing. But when innocent civilians are killed in the course of an aerial bombing, and their death was foreseen, it would seem disingenuous to say, "I'm sorry, those deaths were entirely unintentional." The moral legitimacy of the bombing is irrelevant. The bombing could have been the most unquestionably justified bombing imaginable; biological weapons could have been destroyed that would have otherwise wiped out most of humanity. Nonetheless, it would not sound right to describe the civilian deaths as unintended or unintentional, because that would imply that we had not foreseen the civilian deaths. Therefore, when we are talking about any effect that is foreseen but not intended, it is better to call them not *unintended*, but *nonintended*.[10]

To lay some foundations for future analysis, it is crucial to note that nonintended effects can be either chronologically simultaneous or chronologically subsequent to an action. For example, suppose some students use cheap soap for a carwash fundraiser, knowing that the soap will destroy a neighbor's lawn. They do not intend to destroy the neighbor's lawn, but they foresee what will happen. The lawn's destruction is a chronologically subsequent, nonintended effect. The effect materializes after the action, and it is not intended by the agents. Nonintended effects can also be chronologically simultaneous. For example, Elizabeth Anscombe describes a man pumping water. As he is

[9] In calling these foreseen effects nonintended, rather than unintended, I am developing suggestions from Thomas Cavanaugh and John Finnis, who note that words like "unintentional" and "unintended" connote ignorance of the effects in question. See Cavanaugh, *Double-Effect Reasoning*, 80–2; John Finnis, "Intention and Side-Effects," in *Liability and Responsibility*, ed. R. G. Frey and Christopher W. Morris (Cambridge: Cambridge University Press, 1991), 48–9.

[10] The need for this sort of precision transcends contemporary philosophical concerns and the particularities of the English language. After discussing the differences between voluntary and involuntary actions, and noting that some actions are mixed, Aristotle proposes that some actions should be described as nonvoluntary (see Aristotle, *Nicomachean Ethics*, III.1). Aristotle's analysis here seems to be getting at something very similar to the distinction between intended and nonintended effects.

pumping the water, he realizes that the shadows from the pump's moving arm look strangely like a human face opening and closing its mouth.[11] If the man continues to pump water after this realization, it does not mean that he intends to cause this shadow movement, that is, for the pump's arm to block sunlight in this particular way. Most likely, he simply wants to continue pumping the water. On this particular day, with the sun shining in this particular way, intending to pump the water implies the shadow movement ontologically. It does not, however, imply the shadow movement logically; wanting to pump water does not by definition imply wanting to cause the shadow movement. Consequently, even though the effect is chronologically simultaneous to the action, he need not intend it. There is no transitivity of intention.

INTENTION AND RATIONAL INTENTION

Intention always implies knowledge and desire, but intention is not always rational. The case of animal intentions makes this point especially clear. Even though animals are not capable of rationality, we do not hesitate to ascribe intentions to animals. We regard animal intentions as true intentions. Wittgenstein makes this point in striking fashion:

> What is the natural expression of an intention?—Look at a cat when it stalks a bird; or a beast when it wants to escape.[12]

We often say things like, "That squirrel was trying to get into the birdfeeder again," or, "The cat wants to go outside." These expressions implicitly attribute intentions to animals. Granted, we do not usually talk about what animals "intend." Instead, we usually speak about what animals "want." Still, as discussed above, we typically use the language of desire even when attributing intention to human agents. Furthermore, the grammar of ordinary language does not exclude the explicit attribution of intentions to animals. We can imagine someone saying, "It's a good thing you decided to take a look around the backyard when you did. That fox clearly intended to get into the henhouse." We do not usually talk about the intentions of animals only because they are usually so obvious. Animals are not capable of hidden motives, and observation of an animal's physical behavior usually suffices to discern its intentions. Looking at a cat stalking a bird is enough to know what it intends. The obviousness of what animals intends stems from their incapacity

[11] Anscombe, *Intention*, §23.

[12] Wittgenstein, *Philosophical Investigations*, §647. Aquinas and Anscombe also note that intention can be attributed to animals. See *ST* I–II 12.1, 12.6; Anscombe, *Intention*, §§ 47, 49.

for rationality.[13] Animal intentions are nonrational, and therefore completely transparent (at least in theory) from their physical behavior. Nonetheless, even though animal intentions are nonrational, they remain true intentions. And since animal intentions are true intentions, and yet nonrational, we can conclude that intending always implies knowing and desiring, but it does not always imply rationality.

Reflecting on animal intentions makes it easier to appreciate how many of our own intentions are not rational. For example, on the way home from work we decide to pick up some milk from the store. But our mind wanders and we drive home on automatic pilot, without stopping at the store. What can we say about our intentions? On the one hand, as we are driving home, our actions are not devoid of intention. We stop at stoplights, change lanes, wave on other drivers at intersections, and perform various other intentional actions. On the other hand, our actions are at variance with our rational choices, and we would hesitate to say that our actions are fully rational. Our actions and intentions do not synch with our rationally ratified desires. Similarly, someone who starts a bar fight in a flash of alcohol-fueled anger clearly intends to start the fight, but we would not say that his rationality was fully involved in forming this intention. Our intentional actions do not always fully engage our rationality, nor do they always flow from rationally ratified desires. Our criminal laws enshrine this intuition. For example, those who commit crimes out of passion receive less severe sentences than those who commit crimes in cold blood.

The fact that we are not always fully aware of our own motives further illustrates the possibility of forming intentions that are not completely rational. For example, we might choose a vacation destination close to home, and then only later realize that fear of airplane travel strongly influenced us to make this choice. Our intentions in making our choice were not completely rational; they were only partly rational. Likewise, our intentions can be obvious to an observer and yet not obvious to ourselves. For example, we can imagine someone saying to us, "You're only saying that because you're still angry about yesterday," or, "You're trying to manipulate me by making me feel guilty." Even if these accusations were accurate they might seem absurd to us because our motives were not fully rational and we are genuinely unaware that our actions were informed by them.

[13] The claim that animals are fundamentally incapable of rationality stands regardless of one's concept of rationality. Even if one sees human cognition differing from animal cognition only in its degree of sophistication, and not in its essential structure, to maintain that animals are capable of rationality would evacuate the concept of any practical meaning. It would also lead inevitably to the invention of a replacement concept, in order to be able to distinguish between animal cognition and the sort of cognition proper to humans.

Intending and Willing

Actions informed by rational intentions are not only intended; they are also willed. Rational intending implies rational choice, and rational choice is an act of the will. (This inference does not imply any particular philosophical psychology; it simply follows from our common convention of attributing rational choice to the will.) Therefore, rational intending implies willing. We can also say the reverse: willing implies intending. Anything we will, we also intend. It is impossible to imagine a single instance of willing that does not imply intending.

In fact we can go a step further. However we define what it means to will something, in ordinary language willing always involves knowledge and desire, the two crucial elements of intending. When we will something, we have some knowledge of what we are willing, and we desire it. We can therefore say that willing does not merely imply intending; it *is* intending. Or rather, it is a specific kind of intending, namely rational intending. What sets willing apart from other forms of intending is the kind of knowledge and desire involved. Unlike animal intending or nonrational human intending, willing involves rational cognition and rational desire.

Objections can be raised against this account of willing. The idea that willing always involves intending does not find obvious support from ordinary language. In ordinary language we rarely talk about willing aspects or effects of our actions. In fact, we rarely talk about the *action* of willing at all. Instead, we talk more frequently about people being willing to do something, or doing something willingly, or being forced to do something against their will. We also talk about someone's will, an expression by which we mean the sum total of what an agent wants to be the case. For example, when deciding how to allocate resources, we might ask someone, "What is your will in the matter?" By doing so, we are asking, "How do you want these resources distributed?" We do not, however, typically talk about people engaging in the *action* of willing.

This account of willing can be seen as fully compatible with ordinary language. Arguably, although we rarely talk about agents willing anything, ordinary language does not prejudice against the conclusion that willing implies intending. It simply happens that we rarely have reason to talk about agents willing anything. But if we stop to think about it, we readily agree that rational agents must necessarily will their rational actions. The grammar of intending and willing that permeates ordinary language naturally leads to this conclusion. We rarely have any reason to think about whether agents will their own actions, but when we consider the question, the grammar of ordinary language justifies talking about agents willing aspects and effects of their own actions, or concluding that willing always implies intending, and indeed constitutes a species of intending.

ISOLATING INTENTION FROM INTENTIONAL ACTION

Given what we have seen about the logic of intention, how do we go about clarifying what someone intends in specific, concrete, actions? We can say, first of all, that we cannot possibly intend every aspect of our actions. For us to intend something, we must also foresee it, but our finite minds cannot possibly foresee every aspect of our actions. Even the simple action of swinging a baseball bat involves innumerable subatomic particles and biochemical reactions. It can also have future effects far beyond the confines of a ballpark: for example, on televisions showing a game and fans watching the broadcast. No finite mind could possibly know all that is involved in the simple action of swinging a baseball bat. Only an infinite, omniscient mind could know an action in all its aspects and effects, and therefore only an infinite, omniscient mind could fully circumscribe any given action with its intending. As finite knowers, we can intend our actions only under a limited number of aspects. But we can still intend many different aspects and effects of our actions. We have two primary means of isolating, out of all the many possibilities, which ones we intend. We can determine an agent's intentions from either physical observation or the agent's own description, or both.

Determining Intention from Physical Observation

Physical observation can lead to some conclusions about what an agent intends in performing some action. From observing a batter swinging his bat, it is clear that the batter intends to swing his arms while gripping his bat. It is enough to observe the batter to know that he intends the movements of his body. Unless a physical action is a purely physiological reaction (for example, a patient's knee kicking forward after being tapped by the doctor), it must be intended by the agent under some description. So we can come to some conclusions about an agent's intentions simply from physical observation.

Nonetheless, physical observation cannot disclose everything. We can conclude that the agent intends the physical action under some description, but from physical observation alone we cannot know under which particular description the action is intended. We know that the batter intends to swing his bat, but we cannot determine the full story of his intentions. It is possible that he does not even intend to hit the ball. Perhaps he intends to miss because he has been paid to throw the game, and so, while he intends to swing the bat in the direction of the baseball, he is not in fact trying to hit it. Perhaps he is swinging his bat for exercise and does not care one way or the other if his bat happens to connect with the ball. Or maybe he is trying to hit the baseball, but his action is informed by a secret motive—he wants to hit a home run in memory of an old coach who has recently died. Physical observation can also come to plausible conclusions about someone's motives and hidden intentions. Although such conclusions are not certain, they can be highly probable. For example, we usually have good grounds to assume that a batter who swings in the direction of the baseball is trying to hit it. Still, only the batter has direct access to his intentions and the observation of his physical actions can be deeply misleading; hence the ever-present possibility of being deceived about someone's true intentions.

Determining Intention from the Agent's Description

We cannot intend every aspect of our actions, but we can fully describe what we do intend, at least in theory, precisely because our intentions presuppose knowledge of what we intend. Our intentions are exactly what we know them to be—no more, no less. The most natural way therefore to determine what an agent intends in performing some action is to ask the agent. It is also the only way for us to know the full story about what an agent intends, because only the agent has direct access to the intentions that inform an action. Determining intention from the agent's own description, however, is not simply a matter of listening to what the agent says. We do not always give reliable descriptions of our intentions. Even when we are being honest about our intentions, our descriptions are sometimes erroneous or significantly incomplete. We need to interpret the agent's descriptions before we can come to any conclusion about their intentions.

First, when describing our intentions, we sometimes leave out important information. For example, suppose that, at the prodding of her parents, a girl starts writing thank you notes for her birthday presents. We might ask her, "What are you doing?" She might say, "I'm obeying my parents," or "I'm writing." Both answers would be accurate, but neither would fully capture her intentions. Further questions might be necessary: "What are you writing? To whom are you writing? Why are you writing?" Eventually we would be able to put together a satisfactory summary of her intentions, such that nothing significant would be left out. As this example illustrates, when we are describing our intentions, we do not always supply enough information to give a complete picture. Sometimes we need to be prompted to say more. This difficulty stems from the ontology of intention. Our intentions are "in" our actions; our intentions are not distinct things that we superimpose on our actions. Consequently, even though we have direct access to our intentions, we do not always find it easy to summarize what exactly we had been intending in performing a certain action. We might need to ask ourselves, "Yes, now why exactly was I doing that?" and call to mind the action, then name all the intentions that informed it.

The difficulty of summarizing even our own intentions raises an important question. By what criteria can we discern that intentions have been completely described? The answer seems to be simply this: when all of the aspects under which an action was intended have been named. Achieving this threshold is not nearly as daunting as the impossible task of describing an action in its full ontological reality. Agents will sooner or later run out of intended aspects because finite minds can intend only so many things at the same time precisely because they are finite. In practice it is not usually necessary for agents to give full descriptions of their intentions. It suffices to name those elements that are relevant to whatever analysis is being undertaken. For example, when analyzing the morality of bank robbery, the various steps along the way—crossing the street, filling the gas tank of the getaway car, etc.—are not of much interest because the intentions associated with such acts, considered in themselves, are obviously acceptable. The only relevant intention to the analysis at hand is the intention to rob a bank. To use Anscombe's expression, this intention "swallows up" the other intentions; once it has been identified, it is not necessary to name the others involved, at least for the most typical kinds of analysis.[14]

Second, when describing our intentions, we sometimes incorrectly claim that we do not intend something that, in fact, we *must* intend, given the intentions that we do acknowledge. For example, after taking someone else's money, a man might claim, "I did not intend to steal; I only intended to feed my family." He can plausibly deny intending to take money that had the specific property of belonging to someone else. He wants money; he does not care where it comes from. However, he cannot deny taking money that he knew belonged to someone else. He did not only intend to feed his family; he also intended to feed his family by taking money that he knew belonged to someone else. His interest, or non-interest, in taking money that had the

[14] Anscombe, *Intention*, §26. Anscombe makes an important caveat: sometimes one intention does not swallow up the rest. For example, when we whistle while we work, our whistling is not swallowed up in our intention to work. Our actions are informed by both intentions simultaneously, but neither intention is subsumed by the other (unless, say, our whistling is what makes our working bearable, and is thus subsumed by our intention to work). Consequently, each non-reducible intention must be analyzed separately. Nonetheless, even in circumstances when one intention does not swallow up the others, our actions are not informed by two ontologically distinct intentions. Ontologically speaking, our actions are still informed by one indivisible intention. In the case we are considering here, that one indivisible intention encompasses both our intending to whistle and our intending to work.

specific property of belonging to someone else are relevant to the question of whether his actions were motivated by malice, but they are not relevant to the question of whether he intended to steal.[15] Certain intentions imply other intentions, no matter how much these other intentions might be against our generic preferences, and no matter how much we might want to deny having them.

Many make this point by saying that we cannot intend ends without also intending the means chosen to achieve those ends.[16] For example, in walking down the street to buy milk, we cannot claim that we intend merely the end of acquiring milk; we also intend the means of walking down the street. This principle is obviously true, and in many cases, probably the great majority, it suffices for the analysis of our intentions. The trouble is that, without additional clarification, this means-end formulation is too vague to be of much help with tricky cases.

The first problem with the means-end formulation is that it is not clear what constitutes "the means" and what does not. For example, a woman runs a marathon, knowing that the running will wear down the soles of her sneakers. She clearly intends to run, and she clearly intends to wear sneakers while she runs, but it seems farfetched to say that she also intends to wear down her sneakers.[17] Yet it is not immediately obvious why wearing down her sneakers should not be considered a means to an end. She cannot run the marathon without wearing down her sneakers with every step. Does her wearing down of her sneakers constitute a means to the end of running the marathon? We have good reason to say that it does. But then it would follow that she intends to wear down her sneakers, and this conclusion contradicts a strong intuition to the contrary. The principle "we cannot intend an end without also intending the chosen means to that end" does not give us enough information. We need

[15] Chisholm argues that someone taking a car that he knows belongs to someone else need not intend to steal that car. He writes: "Our man might plead: 'I didn't intend to steal. If I drove off in a car that belonged to someone else, that was only a *side effect* of what I was doing'" Chisholm, "The Structure of Intention," 636–7. Most thieves, he continues, would be equally justified in pleading that they did not intend to steal.

The trouble with Chisholm's argument is that it implies that "taking something one knows belongs to someone else" is not the same thing as stealing. It is true that some thieves might well intend to take something belonging to someone else, precisely because they know it belongs to someone else, like Augustine in his youthful theft of his neighbor's pears (*Confessions*, II.4). But stealing, to be stealing, only requires the intention of taking something known to belong to someone else. It does not require the additional intention of taking it precisely because it has the specific property of belonging to someone else.

[16] For example, see *ST* I–II 12.4.

[17] The marathon runner example is taken from Michael Bratman. He likewise maintains that she need not intend to wear down her sneakers, as does Adams in his critique of Bratman. See Michael Bratman, "Two Faces of Intention," *The Philosophical Review* 93 (1984): 399–401; Frederick Adams, "Intention and Intentional Action: The Simple View," *Mind and Language* (1986): 295–7.

additional information. We need principles for determining what counts as a means and what does not. The means-end formulation sounds good in the abstract, and it has many useful applications, but it does not suffice for the tricky cases; it is too vague and simplistic.

The second problem is that the means-end formulation lulls us into thinking that we can divide our intentions into those that concern the means and those that concern the end. Our intentions, however, cannot be divided so neatly. Our intentions can be described with endless variation. For example, we can say that study is a means to the end of getting a college degree. But we can also say that study is a means to the end of professional advancement, a more comfortable family life, a financially secure retirement—or even the beatific vision. Depending on the frame of reference in which we consider our actions and intentions, the means-end distinction can be applied in any number of ways. Consequently, while it is true enough that we cannot intend ends without also intending our chosen means to those ends, the principle is not very helpful in the complex situations in which clarification is most needed. Moreover, sometimes the means-end formulation makes analysis even more difficult. It can lead us on a wild goose chase for an action's sole unique means or sole unique end, when no such things exist.

The means-end formulation, though, need not be abandoned. By clarifying what makes something a means, we can purify the means-end formulation of its ambiguity. The logic of intention supplies the missing principles. As we saw earlier, when we intend certain aspects of our actions, our intending implies other aspects in two ways: either ontologically or logically. If our intending implies these other aspects logically, then we must also intend them; otherwise, if our intending only implies them ontologically, then we need not intend them. Now, when we translate the language of means and ends into the language of aspects and effects, what is a means? A means is an intended aspect. More specifically, it is an aspect through which we deliberately bring about something else. Consequently, for aspects to qualify as means, they must be logically implied by that which we are trying to bring about. Otherwise, they are simply nonintended side effects. For aspects to qualify as means, it is not enough for them to be ontologically bound up with bringing about some end. As we saw earlier, effects can be chronologically simultaneous to actions, and yet still nonintended. For instance, in Anscombe's example of the man pumping water, the shadow movement is ontologically bound up with pumping the water, but it is not logically implied by the man's intentions. Consequently, even though blocking the sunlight in this particular way is chronologically simultaneous to his pumping, it is not intended. Therefore, it cannot be considered a means to an end.

As typically employed, the means-end formulation fails to distinguish between means ontologically implied by our intentional actions, but not intended, and those means both intended and ontologically implied. As a result, the means-end formulation frequently leads to confusion. In light of the preceding analysis, this lacuna can be rectified by distinguishing between two sorts of means: those that are ontologically necessary, and those that are both ontologically and logically necessary. Ontologically necessary means are ontologically implied by a causal chain of intentions; logically necessary means are both ontologically and logically implied by a causal chain of intentions. This distinction allows us to rescue the means-end formulation. The standard formulation simply states that agents cannot intend an end without also intending the means to that end. With the distinction between ontologically and logically necessary means, we can put it more precisely. Agents cannot intend an end without also intending the *logically necessary* means to that end. Or to put it another way: for something truly to be the means to an end, in the sense relevant for moral analysis, it must be implied logically, and not just ontologically, by the agent's intending of the end. This clarification dissipates much of the ambiguity that plagues the means-end formulation.

Isolating Intention in Tricky Cases

In tricky cases, even with the principles given above, isolating intention can be difficult. It is helpful, therefore, to see these how these principles work in practice. When we are trying to determine which aspects of an action are intended by the agent, a few practical points are important. First, when we are considering a particular aspect, and trying to determine whether or not the agent intends it, what we are asking, essentially, is whether the agent *wants* to bring about that aspect. Often the answer is immediately apparent. Other times, however, aspects are undesirable for one reason or another, and yet closely connected to what the agent obviously intends. Sometimes, despite their lack of intrinsic desirability, an agent wants to bring about these undesirable aspects because they are useful for some other purpose—that is, as a means to an end. Other times, despite their ontological closeness to the agent's obvious intentions, the agent does not want to bring about these undesirable aspects, and thus, despite the ontological closeness, the agent does not intend them. When we are unsure whether an agent wants to bring about these undesirable aspects, we can ask whether they are logically implied by what the agent obviously intends, either as a means or an end. If so, then the agent must intend them. We can also ask whether the agent can plausibly supply reasons for acting without reference to the aspects in question. If so, then the agent need not intend them. With that said and with these guidelines in mind, let us consider three representative scenarios: the marathon runner, the sniper, and the surgeon.

In the example of the marathon runner discussed above, the marathon runner wears down her sneakers as she runs the marathon. This effect is not desirable, but does she want this effect anyway as a means to her ends? Wearing down her sneakers is ontologically implied by her actions; she cannot run the marathon with sneakers on without wearing them down. This effect, however, is not logically implied by her intentions. In wearing her sneakers, she wants to have greater cushioning and protection as she runs, but the idea of wanting cushioning and protection does not, by definition, include the idea of wearing down her sneakers. Her intentions do not logically imply the effect of wearing down her sneakers, and we need not conclude that she intends this effect. We can also fully explain her actions without referring to the effect of wearing down her sneakers. To accomplish the end of running the marathon, she chooses the means of wearing sneakers and she chooses the means of cushioning and protecting her feet, but the wearing down of her sneakers is not a means to her an end; it is a nonintended side effect of the means she chooses.

In another scenario, a sniper fires his weapon at his target, knowing that the noise will alert the enemy to his presence. The effect of alerting the enemy is not desirable, but his intentions ontologically imply it. Do they also logically imply it? It would seem not. The idea of hitting his target does not include within itself the idea of alerting the enemy to his presence. Therefore this effect cannot be said to be logically implied by his intentions, and we can say that the sniper does not intend it. We can also fully explain his actions without referring to the effect of alerting the enemy. To accomplish the end of hitting his target, he fires his weapon, knowing that the noise will alert the enemy to his presence, but the noise is not a means to his end; it is a nonintended side effect of his chosen means.[18]

Finally, let us consider surgery. By their nature, surgical incisions involve bodily harm to the patient. They damage the patient's skin, blood vessels, and other tissue as well. So when a surgeon makes an incision to remove a cancerous tumor, she necessarily causes bodily harm to her patient. But does she want this undesirable effect to happen? It would seem not. We instinctively balk at saying that surgeons want to cause bodily harm to their patients. The whole point of surgery is to improve and safeguard the patient's bodily health. But perhaps the surgeon's intentions logically imply bodily harm, as a means to her ends? Again, it would seem not. Her idea in making the incision is to create access to the cancerous tumor, and the idea of creating access to the cancerous tumor does not include the idea of causing bodily harm.

[18] This example is taken from Gilbert Harman. He also concludes that the sniper does not intend to alert his enemy. Nonetheless, Harman argues, the sniper alerts his enemy "intentionally." See Gilbert Harman, "Practical Reasoning," *Review of Metaphysics* 29 (1976): 433–4. Harman's distinction is confusing and potentially misleading. It would be more accurate to say that the sniper intentionally performs an action that has the nonintended effect of alerting his enemy.

One might object that making an incision, by definition, involves cutting skin and thus bodily harm. Consequently, the surgeon cannot avoid intending bodily harm if she intends to make an incision, because the idea of making an incision includes the idea of causing bodily harm. The surgeon causes bodily harm as her chosen means to the end of removing the tumor, and thus cannot deny intending bodily harm to her patient. This objection is important, because it puts the spotlight on an important philosophical temptation. It implicitly assumes that any adequate description of the surgeon's intentions must include the intention to cut the skin. Making this assumption is the objection's key move. After this assumption, the conclusion follows easily—if the surgeon intends to cut her patient's skin, then she must intend to cause bodily harm, since cutting skin logically implies bodily harm. But in fact, as counterintuitive as it may seem, the surgeon need not be described as intending to cut her patient's skin. As we have seen, we cannot say with certainty what agents intend by looking at their physical movements. We can say with certainty only that they intend their physical movements *under some description*. To say anything more, we would have to ask the agents about their intentions, since we can intend the physical movements of our bodies under any number of descriptions.

Let us return once again to Anscombe's example of the man pumping water. In one and the same action, the man both pumps water and blocks sunlight. Thus far, we have talked about the man intending to pump water, with the shadow movement as a nonintended side effect of his pumping. However, it could just as easily be the case that the man intends only for the pump arm to block the sun in this particular way, and the actual pumping is the nonintended side effect. In the same way, of all the various ways that the surgeon can intend the physical movements of her body while she is making an incision, she need not intend them under the aspect of cutting the patient's skin; she can also intend them under the aspect of creating access to the tumor.

What makes this point difficult to see is our tendency to equate "making an incision" and "cutting skin," as though the two actions are identical. And indeed, as far as their attendant physical realities go, the two actions might well be identical. But as we have seen, actions and intentions are not two separate realities, as though our intentions are superimposed on our actions. Our actions are indivisible realities that encompass both our intending and our physical movement. For example, a gang member could cut his enemy's abdomen in exactly the same way that the surgeon cuts her patient on the operating table. Even though their actions are physically identical, we would not say that their actions are the same. The gang member's cut and the surgeon's cut are two different kinds of actions, because the gang member intends to cause bodily harm, but the surgeon does not. Hence, perhaps, our linguistic tendency to talk about surgeons making incisions to differentiate their actions from other forms of cutting.[19]

CONCLUSION

Most moral systems rely on some notion of intention in their analysis of human action. Nonetheless, the precise nature of intention remains disputed, often even within the same philosophical tradition. In tricky cases, the question of what agents intend engenders confusion and controversy, and thus muddies the waters of moral analysis. Drawing on the phenomenology of human action and the grammar of intention, this chapter developed an account of intending and willing. It showed that intending is ontologically constitutive of intentional action, and it argued that willing is a form of intending, namely, rational intending. It also identified principles for isolating intention from intentional action. By doing so, this chapter provides a crucial foundation for moral analysis and double effect reasoning and also for talking with more precision about divine willing and the problem of God's will and Christ's crucifixion.

[19] Of course, doctors sometimes talk about cutting their patients in a colloquial sense, but this colloquial expression is the exception that proves the rule. The very fact that we have created an alternative expression for surgery—namely, "making an incision"—points to a deep seated intuition that what surgeons are doing is fundamentally different from other forms of cutting.

2

Moral Value and Moral Obligation

Perceptions of moral value are universal. We consider some human actions morally good; we consider others morally bad. We often disagree, however, about whether particular actions are morally good or morally bad, or whether our moral judgments have any ultimate significance. In tricky cases, we sometimes disagree even with ourselves. They scramble our intuitions, leaving us unsure how to classify particular actions. To address the problem of God's will and Christ's crucifixion, we need to address these disagreements and uncertainties. Once we have established a philosophical framework for analyzing human actions, we will be able to evaluate morally ambiguous actions, and then draw some conclusions about their compatibility with God's will.

This chapter lays out accounts of moral value and moral obligation to provide just such a framework. In later chapters, this framework will be applied to double effect reasoning, the ethics of self-sacrifice, and the problem of God's will and Christ's crucifixion.

MORAL VALUE

Any account of moral value begins from the fact that we perceive moral value and that we make moral judgments. Its task is to tell a story of *why*, and then offer principles for evaluating actions whose moral quality is obscure or controversial. In recent times, especially as a result of the work of Elizabeth Anscombe and Alasdair MacIntyre,[1] there has been renewed interest in virtue ethics. Typically, this approach to ethics places particular stress on ontology and teleology, taking as paradigms the ethical systems of thinkers such as Aristotle and Aquinas. Working within this tradition of ethical reflection, this section tells a story about moral value. Then, without trying to offer a definitive defense, it explains why this account is plausible.

[1] See Anscombe, *Modern Moral Philosophy*; Alasdair MacIntyre, *After Virtue*, 2nd ed. (Notre Dame: University of Notre Dame Press, 1984).

Natural Inclination as the Measure of Moral Value

On this story of moral value, actions are morally good if they are in harmony with the inner structure of things, but morally bad if they are not. The sheer reality of what exists is good, and so, too, are those actions that are in harmony with the inner structure of what exists. Moral evil is nothing more than the intentional corruption of what exists.[2] It corrupts what exists by introducing disharmony between things and their inner structure. An evil action is a deformed action in a very similar sense to the way in which a cat born with only three legs is a deformed cat.

This ontological interpretation of moral value provides a unified account of goodness. The goodness of human action is a subspecies of the goodness of being. In this view, moral value is a species of ontology. It does not stand over and against being; it is, rather, an aspect of being. The dynamism of being when it is involved in some action does not remove it from the category of being. Being-in-action is necessarily a form of being.[3] We do not transcend our own being when we perform intentional actions. Just the opposite: we are more fully ourselves, since our entire being is oriented toward action. With our capacity for rationality, humans obviously stand apart, not only from inanimate things, but also from nonrational animals. This capacity for rationality, however, does not remove human action from the realm of ontology. And since moral value is a property of human action, our capacity for rationality does not remove moral value from the realm of ontology, either.

This approach to moral value hangs on the premise that some actions are in harmony with the inner structure of things and some are not. However, bits of matter do not carry signs declaring their inner structure or announcing how they expect to be treated. Consequently, one might object to any theory premised on knowing which actions are in harmony with the inner structure of things and which are not. If we cannot know which actions are in harmony with the inner structure of things, on what basis could we justify such a theory? According to this objection, trying to derive morality from ontology is like trying to figure out the best way to arrange a collection of Lego blocks. Must every piece on the table be used? Should blocks with different colors be mixed

[2] As will become clearer as this chapter progresses, this understanding of moral evil does not mean that good actions do not sometimes lead to ontological corruption; it means that good actions do not *aim* at ontological corruption.

[3] In fact, it may be impossible to imagine any kind of being that does not involve some inherent dynamism. Aquinas, for instance, sees desire (*appetitus*) as an essential element of being, even in God (see *ST* I 5.1, 19–20). Contemporary scientific knowledge confirms Aquinas's dynamic understanding of being in ways that he could never have imagined. We now know, for example, that physical matter is always in motion, both at the subatomic level, with electrons constantly orbiting atomic nuclei, and at the macroscopic level, with the universe constantly expanding.

together? Are Lego buildings preferable to Lego animals? The blocks can be arranged in any number of ways. Without guidelines external to the blocks themselves, it is impossible to say one arrangement is better than another. Likewise, so this objection runs, there are many ways to arrange the building blocks of being. Without external guidelines, it is impossible to say that one way of arranging being is better than another.

This objection, however, assumes too quickly that nothing in being points the way toward being's fulfillment and completion. To the contrary, humans and all other organic entities are guided by interior principles toward growth and flourishing. (Contemporary physics gives us grounds to say that something analogous happens with inanimate objects, since, as we now know, inanimate objects are attracted or repulsed to other bits of matter by the sheer fact of their existence.) These interior principles, or inclinations, are aspects of every organic entity's being. Through these interior principles, desire bubbles up, directing organic entities toward what sustains their existence and brings them to completion. Life does not come with an instruction manual, but it does come with something pedagogically far more effective—desire. Through the unavoidable reality of desire, life has instructions built into the very experience of being alive.

Natural inclinations manifest the orientation of being toward a perfective *telos*, and therefore constitute the measure of moral value.[4] Just as acorns are naturally oriented toward becoming oak trees, we are naturally oriented toward actions that are perfective of the structure of our being. Natural inclinations, whether for acorns or humans, are entirely unchosen. Our natural inclinations come with being human, whether we like it or not. The difference between ourselves and acorns is that we do not automatically proceed along a pre-programmed trajectory. Unlike acorns, we can choose to cooperate in bringing our natural inclinations to fulfillment or we can choose to rebel against them. We have the potential for rational self-determination.

Since our natural inclinations point the way toward what is perfective of the human person, they also provide a measure against which to measure the moral quality of our actions. Actions that aim at advancing our natural inclinations cooperate with the inner structure of being, and those that aim

[4] In grounding morality in natural inclinations, I am following Aquinas (see esp. *ST* I–II 94.2). The precise place of natural inclinations in his ethics is a matter of controversy. For an overview of the interpretations on offer, see William E. May, "Contemporary Perspectives on Thomistic Natural Law," in *St. Thomas Aquinas and the Natural Law Tradition: Contemporary Perspectives*, ed. John Goyette, Mark S. Latkovic, and Richard S. Myers (Washington, DC: The Catholic University of America Press, 1994), 113–56; Matthew Levering, "Natural Law and Natural Inclinations: Rhonheimer, Pinckaers, McAleer," *The Thomist* 70 (2006): 155–201. For my interpretation, and for an evaluation of Aquinas's relevance for contemporary ethics in his approach to natural inclinations, see Nicholas E. Lombardo, *The Logic of Desire: Aquinas on Emotion* (Washington, DC: The Catholic University of America Press, 2011), 101–17, 229–47.

at frustrating them do not. Consequently, we can measure the moral value of our actions against our natural inclinations. If our actions cooperate with our natural inclinations, they are morally good; otherwise, they are morally defective. On this account, then, moral value is determined by measuring intentional action against natural inclination. When we cooperate with our natural inclinations, our actions are morally good; when instead we intentionally frustrate them, our actions are morally defective.

It should be emphasized, however, that *intentionally* frustrating a natural inclination is very different from either declining to advance it or non-intentionally frustrating it. We must positively intend to act against a natural inclination to render an action morally defective. To bring out this important distinction more clearly, let us consider three different ways that we can act against our natural inclinations. First, when we do not foresee the negative effects of our actions, we *unintentionally* thwart our natural inclinations. For example, when an emperor eats a poisoned apple that he does not realize was poisoned, he unintentionally acts against his inclination toward self-preservation. Second, when we foresee, but do not intend, the negative effects of our actions, we *non-intentionally* thwart our natural inclinations. Were the emperor knowingly to eat the poisoned apple, because it looks incredibly tasty and he cannot help himself, but not because he wants to die, he would be non-intentionally frustrating his inclination toward self-preservation. His actions would be morally defective for other reasons, but he would not be intentionally frustrating his inclination toward self-preservation. Third, when we both foresee and intend the negative effects of our actions, we *intentionally* thwart our natural inclinations. Suppose the emperor, wearied by a lifetime of court intrigue, and aware that he has been betrayed by his most trusted advisor, eats the poisoned apple, knowing that it is poisoned, because he wants to die. Only in this last case does the emperor intentionally thwart his natural inclination toward self-preservation.

This approach to moral value turns on the idea that human nature is intrinsically oriented toward certain definite ends. Many deny, however, that human nature is oriented toward any ends whatsoever; in fact many deny that there is even such a thing as human nature. These denials pull the carpet from under this approach to moral value. Without a common human nature intrinsically oriented toward certain definite ends, this approach to moral value would collapse. Yet it is difficult to deny the existence of human nature and its natural inclinations in a logically consistent fashion. All humans obviously share common properties and inclinations. We have one head and two eyes; we walk on two legs; we hunger and thirst; we feel pain; we desire friendship and affection; etc. Even allowing for birth defects and other physical or mental conditions that deviate from the norm, no one can seriously deny that we all share a number of properties and inclinations. Whether we incline toward a particular end might be controversial, or genuinely unclear, but confusion about particular inclinations does not diminish our certainty about others. These other, uncontested, inclinations suffice to derive moral value from human nature, at least in broad outline.

Although some theories claim to anchor moral value in something other than human nature, they inevitably smuggle in some conception of human nature. No theory attempting to explain moral value can avoid relying on some conception of what it means to be human. Every theory of moral value inevitably uses human nature as a measure of moral value. Even minimalist accounts tend to presume a great deal about human nature and its attendant inclinations. For example, someone might hold that every action is morally good unless it harms another person. This minimalist ethic might seem to avoid any reference to human nature, but in fact it presumes, first, that we are vulnerable to harm and, second, that we have some normative way of functioning which harm disrupts. The inevitability of relying on some conception of human nature goes even deeper. In terms of dissociating ethics from human nature, the most radical account of moral value imaginable is an account where each individual agent is the ultimate arbiter of moral value. Yet even this sort of existentialist account presumes that individual agents are capable of knowing and desiring.

In order to derive moral value from our natural inclinations we need to know what they are. What, then, are our natural inclinations, and how should we go about identifying them? Translating the language of natural inclination into the language of desire makes it easier to answer these questions. Natural inclination is an abstraction; it is a way of talking about an innate tendency to experience desire for specific objects. Unlike the concept of natural inclination, however, the concept of desire is integral to ordinary communication and every ethical tradition. Consequently, it can be helpful to discuss this account of moral value, not in terms of natural inclination, but in terms of desire. Doing so grounds discussion more directly in our experience, and it also makes this approach to moral value more intelligible to those approaching it from other ethical traditions. In the language of desire, then, we can say that natural inclination is the inner structure that undergirds the concrete experience of desire. This inner structure gradually reveals itself through experience and empirical observation. It does not manifest itself except within concrete movements of desire, and it cannot be understood apart from them. And just as natural inclination is the measure of moral value, so too is desire—but desire considered in its inner structure, not in its concrete experience.

Since natural inclination is nothing other than the inner structure of desire, our natural inclinations can be identified by reflecting on our concrete experience of desire. By detecting patterns in human experience, both our own and others' personal experience, we can come to conclusions about the ineradicable tendencies of human nature. It does not matter whether a given tendency concerns our bodies, our emotions, or our minds. Every ineradicable tendency toward some definite goal constitutes an inclination of human nature. And since any ineradicable tendency must sooner or later manifest itself, our concrete experience of desire, taken as a whole, must necessarily supply enough empirical data to chart the inner structure of human desire. Some of our natural inclinations can be thematized more easily than others. For example, it is easy to conclude that we are naturally inclined toward food and drink. Other inclinations may be less obvious and more difficult to identify. For example, our innate orientation toward love of God and proactive love of neighbor are not nearly as easy to identify as our inclination toward food and drink.

Due to the epistemic difficulty of identifying our natural inclinations, it can be helpful to compile lists of our natural inclinations as a way of sharing wisdom and provoking debate and discussion.[5] There is also a danger to these lists, however. They do not always note their limitations or explain adequately how their conclusions were derived. Consequently, lists of natural inclinations can be misleading. We are prone to infer that they are in some sense exhaustive and complete, even if only tentatively so. We can also fall into thinking that their epistemic justification derives from something other than personal experience. We can erroneously grant epistemic priority to "objective" reflection on the structure of the human person and what this structure metaphysically entails, forgetting that this sort of reflection ultimately presupposes the concrete experience of desire.

In this account of moral value, a tendency must be universal to constitute a natural inclination. This specification is important because some tendencies are ineradicable without being universal. Through external influences and our own choices, we can acquire tendencies that are not universal. Our experience of desire can become permanently directed along particular trajectories. For example, the inclination toward socialization is universal, but not everyone has an inclination to participate in *my* society and culture. For each of us, our inclination toward socialization is shaped by the community that surrounds us and the culture in which we were born and raised. Likewise, when we develop our interests and aesthetic tastes in certain definite ways, our choices can permanently shape our desires. In other words, many of our natural inclinations, paradoxically, have a universal tendency toward the particular. Nonetheless, it is only in their universality that they provide a measure for moral value. Even though acquired tendencies are enduring, and even though they shape our natural inclinations, they are not universal, and therefore they do not, in and of themselves, provide a measure for moral value.

[5] Aquinas offers one of the classic lists of our natural inclinations in *ST* I–II 94.2.

Rational Desire, Rational Choice, and the Possibility of Moral Evil

Human action implies unchosen desire. We can develop acquired desires, but these acquired desires presuppose our unchosen ones. Without desire that is just "there," desire that precedes any choice, there would be nothing motivating us to act. Our unchosen desires stir us into action. Without them, we would never act. We would have no reason to bother. We would never make any choices, either. Choice presupposes desire, that is, something motivating us to move beyond our current situation. For this reason, our unchosen desires should not be seen as limitations on our freedom, or boundaries that restrict its range; they are a condition of its possibility.[6] We would not be able to choose if we did not first desire.

As rational agents, we experience an unchosen desire that nonrational agents do not: rational desire, that is, desire for whatever appears good to our intellect and reason. Rational desire does not aim at any particular kind of object. It is a generic orientation, an open-ended orientation to the good. Consequently, rational desire is infinite, in the sense that it has no necessary limits. For instance, we can desire joy greater than anything we have experienced or imagined, because we can conceive the idea of such joy, and then, once we conceive of it, we can desire it. By contrast, our nonrational desires are finite. They aim at sensible objects, and sensible objects, by their nature, are finite. Unlike humans, animals do not experience infinite desire. Animals cannot conceive of objects that transcend their finite experience, and therefore they cannot desire them. The origins and metaphysical status of rational desire are irrelevant. From a materialist point of view, rational desire, like the human mind, can be classified as an emergent property: a complex web of instincts, perceptions, and memories that somehow evolved from its constituent parts and came to transcend them. From a Judeo-Christian point of view, it can be classified as the property of an immortal soul. For our purposes, the important point is that any adequate account of human desire must acknowledge that we have an unchosen and ineradicable tendency to desire whatever appears good to our minds.

Rational desire is what makes rational choice possible. When we make rational choices, we are directing our infinite rational desire toward particular goods, choosing one good over another. Some objects are truly good for us, others only appear so, but our desire for the good drives us to seek them out

[6] This discussion of the relationship between freedom and natural inclination is partly inspired by Servais Pinckaers. See Servais Pinckaers, *The Sources of Christian Ethics*, trans. Mary Thomas Noble (Washington, DC: The Catholic University of America Press, 1995), 354–456. See also Lombardo, *The Logic of Desire*, 78–82, 244–5.

and choose between them.[7] Our desire for the good does not merely make rational choice possible; it also makes rational choice compulsory. It pushes us to seek whatever limited goods are within our grasp, and since we cannot have them all, it compels us to choose between them. Nothing in this life is so overwhelmingly satisfying that we could not make a rational choice for something else, no matter how frivolous our reason—our *ratio*—for preferring it. If we were to come across something infinitely desirable, we would not be able to choose anything else; in comparison, finite goods would not seem remotely attractive.

Our capacity for rational choice explains the possibility of moral evil. As we have noted, action implies unchosen desire, and human action presupposes the unchosen desires intrinsic to human nature. Our natural inclinations prompt us to act, and without them, we would not choose to do anything. It follows that each of our actions necessarily advances at least one natural inclination: namely, whichever inclination(s) were prompting us to act in the first place. But this observation raises a question. If human actions are morally good insofar as they advance our natural inclinations, how could they ever fail to be morally good? If human actions necessarily advance at least one natural inclination, it would seem that every human action would have to be morally good. But many human actions are obviously not morally good. So it seems that this account of moral value cannot explain the possibility of moral evil. To answer this objection, we need to recall that, for an action to be morally good, it must do more than simply advance our natural inclinations: it must also avoid frustrating them. Only actions that both advance our natural inclinations and avoid frustrating them are morally good.

This response, however, can seem to create the opposite problem. If the frustration of a single inclination is all it takes to make an action morally evil, then we must regard many ordinary actions as morally evil. We have many different natural inclinations, and our actions often advance one inclination at the expense of another. For example, we sometimes fast before a medical test. In doing so, we advance our inclination to preserve our life, but we also

[7] Some contemporary philosophers have challenged the Aristotelian notion that our desires are attracted to objects only insofar as they seem good to us. The force of their argument rests on the observation that rational agents can desire something that they know is bad, precisely because it is bad. See, for example, Michael Stocker, "Desiring the Bad: An Essay in Moral Psychology," *The Journal of Philosophy* 76 (1979): 738–53; J. David Velleman, "The Guise of the Good," *Noûs* 26 (1992): 3–26.

This line of argument, however, conflates two different types of value judgments. One type judges whether an object is good with respect to our unchosen ends, that is, the attainment of our natural *telos*. The other type judges whether the same object is good with respect to a particular agent's chosen ends. It is easy to show that we can desire objects that we know are bad with respect to our unchosen ends. But, in order to be successful, this objection must show that we see these objects as bad with respect to our chosen ends—an impossible task, because these objects are means to our chosen ends, and thus necessarily good with respect to their attainment.

frustrate our desire to eat and drink. According to this account of moral value, it seems that we have to regard this innocuous action as morally evil—and that seems absurd. To answer this second objection, we need to recall that for an action to be morally defective, it does not suffice for the action to frustrate our natural inclinations. It must *intentionally* frustrate our natural inclinations. This requirement raises the bar considerably on what it takes for an action to qualify as morally evil. It is not enough for us to frustrate our inclinations non-intentionally. We have to *want* to frustrate our inclinations.

Someone might object, but how could we ever *want* to frustrate our natural inclinations? It seems absurd. If our natural inclinations are what prompt us to act in the first place, how could we ever act against them? Our capacity for rational choice is what makes it possible. Through our capacity for rational choice, we can choose anything that appears good to our reason and intellect. But anything can look good to our reason and intellect, at least from some perspective. So that means we can choose anything, no matter how self-destructive, and no matter how much it frustrates our natural inclinations. And whenever we intentionally frustrate our natural inclinations in pursuit of some chimerical good, we have performed a morally defective action.

Unlike humans, animals cannot intentionally thwart their natural inclinations, precisely because they are incapable of rational cognition and rational desire, and thus also of rational choice. For example, animals cannot commit suicide. They cannot intentionally thwart their natural inclination toward self-preservation. They might do something stupid that brings about their own death, but animals cannot *intend* to kill themselves. Dogs do not jump off bridges. They might wolf down chicken bones and get them caught in their throat and die, but they cannot kill themselves intentionally. They can only kill themselves accidentally or inadvertently, as the nonintended side effect of advancing their natural inclinations. Since animals cannot intentionally thwart their natural inclinations, they cannot perform morally evil actions. We can, however, because our capacity for rational choice allows us to make choices against our own best interests. Nature cannot go wrong, but reason can and does.

Nonintended Effects and Moral Value

Above and beyond its role in making rational choice possible, rational desire plays a special role in the determination of moral value. Since rational desire expresses a tendency toward whatever appears good to our reason and intellect, and since this tendency is universal, this tendency constitutes a natural inclination. We might call it our inclination toward the universal good. Consequently, since this tendency is a natural inclination, any action that thwarts it intentionally is morally defective. This straightforward conclusion has powerful consequences. It means that nonintended effects, and not simply intended effects, affect the moral value of actions. When we perform some intentional action, we do not intend only individual aspects and effects of that action. We also intend the sheer coming-to-be of that action, in all its foreseen aspects and effects, whether intended or nonintended.[8] Consequently, for an action to be morally good, it cannot intentionally frustrate our inclination toward the universal good with its aggregate ontological reality.

Nonintended effects, therefore, can affect the moral value of our actions. Even when negative effects are not intended, they diminish the aggregate ontological goodness of our actions.[9] When an action's negative effects frustrate our natural inclinations more than the action's positive effects advance them, the sheer coming-to-be of the action is not good. We are better off not performing such actions. When we know that an action's effects are more negative than positive, and we choose to perform it anyway, we are intentionally acting against our inclination toward the universal good. The action is morally defective.

For example, when a doctor prescribes medication that will cure a patient's illness, we normally regard the doctor's actions as morally good. If, however, the doctor knows that his patient will have painful allergic reactions to this medication and that another drug is easily available, we would evaluate the doctor's actions differently. Even if the doctor does not intend the patient any harm, but, say, can't remember the exact name of the other drug and does not want to look it up, we would not regard his actions as morally good. The negative, nonintended effects of his actions render them defective. In other circumstances, the positive effects of prescribing the medication might outweigh the negative, and thus alter our evaluation of the doctor's actions. For example, if the doctor and the patient were stranded on a desert

[8] The unintended effects of our actions—those effects that we do not foresee—are entirely irrelevant to their moral value, except when these unintended effects stem from prior intentional actions. For example, if a doctor is given false information about a patient, and as a result prescribes a medication that kills the patient, we do not hold the doctor morally responsible. The situation is tragic, but we do not blame the doctor; the unintended effects of his prescribing the medication are irrelevant to our evaluation of his actions. But if we could trace the doctor's mistake back to negligence—say, because he was a lousy student in medical school, or because he did not bother to consult the patient's medical chart—then we would consider him culpable. Even though the patient's death was unintended, the doctor should have known better, and so this unintended effect factors into our evaluation of his actions.

[9] Nonintended aspects can also advance our natural inclinations, and thus increase the aggregate ontological goodness of our actions. For example, we might help a friend who is hungry simply because he is hungry, and nonetheless realize that, as a result, he will be more likely to help us when we are hungry. This nonintended effect advances our natural inclinations and contributes to the aggregate ontological goodness of our actions. So positive, nonintended effects also affect the moral value of our actions. This study, however, focuses on negative nonintended effects, because we usually intend the positive effects of our actions, and even when we do not, our moral judgments rarely take into consideration the positive, nonintended effects of intentional actions.

island and the doctor only had this medication with him, then the positive effects of the medication might well be judged to outweigh the negative. In both circumstances, the doctor's sheer prescription of the medication is compatible with his natural inclinations. The difference is that the negative effects outweigh the positive effects in the first case, because a better drug is available, but on the desert island the positive effects outweigh the negative effects, because the better drug is not available.

In some situations, it can be very difficult to determine whether an action's negative effects outweigh its positive effects. For example, say an infant and a brilliant but aged scientist are both poisoned, and you have only one vial of antidote. To whom do you give the antidote: the infant who has just been born, or the aged scientist who might discover the cure for cancer? What if, instead of a brilliant scientist, it is the world's most famous poet, who would go on to write transcendently beautiful books of poetry after being given the antidote?

It is impossible to formulate certain answers to these sorts of questions. The impossibility does not stem from uncertainty about what is good and valuable; it stems, rather, from the impossibility of ranking incommensurable goods with anything like mathematical precision. Nonetheless, even when incommensurable goods are at stake, we can still make provisional judgments about their relative value (with value, again, measured against our natural inclinations). These provisional judgments are intrinsically prudential. They require us to weigh circumstances proper to particular situations and the foreseen consequences of our actions, and so require prudence. Consequently, as with anything involving prudence, things such as wisdom, experience, and sound theory help us to make better judgments. Those with more experience of the world, and those who are better informed, are better able to estimate future consequences and compare incommensurable goods, and thus better able to make good judgments about an action's balance of positive and negative effects. In some situations, judgments are very easy to make. For example, although an exceptional meal and life-saving medication advance our natural inclinations in different ways, it is obvious that anyone who chooses the meal over the medication has chosen the lesser good. In other situations, even for those who are especially prudent, judgments are very difficult to make. In complex situations, it is far from obvious whether a particular action, on balance, advances our natural inclinations more than it frustrates them.

The Plausibility of This Account of Moral Value

This account of moral value tells a story about our moral intuitions. It also provides a framework for judging morally ambiguous actions. But is its story plausible, and can its framework be trusted to provide reliable moral judgments?

We can answer these questions by considering three of our moral intuitions, one by one, and observing how this account of moral value harmonizes with them. (The analysis that follows, it should be emphasized, does not offer a definitive defense of this account of moral value. To begin, it simply asserts that we experience three moral intuitions, without attempting to prove that they are indeed universally experienced, and without meaning to imply that just because we experience them they must be right. Then, it argues that the account of moral value given here offers a plausible explanation for why we experience these intuitions, and thus provides a trustworthy framework for making moral judgments. It does not argue for anything more, nor does it hope to persuade those who disagree about the universality of these intuitions.)

First, we have a powerful intuition that some actions can never be morally justified, no matter how many positive consequences follow. Various meta-ethical theories attempt to explain why, but the relative merits of their explanations are secondary to the phenomenological "given" of this fundamental moral intuition.[10] If there were no space for judging actions apart from their effects, any action could be justified if its benefits were great enough. No crime could be ruled out without first considering its advantages. And this is absurd. In *The Brothers Karamazov*, Ivan Karamazov asks his brother Alyosha whether the torture and murder of one innocent child would be acceptable if it resulted in universal peace and harmony. Alyosha agrees with Ivan that it would not be acceptable.[11] Ivan's point resonates with our moral intuitions. Even if we cannot explain why, we sense that some actions can never be morally justified.[12] Otherwise, not only would it be acceptable to torture a child for universal peace and harmony, it would be unacceptable *not* to torture

[10] After acknowledging the difficulties of explaining this intuition, Anscombe excludes the possibility of seriously questioning its validity: "But if someone really thinks, *in advance*, that it is open to question whether such an action as procuring the judicial execution of the innocent should be quite excluded from consideration—I do not want to argue with him; he shows a corrupt mind" (Anscombe, "Modern Moral Philosophy," 17). Her refusal to acknowledge such questioning as intellectually legitimate is refreshing: radical moral relativism does not deserve full diplomatic relations.

Nonetheless, there are good reasons for doubting whether in today's culture the sheer questioning of such moral intuitions manifests a corrupt mind, or even a lack of sincerity in philosophical investigation. The present confusion in moral discourse that Anscombe's article names, and which Alasdair MacIntyre further identifies in *After Virtue*, requires serious and sympathetic engagement. Such engagement must walk a fine line: on the one hand, questions about the status of fundamental moral intuitions should be taken seriously; on the other, giving such questioning an equal place at the table gives it more status than it deserves.

[11] *The Brothers Karamazov* Part II, Book 5.4.

[12] Granted, there are some who would dispute the validity of this intuition. But even those subscribing to strict consequentialism must contend with our instinct to rule out certain actions without exception. They cannot claim their position without a fight; they must explain why we are "misled" into thinking that it is immoral to torture a child to save the world.

the child—it would be putting the discomfort of one torturer and one tortured child above the sufferings of billions.

Second, we have an intuition that moral value is profoundly related to personal happiness and the common good. We sense that our actions, in order to be morally good, should somehow contribute to our flourishing and the wellbeing of others, and that their positive effects should outweigh their negative effects. But we also sense that sometimes, when important interests are at stake, it is acceptable, and even praiseworthy, to act in a way that results in very serious negative effects. For instance, those who would never consider torturing a child might support bombing a critical military target in a just war, even knowing that it will cause the collateral deaths of several children.

Third, we recognize that we have difficulty determining the moral value of many actions, sometimes even after lengthy deliberation. Moreover, especially in pluralistic societies, we cannot help but notice widespread disagreement about morality. Sometimes we find ourselves certain about the moral value of an action, and uncertain about another, without necessarily knowing exactly why we are certain about the one and uncertain about the other. We also find ourselves disagreeing with others about actions whose goodness or badness seems obvious to us. We feel certain about our conclusions, and our opponents seem to express comparable certainty about theirs. Our disagreements are sometimes so profound that they make us wonder: on what grounds can we claim certainty about anything related to moral value, since someone else seems to have reached the opposite conclusion with comparable conviction?

The account of moral value given here can explain these intuitions and observations without doing violence to their phenomenological face value. First, by holding that actions that intentionally frustrate our natural inclinations are always morally bad, it explains our sense that some actions are always morally defective, regardless of their positive effects.

Second, by grounding moral value in our natural inclinations, that is, in our intrinsic orientations toward flourishing and fulfillment, this account explains our sense that moral goodness is closely connected to the attainment of happiness, both personal happiness and the happiness of others. Moral evil does not come from desiring too much happiness; it comes from desiring too little. It also accounts for the strong sense, at least in Anglo-American society, that the social sciences and their empirical conclusions are somehow relevant to our reasoning about moral questions. Since our desires are normative for morality, empirical conclusions about human nature are deeply relevant to ethics. Rather than comparing particular desires to some apodictic system of morality, and then determining which are morally appropriate, this account proposes the opposite. We first discern the inner structure of desire from empirical data, and then we measure our actions against it.[13] And because this

[13] This view of the relationship between desire and moral value is derived from Aquinas (or at least, my interpretation of Aquinas). Like Aquinas's approach to desire and moral value, this

account of moral value rules out only the *intentional* frustration of natural inclination, it can also explain why we are sometimes open to weighing positive effects against negative effects. The distinction between intended and nonintended effects explains our intuition that otherwise praiseworthy actions can be morally defective when they cause excessive harm (as when we help our neighbor solve his bug infestation problem by burning down his house), while other actions are morally good even though they involve considerable negative effects (as when we bomb an important military target, knowing that there will be significant collateral damage).

Third, this account of moral value can explain why we find some moral questions so difficult to answer, and why there is so much disagreement. This account maintains that an accurate understanding of human desire is necessary to evaluate human action accurately. But such understanding is hard to come by. As Jeremiah writes, "More tortuous than all else is the human heart, beyond remedy; who can understand it?" (Jer 17:9, NAB). Our concrete experience of desire is complex and confusing, and when we try to make sense of it, we are prone to error. Unfortunately, error about the inner structure of human desire, however innocent, has enormous implications for moral analysis. If we are unaware of certain natural inclinations, then we will not regard their intentional frustration to be morally defective, nor will we regard their advancement worth the price of negative, nonintended effects, no matter how proportionate. And if we posit natural inclinations that do not actually exist, we will make similar mistakes.

Furthermore, this account also maintains that, whether we realize it or not, whenever we make moral judgments we are implicitly considering whether actions harmonize with the inner structure of human desire. As a result, whenever we make moral judgments we are not relying exclusively on our cognitive faculties; we are implicitly measuring the actions in question against our experience of desire. So when we feel certain about a moral judgment, we are feeling certain that a particular action does, or does not, correspond to

proposal has considerable affinities—but also considerable dissimilarities—to David Hume's provocative assertion of the primacy of the passions over reason, and to the expressivist theories characteristic of moral philosophers such as Simon Blackburn. See David Hume, *A Treatise of Human Nature*, ed. David F. Norton and Mary J. Norton (Oxford: Clarendon Press, 2007), 2.3.3; Simon Blackburn, *Ruling Passions: A Theory of Practical Reasoning* (Oxford: Oxford University Press, 1998).

Although Aquinas is often caricatured as coldly rationalistic, he takes the structure of human desire and human emotion as morally normative. In making this move, Aquinas shares much in common with Hume. But because Aquinas sees human desire and human emotion as intrinsically dependent upon cognition and inherently oriented toward reason's guidance, he also grants a normative, supervisory role to reason—and thus avoids many of the problems present in Hume's moral philosophy. For a fuller discussion of these issues and a comparison of Aquinas and Hume on the relationship between passion and moral value, see Lombardo, *The Logic of Desire*, 116n98.

our desires—a very different kind of certainty from purely intellectual certainty. As a result, when two persons with divergent understandings of human desire evaluate the same action, they may come to different conclusions, but still experience the same subjective sense of certainty. And since we are so easily confused about our desires, it is easy to see why two persons might come to different moral judgments. In this way, this account of moral value can explain why persons holding differing views each might honestly claim to feel certain about their moral judgments—yet without affirming moral relativism, and without denying that at least one of them is wrong.

Finally, although this account holds that we should weigh positive against negative effects when judging an action's moral value, it recognizes that our weighing of effects does not admit of mathematical precision or geometric certainty, and that it is especially difficult to predict an action's future effects. It also leaves room for those coming from different cultures, backgrounds, and life experiences to have legitimate differences in their criteria for comparing positive and negative effects. Consequently, even while providing universal guidelines, this account of moral value does not micromanage every instance of moral evaluation. It allows for non-relativistic pluralism.

MORAL OBLIGATION

We do not just think that murder is morally wrong; we also feel morally obliged not to murder. Showing how moral value can be derived from our natural inclinations does not, of itself, explain the subjective experience of moral obligation. It is one thing to explain the origins of moral value. It is another to explain why we experience moral judgments as imperative and obligatory. Can this study's account of moral value explain our experience of moral obligation? If not, surely there must be something lacking about it.

David Hume is the troll guarding the bridge between this account of moral value and our experience of moral obligation. He famously argues that it is not possible to derive an "ought" from an "is." He holds that we cannot move from consideration of "what is" to "what one ought to do," and that we cannot derive propositions about moral obligation from propositions about being.[14] Pithy and powerful, the historical influence of his argument has been enormous, even among those hostile to many of Hume's other conclusions.[15] For all its influence, though, there is considerable controversy about what exactly

[14] See Hume, *A Treatise of Human Nature*, III.1.1.

[15] For example, Anscombe, even though highly critical of Hume, concedes that "it remains impossible to infer *'morally ought'* from 'is' sentences" (Anscombe, "Modern Moral Philosophy," 8).

the point of his argument is. Some, for example, have seen it as an argument against "the naturalistic fallacy" of moving from facts to values. But since Hume himself attempts to ground moral value in the facts of human nature, it seems inaccurate to see this claim as the point of Hume's argument.[16] Furthermore, if that were the point of his argument, it would be a weak one. It could be easily overcome by appealing to Aristotelian teleology, which offers a plausible account of how we can move from facts to values: namely, by comparing facts to their inner teleological orientation. Instead, Hume should be read as objecting to something else. He is objecting to the idea of explaining moral obligation on the basis of *either* facts *or* values. Not only does this reading seem to interpret Hume more accurately, it is also a stronger argument.

Hume does not object to moving from facts to values. He objects to moving to moral obligation from either facts or values. To put it another way, he objects to moving from observations about the way things are to an *obligation* to act accordingly. For example, it is one thing to prove that a movie is worth seeing; it is another thing to prove that we ought to see it. Likewise, it is one thing to evaluate actions as morally good or morally bad based on their ontology; it is another to explain why we must act accordingly. So robbing banks is bad. But what obligates us not to rob banks? Ontological analysis can provide us with endless reasons for why robbing banks is bad for others, bad for society, and even bad for ourselves, but these reasons do not explain why we *ought* to avoid robbing banks. They only explain why, if we were to rob a bank, our actions would be morally bad. They do not touch on the more basic question of why there is any such thing as moral obligation in the first place. Talk about moral value presumes the existential experience of moral obligation (otherwise, why would we talk about moral value?), but just as Euclid's five axioms lie outside his geometry even while providing its foundation, moral obligation itself lies outside the language game of moral value. Consequently, we cannot move from "is" to "ought" any more than we can drive to Europe from North America; there is nothing to bridge the gap. Or so runs this reconstruction of Hume's argument.

Despite Hume's objections, a bridge between moral value and moral obligation does exist: our orientation toward whatever appears good to our minds. Desire for the good, which makes rational choice possible, also explains and underwrites our experience of moral obligation. Objectively, desire for the good orients us toward the advancement of our other natural inclinations, and thus our own personal perfection and completion. Subjectively, we experience desire for the good as commanding and obligating—as the voice of conscience—insofar as it directs us toward actions compatible with our natural inclinations, and thus perfective of our own ontological goodness. *The*

[16] MacIntyre offers a similar reading of Hume on this point. See Alasdair MacIntyre, "Hume on 'Is' and 'Ought'," *The Philosophical Review* 68 (1959): 451–68.

experience of moral obligation is nothing other than experience of our inclination toward the universal good, the same inclination that grounds the very possibility of rational choice. Our desire for the good, and the trajectory of our nature toward its own proper perfection, is the font, not only of moral value, but also of moral obligation. Because both moral value and moral obligation originate in our desire for the good, moral obligation perfectly shadows our capacity to make rational choices. Our experience of moral obligation is just as inescapable as our experience of freedom.

Since our experience of moral obligation flows from our experience of desire, diminished awareness of our true desires can diminish our experience of moral obligation. Consequently, because they engender confusion and ignorance about our true desires, social factors, habitual vice, and the sheer obscurity of some natural inclinations can dull or distort our experience of moral obligation. Nonetheless, although our experience of moral obligation—that is, our experience of conscience—can be dulled or distorted, it can never be entirely eradicated, because knowledge of our natural inclinations can never be entirely eradicated. And just as social factors and our own actions can weaken our conscience, they can also strengthen it. The more we seek to cooperate with our natural inclinations, the more we experience how they lead us to happiness. The more our environment and upbringing helps us to grasp the world as it is, the more we understand our natural inclinations and what they tend toward. In this way, sound education and authentically human culture perform a great service. They help individuals and societies to grasp how non-obvious goods are, in fact, desirable. By doing so, they lead us to understand our natural inclinations with greater insight, and, hopefully, to cooperate with them more effectively.

This account of moral value and moral obligation can claim Friedrich Nietzsche as an unlikely ally. In many respects, Nietzsche's primary philosophical project was the affirmation of life and the overcoming of nihilism and the pessimism of Schopenhauer.[17] The way to overcome nihilism and pessimism, Nietzsche suggests, is by "the revaluation of all values," which he proposes to accomplish by measuring all values against the norm of "the will to power."[18] The precise nature of this will to power is contested, but it can be plausibly understood as a drive toward growth and expansion, and the sort of personal greatness that comes only at a cost, and whose greatness is somehow verified by this cost. He writes:

> I consider life itself instinct for growth, for continuance, for accumulation of forces, for *power*: where the will to power is lacking there is decline.[19]

[17] Bernard Reginster, *The Affirmation of Life: Nietzsche on Overcoming Nihilism* (Cambridge: Harvard University Press, 2006).

[18] Reginster, *The Affirmation of Life*, 148–200.

[19] Friedrich Nietzsche, *The Anti-Christ*, trans. R. J. Hollingdale (Harmondsworth: Penguin Books, 1968), 6.

In his polemic against Christianity, he is particularly implacable against those Christian teachings that, according to his understanding, seek to restrain the will to power. He is especially hostile toward Christian asceticism, which he sees as fighting against the instincts and inclinations natural to the human person. Nietzsche, instead, proposes that we measure human activity against the will to power: human activity is morally good when it advances the will to power, and morally defective when it frustrates it.[20]

If this interpretation of the will to power is correct—if the will to power is the will to seize, affirm, and expand whatever good can be found in ourselves and in the world, with a readiness to pay whatever price is necessary—then Nietzsche's project of revaluating all values against the will to power, not only can be endorsed from a Christian perspective, but *must* be endorsed. Disentangled from his terminology and his larger philosophical system, Nietzsche's point is that we must measure moral values, first and foremost, against our infinite desire for the good, and not anything else, no matter how worthy in itself. This project is eminently compatible with virtue ethics and Christianity, because neither sound philosophy nor good theology can countenance the idea that the unquenchable desires of the human spirit should be satisfied with mere rule-following or, worse, a misguided asceticism that calls for the intentional obstruction of our natural inclinations.

The driving insight behind Nietzsche's project, then, complements the accounts of moral value and moral obligation given in this study, since they also hold that the ultimate norm of moral value, and the only plausible anchor for moral obligation, is nothing other than our drive toward whatever is good—toward whatever affirms life and brings it to perfection. Nietzsche's insight is obscured by his sense that this drive toward what is good necessarily involves domination, but he is right that the robust affirmation of life constitutes the most essential measure of moral value.[21]

CONCLUSION

This chapter has told a story to explain our intuitions about moral value and moral obligation. According to its account of moral value, moral value derives from our natural inclinations—from the inner structure of our desires. When we advance our natural inclinations and avoid intentionally frustrating them,

[20] Reginster, *The Affirmation of Life*, 185–97.

[21] Nietzsche's formulation of the will to power is a response to Schopenhauer. Nietzsche thinks Schopenhauer errs by making "the will to life," or the will to biological survival, the essential principle of life. In place of Schopenhauer's will to life, Nietzsche proposes the will to power, perhaps because he gives too much weight to the observation that biological survival necessarily involves struggle and competition. See Reginster, *The Affirmation of Life*, 124–6.

and when the positive effects of our actions outweigh their negative effects, our actions are morally good. But when we intentionally thwart our natural inclinations, or when the nonintended, negative effects of our actions outweigh their positive effects, our actions are morally bad. On this account of moral value, the experience of moral obligation is simply the subjective experience of our unchosen and inescapable inclination toward the universal good. Even when we do not choose to act on it, this inclination drives us toward actions that cooperate with our natural inclinations, and we subjectively experience this inclination as a feeling of moral obligation. The accounts of moral value and moral obligation given in this chapter provide a basis for analyzing morally ambiguous actions, and thus for discussing the ethics of self-sacrifice and the problem of God's will and Christ's crucifixion.

3

Double Effect Reasoning

Many ethicists invoke double effect reasoning to argue for the moral goodness of seemingly problematic actions.[1] Through this form of moral analysis, actions with negative effects are justified on the grounds that their negative effects are not intended. In recent decades, double effect reasoning has become increasingly popular as a way to resolve difficult moral questions. But while many ethicists employ double effect reasoning, they disagree among themselves about many crucial points. To an extent often overlooked, they do not agree about either its appropriate application or its theoretical justification.

Drawing on the accounts of intention and moral value given earlier, and delving into the controversies surrounding this form of moral analysis, this chapter offers an account of double effect reasoning. It also proposes practical guidelines for applying this account to concrete situations. In the process, it argues that double effect reasoning is not a special mode of moral reasoning, but rather the application of our most basic intuitions about intention and moral value to difficult cases. Subsequent chapters build on these conclusions to distinguish between self-sacrifice and suicide, and then to discuss the ethical implications of different theological narratives of the crucifixion.

HISTORICAL ORIGINS AND CONTEMPORARY INTERPRETATIONS

Double effect reasoning has its origins in the moral theory of Thomas Aquinas and especially his treatment of killing in self-defense in *Summa theologiae* II–II 64.7.[2] Interpreters dispute whether Aquinas actually proposed anything

[1] Following Thomas Cavanaugh, this study prefers to speak of double effect reasoning, rather than a principle or doctrine of double effect. See Cavanaugh, *Double-Effect Reasoning*.

[2] For the story of the origins of double effect reasoning, see Joseph T. Mangan, "An Historical Analysis of the Principle of Double Effect," *Theological Studies* 10 (1949): 41–61; Cavanaugh, *Double-Effect Reasoning*, 1–37; Christopher Kaczor, "Double-Effect Reasoning from Jean Pierre Gury to Peter Knauer," *Theological Studies* 59 (1998): 297–316.

like a principle of double effect,[3] but all agree that double effect reasoning has its origins in his writings and subsequent commentaries on them. Over the past few decades, interest in double effect reasoning has grown, particularly among analytic philosophers.[4] Once employed almost exclusively by Catholic philosophers and moral theologians, double effect reasoning is now seen as a

[3] Whether Aquinas actually employs a principle of double effect is a point of long standing dispute among his interpreters. Mangan provides an overview of the history of this debate. See Mangan, "An Historical Analysis," 43–9. Among more recent authors, those who call into question the idea that Aquinas used such a principle include G. E. M. Anscombe, "Medalist's Address: Action, Intention and 'Double Effect,'" *Proceedings of the American Catholic Philosophical Association* 56 (1982): 24–5; Gareth B. Matthews, "Saint Thomas and the Principle of Double Effect," in *Aquinas' Moral Theory: Essays in Honor of Norman Kreztmann*, ed. Scott MacDonald and Eleonore Stump (Ithaca, NY: Cornell University Press, 1999), 78; Peter A. Redpath, "Why Double Effect and Proportionality Are Not Moral Principles for St. Thomas," *Vera Lex* 5 (2004): 25–42. Those who affirm that Aquinas did make use of some version of the principle of double effect, at least implicitly, include Gregory M. Reichberg, "Aquinas on Defensive Killing: A Case of Double Effect?," *The Thomist* 69 (2005): 370; Cavanaugh, *Double-Effect Reasoning*, 1–2.

[4] Philippa Foot offers striking evidence of the improving fortunes of double effect reasoning. She first published an article repudiating the principle of double effect and later came to accept it. See Philippa Foot, "The Problem of Abortion and the Doctrine of the Double Effect," *Oxford Review* 5 (1967): 5–15; Philippa Foot, "Morality, Action, and Outcome," in *Morality and Objectivity: A Tribute to J. L. Mackier*, ed. Ted Honderich (London and Boston: Routledge and Kegan Paul, 1985), 25–38. Among analytic philosophers, Warren Quinn's Kantian interpretation of the principle of double effect has generated much interest and discussion. See Warren S. Quinn, "Actions, Intentions, and Consequences: The Doctrine of Double Effect," *Philosophy and Public Affairs* 18 (1989): 334–51.

Other defenses of the principle of double effect include Philip E. Devine, "The Principle of Double Effect," *American Journal of Jurisprudence* 19 (1974): 44–60; James G. Hanink, "Some Light on Double Effect," *Analysis* 35 (1975): 147–51; Daniel F. Montaldi, "A Defense of St Thomas and the Principle of Double Effect," *Journal of Religious Ethics* 14 (1986): 296–332; Aulisio, "On the Importance"; Paulinus Ikechukwu Odozor, "Proportionalists and the Principle of Double Effect: A Review Discussion," *Christian Bioethics: Non-Ecumenical Studies in Medical Ethics* 3 (1997): 115–30; Anthony Kenny, "Philippa Foot on Double Effect," in *Virtues and Reasons: Philippa Foot and Moral Theory: Essays in Honour of Philippa Foot* ed. Rosalind Hursthouse, Gavin Lawrence, and Warren Quinn (Oxford Clarendon Press, 1995), 77–87; Daniel P. Sulmasy, "Commentary: Double Effect—Intention is the Solution, Not the Problem," *Journal of Law, Medicine and Ethics* 28 (2000): 26–9; D. R. Mapel, "Revising the Doctrine of Double Effect," *Journal of Applied Philosophy* 18 (2001): 257–72; William J. FitzPatrick, "Acts, Intentions, and Moral Permissibility: In Defence of the Doctrine of Double Effect," *Analysis* 63 (2003): 317–21; Alison Hills, "Defending Double Effect," *Philosophical Studies* 116 (2003): 133–52; P. A. Woodward, "Nancy Davis and the Means-End Relation: Toward a Defense of the Doctrine of Double Effect," *American Catholic Philosophical Quarterly* 77 (2003): 437–59; John Zeis, "Killing Innocents and the Doctrine of Double Effect," *Proceedings of the American Catholic Philosophical Association* 78 (2004): 133–44; Cavanaugh, *Double-Effect Reasoning*; Robert Anderson, "Boyle and the Principle of Double Effect," *American Journal of Jurisprudence* 52 (2007): 259–72; Neil Francis Delaney, "A Note on Intention and the Doctrine of Double Effect," *Philosophical Studies* 134 (2007): 103–10; Alison Hills, "Intentions, Foreseen Consequences and the Doctrine of Double Effect," *Philosophical Studies* 133 (2007): 257–83; Ian A. Smith, "A New Defense of Quinn's Principle of Double Effect," *Journal of Social Philosophy* 38 (2007): 349–64; Neil Delaney, "Two Cheers for 'Closeness': Terror, Targeting and Double Effect," *Philosophical Studies* 137 (2008): 335–67.

serious option among non-religious philosophers, even by those who ultimately reject it.[5] This new interest has been driven in part by the revived interest in virtue ethics and Aquinas, but also by the pressing need for answers to new and previously unimagined bioethical questions.[6]

In its most widespread and traditional form, double effect reasoning is known as a principle or a doctrine, and it is used to provide moral justification, under very specific circumstances, for actions that involve foreseen negative effects. The principle of double effect can be summarized with deceptive ease. After noting certain minor differences among its modern formulations, Joseph Mangan gives this summary:

> Formulated, therefore, in its full modern dress, it may be expressed as follows: A person may licitly perform an action that he foresees will produce a good and a bad effect provided that four conditions are verified at one and the same time: 1)

[5] In a widely read article, Jonathan Bennett claims to offer the first sustained philosophical criticism of the principle of double effect. See Jonathan Bennett, "Whatever the Consequences," *Analysis* 26 (1966): 83–102.

For other philosophical arguments against double effect reasoning, see R. G. Frey, "Some Aspects of the Doctrine of Double Effect," *Canadian Journal of Philosophy* 5 (1975): 259–83; Donald B. Marquis, "Some Difficulties with Double Effect," *Southwestern Journal of Philosophy* 9 (1978): 27–34; L. I. Ugorji, *The Principle of Double Effect: A Critical Appraisal of Its Traditional Understanding and Its Modern Reinterpretation* (Frankfurt: Peter Lang, 1985); Sanford S. Levy, "Paul Ramsey and the Rule of Double Effect," *Journal of Religious Ethics* 15 (1987): 59–71; Haig Khatchadourian, "Is the Principle of Double Effect Morally Acceptable?," *International Philosophical Quarterly* 28 (1988): 21–30; Frances M. Kamm, "The Doctrine of Double Effect: Reflections on Theoretical and Practical Issues," *Journal of Medicine and Philosophy* (1991): 571–85; Donald B. Marquis, "Four Versions of Double Effect," *Journal of Medicine and Philosophy* (1991): 515–44; William N. Nelson, "Conceptions of Morality and the Doctrine of Double Effect," *Journal of Medicine and Philosophy* (1991): 545–64; Jonathan Bennett, "Foreseen Side Effects versus Intended Consequences," in *The Act Itself* (Oxford: Oxford University Press, 1995), 196–200; Sophia Reibetanz, "A Problem for the Doctrine of Double Effect," *Proceedings of the Aristotelian Society* 98 (1998): 217–23; Richard Hull, "Deconstructing the Doctrine of Double Effect," *Ethical Theory and Moral Practice* 3 (2000): 195–207; Alison McIntyre, "Doing Away with Double Effect," *Ethics* 111 (2001): 219–55; Stefano Predelli, "Bombers: Some Comments on Double Effect and Harmful Involvement," *Journal of Military Ethics* 3 (2004): 16–26.

[6] For a collection of classic articles on double effect reasoning, including some of those listed above, see P. A. Woodward, ed. *The Doctrine of Double Effect: Philosophers Debate a Controversial Moral Principle* (Notre Dame: University of Notre Dame Press, 2001). For an overview of contemporary discussion among moral theologians, see John Berkman, "How Important is the Doctrine of Double Effect for Moral Theology? Contextualizing the Controversy," *Christian Bioethics: Non-Ecumenical Studies in Medical Ethics* 3 (1997): 89–114.

Within some circles, debates over the proper application of double effect reasoning has centered especially on bioethical questions and the extent to which the scope of our intentions is defined by the physical aspects of our actions. These debates have been helpful to my thinking through of the issues surrounding intention and double effect reasoning. See, for example, John Finnis, Germain Grisez, and Joseph Boyle, "'Direct' and 'Indirect': A Reply to Critics of Our Action Theory," *The Thomist* 65 (2001): 1–44; Martin Rhonheimer, *Vital Conflicts in Medical Ethics: A Virtue Approach to Craniotomy and Tubal Pregnancies* (Washington, DC: The Catholic University of America Press, 2009); Nicanor Austriaco, *Biomedicine and Beatitude: An Introduction to Catholic Bioethics* (Washington, DC: The Catholic University of America, 2011).

> that the action in itself from its very object be good or at least indifferent; 2) that the good effect and not the evil effect be intended; 3) that the good effect be not produced by means of the evil effect; 4) that there be a proportionately grave reason for permitting the evil effect.[7]

Formulated in these terms, the principle of double effect seems straightforward. Moreover, judging from the recent literature, few would question the basic accuracy of Mangan's summary, even though it was written more than sixty years ago.

Nonetheless, the principle of double effect appears much more straightforward than it actually is. In most formulations, including Mangan's, key concepts are left unexplained and unexamined. As a result, while interpreters might nominally espouse the same account of the principle of double effect, they often disagree about questions fundamental to its interpretation and application. Consequently, despite its frequent invocation, there is no consensus among philosophers and moral theologians about exactly what it is. A cursory scan of recent literature reveals a great deal of confusion, and it is explicitly addressed as such by various authors. Controversy centers on questions of metaethical justification and how to determine whether or not negative effects are intended.

The lack of consensus and outright confusion about the principle of double effect points to deeper problems and deeper confusions. Wittgenstein once wrote, "Sometimes an expression has to be withdrawn from language and sent for cleaning—then it can be put back in circulation."[8] The principle of double effect certainly seems ready for a trip to the dry cleaners. Speaking of double effect reasoning rather than the principle of double effect, as Thomas Cavanaugh does, is a small step in the right direction. Although roughly synonymous, the phrase better signifies that this philosophical resource is a mode of moral analysis, with its own internal controversies, rather than a self-interpreting doctrine.

DOUBLE EFFECT AND MORAL VALUE: A PROPOSAL

From this study's earlier accounts of intention and moral value, it follows that double effect reasoning is not a special mode of moral reasoning, functioning according to its own special rules. It simply applies ordinary intuitions to morally ambiguous actions with a heightened sensitivity to the intentions of the agent. This heightened sensitivity becomes necessary when actions

[7] Mangan, "An Historical Analysis."

[8] Ludwig Wittgenstein, *Culture and Value*, ed. G. H. von Wright and Heikki Nyman, trans. Peter Winch (Oxford: Blackwell, 1980), 39.

cause a jumble of morally significant effects, and when the line between what is intended and what is nonintended becomes blurry. Even in these complex cases, however, accounts of intention and moral value can suffice to determine the moral value of particular actions. There is no need for supplementary principles or doctrines. The difficult cases are difficult, but they are not exceptions.[9]

Disagreements about double effect reasoning, then, are ultimately disagreements about intention and moral value. We generally invoke double effect reasoning to resolve vivid, emotionally-charged dilemmas, and these dilemmas bring basic disagreements to the surface. They force us to confront assumptions about intention and moral value that usually remain unexamined. And because little consensus exists about intention and moral value, either in ordinary language or in philosophy, disagreements are inevitable. Consequently, we should not look at these disagreements as though they pertained only to a special ethical principle and a narrow range of actions. Instead, we should see them as concerning ethical concepts that apply to every human action.

The plausibility of this approach to double effect reasoning becomes more evident in its practical application. Let us turn, therefore, to some typical double effect scenarios and see how this study's earlier accounts of intention and moral value can be applied to them.

The Ethics of Self-Defense

Self-defense is the paradigmatic double effect scenario. Few question the proportionate use of violence in self-defense, but there is great controversy about its precise ethical justification, partly because it has bearing on more difficult questions. Disagreement centers on exactly what we may legitimately intend in defending ourselves, and especially whether we may *intend* to kill our aggressors. Since double effect reasoning has its historical origins in Aquinas's treatment of killing in self-defense, and since literature on self-defense continues to give Aquinas special attention, his views provide a good starting point. According to the dominant commentarial tradition, which can be traced back to Tommaso de Vio Cajetan in the sixteenth century, Aquinas

[9] The account of double effect reasoning given here, along with the accounts of intention and moral value on which it relies, was developed in conversation with the recent literature on the subject. I am especially indebted to Anscombe, "Medalist's Address"; Stephen A. Long, "A Brief Disquisition Regarding the Nature of the Object of the Moral Act According to St. Thomas Aquinas," *The Thomist* 67 (2003): 45–71; Reichberg, "Aquinas on Defensive Killing"; Cavanaugh, *Double-Effect Reasoning*. Particularly helpful was Anscombe's observation that the doctrine of double effect is best understood, not as a unitary principle, but as a "package deal" which comprises several elements, and therefore should be split up.

holds that one may neither kill the aggressor intentionally, nor perform actions that necessarily kill the aggressor.[10] This interpretation, however, seems to misread Aquinas.[11] Aquinas does hold that the aggressor's death is *praeter intentionem*, or beyond the defender's intention.[12] What this phrase "*praeter intentionem*" means, though, is highly contested, and Cajetan does not seem to interpret it correctly. Contrary to Cajetan's reading, Aquinas does not seem to object to actions that necessarily kill the aggressor. This alternative reading of Aquinas also claims an impressive Thomistic pedigree. It may not have been the opinion of Cajetan, but it was the opinion of Francisco de Vitoria, the founder of international law, in his commentary on Aquinas's *Secunda secundae*.[13] When interpreted according to the reading of Francisco de Vitoria or others like it, Aquinas's treatment of self-defense coheres well with this study's accounts of intention and moral value. Nonetheless, as its widespread misreading suggests, Aquinas's treatment of self-defense is neither sufficiently clear nor adequately developed. Consequently, although his position on self-defense provides a helpful starting point, it is better to tackle the question afresh, without explicit reference to Aquinas.

Suppose that we are walking down a dark alley, and suddenly, a menacing-looking thug jumps out and starts chasing us with a knife. We recognize him immediately as the escaped mental patient the news has been talking about. We also notice that he has a bomb strapped to his chest. We remember that he has a known history of random violence, and the public has been warned that he is dangerous and suicidal. Now, as it happens, we are not defenseless. We are carrying a firearm, and in fact have just left the shooting range, where we just won a marksmanship competition. Sizing up the situation, we know that our skills are good enough to shoot our aggressor wherever we choose. We could shoot him in the leg, which would stop him coming after us with a knife. He would still be able to detonate the bomb, however, and with the reports about him being suicidal, there seems to be a distinct possibility that he would do so, killing both himself and us in the process. So we shoot to kill.

[10] Mangan, "An Historical Analysis," 43–52; Joseph Boyle, "*Praeter intentionem* in Aquinas," *The Thomist* 42 (1978): 649–65; Denis Sullivan, "The Doctrine of Double Effect and the Domains of Moral Responsibility," *The Thomist* 64 (2000): 433–7; Cavanaugh, *Double-Effect Reasoning*, 1–14.

[11] Various authors have argued this point convincingly: Matthews, "Saint Thomas and the Principle of Double Effect"; Long, "A Brief Disquisition," 56–62; Reichberg, "Aquinas on Defensive Killing."

[12] *ST* II–II 64.7. For discussions of Aquinas's account of intention, see Boyle, "*Praeter intentionem* in Aquinas; John Finnis, "Object and Intention in Moral Judgments According to Aquinas," *The Thomist* 55 (1991): 1–27; Long, "A Brief Disquisition"; Joseph Pilsner, *The Specification of Human Actions in St Thomas Aquinas* (Oxford: Oxford University Press, 2006).

[13] Francisco de Vitoria, *Comentarios a la Secunda secundae de santo Tomás*, ed. Vicente Beltrán de Heredia, vol. 3 (Salamanca 1932–35); Long, "A Brief Disquisition," 71n32.

What do we intend in this scenario? Let us begin by asking what we want to happen. Well, we want the movements of our body. We want to raise our arm, take aim, pull the trigger, etc. We also want to prevent the aggressor from harming us. But do we want the aggressor's death? The aggressor's death is ontologically implied by our intentions, but we do not want to see the aggressor die. We want to neutralize him. If we miraculously neutralized the aggressor without killing him, we would not stand over him and shoot him in the head; the point of our actions was not to kill him. But perhaps the aggressor's death is logically implied by what we intend? The idea of killing the aggressor is not included within the idea of neutralizing the aggressor. Killing the aggressor is not a means to the end of neutralizing him, either; for something to be a means to an end, it must be intended in its own right. The aggressor's death is a nonintended side effect. Although the aggressor's death happens simultaneously to the intended effect of his neutralization, nonintended effects, as we saw earlier, often happen simultaneously to intended effects.

In considering this scenario, it is helpful to recall the example of the surgeon and the tumor. The surgeon does not intend to cut her patient's skin and thus cause bodily harm; she intends to create access to the tumor. Consequently, her actions are intrinsically different from the actions of a gang member who performs the same physical movements. From a physical point of view their actions might be identical, but human actions cannot be described solely by reference to physicality; some reference to intention is also necessary. Likewise, even if our actions were completely identical from a physical point of view, our killing of the aggressor in self-defense would not be identical with the actions of someone who kills him out of hatred or revenge. In their ontological totality, the surgeon's actions include bodily harm to her patient, but she does not intend this aspect of her actions. Likewise, the ontological totality of our actions includes the aggressor's death, but we do not intend this aspect of our actions. The aggressor's death is *praeter intentionem*.

This analysis answers the question of what we intend in a self-defense scenario. What can we say about the moral value of our actions? Our actions intentionally advance our inclinations, insofar as they advance our inclination toward self-preservation. Although they also frustrate our inclinations, insofar as killing the aggressor frustrates our inclination toward harmonious relationships with others, they do not do so intentionally. The thwarting of this inclination, like the aggressor's death itself, is nonintended. So our actions fulfill the basic requirement for moral goodness; they advance our natural inclinations without intentionally frustrating them. One question remains, however. Do the positive effects of our actions outweigh the negative, nonintended effects? From the aggressor's perspective, the negative effects might seem to outweigh the positive effects of our actions. After all, we remain alive, but the aggressor is killed. But the aggressor's perspective is irrelevant. Effects are weighed against the agent's inclinations, not generic human inclinations, and not the inclinations of anyone else. And clearly, from our perspective, the positive effects of our actions outweigh the negative, and so our actions should be considered morally good.

This analysis applies to a related scenario as well. Due to its dramatic and irreversible outcome, killing in self-defense gets a great deal of philosophical attention from ethicists. Nonetheless, causing physical harm of any sort in self-defense presents essentially the same moral problem.[14] When police officers pacify aggressors by hitting them with their nightsticks, they knowingly cause bodily harm to their aggressors. Their actions can be justified along similar lines as killing in self-defense. They do not intend the physical harm; they intend only to pacify their aggressors, and this positive effect outweighs the negative, nonintended effect of causing bodily harm. Consequently, their actions are morally good.

These conclusions, of course, harmonize with ordinary moral intuitions, but many other analyses would produce similar results and likewise harmonize with our intuitions about these scenarios. The approach to double effect reasoning given here, though, stands out for its flexibility and wide-ranging applications. When crucial elements of the scenario change, it can evaluate them without reaching for other principles. For example, many would say that we do in fact intend to kill the aggressor in the dark alley scenario, but the aggressor's hostility justifies this intention, and, consequently, our actions are morally good. But consider a different scenario. Instead of confronting a heavily armed mental patient, let us suppose an evil genius has constructed a human catapult and sent an innocent person hurtling toward us. Suppose that unless we shoot this innocent person, and thus jar his trajectory, we will be killed, or at least seriously harmed. In this scenario, even though the threat to our life is not posed by someone with hostile intent, we have a strong intuition that it would be morally acceptable to shoot. With the approach to double effect reasoning proposed here, this scenario would be analyzed in nearly the same way as the scenario with the hostile aggressor. Our actions in that scenario were judged morally good, not because a moral principle allowed for intending harm to an aggressor, but because we did not intend the aggressor's death. Likewise, shooting the innocent person in the catapult scenario would be acceptable because we intend our self-preservation but not the innocent person's death. Those who justify killing in self-defense on the basis of the aggressor's hostile intent are, however, in a bind. That principle does not apply to the catapult scenario; they need another one. While a multiplicity of moral principles does not, of itself, point to a philosophical error, Ockham's razor favors those analyses that rely on fewer—all else being equal, the simpler explanation is better.

[14] Reichberg, "Aquinas on Defensive Killing," 345–6.

It can seem counterintuitive to say that we do not intend harm to an aggressor killed in self-defense. It is not entirely counterintuitive, however. It is obvious that we do not want to kill our aggressor in the way that someone seeking revenge might want to kill him. Moreover, we intuitively recognize that the presence or absence of this "wanting" greatly affects the moral value of an act that results in someone's death. Watching a movie, we might approve when the hero of the movie kills his nemesis in a final confrontation, but cringe if the hero kills him after he has been neutralized and no longer constitutes a threat. We know intuitively that a line has been crossed.

Military Targets and Hostage Situations

Bombing military targets when civilian deaths are foreseen is another typical double effect scenario.[15] According to the conventions of modern warfare, the collateral death of civilians is sometimes considered morally justifiable. At the same time, targeting civilians to instill terror or cripple the enemy's morale is always regarded as morally reprehensible. Various ethical theories have been proposed to explain the difference. According to most theories, including the one given here, the crucial difference comes down to intention. If we do not intend the civilian deaths, and if the positive effects of the bombing outweigh the negative, our actions are morally acceptable. If we intend to bring about the civilian deaths, however, then our actions can never be morally acceptable, no matter the positive effects of our actions.

While there is great consensus about the basic principle, some scenarios are not so straightforward. For example, suppose that the enemy places an important military target directly underneath a popular restaurant, so that the bomb would have to pass through the restaurant before reaching the target. At first glance, this scenario seems different. Because the bomb kills civilians on its way to the target, rather than simultaneous with or subsequent to the target's destruction, it can seem more problematic. In fact, however, the civilian casualties are nonintended in this scenario as well. The civilian deaths are ontologically implied by the bombing, but they are not logically implied by the intention to bomb the target. The idea of bombing the military target does not include the idea of killing the civilians. The generals here do not *want* to kill civilians. Nor are the civilian deaths a means to an end; they are ontologically bound up with the bombing but they are not intended. Consequently,

[15] For discussions of double effect and military ethics, see Judith Lichtenberg, "War, Innocence, and the Doctrine of Double Effect," *Philosophical Studies* 74 (1994): 347–68; Timothy M. Renick, "Charity Lost: The Secularization of the Principle of Double Effect in the Just-War Tradition," *The Thomist* 58 (1994): 441–62; Steven Lee, "Double Effect, Double Intention, and Asymmetric Warfare," *Journal of Military Ethics* 3 (2004): 233–51; Predelli, "Bombers."

provided that the positive effects outweigh the negative, bombing a critical military target under these circumstances could be morally acceptable.

Hostage scenarios raise similar questions. For example, suppose that a terrorist surrounds himself with a human shield of hostages so that he can detonate a nuclear bomb. Two snipers each have a shot at the terrorist. The first sniper has a clear shot, but the bullet would pass through the terrorist and kill a hostage on the other side. The second sniper also has a good shot, but his bullet would pass through a hostage before it hit the terrorist. At first glance, the first shot might seem morally preferable, because the second shot seems to kill an innocent hostage as a means to an end. Nonetheless, there is no moral difference between the first and second shots. In both instances, the hostage's death is nonintended. Like the first sniper, the second sniper does not want to kill the hostage; he wants to stop the terrorist from detonating the bomb. Although in the second case the hostage's death chronologically precedes the intended effect, it is not chosen as the means to an end; it is simply the nonintended side effect of shooting the terrorist. Epistemic uncertainty, not moral theory, explains our instinctive preference for the first sniper's shot. We prefer the first shot because it is more obvious to us that the first sniper does not intend the hostage's death. We are wary about the second shot because we find it more difficult to isolate the second sniper's intentions from his actions. Because the second sniper kills the hostage before he kills the terrorist, it can seem as though the second sniper is choosing an evil means to accomplish a good end. Once we realize that the second sniper does not intend the hostage's death either, it becomes clear to us that his shot is also morally acceptable.

A Worry about Double Effect Reasoning

As we consider these scenarios, a worry about double effect reasoning might occur to us. The approach given here produces a good result when applied to typical double effect scenarios, but what happens when it is applied to other scenarios? Could it be used to justify actions that we otherwise judge morally evil? According to the analysis given above, when a dangerous aggressor comes charging at us, we can shoot to kill, and yet not intend the aggressor's death. That can seem to open the door to justifying morally evil actions. For example, what is stopping a hit man from saying that he does not intend to kill people; he intends only to earn some money? Of the various aspects and effects of his actions, he might say, he intends only the effect of getting his payoff. He does not want to his victim to die; he wants only to receive his payoff. Consequently, shooting his victim is not a means to an end. It is merely the nonintended effect of what he intends: namely, getting his payoff. And if enough positive effects follow—say, he will now finally have enough money for the leper colony he has always wanted to start—then his action would be morally good.

This worry is understandable, but it can be put to rest. The force of the hit man's sophistry comes from the way he defines his actions. He says that he intends only to earn some money. But for us to describe our intentions fully, we must somehow relate our bodily movements to our intentions. As we discussed earlier, assuming that they are not purely physiological, our bodily movements must always be intended under some description. Consequently, any adequate description of our intentions must be able to explain our bodily movements. The hit man says that he simply wants some money, but this intention alone cannot explain his bodily movements. By itself, it cannot explain why he is choking his victim and not, say, working as a barista and making espresso. To explain his bodily movements, the hit man must also acknowledge that he does not intend only to earn some money; he also intends to earn that money by means of killing. And because killing is the chosen means to his end, he must also intend his victim's death.

This lengthy analysis, however, is not necessary; imagining how the hit man might justify his actions can throw us, but mental gymnastics are not usually necessary to recognize that the hit man intends his victim's death. When we consider the hit man scenario, and compare it to the self-defense scenario, it is immediately obvious that the hit man wants his victim's death—and therefore intends it—in a way that someone killing an aggressor in self-defense does not want or intend his aggressor's death. The hit man's intentions logically imply his victim's death because he is not simply intending to earn some money. He is intending to earn some money by means of killing. When we kill someone in self-defense, however, our intentions do not logically imply the aggressor's death; the aggressor's death is merely the nonintended side effect of our efforts to stop the aggressor and thus preserve our life.

While ultimately unfounded, this worry about double effect reasoning and its potential misuse shines a light on some significant ambiguities in ordinary language. As noted above, our analysis of the self-defense scenario brought us to the conclusion that when a dangerous aggressor comes charging at us, we can shoot to kill and yet not intend the aggressor's death. At first glance, this conclusion seems like an exercise in doublespeak. How can we shoot to kill and yet not intend to kill the aggressor? It seems preposterous. If we look closer, however, we see that ordinary language talk about such scenarios is filled with ambiguity. We often use the same words with different meanings. Unless we acknowledge these equivocations, our talk about intention will remain trapped in paradox and dead-end analysis, like a fly in a fly-bottle.[16] To find our way out of the fly-bottle, we need to take a closer look at ordinary language and the way we talk about double effect scenarios.

[16] See Wittgenstein, *Philosophical Investigations*, §309.

When we compare the self-defense scenario and the hit man scenario, we instinctively recognize that they involve very different actions, with very different moral values. We call the first action morally good, and the second action morally evil. Nonetheless, we use the same word, killing, to describe both actions. Yet we do not think that their respective agents have performed the same kind of action. If we wanted to eliminate this ambiguity, we would need two different words—say, killing_1 and killing_2—to differentiate between these two kinds of actions. When we do not intend someone's death, we could describe our actions as killing_1, and when we do, we could call them killing_2. This proposal might seem far-fetched, but in fact ordinary language already allows for precisely this distinction. We tend to call killing_1 "killing" and killing_2 "murder." Our moral intuitions about the significance of intending someone's death seem to have pushed us to invent this linguistic distinction. Of course, for reasons of style and expediency, we often describe an act of murder as "killing," and (typically for dramatic effect) we sometimes call non-intentional killing "murder." Still, the very fact that we invented the distinction between these two words makes it all the more plausible that we can indeed shoot to kill and yet not intend the aggressor's death. When we say that we are shooting to kill without intending to kill, we are not contradicting ourselves; what we mean is that we are shooting to kill_1 without intending to kill_2.

CONCLUSION

Double effect reasoning should not be seen as a special sort of moral reasoning, functioning according to its own unique rules. It simply applies ordinary intuitions about intention and moral value to morally ambiguous actions, with a heightened sensitivity to intention. For this reason, it can be misleading to talk about a principle of double effect. Talking in this way can make it sound as though this form of moral analysis is self-standing and self-justifying. Properly understood, the principle of double effect is merely an algorithm for applying basic concepts to morally ambiguous actions. According to the accounts of intention and moral value given earlier, this algorithm could be summarized in the following fashion:

1. Do all of the action's intended effects advance our natural inclinations? If so, the action may be morally good, depending on the answer to the next question. If not, and if the action intentionally frustrates a single natural inclination, then the action is morally defective, regardless of the answer to the next question.

2. Do the action's positive, intended effects outweigh the action's negative, nonintended effects? If so, and if the answer to the first question was also affirmative, then the action is morally good. If not, the action is morally defective.

While this summary is designed especially to help resolve double effect scenarios, it could, in theory, be used to determine the moral value of any human action.[17]

[17] This algorithm only renders a judgment about an action's moral value. When it determines that an action is morally good, it does not follow that the action should be performed; it follows only that the action should be considered morally acceptable. We might well have other acceptable options, some of which might be morally superior.

4

The Ethics of Self-Sacrifice

When a soldier throws himself on a grenade to save innocent bystanders, we have no doubt that he has done something good, and even heroic. But when a police officer deliberately gets himself killed in the line of duty so that his family will receive financial compensation, our assessment is different. We might find the police officer's actions understandable, and we might even praise his desire to help his family, but we would find his actions deeply problematic. Since both men give their life for others, and achieve their end through actions that necessarily involve their death, why do we praise the soldier's actions but not the police officer's? We do not find it difficult to see that the soldier's actions are heroic, or that the police officer's actions are morally flawed, but it is surprisingly difficult to explain why.

Drawing on the preceding accounts of intention, moral value, and double effect reasoning, this chapter proposes an ethics of self-sacrifice that can explain why we praise the soldier's actions and regret those of the police officer. In future chapters, these principles will be applied to theological narratives of the crucifixion and their implicit portrayals of Christ's self-sacrifice.

SACRIFICE AND SELF-SACRIFICE

Sacrifice, in the sense of giving up one good for the sake of another, is an unavoidable feature of human life. We are constantly sacrificing one good for another. Children sacrifice their opportunity for vanilla ice cream by choosing chocolate, and Olympic athletes sacrifice business opportunities to hone their athletic skills. When we talk about sacrifice, we are usually talking about self-sacrifice, a particular kind of sacrifice, where agents give up personal goods for the benefit of others. We speak about firemen sacrificing their safety when they go into burning buildings to save lives; we also speak about mothers sacrificing their sleep for their newborn infants, and star athletes sacrificing scoring opportunities by passing the ball to teammates. In each case, we regard the agents as performing acts of sacrifice—and acts not only of sacrifice, but also of self-sacrifice.

Our ways of talking about sacrifice and self-sacrifice can be misleading. Although sacrifice has positive connotations, particular instances of sacrifice can be morally defective, as when drug addicts sacrifice their physical health and financial security for the sake of their drug use. Likewise, although self-sacrifice has very positive connotations, particular instances of self-sacrifice can be morally defective. Sacrificing our personal goods for the benefit of others is not always praiseworthy. Whenever we intentionally frustrate our inclination to self-preservation, our actions are morally defective, no matter the positive effects. For example, when an elderly person kills himself so that his family is not burdened by having to care for him, he is intentionally acting against his inclination toward self-preservation. Consequently, no amount of positive effects could justify his actions.

Acts of self-sacrifice can also be morally defective if their negative effects outweigh the positive. When people subject themselves to extreme humiliation and self-abnegation to serve others, and the benefit of their service does not justify the nonintended harm to themselves, their actions are morally defective. For example, we might not praise those in positions of great responsibility, such as presidents or prime ministers, for running into burning buildings to rescue people. By putting their lives in jeopardy they are risking the common good of their nations (assuming that they are good leaders), and thus the nonintended effects of their heroism outweigh its positive effects. Likewise, we would be puzzled if a president took a bullet for his bodyguard. We might admire his generosity, but we would also see the president doing something bizarre. Presidential bodyguards give their lives to save the president, not the other way around. (It might not always be morally problematic for presidents or prime ministers to give their lives for their bodyguards; incompetent leaders might have reason to think that their deaths would not harm and perhaps might even benefit their countries.)

When morally good, our acts of self-sacrifice never fail to benefit us, because they necessarily advance our deeper desires. For example, when a father sacrifices his desire to watch a football game to be present with his son at an important moment, he is not only benefitting his son, he is also advancing his own true self-interest because his relationship with his son is more essential to his own happiness than staying home and watching the game. Consequently, when ethical self-sacrifice involves sacrificing material or social goods, it can be said to sacrifice personal goods only in a very narrow sense. We are inclined toward communion with others, and ethical self-sacrifice advances this inclination and thus our personal flourishing. Although it necessarily forfeits goods of one sort or another, ethical self-sacrifice always gains others in their place. Otherwise, it might be self-sacrifice, but it would not be ethical.

SACRIFICING ONE'S LIFE FOR OTHERS

In all societies, sacrificing one's life for others ranks among the noblest possible acts. The words of Jesus echo this judgment: "Greater love has no man than this, that a man lay down his life for his friends" (John 15:13). But sacrificing one's life for others is not always heroic; there are also morally defective ways to give one's life for others.[1] For the sacrifice of our life to be morally good, we must not intend our own death, and the positive effects of our sacrifice must outweigh the negative. When we intend our own deaths, we are committing suicide, no matter the positive effects. Even if he does not pull the trigger, a police officer who deliberately gets himself killed in the line of duty has committed suicide. No matter the financial compensation to his family, his actions cannot be justified. When we do not intend our own deaths but their positive effects do not outweigh the negative, then our actions may not constitute suicide, yet they are still morally defective, as in the case of a president who takes a bullet for his bodyguard.

In some forms of ethical self-sacrifice, we perform actions that we know will lead to our death. The nonintended effect of our death occurs after the intended effects. For example, suppose that a woman helps a fugitive to escape from corrupt government officials, knowing that her assistance will become known and lead to her execution. Her actions are morally good, because she does not intend her own death and the positive effects outweigh the negative. (If she were the secret leader of an underground resistance movement, however, and she knew that her death would cause the resistance movement to collapse, it is not clear whether it would be morally good for her to get involved.) Likewise, we might protest a corrupt government, knowing that we will be killed as a result of our actions. Assuming that we do not want to die, and thus intend our death, and assuming the positive effects are significant enough, our actions would be morally good.

In other instances of self-sacrifice, rather than coming afterward, the nonintended effects are chronologically simultaneous with the intended effects. In these cases, it is more difficult to distinguish between what we intend and what we cause without intending. The classic example is a soldier jumping on a grenade to save others from certain death. His actions ontologically imply his

[1] For collections of essays and articles on self-sacrifice and the distinction between suicide and self-sacrifice, see M. Pabst Battin and David J. Mayo, eds., *Suicide: The Philosophical Issues* (London: Peter Owen, 1980); John Donnelly, ed. *Suicide: Right or Wrong?*, 2nd ed. (Amherst, NY: Promotheus Books, 1998). See also Paul Weiss, "Sacrifice and Self-Sacrifice," *Review of Metaphysics* 2 (1949): 76–98; William E. Stempsey, "Laying Down One's Life for Oneself," *Christian Bioethics: Non-Ecumenical Studies in Medical Ethics* 4 (1998): 202–24; David C. Thomasma, "Assisted Death and Martyrdom," *Christian Bioethics: Non-Ecumenical Studies in Medical Ethics* 4 (1998): 122–42; M. David Litwa, "Self-Sacrifice to Save the Life of Another in Jewish and Christian Traditions," *The Heythrop Journal* 50 (2009): 912–22.

death. Do his intentions logically imply his death? He wants to cover the grenade, he wants to absorb its blast, he wants to save others, and he accomplishes these objectives by jumping on a grenade. So it can seem as though he is using his death as a means to an end and thus intends his death. Let us look more closely at the implications of his intentions, however. Neither the idea of wanting to cover the grenade, nor the idea of wanting to absorb its blast, nor the idea of wanting to save others, includes the idea of wanting his own death. Therefore, his intentions do not logically imply that he intends his death. It is not a means to an end; it is the nonintended side effect of what he does intend. Because his death happens simultaneously to his saving of others, it can seem as if he must intend his death, too. But he need not, because his death is not logically implied by his intentions. His actions have many aspects and effects besides his death and can be fully explained by reference to these other aspects and effects.

Ethical self-sacrifice can also be deliberately provocative. In this form of self-sacrifice, we deliberately provoke our opponents to violence so that we can overcome them. There are many military examples of this sort of provocation. For example, soldiers might charge the left flank of the enemy, provoking the enemy to attack, knowing that they will probably be overwhelmed and killed, so that the rest of their army can surprise the enemy on the right and win a decisive victory. Or let us suppose that some prisoners of war have escaped. They are just about to cross back into friendly territory but there is one guard at the border. By counting bullets, the escaped prisoners know he has only one bullet left. They also know that he will shoot and kill whoever comes out first. So one of the prisoners volunteers to charge into the open, knowing that he will be killed, but also knowing that afterward the remaining prisoners will be able to cross the border safely. In these two examples, even though the soldiers and the escaped prisoner intentionally provoke their enemies and thus bring about their own deaths, they do not intend their own deaths. They intend only to weaken their enemies. Hence their actions are morally good.

Certain forms of nonviolent protest are another example of provocative self-sacrifice. In itself, nonviolent protest simply aims to publicize injustice and pressure authorities to do something about it. Protestors, however, can have another layer of intentions in their actions. In a particularly corrupt situation, there might be little hope that nonviolent protest of itself would prompt any change. In such a situation, some might protest precisely in order to provoke the civil authorities, anticipating that they will react with violence, and calculating that the resulting public outrage will hasten their objectives more effectively than anything they could do on their own. In this scenario, although the protestors intentionally provoke the civil authorities to violence, and thus knowingly cause their own deaths, they do not intend them. They intend only to lure their opponents to overstep and bring their corruption down on their own heads, thus clearing the ground for something positive to happen. In this way, protesting in hope of provoking a violent reaction can be morally good.

These guidelines give us tools to evaluate controversial instances of self-sacrifice. Take the story of Captain Lawrence Oates, a member of Robert Scott's ill-fated polar expedition. On the way back from the South Pole in 1912, Captain Oates became disabled and his pace slowed considerably. Realizing that he was jeopardizing his companions' hope of reaching safety, he walked out of their tent into a blizzard, saying, "I am just going outside and may be some time," and did not return. His actions are widely regarded as heroic, but there is disagreement about their moral justification, and especially, since he knowingly caused his own death, whether or not he could be said to have intended to kill himself.[2] According to this study's account of intention, Captain Oates need not have intended to kill himself. He intended to walk outside and he intended to leave his companions so that they would not feel any obligation to stay behind with him. Nonetheless, even though he knew he was walking into certain death, he need not have wanted his own death; he might have wanted only to get away from his companions and thus free them to move on without him. The idea of walking outside and leaving one's companions to unburden them does not include the idea of killing oneself. It is possible that, as a matter of fact, Captain Oates did intend to kill himself, but from what we know of his actions, he need not have. Consequently, his death need not have been chosen as a means to an end; it could have been—and almost certainly was—merely the nonintended side effect of his actions. Since the positive effects of his actions outweigh the negative effects, his actions were morally good, and even heroic. If he had pulled out a weapon and shot himself, it would be a different matter; then his actions would have been suicidal.

[2] The case of Captain Oates has been widely discussed in the literature on suicide and self-sacrifice. See R. F. Holland, "Suicide," in *Talk of God*, ed. G. N. Vesey (London: MacMillan, 1967–68), 72–85; R. A. Duff, "Absolute Principles and Double Effect," *Analysis* 36 (1976): 68–80; Tom L. Beauchamp, "What is Suicide?," in *Ethical Issues in Death and Dying*, ed. Tom Beauchamp and Seymour Perlin (Englewood Cliffs, NJ: Prentice-Hall, 1978), 97–102; Marquis, "Some Difficulties with Double Effect; R. G. Frey, "Did Socrates Commit Suicide?," *Philosophy* 53 (1978): 106–8; Robert M. Martin, in *Suicide: The Philosophical Issues*, ed. M. Pabst Battin and David J. Mayo (London: Peter Owen, 1980), 48–68; R. G. Frey, "Suicide and Self-Inflicted Death," *Philosophy* 56 (1981): 193–202; R. A. Duff, "Socratic Suicide?," *Proceedings of the Aristotelian Society* 83 (1982–83): 35–47; James W. McGray, "Bobby Sands, Suicide, and Self-Starvation," *Journal of Value Inquiry* 17 (1983): 65–75; Terence M. O'Keeffe, "Suicide and Self-Starvation," *Philosophy* 59 (1984): 349–64; Suzanne Stern-Gillet, "The Rhetoric of Suicide," *Philosophy and Rhetoric* 20 (1987): 160–70; Joseph Kupfer, "Suicide: Its Nature and Moral Evaluation," *Journal of Value Inquiry* 24 (1990): 67–81; Duncan Richter, "The Ethics of Suicide," in *Ethics After Anscombe: Post "Modern Moral Philosophy"* (Dordrecht, The Netherlands: Kluwer Academic Publishers, 2000), 76–93.

Hunger strikes are another controversial instance of self-sacrifice.[3] In hunger strikes, individuals protest injustice by refusing to eat, even to the point of starvation. They start their hunger strikes as a way of protesting an unjust government or an unjust situation, with the understanding that they will begin to eat as soon as their demands are met. Sometimes hunger strikes end in death; sometimes they do not, because the demands are met. Either way, however, hunger strikes are morally defective, because either way hunger strikers are prepared to kill themselves as a chosen means to their ends. Morally speaking, they are like terrorists threatening to kill their hostages if their demands are not met. The only difference is that they themselves are the hostages.

CONCLUSION

We often talk about sacrifice as though it is inherently good and admirable. It is not. Acts of sacrifice or self-sacrifice are morally good only when they do not intentionally frustrate our natural inclinations and we gain more than we lose. Otherwise, they are morally defective. The same applies to scenarios where we sacrifice our own lives. While it is never morally acceptable to intend our own death, no matter the benefits to others, double effect reasoning shows that it can be acceptable, and even heroic, to cause our own death non-intentionally for the sake of some greater good. In future chapters, these conclusions about sacrifice and self-sacrifice will be applied to theological narratives of the crucifixion, and especially Christ's supreme act of self-sacrifice on the cross.

[3] On the morality of hunger strikes, see McGray, "Bobby Sands, Suicide, and Self-Starvation"; O'Keeffe, "Suicide and Self-Starvation."

5

God's Will, Moral Evil, and the Crucifying of Christ

God's goodness has no limits, and it far exceeds our capacity to imagine or describe. Nonetheless, Christians have never hesitated to make positive claims about divine goodness, and especially God's implacable opposition to evil. "God cannot be tempted with evil and he himself tempts no one" (Jas 1:13), James writes. This passage does not reflect any insight original to Christianity; James is simply reaffirming the faith of the Jewish people in a Christian context. God cannot be tempted with evil because God does not find evil attractive. Being all good, God never wants moral evil, and even *cannot* want moral evil. Sound Christian theology, therefore, must keep a clear distance between God's will and the moral evil of Christ's crucifixion. Any theological narrative that suggests that God wills human evil, whether implicitly or explicitly, must be ruled out as logically incoherent. This simple criterion provides a powerful tool for sifting through competing interpretations of the crucifixion and narrowing the range of viable options.

Building on the accounts of intention and moral value given earlier, this chapter clarifies what it means to talk about divine willing and discusses God's non-willing of moral evil. It also argues for the possibility of categorizing human actions as morally evil, definitively and without exception, "in advance" of any special divine revelation. Then, drawing on double effect reasoning and the ethics of self-sacrifice, this chapter evaluates different theological narratives of the crucifixion, considered in broad logical categories. It discusses which theological narratives are philosophically compatible with God's absolute opposition to evil, and which ones must be ruled out, and thus brings the *via negativa* of this first part to its conclusion.

GOD'S WILL AND MORAL EVIL

This study argued earlier that human willing is nothing other than rational intending; that is, the kind of intending that involves not merely knowledge and desire, but also rationality. So, when we talk about God willing something, it follows that we are saying that God rationally intends it, and also that he knows it and wants it. Unlike human intending, divine intending comes in only one variety. Due to their corporeality, humans and animals experience nonrational forms of cognition and nonrational desires, and are thus capable of nonrational intending. Nonrational cognition and nonrational desire, however, are foreign to the divine nature. Being bodiless and immaterial, God does not cognize anything nonrationally, nor does he desire anything nonrationally. When God intends something, he always intends it rationally. In other words, whenever God intends something, he always wills it. Likewise, divine wanting always amounts to divine willing, because God is incapable of any kind of wanting except rational wanting. This understanding of divine willing finds support in ordinary language. For example, we often affirm that God wills something. What do we mean when we say this? We mean that God wants something to be the case. We are describing God's desire. And since saying that God wants something presumes that God knows what he wants, we are also describing what God knows. In short, ordinary ways of talking about God's will presume that divine willing, like human willing, is a kind of rational intending.

Metaphysically, divine willing differs from human willing in one crucial respect. Human willing is tensed and variable. Our willing varies from moment to moment, and individual acts of willing have a temporal duration. As the author of time, however, God is outside of time and eternal. God is also unchanging, because he is one eternal act of divine being. Consequently, unlike human willing, divine willing is eternal and immutable. It has no beginning or end and it does not vary or change. The eternity of divine willing sits uneasily with some of our linguistic habits. We often speak as though God willed something in the past and no longer wills it now. For example, we might say, "God willed for the world to exist," or "God must have willed for us to meet." This language, though, need not be seen as committing us to hidden metaphysical assumptions. We understand implicitly that if God willed for us to meet at some moment in the past, then he still wills for us to have met in the present. In fact, the very idea of "God willing us to meet" presupposes that God orders human events from a vantage point that is atemporal and eternal. So, although we talk about divine willing in tensed terms, this way of speaking does not commit us to a tensed understanding of divine willing. Indeed, since our talk about divine willing often presupposes divine eternity, we might even argue that only a tenseless account of divine willing can resolve the inherent tensions of ordinary language.[1]

[1] The Christian theological tradition has often distinguished between God's antecedent and consequent will. (See, for example, John Damascene, *De orthodoxa fide*, 2.29 and *ST* I 19.6 ad 1.) God's antecedent will is what God wills generically, and God's consequent will is what God wills in actuality, after taking into account our free choices. This distinction, however, can be

Despite their metaphysical differences, divine willing and human willing relate to their objects in similar ways. Like human willing, divine willing can focus on individual aspects of actions to the exclusion of others. God can will particular aspects of actions without willing absolutely everything about them. When we say that God wills something, we do not mean that God necessarily wills everything ontologically bound up with it. Otherwise, our linguistic habit of distinguishing between what God wills and what God does not will would not make any sense. Since God wills the world to exist, and since everything that happens in the world is ontologically bound up with the world's existence, it would follow that God willed absolutely everything that happens, and everything that each of his creatures does. But we do not think that God wills absolutely everything that happens. Our strongest and most certain intuition about the need for distinguishing between what God wills and what God does not will concerns the phenomenon of moral evil. We see wanting or condoning moral evil as completely incompatible with God's goodness, and so we immediately rule out the possibility that God could ever will moral evil. We might affirm that God wills for his rational creatures to exist, or for his rational creatures to exercise free choice, but we would never affirm that God wills moral evil. As the source of all goodness, God cannot be anything other than implacably opposed to moral evil.

Due to an important difference between human willing and divine willing, however, God cannot distance himself as thoroughly from moral evil as we can. Unlike God, we can refuse to will that something exist in any respect whatsoever. We can even refuse to will that we ourselves exist. Consequently, we can completely distance ourselves, volitionally, from moral evil; we can refuse to will that morally evil actions ever happen, under any aspect, for any reason. But God cannot so completely distance himself, volitionally, from moral evil. God did not only create the world; he also sustains it in being. And since it is God who created us with freedom and sustains us in being at every moment of our existence, it is also God who provides the ontological ground for us to stand on at the very moment when we perform morally evil actions. As a result, we cannot say that God has nothing to do with human evil. As the creator and sustainer of all that exists, God underwrites the ontology of every evil action. Consequently, to deny that God has anything to do with human evil would deny his authorship of everything that exists. Since we cannot say that God has nothing to do with human evil, how should we describe God's relationship to morally evil actions?

misleading. Because the words "antecedent" and "consequent" usually imply chronological sequence, the distinction subtly suggests that God undergoes a process of reflection before settling on what he wills. Those using the distinction generally do not mean to attribute any such temporal succession to God's willing, but its terminology inadvertently raises the question. Consequently, although the distinction allows for a certain amount of precision about God's will, it also invites confusion. For this reason, the distinction admits of only limited usefulness. It seems better and safer to use ordinary categories for intending and willing, and then note as necessary when our meaning transcends them.

The first and most popular option is to say that God allows or permits moral evil. According to this proposal, God wills our essential being, which is good, but even though our morally evil actions are ontologically bound up with our essential being, he does not will them. He only permits them. This phrasing suffices in many contexts, but it is not entirely satisfactory. To say that God only permits our evil actions seems too weak. In ordinary contexts, when we allow others to behave badly, it means that we are declining to intervene. For example, we might allow someone to get away with murder (literally or figuratively) because intervening might make things worse. But God does not only refrain from preventing morally evil actions; he also sustains us in existence precisely as we perform our evil actions. So it seems misleading to say that God only permits our evil actions. More precision is necessary.

Another option is to say that God directly wills the existence of rational creatures and their capacity for free choice, but only indirectly wills their morally evil actions. This phrasing has some advantages. It implicitly acknowledges that morally evil actions can be traced back to God's creating and sustaining of the world in existence. In this sense, it is an improvement over saying that God permits or allows evil actions. But this phrasing also seems too strong. It misleadingly suggests that there is some minimal sense in which God wants morally evil actions.

Our earlier reflections on intending and willing open up a third and better option for talking about God's relationship to morally evil actions. Since divine willing, like human willing, is a form of intending, we can talk about what God intends and does not intend. We can say that God intends and wills our existence and our capacity for free choice, but only non-intentionally underwrites our evil actions. He does not will our evil actions; they are the nonintended effects of what he does will. This phrasing captures God's ontological underwriting of our evil actions, and at the same time it explicitly denies that God in any sense wants us to perform them. This solution acknowledges that God holds a certain amount of ontological responsibility for the evil actions of his creatures. After all, God could have chosen not to create free creatures and thus avoided all kinds of problems (also for himself). At the same time, it robustly affirms God's non-willing of moral evil, and it avoids any implication that God condones our evil actions.

RULING OUT HUMAN ACTIONS AS INCOMPATIBLE WITH GOD'S WILL

God does not will morally evil actions; that much is clear. For some theists, however, this principle does not allow us to make absolute determinations about which human actions God might or might not will. Tomorrow, God might ask us to do something that we would otherwise consider morally evil. By the sheer fact of God's command, it would suddenly become morally good for us to perform that action. Indeed, it would become morally evil *not* to perform it. According to this line of reasoning, because God is the highest moral authority, we cannot move from human concepts of morality to absolute conclusions about moral evil. God's will is the ground of all moral value, and so whatever God wills is automatically morally good. In the words of Kierkegaard, God might command a "teleological suspension of the ethical" to accomplish his purposes, and then the actions that God commanded would be morally good no matter what they were.[2] By the very fact of commanding them and thus implicitly willing them, God would render those actions morally good.[3] This position poses a serious challenge to the very idea of ruling out theological narratives for implying that God wills moral evil. It removes any grounds for bringing philosophical questions to theological narratives. The only relevant questions become historical: whether or not God wants particular actions to happen. If he does, by the very fact of his wanting them to happen, those actions are morally good.

In response, it can be agreed that there is no higher moral authority than God, and that God's will is indeed the benchmark against which we must measure every human action. Creation itself is a revelation of God's will, however, and the geography of creation includes the peaks and valleys of moral value. Consequently, when our actions intentionally frustrate our natural inclinations, God cannot morally sanitize them by sheer fiat. He would be contradicting his own will, already manifested in the order of creation, and God cannot contradict himself. It is not just that it would be unworthy of God to contradict himself, or that God does not make mistakes. God is metaphysically incapable of contradicting himself. By virtue of his eternity, God wills what he wills in one eternal act of willing, and this single act is immutable and unchanging.

[2] Soren Kierkegaard, *Fear and Trembling*, trans. Sylvia Walsh (Cambridge: Cambridge University Press, 2006), 46–59.

[3] For an overview of the history of divine command ethics and representative texts from the Middle Ages through the present day, see Janine Marie Idziak, *Divine Command Morality: Historical and Contemporary Readings* (New York: Edwin Mellen Press, 1979).

For some attempts by divine command theorists to explain why the hypothetical possibility of morally unsettling commands does not undermine their ethical theory, see Robert Merrihew Adams, "A Modified Divine Command Theory of Ethical Wrongness," in *Divine Commands and Morality* (Oxford: Oxford University Press, 1981), 83–108; Paul Rooney, *Divine Command Morality* (Aldershot: Avebury, 1996), 97–114; C. Stephen Evans, *Kierkegaard's Ethics of Love: Divine Commands and Moral Obligations* (Oxford: Oxford University Press, 2004), 304–18. For a comprehensive account of divine command ethics, see Robert Merrihew Adams, *Finite and Infinite Goods: A Framework for Ethics* (Oxford: Oxford University Press, 1999).

For a persuasive rebuttal, see Wes Morriston, "What If God Commanded Something Terrible? A Worry for Divine-Command Meta-Ethics," *Religious Studies* 45 (2009): 249–67.

Since moral value derives from ontology, and especially natural inclination, actions that intentionally frustrate our natural inclinations could become morally good only if God were first to change human nature. For example, adultery intentionally frustrates our natural inclination toward exclusive spousal love. Consequently, God cannot command us to commit adultery, because this command would do violence to the inner structure of our desires. He would first have to change human nature into something else, and then he could command adultery. At that point, however, God would no longer be commanding humans to commit adultery; he would be commanding some other kind of creature to commit adultery. God cannot simply declare a problematic action morally good; he first has to change the world, or else create a new one.[4]

This conclusion harmonizes with our intuitions. We have a strong sense that some human actions are always out of bounds, even for God. Those who think that God can sanitize any human action by sheer divine fiat must nonetheless concede that we have a strong intuition to the contrary. When Christians say that God never wills moral evil, they do not think that they are saying something tautological; they think that they are saying something meaningful. But on the view that God could always surprise us tomorrow with a new command, our claims about God's non-willing of moral evil would reduce to tautology. They would convey no useful information about the sort of actions that God does not will. At most, they would be saying that *usually* God does not will those actions we normally consider evil.

Not every moral theory is sturdy enough to rule out actions as necessarily incompatible with God's goodness. To be adequate to the task, a moral theory must possess two characteristics. First, it must derive moral value from ontology. Otherwise, the world would not contain within itself the principles of moral value, and creation would not suffice to reveal God's will. God could transform moral defect into moral goodness simply by changing the rules. Second, it must judge some actions to be inherently defective apart from any consideration of their consequences. Otherwise, if the positive effects were great enough, the most problematic action would become morally good, and God could command any action conceivable, provided that its positive effects outweighed the negative. This criterion is particularly important when it

[4] There is no philosophical problem, however, with God restricting the range of ethical options available to us by sheer divine fiat. Although God cannot command actions that would intentionally frustrate our natural inclinations, and thus transform something morally evil into something morally good, he can make ordinary actions obligatory. That is, over and above the moral demands of our natural inclinations, God can command or forbid additional actions, as long as these additional commands and prohibitions do not intentionally frustrate our inclinations. For example, according to Exodus, God commands us to keep holy the Sabbath, and this command creates a new obligation. Nonetheless, this command does not contradict our natural inclinations. In fact, by leading us to carve out time for rest and worship, it fulfills them.

comes to evaluating theological interpretations of the crucifixion. The most suspect forms of self-sacrifice would surely be morally justified when weighed against the salvation of the world.

Abraham's Sacrifice of Isaac

These questions about the possibility of God commanding otherwise unjust actions do not arise from everyday living. Religious believers are not usually worried that, at any moment, God might command them to do something he had previously forbidden, and thus turn the foundations of human morality upside down. Rather, these questions arise from reading texts in sacred scripture where God commands something shocking.[5] On the one hand, these difficult texts seem to suggest that, when it suits his divine purposes, God can suspend the normal rules of morality. On the other hand, Jews and Christians find the idea of God commanding otherwise unjust actions unsettling, and therefore have often sought to explain these texts in ways that leave ordinary moral intuitions intact. Among the difficult texts that have prompted sustained exegetical reflection, pride of place belongs to Genesis 22, in which God commands Abraham to sacrifice his son Isaac, stopping him only at the last minute. Historically, it was commentary on this story that first gave rise to questions about the possibility of God commanding otherwise unjust actions. To bring our discussion full circle, therefore, we need to apply our conclusions about God's non-willing of moral evil to the Akedah, the binding of Isaac.

Before proposing an interpretation, a historical survey of exegesis on Genesis 22 provides some helpful context.[6] The earliest commentaries, both Jewish and Christian, give special attention to God's apparent injustice in asking Abraham to sacrifice his son, and then devote great energy to explaining why it is not as unjust as it seems. For example, in order to make the sacrifice seem more acceptable, without any textual warrant in Genesis, they often suggest that Isaac voluntarily offered himself to be sacrificed.[7] Many later authors also look for ways to reconcile the biblical story with our ordinary intuitions about right and wrong. Aquinas, for example, argues that God is justified in commanding Abraham to sacrifice Isaac, since original sin makes everyone liable

[5] On these difficult scripture texts that seem to call God's goodness into question, see the excellent collection of essays in Michael Bergmann, Michael J. Murray, and Michael C. Rea, eds., *Divine Evil? The Moral Character of the God of Abraham* (Oxford: Oxford University Press, 2011).

[6] For an overview of Jewish and Christian commentaries on the Akedah, with special attention to the exegetical influence that Jews and Christians have exerted on each other over the centuries, see Edward Kessler, *Bound by the Bible: Jews, Christians and the Sacrifice of Isaac* (Cambridge: Cambridge University Press, 2004).

[7] Kessler, *Bound by the Bible*, passim.

to the penalty of death, and so God's command simply hastens Isaac's just punishment.[8]

Other later authors abandon the project of reconciling ordinary moral norms with Abraham's sacrifice of Isaac. Some reject the universal applicability of ordinary moral norms. Scotus maintains that God's command trumps the normal order of morality,[9] and Kierkegaard likewise holds that God sometimes calls for a "teleological suspension of the ethical."[10] Others reject the justice of Abraham's behavior. Kant maintains that moral norms can never lose their force and that Abraham should have disobeyed the command to sacrifice Isaac, because moral norms are more certain than the authenticity of any private revelation. According to Kant, if a supernatural voice commands someone to do something contrary to the moral law, "then no matter how majestic the apparition may be, and no matter how it may seem to surpass the whole of nature, he must consider it an illusion."[11]

According to the account of God's non-willing of moral evil given here, God could never command a father to sacrifice his son. Human sacrifice, much less a father's sacrifice of his only son, runs against our natural inclinations, and therefore is intrinsically incompatible with God's will. Even if God planned to stop the father before he actually killed his son, God would still be asking him to perform actions with the intention of eventually killing his son. Even though they would not involve any actual killing, these preliminary actions would be performed with the intention of killing, and thus would intentionally frustrate the father's natural inclinations. It follows that the God of Israel could never have asked Abraham to sacrifice Isaac.

This philosophical conviction, however, does not require us to reject the authority of sacred scripture, nor does it place human knowledge and human reason over and above divine revelation. It simply pushes us toward non-literal, non-historical interpretations of Genesis 22. We might want to grant some historical kernels to the story, such as Abraham's historicity or his wholehearted faith in God, or perhaps even some historical episode in which Abraham demonstrated remarkable devotion to God. Nonetheless, we have no reason to think that the human author ever intended for the story of the Akedah to be taken as history in the modern sense. The text makes no explicit

[8] *ST* I–II 94.5 ad 2.

[9] See Scotus *Ordinatio* I dist. 44; *Ordinatio* III suppl. dist. 37 in John Duns Scotus, *Duns Scotus on the Will and Morality*, ed. and trans. Allan B. Wolter (Washington, DC: The Catholic University of America Press, 1986), 254–61, 68–87, esp. 71, 85. For more on his account of natural law and the possibility of divine dispensation, see Hannes Möhle, "Scotus's Theory of Natural Law," in *The Cambridge Companion to Duns Scotus*, ed. Thomas Williams (Cambridge: Cambridge University Press, 2003).

[10] Kierkegaard, *Fear and Trembling*, 46–59.

[11] Immanuel Kant, trans. Mary J. Gregor (New York: Abaris, 1979), 115. For a discussion of Aquinas, Scotus, and Kant on the Akedah and natural law, see Matthew Levering, "God and Natural Law: Reflections on Genesis 22," *Modern Theology* 24 (2008): 151–77.

claims about the historicity of the event, and it would be anachronistic to expect ancient authors to share modern historiographical prejudices against mingling fact and fiction. By reading Genesis 22 as something other than a strictly historical account, we can appreciate its provocative elements without being scandalized by them, seeing it as a dramatic illustration of faith calling us beyond our ordinary horizons. With the early Christians, we can also see the story as a prophetic foreshadowing of God the Father offering his Son for our salvation (noting as they did, for instance, that Isaac, like Christ, carries wood for the sacrifice on his shoulders). This sort of reading defuses the challenge it presents to our moral intuitions, yet without undermining its relevance to questions of faith and ethics, and without requiring us to repudiate it as an embarrassing remnant from a more primitive culture. The same hermeneutic can be applied to other difficult texts in sacred scripture, thus drying up the main wellspring of theological resistance to the idea of ruling out human actions as categorically incompatible with God's will.

This exegetical approach to Genesis 22, which has now become common, is not entirely original to modern times. As we have seen, over the centuries, Jewish and Christian commentators have never countenanced the idea that God would ever command Abraham to do something morally evil. Some commentators supply details to make God's command more acceptable; others assert that whatever God commands is necessarily good; still others flatly reject the possibility that God could have given Abraham such a command; but all of them find the sacrifice of Isaac provoking, and none of them think that God would ever will moral evil. In other words, Jewish and Christian reading of Genesis 22 has always given hermeneutic primacy to God's non-willing of moral evil. Today, due to our greater attentiveness to historical context and literary form, we can move the conversation forward. We can maintain this hermeneutic primacy without denying divine inspiration, and without affirming that the God of Israel actually commanded a father to sacrifice his son. It is important, however, to see this interpretation in continuity with earlier Jewish and Christian exegesis. Earlier generations may have lacked the tools to balance faith in divine inspiration with historical-critical sophistication, but they shared an instinctual aversion to any reading that would undermine God's non-willing of moral evil.

GOD'S WILL AND THE CRUCIFYING OF CHRIST

Since God cannot will human evil, God cannot will the moral evil associated with Christ's crucifixion. This simple principle has many interpretative consequences. It means that any theological narrative in which God wills the actual crucifying of Christ must be ruled out as incompatible with God's goodness. It does not, however, rule out God willing the crucifixion in any sense whatsoever. It excludes only God willing the moral evil associated with it. For example, by virtue of the fact that it happened, God must have willed to sustain those crucifying Christ in existence at the very moment when they were crucifying Christ. He did not merely allow his Son to be crucified; he sustained in existence the arms of the Roman soldiers as they hammered nails into Christ's hands and feet. Most theological interpretations of the crucifixion would also maintain that God wills Christ's heroic endurance of his suffering. We might say, therefore, that God wills the crucifixion event under some aspects of its ontological totality, but he does not will the moral evil associated with the crucifying of Christ. God non-intentionally underwrites the evil actions of those crucifying Christ, and he incorporates them into his plan of salvation, but he does not want, intend, or will the moral evil associated with those actions.

Which precise aspects of the crucifixion event, then, does God will? To answer this question positively, we would have to appeal to sacred scripture, and we will do so in later chapters. In the meantime, we can still answer this question negatively, insofar as we can rule out aspects of the crucifixion event that God cannot will. Most obviously, we can rule out God willing the moral evil of those who orchestrated Christ's crucifixion or actually brought it about, and any theological narrative that would imply as much. We can also rule out God willing Christ's sheer *experience* of crucifixion, for whatever salvific reason, because willing Christ's experience of crucifixion logically implies willing the actual crucifying. In Aristotelian terms, it is impossible to want someone to experience a specific passion without willing its corresponding action, just as it is impossible to want someone to become a father without also wanting him to have a child. The idea of any specific passion includes the idea of its corresponding specific action. Therefore, any theological narrative in which God wills Christ's sheer experience of crucifixion can also be ruled out.

Some might agree that God cannot will Christ's sheer experience of crucifixion, but then argue that God could will for Christ to manifest virtues that can be manifested only while one is being crucified. Here, a distinction must be made between two different scenarios that look deceptively similar. In the first scenario, God sends his Son to manifest virtues that eventually cause his death. God wills that Christ exercise these virtues no matter what happens, but God does not send Christ for the specific purpose of exercising them on the cross. Whether Christ is crucified or not is irrelevant to God's will for Christ. God wants his Son to persevere in goodness; the circumstances of that perseverance are secondary. This sort of scenario avoids implying that God wills moral evil or the actual crucifying of Christ. For example, suppose someone is imprisoned for protesting an injustice. Afterward, he is told that if he renounces his complaint, he will be set free; if he holds fast, he will be executed. In the face of this difficult situation, the protestor's father might want his son to endure death bravely rather than renounce his complaint. Still, the father does not will for his son to suffer virtuously simply for the sake of suffering virtuously; much less does he want his son to experience suffering. Rather, he wants his son to remain steadfast in the face of obstacles and difficulties. In the same way, in this first scenario, God does not will for his Son to suffer virtuously for the sake of suffering virtuously. He wills only Christ's continued exercise of virtue even in the face of suffering.

In a second scenario, God sends his Son for the specific purpose of exercising these virtues on the cross. He does not merely want his Son to exercise these virtues come what may. He wants him to suffer crucifixion to exercise these virtues precisely while being crucified. To put it otherwise, God wants his Son to manifest virtues that have the specific property of being exercised while one is being crucified. Yet, willing Christ to exercise such virtues requires willing the sheer experience of crucifixion which, in turn, implies willing the actual crucifying. For example, if a general starts a war because he wants an opportunity to exercise his military skills, he cannot deny that he wants to start a war, even if he starts the war only for the sake of exercising his military skills. Starting the war is the chosen means of attaining his end. Likewise, if God sends his Son so that he will manifest virtues that can be exercised only on the cross, then he has chosen Christ's experience of crucifixion as the means to an end, and he cannot avoid willing the actual crucifying of Christ and its associated moral evil. In other words, God cannot will for Christ to manifest virtues that have the specific property of being exercised while he is being crucified, without also willing the crucifying of Christ. Therefore, any interpretation of the crucifixion implying that God wills Christ to manifest such virtues must be ruled out from consideration.

We can also say that any theological narrative in which Christ wants or intends his own death is doubly ruled out. Such narratives imply that God wills human evil both in his divine nature, insofar as the Trinity uses suicide as a means to an end, and in his human nature, insofar as God the Son is the subject of Christ's human actions. Consequently, when it comes to evaluating theological narratives, it is important to pay attention to Christ's attitude toward his death. Sometimes it is obvious that Christ does not intend his own death. Theological narratives in which Jesus is surprised by his crucifixion, and thus could not possibly intend it, obviously imply an ethical attitude toward his death. So do theological narratives where Jesus knowingly causes his crucifixion solely out of unswerving fidelity to the truth. These narratives are philosophically plausible and cannot be ruled out in advance.

In many theological narratives, however, it is not immediately obvious whether or not Christ intends his death. For these difficult cases, double effect reasoning and the ethics of self-sacrifice can help us to isolate Christ's intentions. Sometimes they show that a particular narrative has Christ choosing his death as a means to an end, and therefore intending his death. Other times they help us to see how Christ's actions do not imply a suicidal intention, as when a narrative has Christ intending something that ontologically, but not logically, implies his death. Just as a soldier can jump on a grenade to save others without intending his death, so too Christ can intend something ontologically bound up with his death without actually intending his death. When we apply this conclusion to Christ's actions leading up to his crucifixion, we discover a startling result: as long as he does not intend his death, narratives in which Christ deliberately provokes his opponents to crucify him are philosophically viable.

Albert Schweitzer's historical reconstruction of Christ's attitude toward his death provides an excellent example. In his telling, Christ provokes his own death, and yet, because he intends something other than his death, we would not say that his actions constitute suicide. Schweitzer summarizes his narrative of the crucifixion in a famous passage:

> There is silence all around. The Baptist appears, and cries: "Repent, for the Kingdom of Heaven is at hand." Soon after that comes Jesus, and in the knowledge that He is the coming Son of Man lays hold of the wheel of the world to set it moving on that last revolution which is to bring all ordinary history to a close. It refuses to turn, and He throws Himself upon it. Then it does turn; and crushes Him. Instead of bringing in the eschatological conditions, He has destroyed them. The wheel rolls onward, and the mangled body of the one immeasurably great Man, who is strong enough to think of Himself as the spiritual ruler of mankind and to bend history to His purpose, is hanging upon it still. That is His victory and His reign.[12]

In Schweitzer's narrative, Jesus throws himself on "the wheel of the world." His actions, however, are not suicide. Jesus does not intend his own death any more than a soldier throwing himself on a grenade intends his own death. He acts to change the course of history, not to bring about his own death. For Schweitzer, Jesus is like a nonviolent protestor who provokes a corrupt government to overreact and thus bring about its own downfall. And so, whatever the merits of his narrative, it cannot be ruled out on philosophical grounds.

[12] Albert Schweitzer, *The Quest of the Historical Jesus: A Critical Study of Its Progress from Reimarus to Wrede*, trans. William Montgomery (London: A. & C. Black, 1911), 368–9. Along with N. T. Wright's similar reconstruction of Christ's attitude toward his death and René Girard's scapegoat theory of redemption, Schweitzer's imagery in this passage played a crucial role in my thinking about the crucifixion. They prompted me to take seriously the possibility that Christ could have deliberately provoked his own crucifixion in an ethically justified manner. For N. T. Wright's reconstruction, see N. T. Wright, *Jesus and the Victory of God* (Minneapolis: Fortress Press, 1996); for René Girard's theory, see Girard, *The Scapegoat*.

CONCLUSION

God does not will moral evil because divine goodness and human evil are entirely incompatible. This truth about God is foundational for Christian theology. If moral value were derived purely from God's will, though, we would not be able to draw many practical applications from this truth. At any moment, God could decree that an otherwise reprehensible action was suddenly morally good or even heroic. The account of moral value given in earlier chapters, however, derives moral value from ontology. It therefore sees the order of creation as a revelation of God's will for humanity and the measuring stick of moral value. Since God manifests his will in the ontology of creation, and since God is metaphysically incapable of contradicting himself, inherently evil human actions—that is, human actions that intentionally frustrate our natural inclinations—could never be made morally good by divine decree. Therefore, if we determine that a particular human action is inherently evil, we can rule out the possibility that God would or could ever will it. On the basis of these considerations, we can rule out any theological narrative in which God wills the actual crucifying of Christ, or Christ intends his own death. Yet as long as he does not intend his death, theological narratives in which Christ knowingly causes his death, or even provokes it, can nonetheless be philosophically viable.

Part II

New Testament Evidence

6

Jesus' Attitude Toward His Death

In the Gospels, Jesus foresees his death and moves toward it as though it were the culmination of his public ministry. But is this narrative historically accurate? Historical-critical exegesis has led many to doubt that it is. Many suspect that this narrative is a later construction, superimposed on the life of Jesus to emphasize his mastery over events. Others tend to trust its accuracy but do not think that they can rule out alternative possibilities, let alone come to any historically certain conclusions.

This chapter examines the Gospel portrayals of Jesus' intentional attitude toward his death, focusing only on broad thematic questions (such as whether he expected to be killed, and whether he expected his death to advance his objectives), and then assesses their historicity. It shows that the Gospel portrayals of Jesus' attitude toward his death are clear, consistent, and pervasive. Then, with this textual analysis complete, it argues that, should the Gospels be granted any degree of historical reliability, we must conclude that Jesus of Nazareth expected to be killed and expected his death to advance his objectives. In later chapters, this conclusion is used to evaluate theological narratives of the crucifixion.[1]

METHOD AND APPROACH

The argument of this chapter is straightforward. It argues that, throughout their narratives, on many different levels, the Gospels consistently and repeatedly portray Jesus as knowing that he will be killed, and as seeing his death as somehow advancing his objectives. Consequently, if we grant the Gospels any degree of historical reliability, we must regard this portrayal of Jesus' attitude toward his death as historically accurate. We cannot avoid the conclusion that

[1] Historical studies often avoid referring to Jesus of Nazareth by the theological title of "Christ" to avoid compromising their methodological objectivity. Since this chapter focuses on historical questions, it likewise avoids referring to Jesus as Christ.

Jesus expected to be killed, and that he expected his death to advance his objectives. Or so the argument of this chapter runs.[2]

While this argument is straightforward, it requires a great deal of textual evidence. For the argument to work, it must prove that the Gospels portray Jesus' attitude toward his death so frequently, so consistently, and in a way so intertwined with their narratives, that their historical reliability on this point cannot be denied without denying their historical reliability about nearly everything else. The argument, therefore, must offer overwhelming corroborating evidence. It needs to show that there are so many instances where Jesus alludes to his coming death, or assigns it some positive value, that either this depiction traces back to the historical words and actions of Jesus or else the Gospels completely lack historical trustworthiness. The argument does not turn on any single piece of evidence, such as the historicity of a particular Gospel story, or the interpretation of a particular scripture passage. By the very nature of the argument, no single piece of evidence could suffice to establish its conclusions. The argument seeks to generate a cumulative effect by citing numerous examples; it does not deduce wide ranging conclusions from a handful of key scripture texts. As a result, no single instance where Jesus anticipates his death must be taken as historically accurate for the argument to work. Any particular instance can be discarded as historically inaccurate as long as a good number of other instances remain historically plausible.

There is enormous controversy about the historicity of particular sayings and events related to Jesus' attitude toward his death.[3] For example, since Rudolf Bultmann, many scholars have argued that the passion predictions are *vaticinia ex eventu*: prophecies constructed in the wake of the crucifixion, and then placed on Jesus' lips in the Gospels.[4] Conversely, many scholars have argued for the historical authenticity of the ransom saying of Mark 10:45 and Matt 20:28.[5] For the most part, this chapter avoids these debates. The literature is too vast to engage them adequately. More importantly, this chapter's argument does not stand or fall on the historicity of any particular saying or

[2] This argument was inspired in large part by Scot McKnight's observations in Scot McKnight, *Jesus and His Death: Historiography, the Historical Jesus, and Atonement Theory* (Waco, TX: Baylor University Press, 2005), 79–82. Other scholars argue by different means for similar conclusions about Jesus' historical attitude toward his death, most notably: Heinz Schürmann, *Jesu ureigener Tod: Exegetische Besinnungen und Ausblick* (Freiburg: Herder, 1975); B. F. Meyer, *The Aims of Jesus* (London: S.C.M. Press, 1979); Martin Hengel, *The Atonement: The Origins of the Doctrine in the New Testament*, trans. J. Bowden (Philadelphia: Fortress Press, 1981); Wright, *Jesus and the Victory of God.*

[3] For the current state of the question regarding several key sayings and events, see McKnight, *Jesus and His Death.*

[4] See Rudolf Bultmann, *Theology of the New Testament*, vol. 1 (Waco, TX: Baylor University Press, 2007), 29.

[5] On the question of the ransom saying's authenticity in current scholarship, see McKnight, *Jesus and His Death*, 159–75.

event, and so it does not need to engage them. Instead, its main task is to document the Gospel portrayals of Jesus' attitude toward his death. It seeks to demonstrate their underlying clarity and consistency, and thus lay the groundwork for historical conclusions. To this end, it examines passages in the Gospels that indicate something about Jesus' attitude toward his death. Since this chapter's argument does not rest on any single piece of evidence, it avoids spending much time on passages whose portrayal of Jesus is ambiguous or controversial. It focuses instead on assembling evidence that would be accepted by the vast majority of scripture exegetes.[6]

After showing that the Gospel portrayals are overwhelmingly clear and consistent, the chapter argues for their historicity. It approaches this task in two phases. First, it examines the literary form of the Gospels and argues that, at least to some extent, the evangelists intended to convey historically accurate information about Jesus. Then, it argues that, given the literary form of the Gospels, and given their consistent portrayals of Jesus' attitude toward his death, we must conclude that these portrayals are historically accurate—that is, if we grant any degree of historical reliability to the Gospels. It should be emphasized that this study does not seek to establish the historical reliability of the Gospels; that task lies beyond its scope.

THE GOSPEL PORTRAYALS IN OVERVIEW

Before turning to individual pieces of textual evidence, we will first look at the Gospel portrayals in broad outline. This overview will give us a framework in which to place the various points of data. Then, with this broad outline in mind, we will turn to the individual points of data from which it was constructed.

The Gospel narratives are constructed around the crucifixion. They build to a tragic dénouement on Golgotha, and then abruptly pivot and recount the story of the resurrection. Jesus' attitude toward his death and eventual resurrection echoes this narrative structure. He heads toward his crucifixion with steady deliberation, just as the Gospel narratives do, as though it were the inevitable culmination of his public ministry. The Gospels show Jesus knowing the true contours of events before they happen, in stark contrast to his apostles and those who eventually crucify him. Besides the narrators, he alone

[6] Since most of the evidence assembled is noncontroversial, this chapter does not usually engage with secondary literature about particular passages. For most passages considered in this chapter, the exegetical consensus is overwhelming, making such engagement unnecessary. This chapter does, however, engage the secondary literature in the notes when commenting on ambiguous or controversial passages, offering support for its interpretations as necessary.

knows what to expect. The others do not understand where things are going, but Jesus does, from the beginning.

While the evangelists make it clear that Jesus foresees his crucifixion, they do not make his interpretation of the crucifixion nearly as clear. In the Gospels, Jesus habitually maintains a certain reserve with others, even with those favorably disposed toward him (John 2:23–25), and he often speaks in parables (Mark 4:2–34; Matt 13:3–53). This *modus operandi* is particularly evident in how he speaks about his death. Jesus often alludes to his coming death, but he rarely addresses it in explicit terms. When he does, he says little by way of interpretation. He typically states or implies that the Son of Man must suffer, but without explaining why he must suffer. He keeps his cards close to his chest.

Nonetheless, some of Jesus' words and actions in the Gospels do interpret his coming death. Through scattered indications and clues, the four Gospel narratives provide a strikingly consistent picture of Jesus' interpretation of his crucifixion. First, Jesus does not view his crucifixion as the frustration of his mission, that is, of his overarching intentions and objectives.[7] He foresees that he will be crucified, but he is confident that his crucifixion will not prevent him from attaining his objectives—that his rejection will not thwart his mission. Second, Jesus interprets his crucifixion as itself somehow advancing his mission. The crucifixion is not something he simply endures and overcomes as the unfortunate consequence of fidelity to his mission; somehow it actually advances his mission. Third, in the Gospels, Jesus sees his death as somehow integral and necessary to the accomplishment of his mission. It is not part of a contingency plan. It is intrinsic, not extrinsic, to the accomplishment of his mission. From this broad overview, we now turn to individual pieces of textual evidence.

JESUS' PROPHETIC EXPECTATION OF HIS DEATH IN THE GOSPELS

The Gospel narratives depict Jesus knowing that he will meet a violent death and nonetheless proceeding toward it resolutely.[8] His prophetic expectation

[7] When this chapter speaks of Jesus' mission, it is referring simply to Jesus' overarching intentions and objectives, considered as a collective whole.

[8] The following studies merit special note for their treatment of the Gospels accounts of Jesus' death and Jesus' attitude toward his death: Morna Hooker, *Jesus and the Servant: The Influence of the Servant Concept of Deutero-Isaiah in the New Testament* (London: S.P.C.K., 1959); Schürmann, *Jesu ureigener Tod*; Karl Kertlege, ed. *Der Tod Jesu. Deutungen im Neuen Testament* (Freiburg: Herder, 1976); Meyer, *Aims of Jesus*; E. P. Sanders, *Jesus and Judaism* (Philadelphia: Fortress Press, 1985); Joel B. Green, *The Death of Jesus: Tradition and Interpretation in the*

manifests itself in explicit predictions, vague allusions, prophetic actions, and the unspoken presuppositions that lie behind his warnings and ethical teachings.

Predictions of Suffering and Death

The synoptic Gospels recount three occasions when, speaking only to the twelve apostles, Jesus predicts that he will be rejected and killed, and then rise again after three days. These three passion predictions are Jesus' most direct and explicit indications, before the last supper, of what he expects to happen. On each occasion, the apostles do not grasp the meaning of Jesus' predictions; it is only after the crucifixion that they understand.

The first prediction takes place in Caesarea Philippi after the execution of John the Baptist, when Jesus' public ministry has already taken a sour turn, and immediately after Peter's confession of faith. Jesus charges his apostles to tell no one that he is the Christ, and then teaches them that the Son of Man will be rejected and killed, and then rise after three days (Mark 8:31; Matt 16:21–23; Luke 9:22). By making the first prediction after he has begun to encounter resistance and John the Baptist has been executed, Jesus implicitly suggests that, despite appearances, things are still unfolding according to plan, and that his current difficulties were not unexpected. Then, as they are passing through Galilee, after being exasperated by his apostles' lack of faith, Jesus predicts his passion again, telling his apostles that the Son of Man will be delivered into the hands of men and killed, and then rise again (Mark 9:31; Matt 17:22–23; cf. Luke 9:44–45). The timing of the second prediction indicates that Jesus sees his apostles' lack of faith as a foretaste of his public rejection and that, even so, he remains confident that neither their lack of faith nor his public rejection will be able to thwart his objectives. The third prediction comes shortly before

Passion Narrative (Tübingen: J.C.B. Mohr, 1988); Raymond E. Brown, *The Death of the Messiah: From Gethsemane to the Grave. A Commentary on the Passion Narratives in the Four Gospels.*, 2 vols. (New York: Doubleday, 1994); John T. Carroll and Joel B. Green, *The Death of Jesus in Early Christianity* (Peabody, MA: Hendrickson, 1995); Wright, *Jesus and the Victory of God*; William H. Bellinger and William R. Farmer, eds., *Jesus and the Suffering Servant: Isaiah 53 and Christian Origins* (Harrisburg: Trinity, 1998); Delbert R. Burkett, *The Son of Man Debate: A History and Evaluation* (Cambridge: Cambridge University Press, 1999); Bernd Janowski and Peter Stuhlmacher, eds., *The Suffering Servant: Isaiah 53 in Jewish and Christian Sources* (Grand Rapids, MI: Eerdmans, 2004); McKnight, *Jesus and His Death*; Brant J. Pitre, *Jesus, the Tribulation, and the End of the Exile: Restoration Eschatology and the Origin of the Atonement* (Tübingen: J.C. B. Mohr, 2005); Geert Van Oyen and Tom Shepherd, eds., *The Trial and Death of Jesus: Essays on the Passion Narrative in Mark* (Leuven: Peeters, 2006); Gilbert Van Belle, ed. *The Death of Jesus in the Fourth Gospel* (Leuven: Leuven University Press, 2007); Ernest R. Martinez, *Gospel Accounts of the Death Of Jesus: A Study of the Death Accounts Made in the Light of the New Testament Traditions, the Redaction, and the Theology of the Four Evangelists* (Rome: Editrice Pontificia Università Gregoriana, 2008).

the procession into Jerusalem, tingeing this moment of public triumph with a hint of the rejection to come. Jesus includes more details about the abuse that the Son of Man will suffer (in Matthew, he mentions being crucified), and, for the first time, he tells them that he will be handed over to the Gentiles (Mark 10:32–34; Matt 20:17–19; Luke 18:31–33). The narrative placement of the third prediction serves to emphasize Jesus' calm self-possession in the face of seeming success. His apostles and disciples might misunderstand the significance of his messianic entrance into Jerusalem, but Jesus does not, because he knows what comes afterward. In sum, the three passion predictions are integrated into the Gospel narratives; they are not jarring, disruptive asides. Their immediate contexts heighten their meaning and dramatic significance. The first two predictions indicate that Jesus is not surprised by the problems he encounters on the way to Golgotha, and the third prediction indicates that the appearance of success does not lull Jesus into complacency.

Besides these three passion predictions, which are common to all three synoptic Gospels, there are other explicit passion predictions. In Mark and Matthew, Jesus foretells his death in a saying about Elijah and John the Baptist. His disciples ask him why the scribes say that Elijah must come before the Messiah. Jesus responds that Elijah has already come—meaning John the Baptist—and suffered rejection, and then tells them that the Son of Man will suffer in the same way (Mark 9:12–13; Matt 17:11–13). In Matthew, two days before Passover, he prophesies that the Son of Man will be delivered up to be crucified (Matt 26:2). In Luke, the Pharisees warn Jesus that Herod is trying to kill him, and in his response Jesus says he must continue on toward Jerusalem because a prophet cannot die anywhere else (Luke 13:33). Later, Jesus explains that the Son of Man must suffer "many things" at the hands of the present generation before he comes into his glory (Luke 17:25). After the resurrection, on the road to Emmaus, Jesus explains to two disciples how the scriptures foretold the suffering of the Christ (Luke 24:25–27, 44–47). This final explanation recalls and validates Jesus' self-possession when his public ministry seemed to be foundering, and it implicitly affirms that, contrary to appearances, everything had been unfolding according to God's plan.

During the last supper and its preparations, Jesus makes many predictions about his rejection and suffering, often connecting these claims to the fulfillment of scripture. As he instructs his disciples about preparations for the Passover, he charges them to convey to another disciple the message, "My time is at hand" (Matt 26:18), a message that refers obliquely to his passion. Then, at the beginning of the meal, he tells his disciples, "I have earnestly desired to eat this Passover with you before I suffer" (Luke 22:15). In the middle of the meal, he tells his apostles that one of them is about to betray him in fulfillment of scripture (Mark 14:18–21; Matt 26:21–25; Luke 22:21–23; John 13:10–11, 13:21–30, 17:12; cf. John 6:70–71). Jesus says, "For the Son of Man goes as it is written of him, but woe to that man by whom the Son of Man is betrayed! It would have been better for that man if he had not been born" (Mark 14:21; cf. Matt 26:25, Luke 22:23). Jesus' foretelling of his betrayal, and his affirmation that it will fulfill scripture, are central to each of the Gospel narratives. The betrayal epitomizes the cruelty of Jesus' rejection, and his foreknowledge epitomizes his command of his destiny. Jesus also predicts that the disciples will scatter and fall away, in fulfillment of scripture (Mark 14:27–28; Matt 26:31–32; John 16:32; cf. Zech 13:7), and that he will be "reckoned with transgressors," also in fulfillment of scripture (Luke 22:37; cf. Isa 53:12). He foretells that Peter will deny him three times (Mark 14:30; Matt 26:34; Luke 22:31–34; John 13:38). Like his prophecies about his betrayal, these predictions demonstrate his foreknowledge of his imminent death and his acceptance of it. The most significant prediction during the last supper comes in the Eucharistic blessing of the bread and wine. Through the Eucharistic blessing, Jesus indicates that he will give his life for his disciples (Mark 14:22–25; Matt 26:26–29, Luke 22:17–20; 1 Cor 11:23–25). He indicates that his death will be violent in two different ways: by saying that his blood will be poured out, and by blessing the bread and wine separately, a gesture that symbolizes the separation of his blood from his body.

After the meal, Jesus gives further indication of his prophetic expectation. In the garden of Gethsemane, Jesus prays for the cup of suffering to pass from him, but he concludes his prayer resigned to the inevitability of his passion (Mark 14:36; Matt 26:39, 26:42; Luke 22:42; cf. John 18:11). He does not resist those who come to seize him, stating instead that it is the hour of the power of darkness (Luke 22:53) and that his arrest must happen to fulfill the scriptures (Mark 14:49; Matt 26:52–54, 56). On the cross, Jesus cries out to God in words that are identical to the first line of Psalm 22 (Mark 15:34; Matt 27:46), possibly suggesting that he sees his suffering as the prophetic fulfillment of the psalms.[9]

Allusions to a Violent Death

Besides his explicit predictions, there are many passages where Jesus implies or hints that he will be killed. His earliest allusion to his death in the synoptic Gospels comes in a saying about fasting. He explains that his disciples do not fast because wedding guests do not fast in the presence of the bridegroom. But, he adds, the days will come when the bridegroom is taken away from them—the passive tense hinting that he will be removed from their midst by violence—and then they will fast (Mark 2:20; Matt 9:15; Luke 5:35). Jesus

[9] It is not clear whether the evangelists mean to portray Jesus' cry of dereliction as a deliberate allusion to Psalm 22. Nonetheless, it is a real possibility that they do, as another way of indicating that Jesus sees his death as the fulfillment of prophecy.

also alludes to his coming death in the accounts of the transfiguration, which happens immediately after the first passion prediction. During the transfiguration, Jesus speaks with Moses and Elijah about his coming departure—literally, his exodus (ἔξοδος), a word charged with theological significance—that will take place in Jerusalem (Luke 9:31). Afterward, he commands Peter, James, and John to tell no one what happened "until the Son of Man should have risen from the dead" (Mark 9:9; cf. Matt 17:9). Both references allude to a violent death. Then, in the wake of his disciples' failure to exorcise a possessed boy, and shortly before the second passion prediction, an exasperated Jesus wonders aloud how long he must bear with them (Mark 9:19; cf. Matt 17:17, Luke 9:41). Given the context of his complaint, this passage indicates that Jesus expects his presence in their midst to be cut short, or at least that he will not be with them much longer. Shortly before his death, Jesus defends the woman who anoints him with a flask of costly ointment in Bethany, and says that she has anointed his body for his burial, thus indicating that he expects to die soon (Mark 14:6–9; cf Matt 26:6–14, John 12:1–8). This saying also manifests a prophetic expectation of death, and given the narrative context, a violent death.

In the ransom saying, Jesus teaches his disciples that they must serve each other, "for the Son of Man also came not to be served but to serve, and to give his life as a ransom for many" (Mark 10:45; cf. Matt 20:28). The ransom saying does not explicitly predict a violent death, as Jesus could mean that he came to spend his life in service to others. It does, however, imply a violent death, especially since the third passion prediction immediately precedes this pericope. Similarly, in Matthew, while denouncing the scribes and Pharisees, Jesus tells them, "Fill up, then, the measure of your fathers" (Matt 23:32), meaning that he expects them to kill him just as their fathers killed the prophets. By suggesting that his rejection continues a historical pattern, Jesus also implies that he expects to be vindicated, just as the prophets were vindicated.[10]

Jesus also alludes to his suffering and death—indirectly, but unmistakably—through metaphors and parables. After his third prediction of the passion, the sons of Zebedee approach Jesus, asking to be seated at his right and left hand when he comes into his kingdom. He tells them that they do not know what they are asking, and he asks them, "Can you drink the cup that I drink or be baptized with the baptism with which I am baptized?" (Mark 10:38; cf. Matt

[10] The expectation of both rejection and vindication becomes more obvious when paying attention to what Jesus says next. In the same pericope, Jesus goes on to quote Psalm 118, saying, "For I tell you, you will not see me again, until you say, 'Blessed is he who comes in the name of the Lord'" (Matt 23:39; cf. Luke 13:35, Ps 118:26). In itself, the quoted verse expresses expectation of eventual vindication. Given its context, however, it also expresses expectation of rejection, insofar as it comes shortly after a reference to the stone rejected by the builders becoming the cornerstone (Ps 118:22).

20:22). Jesus does not clarify exactly what the cup and baptism symbolize. It is obvious, though, that he is talking about his suffering and death. This exchange immediately follows the third prediction of the passion, and, in all four Gospels, Jesus calls his passion a "cup" in the garden of Gethsemane (Mark 14:36; cf. Matt 26:39, 26:42; Luke 22:42; John 18:11). While there is no parallel to this exchange in Luke or John, Jesus uses the baptism metaphor in a saying unique to Luke. He exclaims, "I have a baptism to be baptized with; and how I am constrained until it is accomplished!" (Luke 12:50). Like the exchange in Mark and Matthew, this saying in Luke also clearly alludes to his passion. The allusion to a violent death becomes even more evident as Jesus goes on to say that he has come to bring not peace but a sword, thus implying that his baptism involves conflict and division.

After his triumphal entrance into Jerusalem, Jesus tells a parable that foretells his crucifixion (Mark 12:1–12; Matt 21:22–46; Luke 20:9–19; cf. Isa 5:1–7). In the parable, a vineyard owner sends his son to collect his share of the harvest, but the tenants kill the son, thinking that they will claim his inheritance. Jesus observes that the vineyard owner will surely come and destroy the tenants, and give the vineyard to others. Then he concludes with a quotation from the psalms: "The very stone which the builders rejected has become the head of the corner" (Mark 12:10; cf. Ps 118:22–23). Afterward, his opponents want to arrest him, because, the evangelists explain, "they perceived that he had told the parable against them" (Mark 12:12; cf. Matt 21:45; Luke 20:19). This parable predicts a violent death, and the concluding scripture quotation about the rejected cornerstone also foretells Jesus' ultimate vindication.[11]

In Matthew, immediately after the vineyard parable, Jesus tells a parable about a king who holds a feast to celebrate his son's wedding (Matt 22:1–14). Those invited do not come. In response, the king invites other guests in their place, just as the vineyard owner found new tenants and thus vindicated his son against those who rejected him. As with the vineyard parable, this parable also alludes to both Jesus' public rejection and his eventual vindication.

In the parable of the rich man and Lazarus (Luke 16:19–31), Jesus alludes to his resurrection, and thus, implicitly, to his approaching death. In the parable, the rich man and Lazarus die. The rich man goes to a place of torment, and he begs Abraham to send Lazarus to warn his brothers so that they will repent.

[11] Jesus describes the vineyard owner's son as "beloved" (Mark 12:6; Luke 20:13). This adjective echoes the language of Genesis in its description of Abraham's sacrifice of Isaac, his "beloved son" (Gen 22:2, 12, 16). See Jon D. Levenson, *The Death and Resurrection of the Beloved Son: The Transformation of Child Sacrifice in Judaism and Christianity* (New Haven: Yale University Press, 1993), 200–19. It also echoes the words of the Father at Jesus' baptism, "You are my beloved Son" (Mark 1:11; cf. Matt 3:17; Luke 3:22), and at his transfiguration, "This is my beloved Son" (Mark 9:7; cf. Matt 17:5). Consequently, in this parable, by describing the vineyard owner's son as "beloved," Jesus may be hinting that his death will bring Abraham's sacrifice of Isaac to prophetic fulfillment.

Abraham tells the rich man, "If they do not hear Moses and the prophets, neither will they be convinced if someone should rise from the dead" (Luke 16:31). In this saying, Jesus ironically alludes to his own resurrection and thus also his imminent death.

The Sign of Jonah

In Matthew and Luke, the scribes and Pharisees ask for a sign, and Jesus tells them, "An evil and adulterous generation seeks for a sign; but no sign shall be given to it except the sign of the prophet Jonah" (Matt 12:39; cf. Matt 16:4, Luke 11:29–30).[12] In Matthew, Jesus explains the sign of Jonah by prophesying that the Son of Man will spend three days and three nights in the heart of the earth, just as Jonah spent three days and three nights in the belly of the whale (Matt 12:40). This explanation connects the sign of Jonah to Jesus' burial and resurrection, and it indicates that Jesus expects to die and rise again.

Luke tells the story differently. At first glance, it seems that Luke does not relate the sign of Jonah to Jesus' death. In Luke's account, Jesus says, "For as Jonah became a sign to the men of Nineveh, so will the Son of Man be to this generation" (Luke 11:30). Then Jesus says that the men of Nineveh will rise at the judgment and condemn this generation, because they repented at the preaching of Jonah, and "something greater than Jonah is here" (Luke 11:32). So it can seem that in Matthew's version the sign of Jonah refers to Jesus' death and resurrection, whereas in Luke's version it refers to Jesus' preaching. On closer inspection, however, the explanations given in Luke and Matthew are not as different as they first appear.

From the Jewish literature of this period, we have strong reason to think that Luke's version of the Jonah saying does in fact allude to Jesus' death and resurrection. First, in the Jewish literature of this period, Jonah's miraculous rescue from the whale generally features much more prominently than Jonah's preaching.[13] Second, the evangelists were writing in a milieu where Jonah's miraculous rescue had symbolic associations with rebirth and resurrection. For example, *The Lives of the Prophets* (first cen. AD) identifies Jonah as the widow's son whom Elijah raised from the dead in 1 Kings 17:17–24—a

[12] Among recent studies on this saying, especially notable are Richard Alan Edwards, *The Sign of Jonah in the Theology of the Evangelists and Q* (London: S.C.M. Press, 1971); Simon Chow, *The Sign of Jonah Reconsidered: A Study of Its Meaning in the Gospel Traditions* (Stockholm: Almqvist & Wiksel International, 1995).

[13] Chow, *Sign of Jonah Reconsidered*, 42–4. In 3 Maccabees (first cen. BC), a passage referring to Jonah focuses on God's miraculous rescue and does not mention his preaching (3 Mac 6:8). Likewise, in his history of the Jews (first cen. AD), Josephus recounts the story of Jonah and the whale at some length, but he mentions the preaching in Nineveh only briefly (*Jewish Antiquities* 9.205–214). Chow, *Sign of Jonah Reconsidered*, 27–34.

common identification in this period—and speaks of Elijah raising Jonah from the dead "again," as though Jonah's miraculous rescue had been a kind of resurrection.[14] Third, at least in some circles, being rescued from the whale seems to have been taken as a supernatural "sign." In an early Jewish homily (first cen. BC to second cen. AD), after his miraculous rescue, Jonah says, "I was taken out of the sleep to be a sign of rebirth, and I shall be a warrant to everyone of his own life."[15] Consequently, when Jesus describes Jonah as a "sign" in Luke's version of the Jonah pericope, we have good grounds for seeing an implicit reference to Jonah's miraculous rescue, with all its connotations of deliverance and renewal, and, therefore, to Jesus' own death and resurrection.[16] Finally, Jesus says that the Son of Man *will* be a sign to this generation. The future tense hints that something must happen before the Son of Man becomes a sign to this generation—implying that the preaching of Jesus' public ministry has not yet sufficed to establish him as that sign.[17] In sum, for Luke as well as for Matthew, Jesus becomes a sign for his generation, not only by his preaching, but also by the divine vindication which authenticates his prophetic status—a vindication that comes only after his passage through death.[18]

[14] For instances of Jewish writers identifying Jonah with the widow's son raised by Elijah, see *The Lives of the Prophets*, 10:6; *The Midrash on Psalms*, 26:7; *Genesis Rabbah*, 98.11; *Pirqe de Rabbi Eliezer* 10. Chow, *Sign of Jonah Reconsidered*, 29–31, 43.

[15] *De Jona*, as translated in Chow, *Sign of Jonah Reconsidered*, 36. The homily was written in Greek but survives in Armenian, and the word for sign in Armenian is *kerparan*. In his German translation of *De Jona*, Siegert translates *kerparan* as *Wahrzeichen* and *Sinnbild*. See F. Siegert, ed. *Drei Hellenistisch-Jüdische Predigten* (Tübingen: J.C.B. Mohr, 1980), 25.

A ninth century Jewish text manifests a similar interpretation of Jonah. It speaks of the sailors seeing the signs and wonders that God performed for Jonah (*Pirqe de Rabbi Eliezer* 10). As such, it may witness to an early rabbinic tradition that Jonah's rescue came to be known by the sailors (and through them, possibly, the Ninevites) and was considered a sign. Hans F. Bayer, *Jesus' Predictions of Vindication and Resurrection: The Provenance, Meaning, and Correlation of the Synoptic Predictions* (Tübingen: J.C.B. Mohr, 1986), 136–7; Joachim Jeremias, "Ἰωνᾶς," in *Theological Dictionary of the New Testament*, ed. Gerhard Kittel and Gerhard Freidrich (Grand Rapids, MI: Eerdmans, 1965), 409n26. Given the late date of this text, however, many dispute its relevance to Jewish interpretative traditions in the first century. Among other things, there may have been Christian influence in the interim between the first and ninth centuries. For the case against the historical relevance of this text, see Joseph A. Fitzmyer, *The Gospel According to Luke*, 2 vols. (New York: Doubleday, 1985), 935–6.

[16] Jeremias and Bayer maintain that first century Jews regarded Jonah's miraculous rescue as a sign, and that Jesus' saying about the sign of Jonah alludes to his death and resurrection in Luke as well as in Matthew. See Jeremias, "Ἰωνᾶς; Bayer, *Jesus' Prediction*, 133–45. Chow, however, disagrees. Chow acknowledges that the designation of Jonah as a figure of resurrection and a sign was present in Judaism before Christianity, but he thinks that, in Luke's version, the sign refers to the preaching of the Church, not Jesus' resurrection. Chow, *Sign of Jonah Reconsidered*, 42–4, 142–5, 212.

[17] Bayer, *Jesus' Prediction*, 142.

[18] Bayer, *Jesus' Prediction*, 141–2.

References to Departure and Return

Many sayings and parables in the Gospels imply that Jesus will depart and return later. Jesus tells a parable about wise and foolish virgins waiting for the bridegroom to return (Matt 25:1–13), and another parable about a master leaving on a journey—in Luke, the master goes to a far country to claim a kingdom—and entrusting servants with his money while he is away (Matt 25:14–30; Luke 19:12–27). He tells parables about servants waiting for their master to return, and he warns his disciples that the Son of Man will return suddenly at an unexpected hour (Mark 13:21–37; Matt 24:23–51; Luke 12:35–48, 17:22–37). He tells them that he will come like a thief (Matt 24:43; Luke 12:39; cf. 1 Thess 5:2–4; 2 Pet 3:10; Rv 3:3, 16:15). Jesus speaks of the Son of Man coming in the glory of his Father with the holy angels (Mark 8:38; Matt 16:28; Luke 9:26) and judging the nations (Matt 25:31–46). He wonders whether the Son of Man will find faith on earth when he comes (Luke 18:8). When the high priest asks Jesus whether he is the Christ, Jesus tells him that he will see the Son of Man "coming with the clouds of heaven" (Mark 14:62; cf. Matt 26:54).[19] None of these sayings and parables refers explicitly to Jesus' suffering, death, or resurrection. The Son of Man can return, however, only if he departs first. Likewise, predictions of eschatological triumph make sense only if Jesus expects difficulties and setbacks before that triumph. Consequently, these various pericopes should be seen as allusions to Jesus' prophetic expectation of his death.

The Destruction of Jerusalem and the Temple

In a number of pericopes, Jesus foretells the destruction of Jerusalem or the temple, and he does so in a way that alludes to his imminent violent death. In Matthew, Jesus mourns over Jerusalem and its pattern of rejecting the prophets sent to it (Matt 23:37). He then prophesies, "Behold, your house is forsaken and desolate. For I tell you, you will not see me again, until you say, 'Blessed is he who comes in the name of the Lord'" (Matt 23:38–39; cf. Luke 13:35, Ps 118:26). With this prophecy, Jesus implies that he expects to be rejected and, as a result of his rejection, for Jerusalem to become forsaken and desolate. In Luke, Jesus weeps over Jerusalem as he makes his final approach. He prophesies that, "because you did not know the time of your visitation,"

[19] Wright argues that these allusions refer primarily to the Lord's return to Zion, which coincides with Jesus' public ministry, rather than Jesus' second coming. See Wright, *Jesus and the Victory of God*, 631–42. The main lines of his argument, however, do not exclude the possibility that Jesus' words also refer to his second coming, as Wright himself seems to acknowledge.

Jerusalem will be destroyed (Luke 19:41–44). Elsewhere, in great detail, Jesus foretells the temple's destruction (Mark 13:1–37; Matt 24:1–36; Luke 21:5–36; cf. John 2:19). He does not give any theological explanation for the temple's coming destruction, but the narrative context implies that Jesus links it to his own destruction.

Jesus' Experience of Rejection and Persecution before the Passion

During the course of the Gospel narratives, Jesus frequently encounters resistance. He is rejected at home, and as he leaves, he tells his disciples, "A prophet is not without honor, except in his own country, and among his own kin, and in his own house" (Mark 6:4; cf. Matt 13:57, Luke 4:24). Towns in Galilee do not respond to his preaching, and he pronounces judgment against them (Matt 11:20–24; Luke 10:12–15). He castigates "this generation" for its failure to repent and accept the Son of Man (Matt 11:16–19, 12:41–42; Luke 11:31–32). Attempts are made on his life and he hears about conspiracies against him. Through these episodes, the evangelists show Jesus having direct experience of rejection and the lengths to which his opponents are willing to go. While these episodes do not, of themselves, indicate that Jesus expects to be killed, they corroborate the larger themes of the Gospel narratives. From a literary point of view, they build dramatic tension and foreshadow the crucifixion. They also complement other pericopes in which Jesus predicts or alludes to his imminent death.

Ethical Teachings and Warnings about Persecution

Many of Jesus' ethical teachings foreshadow his violent rejection, or at least make more sense when interpreted with the crucifixion in view. His disciples must take up their cross and follow him (Mark 8:34; Matt 16:24; Luke 9:23), and those who do not are not worthy of him (Matt 10:38; Luke 14:27). His disciples must serve each another, just as the Son of Man came to serve and give his life as a ransom for the many (Mark 9:35, 10:35–45; Matt 20:20–28, 23:11; Luke 9:48, 12:50, 22:24–27; John 13:4–5, 12–17). Those who would save their lives will lose it, and those who lose their lives for his sake will save it (Mark 8:34–35; Matt 16:25; Luke 9:24; John 12:25).

Jesus also warns his disciples that they will be rejected, persecuted, and handed over to be killed (Mark 10:30, 13:9–13; Matt 10:16–25, 10:34–36, 24:9–14; Luke 12:51–53, 21:12–19; John 15:18–25, 16:1–4, 17:14). They should be concerned when all speak well of them, because that is how the false prophets were treated (Luke 6:26). But when they face their inevitable persecution, they should bless those who curse them (Luke 6:28). He tells them that the meek will inherit the earth (Matt 5:5). His disciples should not resist one who is evil, but, instead, turn the other cheek, love their enemies, and pray for those who persecute them (Matt 5:38–48; Luke 6:27–36). Jesus forgives sins (e.g., Mark 2:5–12; Matt 9:1–8; Luke 5:17–26), he forgives those who crucified him (Luke 23:34), and he commands his disciples to forgive those who sin against them (Mark 11:25; Matt 6:12–15, Matt 18:21–35; Luke 11:4, 17:4). And he tells his disciples to rejoice when they are persecuted for their testimony to him, "for your reward is great in heaven, for so men persecuted the prophets who were before you" (Matt 5:12; cf. Luke 6:23). Jesus instructs his disciples to pray that they are spared from trials (Mark 13:18; Matt 6:13, 24:20; Luke 11:4), suggesting that his disciples should expect trials. He promises that those who mourn will be comforted, and those who hunger will be satisfied—that God eventually will turn his disciples' suffering into joy (Matt 5:4; Luke 6:21)—but he does not promise that his disciples will be spared mourning, hunger, or suffering. He promises vindication, but a vindication that comes only after suffering.

Jesus' crucifixion is the hermeneutic key to these ethical teachings and these warnings about persecution.[20] They do not make sense without it. These teachings and warnings imply that Jesus expects for his disciples to experience suffering and evil, and then, eventually, divine vindication. Implicitly, they suggest that Jesus expects the same for himself. In one saying, Jesus makes the link between his teaching and his personal experience explicit: "If they have called the master of the house Beelzebul, how much more will they malign those of his household" (Matt 10:25; cf. Luke 23:31; John 15:18–20, 17:14).

Allusions to the Passion Specific to John's Gospel

There are many sayings specific to John's Gospel where Jesus alludes to his death.[21] These allusions are more frequent and explicit in John than in the other Gospels. Still, as with the synoptic Gospels, in John, Jesus rarely speaks explicitly about his death—for the most part, he speaks in figures (see John 16:25)—and his audience frequently misses his meaning when he refers to his death and resurrection. Allusions to his death are found throughout the Gospel of John, and they take a variety of forms. In the first chapter, he tells Nathaniel that "you will see heaven opened, and the angels of God ascending and descending upon the Son of Man" (John 1:51), an enigmatic saying that is

[20] For a similar evaluation of the centrality of the cross to Jesus' ethical teaching, see Richard B. Hays, *Moral Vision of the New Testament: Community, Cross, New Creation* (San Francisco: Harper, 1996), 73–92, 193–206; Richard A. Burridge, *Imitating Jesus: An Inclusive Approach to New Testament Ethics* (Grand Rapids, MI: Eerdmans, 2007), 155–85.

[21] For a wide-ranging collection of articles on the death of Jesus in John, see Van Belle, ed. *Death of Jesus.*

often read in light of the crucifixion. After driving out the money-changers in the temple, Jesus alludes to his death and resurrection, saying: "Destroy this temple, and in three days I will raise it up" (John 2:19; cf. Mark 14:58, 15:29; Matt 26:61, 27:40; Acts 6:14). On three different occasions, he talks about being "lifted up" (John 3:14, 8:28, 12:32), which, the evangelist explains, he said "to show by what death he was to die" (John 12:33). Jesus will give his flesh for the life of the world, and those who eat his flesh and drink his blood will have life because of him (John 6:51–58). As the good shepherd, he lays down his life for his sheep (John 10:11–18; cf. Matt 18:12–13; Luke 15:4–6), thus exemplifying his teaching that no man has greater love than to lay down his life for his friends (John 15:17).

On numerous occasions he tells people that he is going somewhere they cannot follow, or that he is going to the Father (John 7:33–36, 8:21–22, 13:33–36, 14:28, 16:5–10, 16:28). At the last supper he tells his disciples that he is going to prepare a place for them (John 14:2–3) and send the Holy Spirit (John 16:7). He says to them: "A little while, and you will see me no more; again a little while, and you will see me" (John 16:16; cf. 14:19). He compares his departure to a woman's labor pains, and his return to the joy that follows the birth of her child (John 16:21–22).

Throughout John's Gospel, Jesus often talks about his "hour," an expression that obliquely but unmistakably refers to his passion.[22] This language shows Jesus expecting to suffer a violent death from the beginning and embracing it for some higher purpose. For example, as his hour approaches, he exclaims aloud that his soul is troubled, but he does not ask his Father to save him, because "unless a grain of wheat falls into the earth and dies, it remains alone; but if it dies, it bears much fruit" (John 12:24; cf. Mark 4:31, Matt 13:13, Luke 13:19). As he gives up his spirit, he says, "It is finished" (John 19:30), indicating that his hour of suffering was something he expected and embraced.

JESUS' INTERPRETATION OF HIS DEATH IN THE GOSPELS

In the Gospels, Jesus often interprets his death as advancing his mission. His institution of the Eucharist supplies the most explicit example.

> And as they were eating, he took bread, and blessed, and broke it, and gave it to them, and said, "Take; this is my body." And he took a cup, and when he had

[22] The meaning of the allusion finds confirmation in his parallel use of "hour" in the synoptic Gospels (Mark 14:35, 14:41; Matt 26:45; Luke 22:53).

given thanks he gave it to them, and they all drank of it. And he said to them, 'This is my blood of the covenant, which is poured out for many. Truly, I say to you, I shall not drink again of the fruit of the vine until that day when I drink it new in the kingdom of God' (Mark 14:22–25; cf. Matt 26:26–29; Luke 22:17–20; 1 Cor 11:23–25).

By their descriptions of Jesus' words and actions at the last supper, the Gospels portray Jesus as embracing his death as something that advances his mission and benefits others.[23] By his separate blessing of the bread and wine, and his saying about his blood being poured out, he foretells his violent death. By distributing the Eucharistic elements himself, Jesus signifies that he gives his life freely and that it is not taken from him. Finally, by directing his disciples to consume the Eucharistic elements Jesus is indicating that, through his death, his body and blood will become life-giving in the same way that food and drink are life-giving. In Matthew, Jesus further specifies that he pours out his blood "for the forgiveness of sins" (Matt 26:29).

The covenant language reveals a great deal about Jesus' interpretation of his death. By associating his blood with a covenant, Jesus invokes one of the central theological categories of the Jewish scriptures. The people of Israel understood their relationship to God in terms of a covenant, and specifically a covenant ratified by the shedding of blood. After their exodus from Egypt, Moses sprinkled blood on the people to ratify a covenant between Israel and the Lord (Exodus 24:8; cf. Heb 9:20). The cultural memory of this covenant shaped the theological outlook of the people of Israel, and it became a key reference point for later books of scripture. Jeremiah prophesies a new covenant that the Lord will make with the house of Israel, putting his law within them and writing it upon their hearts (Jer 31:31–34). In the book of Zechariah, the Lord promises, "because of the blood of my covenant with you, I will set your captives free from the waterless pit" (Zech 9:11). Consequently, Jesus' words at the last supper tap into a rich vein of theological concepts and images. At the very least, the evangelists must mean to suggest that Jesus sees his death as bringing about a covenant comparable to the covenant of Moses, and that just as Moses liberated Israel from slavery, so too will Jesus. There may also be deliberate allusions to the prophecies of Jeremiah and Zechariah. But whatever its precise meaning, the covenant language shows Jesus interpreting his death in a positive light and embracing it.

Jesus interprets his death in a similar fashion in a number of sayings. In Mark and Matthew, shortly after his third passion prediction, Jesus tells his disciples that "the Son of Man also came not to be served but to serve, and to give his life as a ransom for many" (Mark 10:45; Matt 20:28). The saying

[23] For a study of the theological significance of the Eucharistic words of Jesus in their historical context, see Joachim Jeremias, *The Eucharistic Words of Jesus*, trans. Norman Perrin, 3rd ed. (London: S.C.M. Press, 1966), 204–62.

indicates that Jesus sees his death—the giving of his life—as advancing his mission, and in fact integral to its accomplishment. In Matthew and Luke, the saying about the sign of Jonah interprets Jesus' death in a similar way (Matt 12:38–42; Luke 11:29–32). This enigmatic saying seems to suggest that, like Jonah, in order to save others, Jesus will allow himself to be put to death. Then, also like Jonah, he will emerge three days later, and his vindication will enhance his preaching, just like Jonah's miraculous rescue from the whale enhanced Jonah's preaching. In John, Jesus compares his crucifixion to the bronze serpent that Moses lifted up at God's command, so that those bitten by serpents would be cured by looking at it (John 3:14–15; Num 21:8–9), saying: "And as Moses lifted up the serpent in the wilderness, so must the Son of Man be lifted up, that whoever believes in him may have eternal life" (John 3:14–15). In this saying, Jesus again interprets his death as not only salvific and life-giving, but also integral to his mission.

Jesus' habit of referring to himself as the Son of Man also hints at a positive interpretation of his death. In the Gospels, the expression puzzles Jesus' contemporaries (John 12:34), and its meaning remains a point of debate among scripture exegetes.[24] Nonetheless, scholars generally agree that, at least in the evangelists' portrayal of Jesus, the expression alludes to the book of Daniel, which describes "one like a son of man" receiving everlasting dominion from the Ancient of Days (Dan 7:12–14).[25] They also agree that, in the Gospels, Jesus associates this title with his suffering and death. For example, in the three passion predictions, Jesus usually refers to himself as the Son of Man, thus associating the title with his passion.[26]

Jesus' Interpretation of Prophecy

In the Gospels, Jesus often interprets his death through the lens of scriptural prophecy. He gives particular attention to the four servant songs of Deutero-Isaiah (Isa 42:1–9; 49:1–6; 50:4–9; 52:13–53:12), in which God chooses a

[24] For an overview of the history of the debate and the various interpretative possibilities, see Burkett, *Son of Man Debate*.

[25] Even Maurice Casey, who maintains that Jesus used "son of man" as an idiomatic Aramaic expression without any special theological significance, acknowledges that the Gospels interpret this expression in relation to Daniel 7. See Maurice Casey, *The Solution to the "Son of Man" Problem* (London: T & T Clark, 2007).

[26] Scholars disagree about whether an apocalyptic Son of Man figure existed in the Jewish imagination before Jesus. (For an overview of the arguments on both sides, see Burkett, *Son of Man Debate*, 22–31, 68–81, 97–120.) They also disagree about whether the text of Daniel offers any real basis for this interpretation of its Son of Man prophecy, or whether Jesus himself associated the title "Son of Man" with his suffering. Nonetheless, scholars generally agree that the *evangelists'* Jesus associates the title "Son of Man" with his suffering, which is all that this chapter needs for its argument to work.

mysterious servant for a mission that involves suffering.[27] By alluding to these servant songs, Jesus indicates that he sees his suffering as integral to his mission, and not just a temporary setback. The most important reference comes during the last supper. Jesus quotes the fourth song, saying to his disciples, "For I tell you that this scripture must be fulfilled in me, 'And he was reckoned with transgressors'; for what is written about me has its fulfillment" (Luke 22:37; cf. Isa 53:12). In the book of Isaiah, the cited verse concludes, "yet he bore the sin of many, and made intercession for the transgressors" (Isa 53:12), and comes shortly after Isaiah has described the servant suffering on behalf of the sins of others (Isa 53:10). By quoting this passage, Jesus shows that he interprets his suffering in light of the servant's suffering. Moreover, by describing Isaiah's prophecy as "what is written about me," Jesus explicitly identifies himself with Isaiah's suffering servant.[28] Jesus seems to allude to the servant songs in other passages as well. In the second passion prediction, Jesus says that the Son of Man will be "treated with contempt" (Mark 9:12), a phrase that seems to allude to the fourth song, insofar as it echoes Isaiah's description of the servant's suffering (Isa 53:3). Likewise, when he tells John's disciples to report to their master that "the blind

[27] Exegetes debate whether the Gospels portray Jesus as consciously identifying himself with the person and mission of the servant. For an overview of contemporary scholarship on this question, see Bellinger and Farmer, eds., *Jesus and the Suffering Servant*; Janowski and Stuhlmacher, eds., *The Suffering Servant*; McKnight, *Jesus and His Death*, 207–24. For a summary of the case that the Gospels portray Jesus as consciously identifying himself with the person and mission of the servant, see O. Betz, "Jesus and Isaiah 53," in *Jesus and the Suffering Servant: Isaiah 53 and Christian Origins*, ed. William H. Bellinger and William R. Farmer (Harrisburg: Trinity, 1998), 70–87. Morna Hooker lays out the case against in Hooker, *Jesus and the Servant*. Forty years later, Hooker reiterates her position in Morna Hooker, "Did the Use of Isaiah 53 to Interpret His Mission Begin with Jesus?," in *Jesus and the Suffering Servant: Isaiah 53 and Christian Origins*, ed. William H. Bellinger and William R. Farmer (Harrisburg: Trinity, 1998).

Scholars also debate whether Jewish literature before Jesus interpreted Isaiah's suffering servant as a messianic figure. After considering the evidence, Sydney Page concludes that the servant songs were interpreted in messianic terms by some strands of Jewish literature. He writes, "Given the diversity in the interpretation of the servant songs in the intertestamental period, and the possibility that some segments of Judaism were well disposed towards a messianic interpretation, it is completely credible that someone possessed with a messianic consciousness could have interpreted his career, and especially his death, in the light of the songs. So far as we know no one prior to Jesus did so, but the raw materials for such a development were already present in late Judaism." Sydney Page, "The Suffering Servant between the Testaments," *New Testament Studies* 31 (1985): 493. His conclusion gives further credence to the idea that the Gospels do indeed portray Jesus as consciously identifying himself with the person and mission of the servant.

[28] Allusions to scripture typically call to mind not only a particular text, but also its larger context. Moreover, by the very fact of alluding to a particular text, they often interpret and reinterpret that text in new ways. See Richard B. Hays, *Echoes of Scripture in the Letters of Paul* (New Haven: Yale University Press, 1989). Luke's portrayal of Jesus here reflects this dynamic. When Jesus quotes this brief passage from the fourth servant song, and says that it will be fulfilled in himself, he is not only making a claim about a specific prophecy from Isaiah. He is also calling to mind the servant songs in their entirety and suggesting that he will bring them to fulfillment—and thus interpreting and reinterpreting Isaiah in the process.

receive their sight" (Luke 7:22; cf. Isa 42:7), Jesus may be referring to the first song. The evangelists also quote or seemingly allude to the servant songs in their narration (Matt 8:17, 12:18–21; Mark 15:28; Luke 2:32, Luke 9:51; John 12:38), and they often draw attention to Jesus' fulfillment of other prophecies of Isaiah. These supplemental allusions amplify those placed on the lips of Jesus, putting them in stronger relief and enhancing their dramatic significance.

During the temple cleansing episode, with an unusually rich conflux of scriptural allusions, Jesus again interprets his death as the fulfillment of prophecy (Mark 11:15–17; Matt 21:12–13; Luke 19:45–46; John 2:14–22). The Gospels all portray Jesus as viewing the temple cleansing as especially significant.[29] At first glance, with the exception of John, none of them shows Jesus interpreting the temple cleansing in light of his imminent death. Closer inspection reveals otherwise. In his use of prophecy, Jesus suggests that the temple cleansing prophetically foreshadows both his own death and his eventual establishment of the messianic kingdom. The connection between the various prophecies takes some work to unravel. First, the very act of driving out the traders and money changers from the temple seems to allude to Zechariah and the messianic kingdom he prophesied (cf. Zech 14:21).[30] Then, Jesus interprets his actions with scripture. To start, he quotes a passage from Isaiah which prophesies that Gentiles will worship in the temple with Jews (Mark 11:17; cf. Matt 21:13; Luke 19:46; Isa 56:7). Then, taking words from Jeremiah's condemnation of the sin and idolatry, Jesus castigates the traders, rebuking them for frustrating the fulfillment of Isaiah's prophecy by their trading (Mark 11:17; cf. Matt 21:13; Luke 19:46; Jer 7:11). So far, it seems

[29] In John's account, the disciples, and not only Jesus, are depicted as regarding the cleansing as especially significant. Overwhelmed by what they have just witnessed, they instinctively turn to scripture—and not just to scripture, but to a psalm of lament often cited in the New Testament as prophetic of Jesus' suffering—in order to make sense of Jesus' dramatic action (John 2:17; Ps 69:9).

[30] Cecil Roth, "The Cleansing of the Temple and Zechariah XIV 21," *Novum Testamentum* 4 (1960): 174–81; Meyer, *Aims of Jesus*, 197–200. Although they do not quote Zechariah, the Gospel narratives about the temple cleansing each seem to allude to Zechariah's prophecies about the coming of a messianic kingdom. In the synoptic Gospels, the cleansing takes place shortly after the triumphal entrance into Jerusalem, an episode that obviously alludes to Zechariah. Moreover, Jesus quotes Isaiah and Jeremiah to explain his cleansing of the temple. It is therefore likely that the Gospels also mean to suggest that the temple cleansing fulfills the prophecies of Zechariah as well as those of Isaiah and Jeremiah.

In John's Gospel, Jesus does not explain the cleansing by quoting Isaiah or Jeremiah, but his words also seem to allude to Zechariah. He tells those who sold the pigeons, "Take these things away; you shall not make my Father's house a house of trade" (John 2:16). In this saying, Jesus seems to echo Zechariah's description of the coming messianic kingdom, who had written that "there shall no longer be a trader in the house of the LORD of hosts on that day" (Zech 14:21). After the cleansing, his disciples think of a verse from Psalm 69, indicating that the evangelist wants to frame the temple cleansing as the fulfillment of prophecy—and thus bolstering the possibility that Jesus' saying alludes to Zechariah.

that Jesus is simply condemning the traders for frustrating the fulfillment of Isaiah's prophecy. But there is more: he is also castigating them for making the temple's destruction inevitable. In the book of Jeremiah, immediately after the passage quoted by Jesus, Jeremiah goes on to predict the destruction of the first temple (Jer 7:12–14). Consequently, by condemning the traders with these words, Jesus is hinting that he expects the second temple to be destroyed on account of their sins. Sin and idolatry led to the first temple's destruction, he seems to be suggesting, and sin and idolatry will lead to the second temple's destruction.

There is yet another dimension to the Gospels' portrayals: each of them, in some fashion, connects the temple cleansing to Jesus' death. The connection is most obvious in John. In John, after the temple cleansing, Jesus says, "Destroy this temple, and in three days I will raise it up" (John 2:19). The connection is also present in the other Gospels in a less obvious way, insofar as the synoptic Gospels each depict the temple cleansing as the proximate cause of Jesus' crucifixion.[31] In short, in the Gospels, Jesus interprets the temple's desecration by the traders as foreshadowing both the temple's destruction and his own rejection. Yet at the same time, he also sees the cleansing of the temple—and, apparently, the temple's pending destruction, along with his own death—as ushering in a new beginning. He relates the temple cleansing to Zechariah's prophecies about the messianic kingdom, and also to Isaiah's prophecies about the Gentiles joining Israel's worship.

The Gospels show Jesus associating himself with the prophecies of Zechariah in other episodes as well. After giving his disciples unusually careful instructions about his mount, Jesus enters Jerusalem riding on a donkey (Mark 11:1–10; Matt 21:1–9; Luke 19:28–40; John 12:12–19). This action corresponds to Zechariah's prophecy about a messianic king who enters Jerusalem riding on a donkey (Zech 9:9). Jesus' detailed instructions make it clear that by choosing to ride into Jerusalem on a donkey, he is claiming to be the messianic king prophesied by Zechariah. Zechariah also prophesies about a stricken shepherd. After the last supper, on the way to the garden of Gethsemane, Jesus tells his disciples that they will be scattered in fulfillment of the stricken shepherd prophecy, saying: "You will all fall away; for it is written, 'I will strike the shepherd, and the sheep will be scattered'" (Mark 14:27; cf. Matt 26:31; Zech 13:7). Zechariah depicts the stricken shepherd as a type of David, the shepherd-king of Israel, and describes him as close to God. Consequently, by interpreting his suffering with reference to Zechariah's stricken shepherd, Jesus is implicitly claiming to be a messianic

[31] See also Mark 14:58, 15:29 and Matt 26:61, 27:40, which give further evidence that the synoptic Gospels connect the temple's destruction to Jesus' death.

figure in the line of David, and to have a mission that somehow involves suffering violence.[32]

Jesus often alludes to the psalms in the Gospels, in a way indicating that he sees himself as bringing them to prophetic fulfillment. He identifies himself with the stone rejected by the builders in Psalm 118, which then becomes the cornerstone (Ps 118: 22–23; Mark 12:10–11; Matt 21:42; Luke 20:17). He also claims to be the proper recipient of the messianic greeting contained in Psalm 118 (Luke 13:35; Ps 118:26). He openly accepts this greeting from the crowds and he defends its appropriateness in the face of criticism (Mark 11:9–10; Matt 21:9, 15–16, Luke 19:38–40; John 12:13). Jesus also quotes four psalms of lament. During the last supper, Jesus foretells his betrayal with a quotation from Psalm 41: "He who ate my bread has lifted his heel against me" (Ps 41:9 as cited by Jesus in John 13:18; cf. Mark 14:18–20; Matt 26:23; Luke 22:21), and he interprets his rejection as the fulfillment of Psalm 69, "They hated me without a cause" (Ps 69:4, as cited by Jesus in John 15:25). In each Gospel, he alludes to a psalm of lament in his final words. In Mark and Matthew, Jesus cries out, "Eloi, Eloi, lama sabachthani?" (Mark 15:34; cf. Matt 27:46), which is the first verse of Psalm 22. In Luke, Jesus commends his spirit into his Father's hands, quoting Psalm 31 (Luke 23:26; Ps 31:5). In John, the evangelist tells us that, in order to fulfill the scriptures, Jesus says, "I thirst," thus prompting those at the foot of the cross to give him vinegar to drink; after taking the vinegar, Jesus says, "It is finished," and dies (John 19:28–30). It is not clear exactly how John sees these words and actions fulfilling the scriptures, but he seems to be alluding to Psalm 22 or Psalm 69, or both.[33] By quoting the

[32] According to Richard Hays' criteria for identifying scriptural echoes (Hays, *Echoes of Scripture*, 29–32), Jesus may also be alluding to a second prophecy from Zechariah in Mark 14:27 and Matt 26:31. Shortly before the verse quoted by Jesus, Zechariah speaks about "him whom they have pierced," a mysterious figure whom the inhabitants of Jerusalem mourn "as one mourns for an only child" (Zech 12:10). Consequently, by placing the stricken shepherd prophecy on Jesus' lips, the evangelists may mean to suggest that Jesus is alluding to this other prophecy as well, and in this way foretelling the manner of his death and claiming to be the only begotten Son of the Father (the "only child" of Zechariah's prophecy). The fact that John 19:37 quotes Zech 12:10 outright heightens the plausibility of this reading.

[33] John may mean that Jesus' words fulfill Psalm 22 (Ps 22:15). In this case, Jesus' words simply highlight how his thirst on the cross prophetically fulfills Psalm 22. But John may also mean that Jesus' words fulfill Psalm 69. In this reading, Jesus' words fulfill the scriptures not only in what they mean, but also in what actions they prompt. By declaring his thirst, Jesus prompts those standing nearby to give him some vinegar, so that they fulfill Psalm 69: "for my thirst they gave me vinegar to drink" (Ps 69:21).

This latter interpretation seems more plausible, since Jesus speaks "to fulfill the scripture" (John 19:28), which suggests that his words will bring about this fulfillment, and do not simply declare that it has already happened. Furthermore, each synoptic Gospel mentions that Jesus was offered vinegar on the cross (Mark 15:36; Matt 27:48; Luke 23:36), which suggests that the other Gospels are also attentive to the fulfillment of Psalm 69. Consequently, on the basis of both internal and external evidence, it seems plausible that John has Psalm 69 in mind when he speaking about Jesus fulfilling the scriptures. (John may also mean that Jesus asks for the vinegar as a deliberate prophetic gesture, with the *intention* of bringing about the fulfillment of Psalm 69;

psalms, Jesus is identifying himself with David, because David is the putative author of the psalms, and, therefore, he is implicitly claiming to be the Messiah.[34] Moreover, by quoting psalms of lament, Jesus is drawing attention to the many passages in the psalms that associate the psalmist—and therefore also David and the Messiah, the Son of David—with suffering. Implicitly, he is suggesting that these passages from the psalms prophesy a suffering Messiah, and that he himself is that suffering Messiah.

The Necessity of Jesus' Suffering

From the beginning, from his earliest allusions in the Gospels, Jesus describes his death, not merely as advancing his mission, but as somehow necessary to its accomplishment. In the first passion prediction, in all three synoptic Gospels, Jesus tells his disciples that it is necessary (δεῖ) that the Son of Man suffer many things (Mark 8:31; cf. Matt 16:21; Luke 9:22). In Luke, Jesus repeats this claim almost verbatim in another pericope (Luke 17:25), and then again after the resurrection, this time in the past tense (Luke 24:26). Later, during the last supper, Jesus tells his disciples that it is necessary for Isaiah's fourth servant song to be fulfilled in him: "For I tell you that this scripture must be fulfilled (δεῖ τελεσθῆναι) in me, 'And he was reckoned with transgressors' (Luke 22:37; cf. Isa 53:12).[35] In John, Jesus tells Nicodemus that it is necessary (δεῖ) for the Son of Man to be lifted up, "that whoever believes in him may have eternal life." (John 3:14–15; cf. John 12:34). In Matthew, as he is being arrested, Jesus explains to his apostles that, according to the scriptures, "it must be so" (οὕτως δεῖ γενέσθαι) (Matt 26:54). In Luke, Jesus says it is not possible (ὅτι οὐκ ἐνδέχεται) for a prophet to perish away from Jerusalem (Luke 13:33). Similarly, in the garden of Gethsemane, Jesus prays, "My Father, if it be possible (εἰ δυνατόν ἐστιν), let this cup pass from me" (Matt 26:39; cf. Mark 14:36). But his cup does not pass from him, and, as his betrayer arrives, Jesus announces that his hour has come (Mark 14:41; Matt 26:45; Luke 22:53),

that is a separate possibility, much more difficult to confirm.) John may be thinking of Psalm 22, too, but his primary reference seems to be Psalm 68.

For a discussion of this passage and its allusion to scripture, see Brown, *Death of the Messiah*, 1072–4. Brown observes that Jesus' words may also allude to the cup given to him by his Father (John 18:11).

[34] Stephen P. Ahearne-Kroll, *The Psalms of Lament in Mark's Passion: Jesus' Davidic Suffering* (Cambridge: Cambridge University Press, 2008); Margaret Daly-Denton, *David in the Fourth Gospel: The Johannine Reception of the Psalms* (Leiden: Brill, 2000).

[35] Another passage in Luke portrays Jesus viewing his rejection as something destined to happen. While predicting the betrayal of Judas, he says, "the Son of Man goes as it has been determined (τὸ ὡρισμένον πορεύεται)" (Luke 22:22). This phrasing stops short of describing his rejection as necessary, but it comes close.

implying that it is not possible for his suffering to pass him by—that it is somehow necessary.

On a few occasions, Jesus states that he has come for a purpose that necessarily involves his death. In Mark and Matthew, he says that the Son of Man came "to give his life as a ransom for many" (Mark 10:45; cf. Matt 20:28). In Luke, Jesus proclaims, "I have a baptism to be baptized with, and how I am constrained until it is accomplished!" (Luke 12:50), implying that Jesus' passion is somehow intrinsic, and therefore necessary, to his mission. In John, Jesus proclaims that his hour has come and that he will not ask the Father to save him, because he has come to this hour "for this purpose" (John 12:23–27). He does not explain what he means by "this purpose," but he does talk about a grain of wheat which dies and then bears much fruit, indicating that, whatever it is, "this purpose" involves his death. Like the ransom saying, the wheat metaphor implies that Jesus sees himself as giving his life for others, and, indeed, for many others.

Jesus' Deliberate Provocation of His Opponents

In the Gospels, Jesus does not merely interpret his death as integral to his mission; he also provokes it. In John's Gospel, after the temple cleansing, he is asked for a sign to justify his actions. In response, he says, referring to the temple of his body, "Destroy this temple, and in three days I will raise it up" (John 2:19). This response contains layers of meaning. On one level, Jesus is saying that he can and will overcome their violence. But that is not all he is doing. On another level, like the temple cleansing itself, his words are deliberately provocative. They are a taunt. It should not be glossed over that Jesus is speaking in the imperative mood. He is not making a conditional statement about what will happen if the temple of his body is destroyed. He is goading his opponents to kill him.[36]

[36] Jesus' saying about the sign of Jonah may also hint at an underlying strategy of provocation. Jonah asks the sailors to throw him into the ocean so that the storm will be calmed and they will be saved (John 1:12), but then, instead of drowning, he is swallowed by the whale and emerges three days later. By comparing himself to Jonah, Jesus may be hinting that his public ministry constitutes a sustained request to be thrown into the heart of the earth by "an evil and adulterous generation," so that he can save it, just as Jonah saved the sailors from the storm, and then emerge vindicated three days later. If so, the saying would shed light on why Jesus suggests that the sign of Jonah is a sign especially suited to an "evil generation" (Matt 12:39; Luke 11:29). Since evil implies opposition to God, a sign that miraculously overcame the rejection of God's emissary would be appropriate to an evil generation.

Admittedly, this reading of the Jonah saying is a stretch. Neither Matthew nor Luke gives us much help in interpreting the Jonah saying, and it is impossible to know whether this sort of reading—although it can be justified—was something they had in mind. But putting aside questions about the evangelists' intentions, should we read the Jonah saying as hinting at a strategy of provocation, the sign of Jonah would become the synoptic equivalent to the sign of the

Jesus' deliberate provocation of his opponents features prominently in other Gospel passages. In Matthew, in the midst of denouncing the scribes and Pharisees, Jesus encourages them to take violent action against him. After pointing out that they are the sons of those who murdered the prophets, Jesus says to them, "Fill up, then, the measure of your fathers" (Matt 23:32), essentially telling them to get it over with and kill him as their fathers killed the prophets. In John, Jesus incites Judas in a similar way during the last supper. After Jesus gives him a morsel of bread, Satan enters Judas, and Jesus says to him, "What you are going to do, do quickly" (John 13:27). Judas leaves immediately. The evangelist notes that the others thought that Jesus was telling Judas to take care of some ordinary task, but then explains that Jesus was referring to Judas' betrayal—thus emphasizing, in case there was any doubt, that the evangelist wants to portray Jesus as actually telling Judas to go ahead and betray him, and that Jesus is so much in control that even his betrayer cannot help but accomplish his will. In sum, in these two episodes, Jesus regards his death as so inevitable that, in order to get it over with, he actively takes steps to hasten it.[37]

Jesus also provokes his opponents by telling the parable about the wicked tenants. In the parable, the wicked tenants kill the vineyard owner's beloved son. The evangelists explain that, after Jesus tells the parable, his opponents perceive that it had been told against them, and they try to arrest him (Mark 12:12; Matt 21:45–46; Luke 20:19). Ironically, by telling the parable, Jesus hastens its fulfillment. The parable is not only a parable; it is also a provocation. With their commentary, the evangelists are making sure we realize that Jesus was being deliberately provocative and knew full well what the ultimate consequences of telling this particular parable would be.

Jesus' silence before his interrogators can also be seen as provocative, or at least as something that deliberately hastens his death (cf. Mark 14:61, 15:5; Matt 26:63, 27:12–14; Luke 23:9; John 19:9). Earlier, Jesus had responded to hostile questions; now, he is silent, and his failure to defend himself hastens his execution. The Gospels do not explain his behavior, but we seem meant to infer that Jesus is silent because he sees his death as inevitable and necessary, and because he is ready to die.[38] Pilate's reaction to his silence is particularly telling (Mark 15:5; Matt 27:12–14; John 19:9). Expecting Jesus to at least try to save his own life, especially given the weak nature of the charges against him, Pilate finds his silence puzzling and even unnerving. By drawing attention to

rebuilt temple promised by Jesus in John's Gospel. Both signs are promised in answer to a request for a sign from skeptical interlocutors; both signs are riddles; both signs follow only after provocation and violence; and both signs involve vindication after a period of three days.

[37] A desire to hasten his own death may also be implicit in Luke 12:49.

[38] E. Schnabel, "The Silence of Jesus," in *Authenticating the Words of Jesus*, ed. Bruce D. Chilton and C. A. Evans (Leiden: Brill, 1999), 203–57. For a survey of alternative interpretations of Jesus' silence, see Schnabel, "Silence of Jesus," 241–56.

Jesus' silence, the evangelists probably intend to evoke the suffering servant of Isaiah: "like a lamb that is led to the slaughter, and like a sheep that before its shearers is dumb, so he opened not his mouth" (Isa 53:7).

Jesus' provocative behavior can be interpreted in a number of ways. Frustration could be said to shape his intentions, at least in part. But something more than frustration appears to be involved. The Gospels seem to present his provocations as deliberate attempts to hasten what he regards as inevitable, so that he can get on with the business of suffering and dying. They reflect a deeper strategy of provocation. During his public ministry, Jesus tells his disciples, "I have not come to bring peace, but a sword" (Matt 10:34). This saying, which places provocation and controversy at the heart of his mission, is of one piece with the various episodes in which Jesus deliberately provokes his opponents or actively hastens his death.

HISTORICITY OF THE GOSPEL PORTRAYALS

Thus far, we have been considering how the Gospels portray Jesus' attitude toward his death. The textual evidence has been unequivocal. With great consistency, the Gospels show Jesus expecting to be killed and thinking that his death will advance his mission. But do these portrayals correspond to Jesus' historical expectations? To answer this question, we must first consider whether the Gospels even purport to make historical claims, and if so, whether we should assign these claims any historical credibility, and on what grounds. We need to look at the literary genre of the Gospels, the trustworthiness of their authors, and the reliability of their sources. Then, after considering these fundamental issues, we will be able to draw some conclusions about the Gospel portrayals of Jesus' attitude toward his death.

The Literary Genre of the Gospels

To determine whether the Gospels even purport to make historical claims, we need to consider their literary genre. When we read a novel we know that its author is not making any claims about the past (other than in passing, as background to the story); conversely, when we read a newspaper article about yesterday's events we know that its author is indeed making claims about the past. It is not only the text's physical packaging as a novel or a newspaper that tells us what the author is doing; the style of writing itself tells us something. From the text alone we can judge whether it is a novel or a newspaper article. Likewise by looking at the Gospels and taking note of their literary features, we can make an informed judgment about their literary genre—and therefore whether or not, and to what extent, the evangelists are purporting to make historical claims.

Scholarly opinion about the Gospels' literary genre has fluctuated over the past two hundred years. Until the twentieth century, scholarly consensus classified the Gospels as ancient biographies with Jesus as their subject. Then in the early twentieth century, German biblical scholars rejected this consensus and began to offer alternative classifications. The paradigm shift is especially associated with Rudolf Bultmann, who held that the Gospels constitute "a new phenomenon in the history of literature," and that they are more legendary and cultic than biographical and historical.[39] Over the past few decades, however, scholarship has shifted back toward the earlier consensus.[40] From analysis of the Gospels' literary features, scholars have established (though not without dissent) that the Gospels belong to the genre of ancient Greco-Roman biography.[41] This classification is intuitively plausible. Apart from the technical literary evidence, it is prima facie more likely that the evangelists would draw upon an existing literary genre rather than invent a new one. And since ancient Greco-Roman biographies make historical claims about their subjects, the Gospels should likewise be taken as making historical claims about Jesus. Ancient Greco-Roman biographies are not like modern biographies in their claims to historical precision—still less are they like court transcripts or newspaper reporting—but their authors do intend to make historical claims about the subjects of their biographies.[42] So if the Gospels indeed belong to this genre, the evangelists must intend to make historical claims about Jesus. Whether or not we should take these claims to be historically reliable, however, is another matter.

Evaluating the Historical Claims of the Gospels

The historical claims of the Gospels are not self-interpreting; they must be evaluated. In this respect, the Gospels are just like any other historical text. No

[39] Rudolf Bultmann, *The History of the Synoptic Tradition*, trans. John Marsh, 2nd ed. (Oxford: Blackwell, 1972), 373–4.

[40] Two books played an especially important role in launching the new movement to classify the Gospels once again in the genre of ancient biography: C. H. Talbert, *What is a Gospel? The Genre of the Canonical Gospels* (Philadelphia: Fortress Press, 1977); P. L. Shuler, *A Genre for the Gospels: The Biographical Character of Matthew* (Philadelphia: Fortress Press, 1982).

[41] The case for this position has been made most thoroughly by Richard Burridge in his influential monograph (from which this brief history of scholarship on the literary genre of the Gospels has been derived). See Richard A. Burridge, *What Are the Gospels? A Comparison with Graeco-Roman Biography* (Cambridge: Cambridge University Press, 1992). In the second edition of his book, published by Eerdmans in 2004, Burridge adds a chapter in which he develops his earlier position and responds to critics. See Richard A. Burridge, *What Are the Gospels? A Comparison with Graeco-Roman Biography*, 2nd ed. (Grand Rapids, MI: Eerdmans, 2004).

[42] Burridge, *What Are the Gospels?*, 128–90.

historical text can prove the historicity of its own claims. Its historical testimony must be judged by its readers. Consequently, when it comes to judging the historical claims of the Gospels, we must approach them as we would the testimony of any witness. We have to weigh the evidence, consider the possibilities, and then draw our conclusions. If the evidence seems sufficient, we judge the testimony to be reliable; if not, we either suspend judgment or reject the testimony as false.

When making judgments about historical claims, we typically consider two types of evidence. The first type supports the credibility of the witness. For example, those who have a history of criminal behavior have less credibility and those who are known for being model citizens have more. Likewise, when it comes to knowing the details of a major World War II battle, a military historian has more credibility than an actor who plays General Patton in a movie. This first type of evidence does not directly confirm or undermine the witness's testimony. It simply gives us reason to trust or mistrust the witness. Questionable sources sometimes tell the truth and respected sources sometimes lie; likewise, experts sometimes get things wrong. Nonetheless, it is a valuable kind of evidence, and when making judgments about historical claims, we often focus to a great extent on the credibility of the witness. The second type of evidence confirms or contradicts the original testimony with its own direct testimony. For example, after an eyewitness identifies a burglar, other eyewitnesses and video records might corroborate the testimony of the first witness. This evidence confirms the original testimony but also does something more. It bolsters the credibility of the original witness because it confirms that the original witness was both telling the truth and capable of identifying the burglar accurately.

No amount of evidence, however, can supplant the necessity of coming to one's own conclusions about the testimony. Evidence does not interpret itself, or even establish itself as evidence. When we judge a witness' testimony to be reliable, we often appeal to evidence, as though the evidence provides independent justification for our judgment. In fact, however, even determining what counts as evidence relies on our judgment. When we evaluate historical claims, the evidence does not declare itself; we must determine what counts as evidence, both in the sense of being reliable and in the sense of being relevant to the question at hand. Even deferring to the opinion of experts implies that we have made some preliminary judgments. It means that we judge the testimony in question neither obviously reliable nor obviously unreliable and that we judge the opinion of experts more reliable than our own. Moreover, once we apprehend testimony of whatever sort, we cannot avoid making a personal judgment about its reliability and the reliability of the supporting evidence. (The decision to suspend judgment also implies a personal judgment, even if only that it is not possible to come to an immediate conclusion.) In ordinary life we are constantly making judgments about the testimony of others, even if only implicitly or unconsciously. When we hear a newscast on the radio we cannot avoid making judgments about its truth value. We cannot help but accept it, reject it, or judge that we do not yet know enough.

We often suffer from the illusion that we can achieve mathematical certainty about the historicity of past events. But we cannot: the certainty proper to mathematics is not the certainty proper to historical knowledge. No amount of evidence—material, oral, or written—can preclude skepticism about the historicity of an event that we did not experience personally. Unless they are self-contradictory, any counterfactual claims about the past are logically possible. They cannot be disproven by deductive reasoning. The impossibility of doing so explains why conspiracy theories find so many adherents in every age. It is logically possible that Julius Caesar never existed and that, in order to bolster his legitimacy as Roman emperor in the eyes of future generations, Augustus ruthlessly cultivated the myth of his existence by planting false evidence. To exclude this counterfactual possibility, it is necessary to trust the historical testimony that indicates otherwise. There is no way around the necessity of trust.

When it comes to judging the historical claims of the Gospels, we cannot rely on external evidence. Besides the Gospels, few documents that mention Jesus survive from the first century. Consequently, we cannot focus on whether the external evidence confirms or contradicts the Gospels' historical claims. There is not enough to make that line of inquiry worthwhile. The lack of external evidence, however, does not mean that it is impossible to judge the Gospels' historical claims. We routinely make judgments about historical claims without external evidence, as long as we have reliable testimony. For example, in court, suspects are often convicted on eyewitness testimony alone as long as the witnesses appear credible. External evidence is often given greater weight, because eyewitness testimony can be unreliable; nonetheless, even when unsupported by external evidence, eyewitness testimony is often deemed sufficient to convict. The absence of external evidence, therefore, does not doom the possibility of evaluating the Gospels' historical claims. It simply means that we have to focus on evaluating the reliability of the evangelists.

Many things can be cited as evidence in favor of the evangelists' reliability. Historians and exegetes often point to the internal coherence of their narratives, the coherence of the Gospels with first century Judaism and the geography of Palestine, and the willingness of the apostles and other early Christians to endure persecution for their claims about Jesus. This evidence, however, neither proves nor confirms the Gospels' historical claims. It only provides reasons to trust the evangelists' testimony. It does not provide independent support for their historical claims. External evidence exists for some of the historical claims made in the Gospels—for example, that there was a temple in Jerusalem—but this sort of independent confirmation does not touch the Gospels' more significant historical claims. Furthermore, it should not be overlooked that the text of the Gospels can also be seen as providing reasons *not* to trust the evangelists. For example, skeptics might argue that the miracle stories in the Gospels run counter to ordinary human experience and thus undermine the evangelists' credibility.

Still, we need not give up on the possibility of historically certain knowledge about Jesus, any more than we need to give up on the possibility of historically certain knowledge about other past events. We simply need to acknowledge that historical judgments are intrinsically subjective and intrinsically dependent on trust.[43] The historicity of the Gospels is a charged topic for many reasons, but there are no special rules for judging their historical claims. Judging the Gospels' historical claims certainly involves subjective judgments about their reliability, a quality that cannot be measured or quantified, but then so does judging any other historical claim. Historical judgments are inherently subjective, and thus inherently exclude the possibility of mathematical certainty. This element of subjectivity, however, does not exclude the possibility of another kind of certainty, and another kind of objectivity—few people seriously doubt the existence of Julius Caesar, or fail to regard his existence as an objective fact—even in the case of the Gospels.

Many arguments can and have been made to establish the historical reliability of the Gospels. These arguments are valuable and useful. In their own way, they confirm the Gospels' historical claims. Nonetheless, these arguments cannot establish the historical reliability of the Gospels in any absolute sense. We can always find the arguments unpersuasive. It is like an acquaintance trying to defend someone's honesty to us. We can always find the defense wanting and decide to withhold our trust. When it comes to the Gospels, the best one could hope to do is show why it is more coherent with our experience of the world to trust, rather than distrust, the Gospels' historical claims. Success in accomplishing this goal cannot be measured in absolute terms, because showing coherence is a different task from deductive reasoning. Success in accomplishing this goal will vary widely according to someone's background, education, personal experience—and willingness to trust others.

So, are the historical claims of the Gospels to be judged reliable? As with all other historical claims, each of us must answer that question personally; no one can answer it for us.

[43] In my thinking about the dependence of human knowledge on interpersonal trust, and the applications of this insight to historical knowledge about Jesus, I am indebted to John Paul II, *Fides et Ratio: On the Relationship between Faith and Reason* (Boston: Pauline Books & Media, 1998), 28–34; Richard Bauckham, *Jesus and the Eyewitnesses: The Gospels as Eyewitness Testimony* (Grand Rapids, MI: Eerdmans, 2006), 1–11, 472–508.

The Gospels, Their Sources, and Degrees of Historical Reliability

Should we find the Gospels reliable, then we have reason to take their historical claims seriously. Even so, the matter is not settled. If we think that the Gospels are reliable, we have reason to take their historical claims seriously, but we may not have grounds to think that their claims are historically accurate. Unless the evangelists are well informed, their historical claims may be inaccurate to some degree. Consequently, if we judge that the evangelists are reliable in their historical claims—that they are being truthful, at least to some significant degree, and that they have some grounds for their assertions—the next step is to determine their degree of historical reliability.

This question about the Gospels' degree of historical reliability turns especially on the question of the evangelists' sources, and whether the evangelists could plausibly have had access to accurate information about Jesus. Scholars have put forward different theories about the evangelists' sources. Most theories maintain that the evangelists drew on a combination of oral and written traditions in constructing the Gospels. Contemporary scholars generally believe that the earliest and most formative traditions were transmitted orally. They disagree, however, about the nature of these oral traditions, and especially about the mechanisms by which stories and sayings about Jesus were transmitted to the evangelists.

The principal theories about early Christian oral tradition can be sorted into four main categories.[44] The first theory is that the evangelists relied on informal, uncontrolled oral tradition. This theory was first advocated by Bultmann and other form critics. According to this theory, early Christians transmitted stories and sayings in small units and they would take great liberty in adapting them to social context. Consequently, the Gospels reveal less about what actually happened and more about the social context in which stories and sayings were originally told. When it comes to the historical accuracy of the Gospels, proponents of this theory have very different opinions. Some proponents, such as Bultmann and other early form critics, rank their historical reliability very low. Other proponents of the theory, especially later ones, believe that the Gospel narratives contain a good amount of accurate historical information about Jesus.

[44] This fourfold division derives from Kenneth Bailey's threefold division. It adds a fourth category to incorporate the work of Samuel Byrskog and Richard Bauckham on eyewitness testimony. Bailey presents his threefold taxonomy in Kenneth E. Bailey, "Informal Controlled Oral Tradition and the Synoptic Gospels," *Themelios* 20 (1995): 4–11. Bailey's article was originally published in Kenneth E. Bailey, "Informal Controlled Oral Tradition and the Synoptic Gospels," *Asia Journal of Theology* 5 (1991): 34–54. See also Bauckham's comments about Bailey's threefold division in Bauckham, *Jesus and the Eyewitnesses*, 257–60.

The second theory is that the evangelists relied on formal, controlled oral tradition. It was proposed by Scandinavian scholars Harald Riesenfeld and Birger Gerhardsson in reaction to form criticism.[45] This theory maintains that the oral traditions used by the evangelists were much more reliable than form critics believe. Memorizing scripture is known to have been a common practice in rabbinic Judaism and, according to this theory, the early Christians memorized stories and sayings with equal dedication because they regarded the words and actions of Jesus as divinely inspired and therefore equivalent to scripture. Individual Christians would dedicate themselves to preserving the tradition by memorizing stories and sayings. Then, eventually, the evangelists recorded these memorized stories and sayings in the Gospels. Consequently, these scholars argue, the traditions recorded in the Gospels have a high degree of historical accuracy.

The third theory is that the evangelists relied on informal, controlled oral tradition. Kenneth Bailey proposed this theory after reflecting on decades of living and teaching in the Middle East, and especially from observing storytelling at community gatherings.[46] During these gatherings he saw how communities preserved the memory of historical events through storytelling. According to Bailey's theory, stories and sayings were transmitted with some flexibility, but the Christian community ensured that their essential content remained constant. The Christian community also ensured that stories and sayings retained certain phrases from one telling to the next. Storytellers were allowed some flexibility in how they recounted stories and sayings, but if they strayed too far from previous versions, they would be corrected by those present who also knew the story.[47] In this way, the community's collective memory served as a kind of control. It ensured that the Christian community maintained a high degree of historical accuracy in its oral traditions until they were written down in the Gospels. At the same time, according to this

[45] See Harald Riesenfeld, *The Gospel Tradition: Essays*, trans. E. Margaret Rowley and Robert A. Kraft (Oxford: Blackwell, 1970); Birger Gerhardsson, *Memory and Manuscript: Oral Tradition and Written Transmission in Rabbinic Judaism and Early Christianity* (Uppsala: Gleerup, 1961); Birger Gerhardsson, *The Gospel Tradition* (Lund: Gleerup, 1986). See also Bailey, "Informal Controlled Oral Tradition; Bauckham, *Jesus and the Eyewitnesses*, 249–52.

[46] Bailey, "Informal Controlled Oral Tradition"; Kenneth E. Bailey, "Middle Eastern Oral Tradition and the Synoptic Gospels," *Expository Times* 106 (1995): 363–7. James Dunn develops Bailey's approach to oral tradition in James D. G. Dunn, *Jesus Remembered* (Grand Rapids, MI: Eerdmans, 2003). Gerhardsson critiques Bailey's theory and its subsequent development by James Dunn in Birger Gerhardsson, "The Secret of the Transmission of the Unwritten Jesus Tradition," *New Testament Studies* 51 (2004): 1–18. He observes that there is no hard evidence that Bailey's experience of contemporary Arab village life corresponds to first century Palestinian Jewish culture.

[47] Arguably, something analogous happens with joke telling. A joke teller is allowed some amount of license in retelling a joke, but if some of those listening already know the joke and think that the joke is being badly bungled, or that the wording of the punch line is not quite right, they will interrupt and correct the joke teller.

theory, the Gospels do not offer the degree of historical precision that we would expect from formal, controlled oral tradition.

The fourth and final theory is that the evangelists relied on oral tradition shaped by eyewitness testimony. According to this theory, early Christian oral tradition featured both flexibility and historical precision. Christian storytellers often transmitted stories and sayings in a flexible manner, as in Bailey's theory of informal, controlled oral tradition, but eyewitnesses ensured that the stories and sayings maintained a high degree of historical accuracy and that the transmission of information was guided and structured, as in the Scandinavian theory of formal, controlled oral tradition.[48] Samuel Byrskog was the first to propose a version of this theory.[49] He shows that ancient historians, following Heraclitus' dictum that "eyes are surer witnesses than ears," considered eyewitness testimony indispensable to good history.[50] He then argues that the evangelists would certainly have been shaped by this historiographical notion. Consequently, they would have every reason to consider eyewitness testimony indispensable to their writing of the Gospels. Moreover, Byrskog argues, both internal and external evidence attests that the evangelists relied on eyewitness testimony.[51]

Richard Bauckham has developed Byrskog's thesis further. He argues that fragments from Papias about the origins of the Gospels, dating from the early second century, provide strong external evidence that the evangelists drew on eyewitness testimony.[52] Bauckham also identifies internal evidence for eyewitness testimony. Pointing out clues in the evangelists' use of personal names, he argues that named persons in the Gospels are often sources for the stories in which they appear.[53] Among other things, based on internal evidence, he makes a strong case that Peter is an eyewitness source for Mark's Gospel.[54]

[48] See Bauckham, *Jesus and the Eyewitnesses*, 264–318. Note that, like Gerhardsson, but not to the same extent, Bauckham argues that memorization—a common ancient practice—played an important role in the early transmission of information about Jesus. See Bauckham, *Jesus and the Eyewitnesses*, 280–7.

[49] Samuel Byrskog, *Story as History—History as Story: The Gospel Tradition in the Context of Ancient Oral History* (Tübingen: J.C.B. Mohr, 2002). In his theory, Bailey also suggests that eyewitnesses played a special role in controlling the community's collective memory, but he does not develop this suggestion. See Bailey, "Informal Controlled Oral Tradition," 10. For a critique of Bailey's incorporation of eyewitness testimony into his theory, see Bauckham, *Jesus and the Eyewitnesses*, 260–3.

[50] Byrskog, *Story as History*, 48–91.

[51] Byrskog, *Story as History*, 165–76, 223–306.

[52] Bauckham, *Jesus and the Eyewitnesses*, 12–38, 202–39, 412–37; Richard Bauckham, *The Testimony of the Beloved Disciple: Narrative, History, and Theology in the Gospel of John* (Grand Rapids, MI: Baker Academic, 2007).

[53] Bauckham, *Jesus and the Eyewitnesses*, 39–66.

[54] Bauckham, *Jesus and the Eyewitnesses*, 155–82.

Following Martin Hengel, he also argues that the author of John's Gospel is an eyewitness, namely, John the Presbyter (who, unlike Hengel, he distinguishes from John the Apostle, the son of Zebedee).[55] Scientific studies and anecdotal evidence have demonstrated that eyewitness memory can be remarkably accurate, even many decades later.[56] Therefore, Bauckham argues, the Gospels' reliance on eyewitness testimony gives great credibility to their historical claims.

Which of these different theories of oral transmission is correct, if any? Choosing between them is not simply a matter of choosing the theory that seems the most plausible on its own terms. It also involves considering other questions. For example, if we think that many Gospel stories are historically implausible, but that the evangelists do not intend to deceive, then we will favor theories that leave more room for distortion in the oral transmission of stories and sayings about Jesus. But if we think that most Gospel stories are historically plausible, then we might favor theories that leave less room for distortion. Our opinions about the plausibility of Gospel stories deeply influence how we evaluate theories of oral transmission. So do our opinions about whether, and to what extent, the evangelists are being truthful. In the end, therefore, our judgments about theories of oral transmission are irreducibly bound up with larger questions about the Gospels. We cannot form an opinion about a particular theory of oral transmission without being influenced by our judgments on the Gospels' historical claims, and vice versa.

With that said, for many reasons, the theories of Bailey, Byrskog, and Bauckham seem more plausible than the alternatives. Some of Jesus' companions must have been alive a few decades after his death (as many early Christian documents claim),[57] and other early Christians would naturally turn to them for information about Jesus. Their memories surely would still be accurate even after many years. We remember consequential events with great accuracy decades afterward; Jesus' companions could not have remembered his words and actions with any less accuracy. But even if we are not persuaded by theories that grant a high degree of historical reliability to the Gospels, we need not doubt that the Gospels contain some amount of historically accurate information. Even the theories of Bultmann and other form critics, which postulate great historical distortion in the Gospel portrayals of Jesus, presume there must be *some* historical kernel to the Gospel stories.

[55] Bauckham, *Jesus and the Eyewitnesses*, 358–83; Bauckham, *The Testimony of the Beloved Disciple*; Martin Hengel, *The Johannine Question*, trans. J. Bowden (London: S.C.M. Press, 1989).

[56] Bauckham, *Jesus and the Eyewitnesses*, 319–57.

[57] For more on the external evidence that indicates that the Gospels were based on eyewitness testimony, see Bauckham, *Jesus and the Eyewitnesses*, 12–38, 202–39, 412–71.

Jesus' Historical Attitude toward His Death

With these broad considerations about judging the historical claims of the Gospels, we can finally turn to Jesus' attitude toward his death. Do the Gospel portrayals correspond to Jesus' historical expectations? Let us review the evidence. In the Gospels, Jesus' prophetic expectation of his death and his positive interpretation of that death permeate his words and actions.[58] They are not confined to a few isolated sayings. If every implicit and explicit reference to them were removed from the Gospels, there would be little left. The Gospel narratives, which are each structured around Jesus' inexorable march to Golgotha, would collapse into incoherence. Attempts to imagine how things would have turned out if Jesus had not been crucified always result in deeply unsatisfying narratives.[59] Just as *Casablanca* can only end with Ingrid Bergman getting on the plane and leaving Humphrey Bogart behind, the story of Jesus can only end on Golgotha. Given its dramatic structure, no other ending would fit. Part of this structural necessity stems from the evangelists' shaping of the narratives, but part of it also stems from the orientation toward the cross that suffuses the words and actions of Jesus.

Consequently, if we grant even minimal reliability to the historical claims of the Gospels, then Jesus must have expected to meet a violent death, and he must have interpreted his death in a positive light, as somehow advancing his mission. He must also have seen his death as particularly important to his mission. Otherwise, he would not have talked about it so much. This conclusion holds true even if we doubt the evangelists' truthfulness about, say, the miracle stories or the resurrection, and even if we think that they or someone else invented many of the sayings they attribute to Jesus.[60] Assuming a skeptical stance toward the Gospels, the evangelists must either have been drawing on some historical kernel or else have completely fabricated their portrayals of Jesus' attitude toward his death. Between these two possibilities, the first one is much more plausible. That Jesus could have expected to be killed for challenging the religious establishment is quite conceivable, as is the idea that he could have assigned some positive significance to his death under such circumstances. The other possibility, that the evangelists invented their

[58] See McKnight, *Jesus and His Death*, 79–82.

[59] In a collection of essays on counterfactual history, Carlos Eire imagines what it would be like if Jesus had not been crucified. His essay is well crafted but nonetheless unsatisfying and implausible. In its failure, the exercise of the essay confirms that there is something about the inner trajectory of the Gospel narratives that can only end with Jesus' crucifixion—a point that Eire may well be intending to highlight. Carlos M. N. Eire, "Pontius Pilate Spares Jesus: Christianity without the Crucifixion," in *More What If? Eminent Historians Imagine What Might Have Been*, ed. Robert Cowley (London: MacMillan, 2001), 48–67.

[60] Even when we intend to deceive, we often reveal truths that we take for granted in spite of ourselves. For example, when being interrogated, criminals often reveal information that they are trying to keep secret, precisely by the way that they lie and dissemble.

portrayals of Jesus' attitude toward his death, would imply that the evangelists dedicated themselves to suffusing innumerable stories and sayings with an expectation of violent death—and that they succeeded without diminishing the genius of those stories and sayings, and without any obvious reason for going to such trouble. So even if we doubt the evangelists' truthfulness and reliability, we still have a strong reason to think that Jesus knew that he was going to be killed, and that he saw his death as somehow advancing his mission.

The institution narratives provide an especially important witness to Jesus' historical expectations. His institution of the Eucharist during the last supper is an action, rather than a saying, and as such it rests on especially reliable historical grounding.[61] The institution of the Eucharist shows deep familiarity with Jewish customs but also radically departs from them; its implied theology also fits remarkably well with New Testament portrayals of Jesus' teachings. Consequently, on internal evidence alone, the Eucharistic transformation of the Passover seder must have been invented by Jesus or someone with a similar sociological profile.[62] Besides the institution narratives, innumerable passages in the New Testament allude, both implicitly and explicitly, to the Christian practice of celebrating the Eucharist. Moreover, early Christian literature overwhelmingly attests to the centrality of the Eucharist to early Christian culture, worship, and theology. Besides the crucifixion and resurrection, no other episode in the life of Jesus is anywhere near as central to early Christian belief and practice as his institution of the Eucharist. The historicity of Jesus' institution of the Eucharist in some form is beyond reasonable doubt.[63] It is often said that the most historically certain fact about Jesus is

[61] E. P. Sanders has argued persuasively that "facts" about the life and public actions of Jesus are especially secure in their historicity, more so than many of the sayings attributed to him, and therefore should enjoy a special place in the historical reconstruction of his life. Sanders, *Jesus and Judaism*, 3–13.

[62] John Meier has observed that, in all three synoptic accounts, Jesus has the disciples drink from his cup, rather than their own cups, as would be the usual Jewish custom for a blessing. In its narrative context, this innovation heightens the symbolism of sacrificial self-donation. From a historical-critical perspective, it gives further support to the historicity of the institution narratives. John P. Meier, "The Eucharist and the Last Supper: Did It Happen?," *Theology Digest* 42 (1995): 349.

[63] For a robust defense of the historicity of the institution narratives through the application of historical-critical principles and a survey of the state of the question, see Meier, "Eucharist and the Last Supper." See also R. Pesch, *Das Abendmahl und Jesu Todesverständnis* (Freiburg: Herder, 1978).

Some who personally accept the historicity of the institution narratives might object to the view that their historicity is beyond reasonable doubt. Yet it should be considered how much intellectual effort it takes to sustain a negative judgment about their historicity, or even an agnostic one. It requires tremendous, thoroughgoing skepticism about the historical reliability of either the Gospels or early Christian literature. It also faces great challenges in explaining the sheer fact of why Christians started celebrating the Eucharist in the first place. It seems logically necessary that any scholar who rejects the historicity of the institution narratives would have to

that he was crucified. If that is true, then the second most historically certain fact is that he instituted the Eucharist.

The historicity of the institution narratives holds great significance for reconstructing Jesus' historical attitude toward his death. The institution narratives vary somewhat among the synoptic Gospels and First Corinthians, especially in the wording that they attribute to Jesus. Yet none of these variations diminish the implication that Jesus expected to meet a violent death, and that he interpreted his death as somehow beneficial and life-giving to his disciples. Moreover, it is difficult to imagine any scenario where Jesus could have done anything like what is recounted in the institution narratives (say, blessed and distributed the bread, but not the cup), and not thereby indicated that he interpreted his death as beneficial and life-giving to his disciples. Consequently, even apart from any other story or saying, the historicity of Jesus' institution of the Eucharist alone suffices to establish the central claim of this chapter: that Jesus expected a violent death, and that he saw his death as advancing his objectives.

Arguably, however, we do not need to presume anything about the historicity of the Gospels, or even the institution narratives, to draw conclusions about Jesus' historical attitude toward his death. As we have seen, the Gospels are filled with sayings and parables that, in a subtle and obscure way, manifest a positive understanding of an imminent death. This positive understanding is not tangential to their meaning. To the contrary, these sayings and parables presuppose it and revolve around it. They would cease to make sense without it. Yet by the fact of their existence, they must have come from somewhere, and by the fact of their wide dissemination in the ancient world, these sayings and parables, or at least the bulk of them, must trace to the first century. Moreover, literary and textual analysis shows that they exhibit great familiarity with Jewish religious practices of the first century. This circumstantial evidence gives us grounds to think that these sayings and parables trace back to a Jewish teacher of the first century who expected to be killed and who saw his death as somehow advancing his objectives—that is, someone who fits the standard profile of Jesus of Nazareth. Alternative interpretations of the evidence are certainly possible. Any such alternative interpretation, however, would face a number of challenges. It is difficult to explain why someone would put so much effort into constructing sayings and parables that revolve around hidden allusions to an imminent death, and then attribute them to Jesus, when most readers would undoubtedly miss the hidden allusions. It is

be equally skeptical about almost every other piece of information about Jesus, and therefore would have to abstain from making nearly any historical claim about Jesus, other than to express doubts about the received testimony. Having ruled out the earliest documents as almost completely unreliable, on what documentary basis could a scholar of such skepticism make any alternative historical claims about Jesus?

also difficult to explain how anyone, no matter how talented, could accomplish this task without compromising the acknowledged genius of these sayings and parables. According to Ockham's razor, the simplest solution is the best. In this case, the simplest solution is that these sayings and parables trace back to Jesus of Nazareth, at least to a great extent, and taken together, they give us a window into his thoughts and feelings as he approached his death on the cross.

CONCLUSION

The Gospels portray Jesus knowing in advance that he will be killed, and seeing his death as advancing his objectives. This portrayal of Jesus' attitude toward his death thoroughly suffuses the Gospels. Given the biographical genre of the Gospels, the evangelists clearly mean to assert that Jesus of Nazareth actually exhibited this attitude during his public ministry. Consequently, it is difficult to grant any degree of historical accuracy to the Gospels without also affirming the historicity of this portrayal of Jesus' attitude toward his death. The institution narratives, which have special claim to historical certainty, confirm its historicity with particular force. These conclusions have important consequences for theological interpretations of the crucifixion. If we grant any degree of historical accuracy to the Gospels, any interpretation that supposes that Jesus did not know that he would be killed, or that he did not see something positive coming from his death, must be ruled as incompatible, not merely with sacred scripture, but also with historical fact.

7

The Crucifixion in God's Plan of Salvation

In the New Testament, the crucifixion is central to God's plan of salvation. Its precise role in that plan of salvation, however, is not always clear. On the one hand, the New Testament presents the crucifixion as happening according to God's will and foreknowledge, and even as necessary to the accomplishment of God's purposes. On the other, the New Testament also suggests that God does not approve of the actions of those crucifying Christ, and that God does not will every aspect of the crucifixion event.

This chapter examines what the New Testament says about the role of Christ's crucifixion in God's plan of salvation. To keep the project manageable, it overlooks the ways in which the theologies of relevant passages might be said to diverge. Instead, it focuses on points of common agreement. Likewise, also to keep the project manageable, this chapter ignores questions about the mechanics of redemption and how exactly the crucifixion fits into God's plan of salvation. It focuses instead on general questions. It looks at the crucifixion's relationship to God's will and God's intentions, and then it considers the salvific necessity of the crucifixion. In doing so, this chapter sets out, in general terms, what the New Testament says about the crucifixion in God's plan of salvation, and thus provides criteria for evaluating theological interpretations of Christ's crucifixion in later chapters.

THE FATHER'S WILL AND CHRIST'S CRUCIFIXION

The Gospels often speak about the will (*θέλημά*) of the Father. Typically, this expression designates the way that God wants his creatures to behave or events to unfold. Most of these references to the Father's will are placed on the lips of Jesus. In his teaching, he tells his disciples that doing his Father's will is the principal criterion for entering the kingdom (Matt 7:21) and membership in his extended family (Matt 12:50; cf. Mark 3:35). He also teaches his disciples to pray for their Father's will to be done, "on earth as it is in heaven" (Matt 6:10). In John, Jesus frequently talks about the will of "him who sent me," meaning the will of his Father (John 4:34; 5:30, 6:38; 7:17). The epistles also refer to God's will. On one occasion, an epistle mentions the Father's will (Gal 1:4). More commonly, however, they refer to God's will. They talk about knowing or doing God's will, usually in relation to some specific behavior (Rom 2:18, 12:2; Eph 6:6; 1 Thess 4:3, 5:18; Heb 10:9; 10:36, 13:21; 1 Pet 2:15, 3:17, 4:19; 1 John 2:17). They also refer to the Lord's will (Eph 5:17) and Christ's will (1 John 5:14).

Given their various references to the Father's will, it is not surprising that the Gospels also frame the crucifixion in relation to the Father's will. In the garden of Gethsemane, Jesus prays to his Father that the cup of his passion pass from him, "yet not what I will, but what you will," (Mark 14:36; cf. Matt 26:39; Luke 22:42), and "if this cannot pass unless I drink it, your will be done" (Matt 26:42; cf. Luke 22:42). During the course of his prayer, Jesus comes to accept that the cup cannot pass from him, as indicated by his final words to his disciples (Mark 14:41–42; cf. Matt 26:45–46). The evangelists do not comment on Christ's prayer, nor do they comment on the Father's apparent response; they allow the story to stand on its own. In doing so, they implicitly affirm that it is the Father's will for Jesus to drink his cup, but without clarifying the precise sense in which it is the Father's will, or why. John's version of the Gethsemane story does not include the prayer, but he does put an allusion to the cup on the lips of Jesus. In fact, in John, Jesus goes so far as to refer to "the cup which the Father has given me" (John 18:11), implying that, for John, the Father does not merely decline to take away the cup; he positively gives it to Jesus to drink.[1]

A few other passages in the New Testament also relate the crucifixion to the Father's will. The first and most important is found in Galatians. In his greeting, Paul writes:

> Grace to you and peace from God the Father and our Lord Jesus Christ, who gave himself for our sins to deliver us from the present evil age, according to the will of our God and Father; to whom be the glory forever and ever. Amen. (Gal 1:3–5).

This greeting constitutes the most explicit affirmation in the New Testament that Jesus gave himself over to death "according to the will of our God and Father." Even so, Paul stops short of claiming that the Father wills the actual crucifying of Christ. Paul affirms that Jesus "gave himself for our sins" according to God's will, not that he is crucified according to God's will. Paul does not exclude the latter possibility, but he does not affirm it, either. Like the

[1] For a study of John's account of human and divine agency in the crucifixion event, see Craig R. Koester, "Why Was the Messiah Crucified? A Study of God, Jesus, Satan, and Human Agency in Johannine Theology," in *The Death of Jesus in the Fourth Gospel*, ed. Gilbert Van Belle (Leuven: Leuven University Press, 2007), 163–80.

passages in the Gospels, Paul affirms that the crucifixion happens according to the Father's will, but he does not clarify in what precise sense.

Two other epistles touch on the relationship between the Father's will and Christ's crucifixion by speaking about Christ's obedience to God. In Philippians, Paul writes that Jesus "humbled himself and became obedient unto death, even death on a cross" (Phil 2:8). In context, the phrase obviously implies that Christ obeys God and, therefore, God's will. Paul does not specify what exactly this obedience entails, however. Consequently, considering the passage on its own, it is not clear whether becoming "obedient unto death" means that Christ was so tenaciously obedient to God's will that he ended up crucified, or that Christ was obedient to a command that necessarily involved his crucifixion. A passage in Hebrews also speaks about Christ's obedience to God. This time, the description of Christ's obedience contains an explicit reference to the will of God:

> Consequently, when Christ came into the world, he said, "Sacrifices and offerings you have not desired, but a body you have prepared for me; in burnt offerings and sin offerings you have taken no pleasure. Then I said, 'Lo, I have come to do your will, O God,' as it is written of me in the roll of the book." . . . And by that will we have been sanctified through the offering of the body of Jesus Christ once for all (Heb 10:5–7, 10; cf. Ps 40:7–9).

According to Hebrews, Christ offers his body—an offering which constitutes "a single sacrifice for sins" (Heb 10:12)—in obedience to God's will. As with the passage from Philippians, this passage from Hebrews does not explain precisely how Christ's crucifixion relates to God's will. Nonetheless, because the passage forms part of an extended argument about how Christ established a new covenant in his blood, Hebrews seems to be suggesting that Christ's suffering and death were intrinsic to his obedience. They were not simply the result of Christ's unwavering obedience; they were somehow integral to what God wanted Christ to do.

The few passages in the New Testament that speak explicitly about the Father's will and Christ's crucifixion affirm unambiguously that Jesus gave himself up to his crucifixion in obedience to the Father's will. They do not, however, specify the precise sense in which God wills the crucifixion event. For clarification about this question, we need to turn to other passages in the New Testament.

GOD'S INTENTIONS AND CHRIST'S CRUCIFIXION

The New Testament often describes God's intentions in performing some action. As discussed earlier, willing is a form of intending. Consequently, descriptions of God's intentions in the New Testament do not shed light only on God's thinking and God's motivations; they also shed light on God's will. With this in mind, let us turn to the New Testament's descriptions of God's intentions in sending his Son and handing him over to be crucified.

God's Intentions in Sending His Son

The New Testament portrays the crucifixion as somehow integral to God's intentions in sending his Son. Various passages communicate this understanding of God's intentions. Some passages suggest that the crucifixion happens according to God's plan; others affirm that God sends his Son for the purpose of giving his life for others. Together these various passages convey a strong sense that God sends his Son for the explicit purpose of redeeming humanity through the blood of his cross.

In the Acts of the Apostles, Christ's crucifixion is twice described as happening according to God's *βουλή*, a word that can be translated as "plan, purpose, or intention."[2] On Pentecost, Peter proclaims that Jesus was "delivered up according to the definite plan (*βουλῇ*) and foreknowledge of God" (Acts 2:23). By saying that Christ was delivered up according to God's *βουλή*, Peter is not merely claiming that God permitted Christ's crucifixion; he is also claiming that God positively used it to accomplish his purposes. Shortly afterward, while praying aloud, the early Church echoes Peter's theological interpretation. It talks about Christ's crucifixion as that which "your hand and your plan (*βουλή*) had predestined to take place" (Act 4:28). In this phrase, the early Church goes beyond what Peter had said on Pentecost. Peter had talked about God accomplishing his purposes through Christ's crucifixion; here, the early Church goes one step further and suggests that God had actually "predestined" (*προώρισεν*) Christ's crucifixion. What precisely Luke means by the word "predestined" is endlessly debatable, as are all other New Testament references to predestination, but whatever else the word means, it indicates that Christ's crucifixion is somehow inextricably bound up with God's plan of salvation.

The New Testament epistles contain two important passages about God's intentions in sending his Son. Each affirms that God sent his Son to suffer on our behalf. In his first letter, John writes: "In this is love, not that we loved God but that he loved us and sent his Son to be the expiation for our sins" (1 John 4:10). John does not explain precisely what "expiation" means, but it obviously involves Christ's suffering and death. Similarly, in his letter to the Galatians,

[2] For a discussion of God's plan and the necessity of the crucifixion in Luke-Acts, see John T. Squires, *The Plan of God in Luke-Acts* (Cambridge: Cambridge University Press, 1993), 52–77, 166–85.

Paul writes, "But when the time had fully come, God sent forth his Son, born of woman, born under the law, to redeem those who were under the law, so that we might receive adoption as sons" (Gal 4:4–5). Taken by itself, this passage states only that the Son redeems those who were under the law; it does not connect redemption to crucifixion. A few verses earlier, however, Paul had claimed that Christ redeemed humanity from the curse of the law by being crucified and thus becoming a curse himself (Gal 3:13). Consequently, this passage from Galatians, like the passage from 1 John, also implies that God's intentions in sending his Son somehow encompassed Christ's sacrificial death on the cross.

As discussed earlier, the New Testament frequently alludes to the servant songs of Isaiah. It suggests, implicitly and explicitly, that these servant songs find their fulfillment in Jesus. In their references to the servant's suffering, these songs also claim that the servant's suffering happens according to God's will, and that this suffering is somehow integral to the servant's mission. For example, in the fourth servant song, Isaiah writes, "it was the will of the LORD to bruise him" (Isa 53:10), and "he was wounded for our transgressions, he was bruised for our iniquities; upon him was the chastisement that made us whole, and with his stripes we are healed" (Isa 53:5). Consequently, when the New Testament suggests that the servant songs find their fulfillment in Jesus, it is implicitly affirming that, just as suffering was integral to the servant's mission, so too suffering is integral to Jesus' mission, and thus also to God's intentions in sending his Son.

God's Intentions in Giving Over His Son

The New Testament claims that God gave Jesus over to his death, and in doing so obtained something for our benefit and salvation. At the same time, it distances God from the moral evil of those who crucify Jesus. It shows God intending aspects of the crucifixion event, but not intending either Jesus' death qua death, or the actual crucifying. To understand more precisely what the New Testament says about God's intentions in giving over his Son, we need to consider, first, the New Testament's choice of words, and second, the way that the New Testament contrasts God's intentions with the intentions of those who crucify Jesus.

God is not the only one who "gives over" Jesus in the New Testament. Jesus is also given over by Judas, the chief priests, and Pilate, and even by himself. Regardless of who is doing the giving over, the New Testament mostly uses the same Greek word, *παραδίδωμι*. The word means, primarily, "to give over, to hand over, to deliver," but it can also mean, "to betray,"[3] and generally carries

[3] For a discussion of the meaning of *παραδίδωμι* in the New Testament, see Frederick W. Danker, *A Greek-English Lexicon of the New Testament and Other Early Christian Literature*,

the connotation of being given over to a hostile force.[4] As with its English equivalents, the precise meaning of the word παραδίδωμι in a given instance must be determined from context. Consequently, the word can be used to describe both malicious giving over, as when Judas betrays Christ, and generous giving over, as when Christ allows himself to be crucified. The intrinsic ambiguity of παραδίδωμι causes some interpretative difficulties. In many passages it is clear who gives over Jesus. Sometimes the agent acts with good intentions, as when God gives over his Son (Acts 2:23; Rom 4:25, 8:32), or Christ gives over himself (Gal 1:14; 2:20; Eph 5:2, 5:25; 1 Tim 2:5–6; Titus 2:13–14). Other times the agent acts with evil intentions, as when Judas goes to the chief priests to give Jesus over to them (Mark 14:10), or the chief priests give Jesus over to Pilate (Mark 15:1), or Pilate gives Jesus over to be crucified (John 19:16). In certain passages, however, it is not clear who is doing the handing over, and whether their intentions are good or evil (Mark 9:31, 14:41; Matt 26:2, 26:45; 1 Cor 11:23).[5]

With this overview in mind, what can we say about God's intentions in giving over his Son? On the one hand, the New Testament affirms that God gave over his Son and that he did so for our benefit. Paul makes the most explicit statement to this effect: "He who did not spare his own Son but gave him up for us all, will he not also give us all things with him?" (Rom 8:32). On the other hand, God does not intend every aspect of this giving over. The whole thrust of Paul's argument in Rom 8:32 hangs on the unspoken premise that it was a great sacrifice for God to give his Son over to death, and that doing so somehow ran counter to God's inclinations. God did not intend his Son's death; he intended only to benefit us. Nonetheless, God still gave his Son over for us, and this generosity, Paul argues, proves that God will not withhold anything from us. Other passages that allude to God's giving over can be read in a similar way (see Acts 2:23; Rom 4:25).

The idea of God giving over Jesus implies a clash of intentions. It implies that God gives Jesus into the hands of those who wish him evil, and whose intentions are therefore diametrically opposed to God's. (The connotations of παραδίδωμι strengthen this implication: as noted above, the word typically indicates that the one being given over is received by a hostile power.) Although God and those crucifying Christ each have a role in the crucifixion event—God does the giving over and the others do the crucifying—their

3rd ed. (Chicago: University of Chicago Press, 2000), 761–3, 867; Anthony Cane, *The Place of Judas Iscariot in Christology* (Aldershot: Ashgate, 2005), 19–24.

[4] Cilliers Breytenbach, "The Septuagint Version of Isaiah 53 and the Early Christian Formula 'He Was Delivered for Our Trespasses,'" *Novum Testamentum* 51 (2009): 339–51.

[5] For discussions of the ambiguity about who does the handing over in the New Testament's use of παραδίδωμι, see Wiard Popkes, *Christus Traditus. Eine Untersuchung zum Begriff der Dahingabe im Neuen Testament* (Zurich: Zwingli Verlag, 1967), 152–69; Cane, *Place of Judas*, 20–1.

actions are informed by very different intentions. God makes the crucifixion possible by giving Jesus into the hands of his enemies, but he does not intend the actual crucifying. Those crucifying Christ, however, obviously intend the actual crucifying. Logically, this clash of intentions is central to the coherence of the New Testament's narrative. The New Testament depicts God as not fully "wanting" Christ's crucifixion. But unless *someone else* wants the crucifying of Christ, by process of elimination God would have to want it; there would be no one else left to want it and thus account for the fact that it happens.

In their various narratives of the crucifixion, the Gospels and the Acts of the Apostles frequently draw attention to this clash of intentions. They make a point of contrasting God's intentions in giving over Jesus with the motives of those crucifying him. By doing so, they emphasize that God's giving over differs in kind from Judas' and the chief priests' giving over. Their intentions are malicious, but God's intentions are generous. The contrast also implicitly distances God from the moral evil of the crucifixion. The Gospels give particular attention to Judas' giving over and the paradox of his betrayal. On the one hand, Judas' betrayal fulfills the scriptures and makes it possible for salvation to come through the cross; on the other hand, his guilt and personal responsibility remain. During the last supper, Jesus proclaims both the necessity of Judas' betrayal and the full weight of his moral responsibility: "For the Son of man goes as it is written of him, but woe to that man by whom the Son of man is betrayed!" (Mark 14:21; cf. Matt 26:25, Luke 22:23). In other words, although God has incorporated Judas' betrayal into his plan of salvation, Judas' guilt is not for that reason excused, precisely because Judas intends evil while God intends only good. By emphasizing the clash of intentions between God and Judas, the Gospels clarify the nature of God's handing over, and they also distance God from the moral evil of Judas' betrayal.

John also contrasts God's intentions with those of Caiaphas and Pilate. The contrast he draws between God and Caiaphas is particularly striking. During a discussion among the chief priests and the Pharisees, John writes:

> But one of them, Caiaphas, who was high priest that year, said to them, "You know nothing at all; you do not understand that it is expedient for you that one man should die for the people, and that the whole nation should not perish." He did not say this of his own accord, but being high priest that year he prophesied that Jesus should die for the nation, and not for the nation only, but to gather into one the children of God who are scattered abroad (John 11:49-52).[6]

[6] For an analysis of this scene, in the context of a study on the figure of Caiaphas, see Helen K. Bond, *Caiaphas: Friend of Rome and Judge of Jesus?* (Louisville: Westminster John Knox Press, 2004), 132–3.

By lingering over Caiaphas' unwitting prophecy, and explaining how it will be fulfilled in unforeseen ways, John underscores the irony of the situation. The irony is not merely that the prophecy will be fulfilled in spite of Caiaphas' evil intentions; the irony is that the prophecy will be fulfilled *through* his evil intentions. God accomplishes his purposes not over and against Caiaphas but with Caiaphas. By drawing attention to this irony, John puts the clash of intentions between God and Caiaphas front and center, emphasizing that God intends the crucifixion event in a way very different from Caiaphas, and thus also distancing God from the moral evil of Christ's crucifixion.

John draws a similar contrast between God and Pilate. During his interrogation, Jesus tells Pilate: "You would have no power over me unless it had been given you from above; therefore he who delivered me to you has the greater sin" (John 19:11).[7] On the one hand, by talking about Pilate's power being given to him from above, Jesus hints that everything is unfolding according to God's plan, or at least with his permission. On the other hand, Pilate is not excused. God has given Pilate power over Jesus, but the grant of this power does not absolve Pilate from its misuse. In short, John is contrasting God's giving over with Pilate's giving over, and thus making obvious that God does not intend the actual crucifying of Christ.

In the Acts of the Apostles, the apostles frequently contrast the intentions of those crucifying Christ with God's intentions in handing him over. The first instance occurs very early in the narrative. On Pentecost, in his first public speech, Peter proclaims:

> Men of Israel, hear these words: Jesus of Nazareth, a man attested to you by God with mighty works and wonders and signs which God did through him in your midst, as you yourselves know—this Jesus, delivered up according to the definite plan and foreknowledge of God, you crucified and killed by the hands of lawless men. But God raised him up, having loosed the pangs of death, because it was not possible for him to be held by it. (Acts 2:22–24)

In this passage, Peter affirms that Jesus was "delivered up according to the definite plan and knowledge of God" (Acts 2:23). Then, immediately afterward, he lays the blame for Christ's death at the feet of those listening to him. The clear implication is that those who crucified Christ are morally responsible for his death, even though God gave him into their hands, but God is not. God may have given him into their hands as part of a larger strategy, but God is not responsible for the actual crucifying of Christ, nor does he approve of it. Peter completes the contrast by noting that his hearers crucified Christ, and

[7] For discussions of this interaction between Pilate and Jesus, see Helen K. Bond, *Pontius Pilate in History and Interpretation* (Cambridge: Cambridge University Press, 1998), 188–9; Ronald A. Piper, "The Characterisation of Pilate and the Death of Jesus in the Fourth Gospel," in *The Death of Jesus in the Fourth Gospel*, ed. Gilbert Van Belle (Leuven: Leuven University Press, 2007), 155–8.

then God raised him up. This contrast—"you/they crucified Christ, and God raised him up"—occurs again and again in Acts (cf. Acts 2:36, 3:13–15, 4:10, 5:30, 10:39–40, 13:29–30). Each time, the refrain calls attention to the clash of intentions between God and those who crucified Christ.

By contrasting God's intentions with those of Christ's enemies, the Gospels and Acts clarify God's intentions in giving over his Son. They make it easier to see that, unlike those who put Jesus to death, God does not desire the actual crucifying of his Son. God might hand his Son over to them and allow them to do their worst, but only in order to obtain our salvation, not because he intends his Son's death.

THE NECESSITY OF THE CRUCIFIXION

Many passages in the New Testament describe the crucifixion as somehow necessary to God's plan of salvation. As discussed in the previous chapter, in the Gospel portrayals, Jesus clearly sees his death as somehow necessary to his mission. His sayings often allude, either implicitly or explicitly, to the necessity of the crucifixion. Peter and Paul echo Christ's self-understanding in Acts. During his stay in Thessalonica, Paul focuses on proving "that it was necessary for the Christ to suffer and to rise from the dead" (Acts 17:3). In his first speech in Acts, Peter comes close to saying the same thing. He declares, "Brethren, the scripture had to be fulfilled, which the Holy Spirit spoke beforehand by the mouth of David, concerning Judas who was guide to those who arrested Jesus" (Acts 1:16). In this passage, Peter is speaking primarily about the necessity of Judas' betrayal, not the necessity of the crucifixion. Nonetheless, since Judas' betrayal is tied inextricably to Jesus' suffering, speaking about the necessity of Judas' betrayal is tantamount to speaking about the necessity of the crucifixion.

While the New Testament affirms repeatedly and unequivocally that Christ's crucifixion is necessary to God's plan of salvation, it does not clarify the precise sense in which it is necessary. In the Gospels, in all his statements about the necessity of his suffering, Jesus does not explain why or in what sense it is necessary. The sayings of Peter and Paul in Acts are also vague and ambiguous. So how are we to interpret the various New Testament statements about the crucifixion's salvific necessity? There are too many passages with different shades of meaning, and possibly different theologies, to give a blanket analysis that would apply to them all. We also cannot go too far into this question without getting entangled in larger theological questions about the theology of redemption, which would take us too far afield. Therefore, rather than looking for a definitive interpretation, we will focus on excluding problematic interpretations, and thus proceed by process of elimination.

In one possible interpretation, the crucifixion is necessary in the sense of being inevitable. Given the state of fallen humanity and the ubiquity of sin and malice, the words and actions of Jesus could only lead to his death. So it is necessary for Jesus to suffer, not because his suffering advances his divinely appointed mission, but because it is the necessary consequence of his mission. This interpretation has many advantages. It explains, in a straightforward way, the necessity of the crucifixion, and it holds together well with the repeated declarations about those who crucify Christ being fully responsible for the guilt of their actions.

This interpretation, however, cannot explain New Testament statements about the crucifixion's necessity when considered in their full context. When we read these statements in the light of other passages that touch on God's will, God's plan, or God's reasons for sending his Son, it becomes evident that these statements about the necessity of the crucifixion are claiming something more than mere historical inevitability. Again and again the New Testament presents the crucifixion as integral to Christ's mission and God's plan, and not simply as the inevitable consequence of some other objective. For example, Peter writes that we are redeemed "with the precious blood of Christ" (1 Pet 1:18–19), and John writes that God sent his Son to be "the expiation for our sins" (1 John 4:10). Whatever it means to be redeemed, and whatever it means for the Son to expiate our sins, it is hard to see how these passages could be compatible with an interpretation of the crucifixion's necessity as mere historical inevitability. Even more telling from a logical point of view is the way the New Testament links its declarations about the crucifixion's necessity to its declarations about the resurrection's necessity (Mark 8:31; Matt 16:21; Luke 9:22, 24:26; Acts 17:3). It is not only the crucifixion that is necessary to Christ's mission; the resurrection is also necessary. And since the crucifixion is what makes the resurrection possible, the New Testament cannot mean that the crucifixion is necessary merely in the sense of being historically inevitable; it must mean that the crucifixion is also necessary in some ontological sense.

According to another interpretation of New Testament statements, the crucifixion is absolutely necessary, such that it would be beyond God's power to save humanity had Christ not been crucified. As a theological opinion, this interpretation has attracted interest since the Middle Ages. It continues to be discussed and it has its strengths and weaknesses. As a reading of the New Testament, however, it cannot be sustained. The New Testament's declarations are vague and ambiguous. They do not make any counterfactual assertions about what God could or could not have done had Christ not been crucified. More importantly for our purposes, they never deny that God could have saved humanity without Christ's crucifixion. Consequently, they cannot be read as stating that the crucifixion is absolutely necessary. While one can argue on theological grounds that, as a matter of fact, the crucifixion is indeed absolutely necessary for salvation, the New Testament does not make any explicit statements to this effect.

Having excluded these two interpretations, what can we say about the proper interpretation of New Testament statements regarding the necessity of the crucifixion? They seem to be asserting something more than mere historical inevitability and something less than absolute metaphysical necessity. Or to put it more positively, the New Testament claims that the crucifixion is ontologically bound up with God's plan of salvation. That is, the crucifixion event is somehow integral to the mechanics of redemption; something in the way that God's plan of salvation "works" involves Christ's crucifixion. Without venturing into controversial exegetical questions, it is difficult to say more.

CONCLUSION

In the New Testament, the relationship between God's will and Christ's crucifixion is portrayed with great consistency. God sends his Son to redeem us, and he gives him over to those who would crucify him. The crucifixion is also somehow integral and necessary to God's plan of salvation. In this way, the crucifixion happens according to both God's will (*θέλημά*) and God's plan (*βουλή*). At the same time, the New Testament always stops short of claiming that God wants, intends, or wills the actual crucifying of his Son. It places the full weight of moral responsibility on the shoulders of those who crucify Christ, and it does not sanitize the violence of the crucifixion or diminish its injustice. Nonetheless, while the New Testament is strikingly consistent about the crucifixion's role in God's plan of salvation, it is also confusing and ambiguous. How could God send his Son to redeem us through his blood, and thus make the crucifixion ontologically necessary to his plan of salvation, and yet not want (and therefore will) the actual crucifying? Many different answers have emerged from reflecting on this enigma. To some of them we now turn in the third and final part of this study.

Part III

Theological Evaluation

8

Anselm and *Cur Deus homo*

In *Cur Deus homo*, Anselm of Canterbury (1033–1109) pioneers a new theological interpretation of the crucifixion. He maintains that the heroism of Christ's self-sacrifice makes satisfaction for the infinite offense of sin, and thus accomplishes the redemption of humanity. He is acutely aware, however, that this interpretation can make God seem cruel and unjust. Consequently, he devotes considerable energy to clarifying the precise sense in which God wills Christ's crucifixion, particularly in Book I.8–10 of *Cur Deus homo*, in order to avoid any implication that God wills the moral evil of Christ's crucifixion or delights in his Son's suffering. Drawing on a form of double effect reasoning, he maintains that God wills the heroism of Christ's self-sacrifice, but not his actual suffering and death. In this way, Anselm attempts to secure the salvific efficacy of the crucifixion event and at the same time avoid implying that God is pleased by cruelty.

In his approach to Christ's crucifixion, Anselm stands out for his sensitivity to the problem of God's apparent injustice to his Son. His lengthy discussion of the precise sense in which God wills Christ's crucifixion is without obvious precedent,[1] and his attention to the question exceeds that of Aquinas and many other medieval theologians who come after him.[2] Nonetheless, Anselm's

[1] The critical edition of *Cur Deus homo* identifies few sources for Book I.8–10, the section where Anselm gives the most attention to the problem of God's apparent injustice and the precise nature of what God wills vis-à-vis Christ's crucifixion. Of these few sources, only Pseudo-Ambrose echoes Anselm's wrestling with the divine injustice seemingly implied by Christ's crucifixion: "Itaque immeritus, qui occiditur, placet Deo; non quia occiditur, sed quia usque ad mortem iustitiam conservavit . . . " Pseudo-Ambrose, *Commentary on Ephesians* 5:2 (*PL* 17:416). See Anselm, *Opera Omnia*, ed. F. S. Schmitt, 6 vols. (Edinburgh: Thomas Nelson and Sons, 1946–1961), II.59–67.

[2] Aquinas touches on the Father's will and Christ's crucifixion in few places, and in none of them does he give the matter as much attention as Anselm in *Cur Deus homo* I.8–10. I have been able to identify relevant passages only in the following places: *Scriptum super libros Sententiarum* I 48, III 20.5; *Summa contra Gentiles* IV 53–5; *Commentary on Philippians*, 2.2; *Commentary on Romans* 5.5; *Commentary on John*, 3.3, 14.8; *Summa theologiae* III 46–7, 50. Aquinas makes fewer distinctions than Anselm, and his treatment seems cursory in comparison. The question does not seem to have ever captured his attention to the same extent. For example, in his earliest treatment of the issue, Aquinas simply affirms that God wills Christ's passion and death, but does

theory of redemption implies that God wills the actual crucifying of Christ—precisely what Anselm wants to deny. This chapter evaluates Anselm's theological interpretation of the crucifixion, focusing on a close reading of Book I.8–10 of *Cur Deus homo*. It concludes that Anselm's theory of redemption cannot avoid implying that God wills moral evil. Then, in light of this exegetical analysis, it identifies structural flaws in Anselm's theory of redemption, especially with respect to his aesthetics and his Trinitarian theology, that make this implication inevitable.

THE CONCERNS DRIVING ANSELM'S THEORY OF REDEMPTION

Anselm develops his new interpretation of the crucifixion in response to two key concerns. The first arises from his rejection of the devil's ransom interpretation, the dominant proposal on offer in his day.[3] According to Anselm's reconstruction of the devil's ransom interpretation, the devil had become the *de jure* ruler of humanity by luring us into sin, and it was only through Christ's crucifixion that God redeemed humanity from the devil's grasp. Since his authority extended only to sinners, the devil overreached by crucifying Jesus and, as a result of this violation, he forfeited his legal jurisdiction back to God. The crucifixion is thus a ransom paid to the devil for humanity's salvation. Anselm rejects this theological interpretation of Christ's crucifixion, arguing that God could never have been obligated to respect demonic jurisdiction, "since in fact neither the devil nor human beings belong to anyone other than God or stand outside God's power."[4]

The devil's ransom interpretation of the crucifixion seems to have been so dominant in Anselm's theological milieu that it lacked any serious alternative. Consequently, it was inevitable that Anselm's rejection of it would lead him to develop a new theological interpretation of the crucifixion. It is hardly plausible that he could have rejected the dominant interpretation of a central Christian mystery without attempting to provide his own.

not will the actions of those crucifying him (*Scriptum super libros Sententiarum* I 48). He stops there, apparently untroubled by the questions that this affirmation leaves unanswered. By the time of Aquinas, Anselm's theory was firmly established, and its influence may have led Aquinas to accept some of Anselm's conclusions without worrying about their derivation or implications.

[3] For a discussion of the devil's ransom interpretation as Anselm knew it, see R. W. Southern, *Saint Anselm: A Portrait in a Landscape* (Cambridge: Cambridge University Press, 1990), 207–11. The critical edition of *Cur Deus homo* does not indicate any sources for his argument against the devil's rights in *CDH* I.6–7. See Anselm, *Opera Omnia*, II.53–59.

[4] *CDH* I.7, in Anselm, *Basic Writings*, trans. Thomas Williams (Indianapolis: Hackett, 2007), 251.

His concerns about the devil's ransom interpretation, therefore, play a major role in the development of his theological interpretation of the crucifixion. In fact, he seems more certain of his rejection of the devil's ransom interpretation than any individual element of his own proposal, as is evident in the decisiveness with which he rejects it,[5] compared to the tentativeness with which he puts forth his alternative.[6] The structure of his argument also indicates the significance of this rejection to his theological agenda. His first move, after adumbrating the aims and scope of his investigation, but before beginning it properly, is to dispose of the devil's ransom interpretation.[7] The interpretation is mentioned only briefly in the text of *Cur Deus homo*, but its influence is pervasive: the entire work can be seen as Anselm's attempt to provide an alternative.[8]

The second concern driving *Cur Deus homo* stems from the problem of God's apparent injustice to his Son. Anselm wants to interpret the crucifixion in a way that does not attribute harshness or cruelty to God. Anselm's theory of redemption has received considerable criticism in recent memory, and much of it is well founded.[9] Anselm, however, is frequently caricatured as

[5] *CDH* I.7. See also his *Meditation on Human Redemption*.

[6] For example, see *CDH* I.1–2, where Anselm repeatedly professes the fallibility of his explanation of why God became man, but not the fallibility of his rejection of the devil's ransom interpretation. While he does not exclude the possibility that he is wrong about the devil's ransom, he does not acknowledge it, either. Anselm clearly wants to prevent his readers from taking his new theory as an authoritative interpretation of Christian doctrine, but, strikingly, he does not indicate any corresponding concern about his readers taking his rejection of the devil's ransom interpretation as definitive.

[7] *CDH* 1.6–7.

[8] Anselm structures his *Meditation on Human Redemption* in a similar way. First, he introduces his meditation with poetic praise of Christ and an exhortation to contemplate divine revelation. Then, immediately after identifying Christ's crucifixion as the locus of redemption, Anselm launches into the devil's ransom interpretation. He first attacks the idea that God became man to deceive the devil, and then the idea that God owes the devil anything except punishment.

[9] Perhaps most notably in Gustaf Aulén, *Christus Victor: An Historical Study of the Three Main Types of the Idea of Atonement*, trans. A. G. Herbert (London: S.P.C.K, 1931). See also, for example, Joanne Carlson Brown and Rebecca Parker, "For God So Loved the World?," in *Christianity, Patriarchy and Abuse: A Feminist Critique*, ed. Joanne Carlson Brown and Carole R. Bohn (New York: Pilgrim Press, 1989) 1–30; Symeon Rodger, "The Soteriology of Anselm of Canterbury, An Orthodox Perspective," *Greek Orthodox Theological Review* 34 (1989): 19–43; Grey, *Redeeming the Dream*, 109–25; Anthony W. Bartlett, *Cross Purposes: The Violent Grammar of the Christian Atonement* (Harrisburg: Trinity, 2001); Stephen Finlan, *Problems with Atonement* (Collegeville, MN: Liturgical Press, 2005), esp. 71–4.

Many other scholars, though, have defended Anselm against his modern critics or offered sympathetic reconstructions of his theory of salvation. For example, see John McIntyre, *St Anselm and His Critics: A Reinterpretation of the Cur Deus Homo* (London: Oliver, 1954); Eugene R. Fairweather, "Incarnation and Atonement: An Anselmian Response to Aulén's Christus Victor," *Canadian Journal of Theology* 7 (1961): 167–75; Christopher Armstrong, "St Anselm and His Critics: Further Reflection on the *Cur Deus Homo*," *Downside Review* 86 (1968): 354–76; Ted Peters, "Atonement in Anselm and Luther, Second Thoughts about Gustaf Aulén's *Christus Victor*," *Lutheran Quarterly* 24 (1972): 301–14; John D. Hannah, "Anselm on

being insensitive to the problem of God's apparent injustice, and this sort of criticism is not justified. Anselm names the problem of God's apparent injustice in strong, vivid language, and he wrestles with it forcefully. He rejects the idea that God requires innocent blood or takes pleasure in it, and he affirms that Christ's actual suffering is distasteful and displeasing to God the Father. Whatever the merits of his theory of redemption, Anselm cannot be accused of indifference to the problem of God's apparent injustice. To the contrary, his sensitivity to the problem ranks as one of the primary stimuli driving his interpretation of the crucifixion.

ANSELM ON GOD'S WILL AND CHRIST'S CRUCIFIXION

In *Cur Deus homo*, Anselm argues that Jesus redeems us by his heroic self-sacrifice on the cross. Since he is both God and man, his actions have infinite value; hence, the infinite value of his heroic generosity compensates for the infinite offense of humanity's sin. Anselm's theory of redemption addresses his two primary concerns. It provides an alternative to the devil's ransom interpretation and avoids giving any role to the devil in the mechanics of redemption. It also solves the problem of God's apparent injustice, because it is Christ's heroic generosity, not his suffering, which pleases God and makes satisfaction for sin.

The trouble is that Anselm's theory of redemption cannot sustain his claim that God wills Christ's heroic self-sacrifice without willing his suffering and death. Despite his best efforts, he cannot avoid implying that God *wants* Christ to be crucified. It is not enough for Anselm to deny that God wills the suffering and death of his Son; he must also demonstrate that his theory can sustain this denial, and on this point he is not successful. His failure is not obvious, however, because Anselm lays out his position with subtle logic and skillful rhetoric. To see the problems with his argument, it is necessary to turn to a close reading of Book I.8–10, the part of *Cur Deus homo* where Anselm most directly engages the problem of God's will and Christ's crucifixion.[10]

the Doctrine of Atonement," *Bibliotheca Sacra* 135 (1978): 333–44; Glenn W. Olsen, "Hans Urs von Balthasar and the Rehabilitation of St Anselm's Doctrine of the Atonement," *Scottish Journal of Theology* 34 (1981): 49–61; Hunter Brown, "Anselm's *Cur Deus Homo* Revisited," *Église et Théologie* 25 (1994): 189–204; Marilyn McCord Adams, "Satisfying Mercy: Saint Anselm's *Cur Deus Homo*, Reconsidered," *Modern Schoolman* 72 (1995): 91–107; David Bentley Hart, "A Gift Exceeding Every Debt: An Eastern Orthodox Appreciation of Anselm's Cur Deus Homo," *Pro Ecclesia* 7 (1998): 333–49; Flora A. Keshgegian, "The Scandal of the Cross: Revisiting Anselm and His Feminist Critics," *Anglican Theological Review* 82 (2000): 475–92; Katherin A. Rogers, "A Defense of Anselm's *Cur Deus Homo* Argument," *Proceedings of the American Catholic Philosophical Association* 74 (2000): 187–200; Gary A. Anderson, *Sin: A History* (New Haven: Yale University Press, 2009), 189–202.

[10] Few scholars comment on Anselm's account of God's will and Christ's crucifixion in *Cur Deus homo*, and John McIntyre offers the only other close reading of Book I.8–10 that I have

The Problem of God's Apparent Injustice (*CDH* I.8)

Anselm opens his discussion of God's will and Christ's crucifixion by stating the problem of God's apparent injustice to his Son. He frames the problem in this way:

> So how can it be shown to be just or reasonable for God to treat him, or allow him to be treated, in this way? What sort of justice is it for the most just human being of all to be handed over to death for the sake of a sinner? If any human being condemned an innocent man in order to set a guilty man free, would he not be judged worthy of condemnation himself?[11]

By naming these potential objections, Anselm acknowledges that attributing salvific significance to Christ's crucifixion can seem to imply injustice on God's part. He also contextualizes the argument that follows. Anselm is indicating which questions he aims to answer with his theory of redemption.

Despite the directness of his opening questions, however, Anselm is not entirely clear about how he defines the problem of God's apparent injustice. He does not specify whether he is concerned with the apparent injustice of the Triune God, or the apparent justice of God the Father; he also fails to specify whether the apparent victim is God the Son in both his divinity and his humanity, or only his humanity. His subsequent argument provides only

found. McIntyre states that Anselm's analysis in Chapters 9–10 "is almost certainly the most obscure passage in the whole work." Like me, he concludes that Anselm's analysis is self-contradictory. See McIntyre, *Anselm and His Critics*, 154–61, esp. 55.

In the Lambeth fragments, written after *Cur Deus homo*, Anselm discusses four different kinds of willing (efficient, approving, concessive, and permissive); then, he applies this fourfold distinction to divine willing and the interpretation of scripture. Anselm does not refer to this fourfold distinction in *Cur Deus homo*. It is likely, therefore, that he developed these categories only afterward, at least as they appear in their final form. According to F. S. Schmitt, it is also likely that Anselm had originally meant to include such a discussion of willing in *Cur Deus homo*. In the preface to *Cur Deus homo*, Anselm laments that "certain people" had copied the first parts of the manuscript "before it was completed and fully thought through," thus forcing him to complete the work hastily. He then comments, "If I had been allowed freedom from distractions and enough time to work on it, I would have included and added quite a few things that I have left unsaid" (*CDH*, pref., 238). See F. S. Schmitt, *Ein neues unvollendetes Werk des hl. Anselm von Canterbury* (Münster: Aschendorff, 1936), 21; Anselm, *Basic Writings*, x. If Anselm had indeed meant to spend more time developing his account of willing before putting *Cur Deus homo* in its final form, and if the early draft not been copied and distributed without his permission, Book I.8–10 might have turned out very different, and his account of God's will and Christ's crucifixion might have been more successful.

For a comparison of Anselm's treatment of willing in the Lambeth fragments and *Cur Deus homo*, see Desmond Paul Henry, *The Logic of Saint Anselm* (Oxford: Oxford University Press, 1967), 201–6. Henry notes that Anselm's four categories of willing also appear in the first version of the *De Concordia*, as well as the *De Voluntate* (whose authenticity is disputed). For an analysis of Anselm's treatment of willing in the *De Voluntate*, with some references to *Cur Deus homo*, see Imelda Choquette, "*Voluntas, Affectio*, and *Potestas* in the *Liber De Voluntate* of St. Anselm," *Mediaeval Studies* 4 (1942): 61–81.

[11] *CDH* I.8, 253. See also *CDH* I.10.

limited clarification. Anselm usually frames the problem in terms of a tension between the Triune God, of whom God the Father is the primary representative and a kind of spokesperson, and God the Son in his humanity. But in some instances, in order to secure certain aspects of his argument, Anselm says things that create an impression of intra-Trinitarian tension between God the Father and God the Son. Consequently, in order to understand how he frames the problem in any given instance, attention to context is crucial. With that said, let us turn to Anselm's solution.

Anselm's Solution (*CDH* I.8–9)

Anselm launches his solution by observing that Christ went to his death voluntarily, a point to which he often returns in *Cur Deus homo*.[12] He argues that God was not unjust since God did not send Christ to his death against his will. It is a weak opening argument. It does not address the central difficulty. Regardless of whether Christ went to his death voluntarily, if God gave his Son an unjust command, then by the very fact of doing so, he treated him unjustly. Anselm seems to agree, because he acknowledges that he must also show that God did not command Christ to endure his crucifixion for unjust reasons. So, after observing that Christ goes to his death voluntarily, Anselm turns to clarify exactly what God commanded Christ to do.

Anselm distinguishes between what God commanded Christ to do, and what God's command entailed in its actual execution. On the one hand, there is "what he did because obedience demanded it"; on the other hand, there is "what was done to him because he preserved obedience, and which he endured, but not because obedience demanded it."[13] Anselm argues that God did not command Christ to endure crucifixion; the crucifixion was merely the consequence of his obedience. God commanded only Christ's justice. He writes:

> God did not compel Christ, in whom there was no sin, to die. On the contrary, Christ endured death of his own accord. His obedience consisted not in abandoning his life, but in preserving justice; and he persevered in justice with such fortitude that he incurred his death. It can also be said that the Father commanded that he die, since he commanded that on account of which he incurred death.[14]

God did not command Christ to die. God gave Christ the same command he gives everyone: to live justly, and to persevere in living justly, whatever the cost. God did not command Jesus to be crucified; he commanded Jesus to

[12] See *CDH* I.9–10, II.10–11, II.16–17. [13] *CDH* I.9, 255. [14] *CDH* I.9, 256.

remain innocent come what may. In this way, Anselm exonerates God of the charges of injustice and cruelty.

Double effect reasoning is very much evident in Anselm's analysis of God's commanding.[15] By focusing on what God intended in commanding Christ, Anselm implicitly draws on double effect reasoning to explain why God's commands were just. According to Anselm, God commanded Christ's perseverance in justice, but God did not command or intend his crucifixion. And since the crucifying of Christ is logically implied neither by persevering in justice, nor by commanding such perseverance, Anselm's analysis of God's command is sound (thus far). God could indeed have commanded Christ's perseverance in justice, and thus knowingly caused the crucifixion, without intending the crucifying of Christ. The crucifixion would have been merely the nonintended effect of God's commanding Christ to persevere in justice.

Anselm's analysis neutralizes the charge of injustice, at least with respect to God's command to Christ. But what Anselm gives with one hand, he takes back with the other. Later in the same chapter, as he comments on Christ's prayer in the garden of Gethsemane, he slips in a certain amount of equivocation:

> Now where he says, "Father if it is possible, let this cup pass from me; yet not as I will, but as you will," and "If this cup cannot pass unless I drink it, let your will be done," by his own will he means the natural desire for well-being by which human flesh shrank from the pain of death. He speaks of the Father's will, not in the sense that the Father wanted the Son's death rather than his life, but because the Father was unwilling (*nolebat*) that the human race should be restored unless a human being accomplished something as great as that death was.[16]

Earlier Anselm had maintained that God commanded Christ's crucifixion only in the sense that God commanded Christ's unwavering justice. Here, though, Anselm claims that God willed Christ's acceptance of death in another sense as well. He claims that the Father "was unwilling" or "did not want" (*nolebat* can be translated either way) for the human race to be restored unless someone accomplished "something as great as that death was"—a category of accomplishments, Anselm implies, which includes nothing besides Christ's persevering in justice to the point of death.[17] When taken to its logical

[15] This observation should not be taken to mean that Anselm had any explicit notion of double effect reasoning; as discussed in Chapter 3, the formal conceptualization of double effect reasoning emerged long after Anselm. Nonetheless, Anselm can be said to employ double effect reasoning, insofar as he is attempting to justify an action on the grounds that the positive consequences outweigh the negative and the negative effects are not intended.

[16] *CDH* I.9, 257.

[17] Although Anselm does not say outright that nothing could ever be as great as Christ's acceptance of death, the premise is implied by his argument, and by what he writes subsequently. See especially *CDH* I.11–15, 22; II.18.

conclusion, this claim revives the charge of injustice that Anselm had defused at the beginning of the chapter.

On the face of it, Anselm's two different claims are not in conflict. According to the first claim, God did not will Christ's suffering in itself; he willed only for Christ to persevere in justice, even to the point of death. According to the second claim, God was not willing for the world to be restored unless Christ endured his passion. These two claims are not in direct tension. God could expect certain behavior from Christ, and then, as a separate matter, God could also have decided that he would not allow the world to be restored unless Christ held fast to truth and justice even unto death. They are two separate issues, and considered in themselves, Anselm's two claims do not contradict each other.

The harmony between these two claims, however, is fragile. It shatters when we add the additional claim that the Father positively willed for the human race to be restored. As soon as we add this third premise, it follows that the Father must have positively willed for his Son to endure death. The Father had already decided that he was only willing for the human race to be restored if the Son were to persevere in justice precisely while being crucified. Consequently, if the Father positively wanted the world to be restored, then he must also have wanted Christ to hold fast to truth and justice precisely while being crucified. As discussed in Chapter 5, God cannot will for Christ to manifest virtues that have the specific property of being exercised while one is being crucified, without also willing Christ's sheer experience of crucifixion. Consequently, once we add the third claim that the Father willed for the human race to be restored, we are back to the problem of God's apparent injustice: God seems to will Christ's suffering and death, and thus the actual crucifying of Christ.

Significantly, though, Anselm never claims that the Father positively willed for the human race to be restored.[18] His silence on this point is not an oversight. Instead, Anselm argues that the Son decided to save the world on his own, without being asked. By this maneuver, Anselm threads the needle and fends off the implication that the Father willed his Son's death qua death, that is, in itself. He explains:

> It is in this sense, then, that the Father willed the death of the Son: he was unwilling for the world to be saved unless a human being accomplished something so great, as I have said. Given that no one else could do this, and that the

[18] Up to this point in the chapter, the closest Anselm comes to making such a claim runs as follows: "[Christ] himself, together with the Father and the Holy Spirit, had ordained that he would reveal to the world the loftiness of his omnipotence in no other way than through death" (*CDH* I.9, 256). This statement, however, does not indicate that the Father positively willed for the world to be restored. It indicates only that the Father, together with the Son and Holy Spirit, had ordained that the human race would not be restored unless Christ gave his life on the cross.

> Son so fervently desired the salvation of human beings, the Father's will had the same effect as if he had commanded the Son to die.[19]

According to Anselm, the Father can only be said to have commanded his Son to die in that he was unwilling for the world to be saved any other way. He did not command his Son to save the world, nor did he command his Son to endure crucifixion. Therefore, Anselm argues, it cannot be said that the Father commanded or willed his Son's death in any straightforward sense. Instead, the Son, wanting to save the world and knowing that the Father was unwilling to save the world unless he endured crucifixion, went to his death on his own initiative. So the world was saved through Christ's crucifixion, but the Father did not will the actual crucifying of Christ. He was merely unwilling for the world to be saved through any other means.

Anselm's solution is ingenious. It not only avoids the implication that God the Father commanded Christ to endure crucifixion; it also avoids the implication that the Father caused the crucifixion. According to Anselm, the Son embraced death on his own initiative and so the Father does not shoulder any responsibility. Anselm's solution, however, does not touch the larger problem. It cannot avoid implying that the Triune God wills the actual crucifying of Christ. According to Anselm's narrative, the Son realized that the Father was unwilling to save the world unless he endured crucifixion, and so he went to his death. But this description of the Son's actions implies that the Son intended his own death as his chosen means to the end of saving the world.[20] He did not physically kill himself, but since he provoked others to kill him (even if only by living justly and holding fast to the truth) precisely in order to experience death, he committed a kind of suicide. Consequently, Anselm's narrative implies that the Son wills the actual crucifying, and since the Son is divine, that the entire Triune God wills it as well.

Anselm's solution not only fails to solve the problem of God's apparent injustice; through his narrative of Trinitarian decision-making, he also creates new problems. The first problem stems from Anselm's silence about the Father positively willing the world's salvation. In Anselm's narrative, the Father sets down conditions for what would need to happen for the world to be saved, but we do not hear anything about the Father either positively willing the world's salvation or setting that salvation in motion. Anselm is not merely silent about the Father setting salvation in motion—his entire narrative depends on the Father *not* setting it in motion. For the narrative to work, the Son, without any pressure from the Father, must volunteer to suffer. So the Father cannot command the Son to suffer, nor can he give any hints about his

[19] *CDH*, I.9, 258.

[20] Later in *Cur Deus homo*, Anselm makes this implication more explicit: "For it is every bit as true that he became a human being in order that he might *will* to die as it is that he became a human being in order that he might die" (*CDH* II.16, 313).

preferences: for such an obedient Son, the slightest hint would be a command. Consequently, in Anselm's narrative, the Father wills for the crucifixion to be a requirement for our restoration, but he does not positively will for that restoration to come about. Of course, put in such stark terms, Anselm would not want to affirm that the Father did not positively will the world's salvation; he would want to affirm the exact opposite. Nonetheless, despite its obvious contradiction with the New Testament (see esp. John 3:16), this conclusion follows from his Trinitarian narrative.

Other problems stem from the way that the Father and the Son act independently of each other. In Anselm's narrative, the Father, on his own, lays down his requirements for the world's salvation and then the Son, also on his own, decides to meet them. The Father decides that the world's salvation requires the Son's crucifixion, but he neither commands the Son to die nor asks him if he would be willing to volunteer. In fact, Anselm does not mention any communication at all. The next thing we read, the Son is reflecting on the Father's unwillingness for the world to be saved unless he allows himself to be crucified (how he figured out what the Father wanted, we are not told), and he decides to regard the Father's preference as his will for him. This narrative paints a very strange picture. It is as though the Father expects the Son to read his mind and figure out how he wants the world to be saved. The Father would be pleased if the Son decided to save the world but feels that it would be too much to ask, so he leaves it entirely up to the Son. This description exaggerates but fairly represents the substance of what Anselm suggests and implies.

What are we to make of this narrative? To answer this question, we must first face a glaring ambiguity in Anselm's telling of the story: namely, when Anselm talks about the Son, is he referring to the Son in his divinity, or the Son in his humanity, or does Anselm perhaps alternate? Anselm does not say. We can safely assume, however, that he would want to be taken as referring to the Son in his humanity throughout his narrative. If he were taken as referring at any point to the Son in his divinity, his narrative would imply that God the Son acted independently of God the Father in taking flesh and allowing himself to be crucified. It would thus attribute a separate divine intellect and divine will to the Son, thereby injecting disunity into the Trinity, something which Anselm could not have intended.

Yet, on the assumption that the Son's independent decision-making took place in his humanity, Anselm's narrative suffers from a serious omission. It fails to explain how the Son came to take flesh in the first place. According to Anselm's narrative, God the Father did not command the Son to suffer; instead, the Son volunteered to suffer. Assuming that the Son volunteered to suffer in his humanity, how is it that the Son came to possess a humanity in which to volunteer? Did the Father send him to take flesh? For what purpose was he sent? Anselm does not even attempt to fill in the gaps of his narrative. If we say that God the Son took flesh on his own initiative, then we compromise divine unity. If we say that God the Son took flesh to redeem us through his death, in execution of the common will of the Triune God, then the Father positively willed for the Son to die for us. But that would conflict with Anselm's apparent reluctance to say so. It would also contradict what Anselm says earlier when he explains that the Father asked Christ to hold "unswervingly to truth and justice,"[21] but did not ask or compel him to die:

> God did not compel Christ, in whom there was no sin, to die. On the contrary, Christ endured death of his own accord. His obedience consisted not in abandoning his life, but in preserving justice; and he persevered in justice with such fortitude that he incurred his death.[22]

Granted, this passage does not describe God's reasons for sending his Son; it describes God's will for his Son in his humanity, after he has already taken flesh. Nonetheless, if God sends his Son for the purpose of dying, then he is necessarily asking the Son in his humanity to die. Since, according to Anselm, the Son in his humanity was not asked by God to die, it follows that he was not sent for the purpose of dying, either. To preserve the coherence of Anselm's narrative, we can only conclude that the Son was instead sent for some initial objective other than our redemption.[23] Then, after taking flesh for the sake of this initial objective, the Son in his humanity volunteered to save the world by his suffering.

This result is not theologically disastrous. Since the New Testament always relates Christ's coming to our redemption, it is difficult to give a rationale besides redemption for the Incarnation, but it is not impossible. For example, Scotus argues that the Son became man first and foremost to bring the created world to its fullest perfection, and only secondarily to accomplish our redemption, and so the Son would have become man even if we had not sinned.[24] Drawing on this position, one could argue that God sent his Son for the initial

[21] *CDH* I.9, 255. [22] *CDH* I.9, 256.

[23] Many early readers of Anselm seem to have reached a similar conclusion. It cannot be a coincidence that, shortly after Anselm, starting with Rupert of Deutz, the question of whether God would have become man even if we had not sinned started to arouse interest among Western theologians. (See Introduction, n10.) It also cannot be a coincidence that this interest persists to the present day in the West, while Eastern theologians, notably immune from Anselm's influence, have never found the question nearly as engaging.

[24] For some relevant texts of Scotus, see *Ordinatio* III 7.3; *Ordinatio* III (suppl.) 19; *Reportatio Parisiensis* III 7.4, *Lectura Completa* III 7.3; *Reportatio Barcinonensis* II 7.3; *Reportatio Valentiensis* III 6.6. All but the last of these writings are excerpted in both Latin and English in Juniper Carol, *Why Jesus Christ? Thomistic, Scotistic, and Conciliatory Perspectives* (Manassas, VA: Trinity Communications, 1988), 121–9. For reconstruction and analysis of Scotus' position on the inevitability of the Incarnation, see Carol, *Why Jesus Christ?*, 121–49; Mary Elizabeth Ingham, "John Duns Scotus: An Integrated Vision," in *The History of Franciscan Theology*, ed. Kenan B. Osborne (St. Bonaventure, NY: The Franciscan Institute, 1994), 219–26; Delio, "Revisiting the Franciscan Doctrine of Christ," 7–9; Horan, "How Original Was Scotus on the Incarnation?", 383–5.

objective of uniting divinity and creation in his own person; it was only after taking flesh that the Son, in his humanity, volunteered to suffer and so redeem humanity.

Yet, even if we grant that the Father sent the Son for an objective other than redemption, we run against the stated purpose of *Cur Deus homo*—to provide an account of why God became man.[25] For Anselm's account to avoid the implication that the Father sent his Son for the purpose of dying, God must have become man for an objective other than humanity's redemption. Anselm, however, is silent about what such an initial objective might have looked like.[26] Consequently, unless we want to maintain that Anselm never even attempts to answer his treatise's eponymous question, "Cur Deus homo?" we can only conclude that his Trinitarian narrative is profoundly incoherent. It does not hang together. Granted, the narrative is imaginative and undeveloped, and only with great care can theological claims be extracted from it. Even so, on some points, its implications are clear and very problematic. The narrative divides the Trinity. As it stands, it does not fill in all the gaps that would need to be filled if the Son's independent acting were to be located in his humanity. Since the narrative turns on the Son acting independently of the Father, and yet cannot coherently locate this independence in the Son's humanity, it subtly leads one to think of God the Father and God the Son as separate centers of knowing and willing. The only way the narrative could work—the only way it could offer a coherent explanation of why God became man—is if God the Father and God the Son had two separate wills. In theological writing, imaginative reconstruction of Trinitarian decision-making is a standard device, and its anthropomorphic quality hardly jeopardizes the doctrinal orthodoxy of Anselm's narrative. Anselm, however, accomplishes his theological purposes precisely through the anthropomorphic features of his Trinitarian narrative, rather than in spite of them. As a result, in a vague, shadowy way, his narrative gives rise to an impression of Trinitarian disunity.

Of course, Anselm is firmly committed to divine unity, as is evident, for example, in *De processione Spiritus Sancti*, his treatise on the Holy Spirit's eternal procession from the Father and the Son. Moreover, in *Cur Deus homo*, in the midst of his discussion of God's will and Christ's crucifixion, Anselm asserts that the Father, the Son, and the Holy Spirit had together ordained that the Son "would reveal to the world the loftiness of his omnipotence in no other

[25] *CDH*, I.1.

[26] The closest Anselm comes to describing such an initial objective is when he argues that God's will for the Son was not for him to die, but to persevere in justice. Anselm claims that the Son's obedience "consisted not in abandoning his life, but in preserving justice; and he persevered in justice with such fortitude that he incurred his death" (*CDH* I.9, 256). This passage, however, describes God's will for the Son *after the Son has already taken flesh*. It does not give an account of God's reasons for sending his Son in the first place.

way than through death."[27] So there can be no question of Anselm meaning to deny the unity of either the divine nature or the divine will. For Anselm's narrative to work, however, the Son must will things apart from the Father; otherwise, it would not absolve the Father from wanting the death of his Son. Yet, as we have seen, Anselm does not supply a coherent rationale for locating the Son's independent willing in the Son's humanity. Consequently, his narrative cannot avoid undermining the unity of the divine will. It lacks the resources to sustain the Son's independent willing within the framework of orthodox Trinitarian doctrine.

Anselm Revisits His Solution (*CDH* I.10)

Anselm seems aware that his first discussion of God's commanding and willing is not entirely satisfactory, because he returns to the same subject in the following chapter, titling it, "Another way in which the same passages can be understood correctly." It is as though he wants a fresh start in tackling the issue. Anselm begins this second discussion by giving another interpretation of the Father's command to the Son. He proposes that the Father's command can also be understood as the gift of an interior desire to endure death for the sake of our salvation. He explains:

> It can also be rightly understood that the Father "commanded him"—but did not compel him—through that generous will by which the Son was willing to die for the salvation of the world; it was in that way that the Father gave him the "cup" of his passion and "did not spare" him "but handed him over for us" and willed his death, and that the Son himself was "obedient to the point of death" and "learned obedience from the things he suffered."[28]

Since Christ preserved this interior desire "of his own accord," Anselm argues, his human freedom was not compromised by the Father's inspiring it within him.[29] He writes:

> For according to this humanity he did not have from himself his will to live justly, but from the Father; and in the same way, it could only be from "the Father of lights," from whom comes "every best gift and every perfect gift," that he had that will by which he was willing to die in order to accomplish so great a good.[30]

[27] *CDH* I.9, 256. As discussed earlier, this passage does not assert that the Triune God had ordained that the Son would reveal the divine omnipotence through his death. Crucially, it asserts only that the Triune God had ruled out the possibility of the Son revealing the divine omnipotence in any other way.

[28] *CDH* I.10, 258; Rom 8:32; Phil 2:8; Heb 5:8.

[29] *CDH* I.10, 259.

[30] *CDH* I.10, 258; Jas 1:17.

Anselm's main point in this second passage—that the Father inspired the Son's humanity with an interior desire to live justly and embrace his crucifixion—is not problematic. He is drawing on orthodox Chalcedonian Christology and a fairly standard interpretation of the dynamism between God's grace and human freedom. Anselm takes the idea that God's grace infuses in us an inclination to live justly, which we can ratify or reject, and applies it to Christ's embrace of his salvific mission. Even though his humanity is united to a divine person, Christ is truly human and therefore required divine grace in his humanity to fulfill the will of his Father. So there is nothing problematic about Anselm's claim that God inspired Christ with an interior desire that Christ then freely ratified, and that this inspiration was a kind of command.

The problems with his argument stem from other issues. First, Anselm again implies that Christ's willingness to suffer justifies God's command. But while Anselm is right that Christ's willingness is theologically significant, Christ's willingness to suffer does not, of itself, resolve the problem of God's apparent injustice. The real issue is not whether Christ went to his death against his will. The real issue is whether God's command was just. A general might command a soldier to go to his death, and the soldier might obey voluntarily, but whether the soldier obeys voluntarily is entirely irrelevant to the justice of the general's command. In these passages, Anselm does not attempt to demonstrate that God's command was just. He devotes his energies instead to showing that Christ went to his death willingly, and this question is beside the point. Second, and more importantly, by claiming that the Father inspires Christ's humanity with "that will by which he was willing to die in order to accomplish so great a good," Anselm undermines the achievements of his first discussion of the Father's will and Christ's crucifixion. For all its problems, Anselm's Trinitarian narrative does not claim that the Father commanded Christ to abandon his life. As a result, it succeeds in avoiding any implication that the Father caused Christ's death. But now even this limited success evaporates because if the Father were to have inspired Christ with an interior desire to go to his death, then the Father would also have necessarily caused that death.

After giving this second interpretation of God's command, Anselm returns to the question of God's will. In the previous chapter he had written about God's unwillingness for the world to be saved unless Christ endured death; now he speaks of what God positively wills. He first offers some principles drawn from human experience:

> Just as we say that someone wills when he does not cause the other person to will, so too we say that someone wills when he does not cause the other person to will but approves of his willing. For example, when we see someone bravely willing to suffer some hardship in order to bring to completion what he rightly wills, we

acknowledge that we will that he endure such suffering; yet we do not will or love his suffering but rather his will.[31]

So far, so good. His observations about our approval of heroic sacrifice, which draw on double effect reasoning, ring true. But then he takes the argument in another direction. He writes:

We are also accustomed to say of someone who can prevent something but does not prevent it that he wills the thing he does not prevent.[32]

This statement is not true. For example, when a secret agent does not act to save an innocent victim from a brutal beating to keep his cover and safeguard his mission, we do not necessarily conclude that the secret agent wants or wills the beating. In fact, we would tend to assume just the opposite. In the previous passage Anselm had made an important distinction between willing the heroism of self-sacrifice and willing its concomitant suffering, but with this statement he blurs that distinction.

This rhetorical sleight of hand sets the stage for the next phase of Anselm's argument. Having offered these observations about human willing, he now applies them to divine willing, and particularly the Father's willing of the Son's crucifixion:

So, since the Son's will was pleasing to the Father, and since the Father did not prevent him from willing or from carrying out what he willed, it is correct to affirm that the Father willed that the Son endure death so generously and for so great a benefit, even though he did not love the Son's suffering.[33]

At first glance, Anselm's description of what the Father wills seems equivalent to willing a just man to stand fast in the face of suffering. The Father seems to will the Son's courage, and only tolerate his suffering, in the same way that we might will the courage of the just man, but only tolerate his suffering. The parallel breaks down, however, with the phrase "for so great a benefit." What is the benefit for which the Son endures death? It is the salvation of the world, which the Father was unwilling to allow unless the Son accomplished "something as great as that death was."[34] Consequently, on Anselm's account, the Father's willing of the Son's suffering is not equivalent to willing a just man to stand fast in the face of suffering. The Father did not merely will the Son's courageous perseverance in justice. Since the Father willed for the Son to save the world, and since the Father was unwilling for the world to be saved unless the Son laid down his life on the cross, the Father also willed the actual crucifying of his Son. He wanted and intended his Son's death.

Anselm tries to avoid this problematic conclusion by suggesting that the salvific significance of Christ's crucifixion stems, not from some arbitrary

[31] *CDH* I.10, 259. [32] *CDH* I.10, 259. [33] *CDH* I.10, 259. [34] *CDH* I.9, 257.

whim, but from an ontological necessity that even the Father had to acknowledge. Anselm adopts two different maneuvers to advance this position. The first maneuver is more rhetorical than substantive. Anselm quietly drops his claim about the Father being unwilling to save the world through any other means and replaces it with a vague affirmation about Christ's passion being somehow necessary for the world's salvation. Anselm makes this move in a passage about Christ's motivation for embracing his suffering:

> Now he said that the cup could not pass unless he drank it, not because he could not have avoided death if he had wanted to, but because (as I have said) it was impossible for the world to be saved in any other way; and he unswervingly willed to suffer death rather than that the world should not be saved.[35]

Yet, according to what Anselm had stated in the previous chapter, the reason why "it was impossible for the world to be saved in any other way" was that the Father was unwilling to save the world in any other way. The Father does not merely will Christ's heroic acceptance of death in pursuit of a worthy goal; the Father also *establishes* Christ's heroic acceptance of death as the goal that Christ must pursue. Anselm's rhetoric obscures this implication but cannot avoid it.

His second maneuver for establishing the crucifixion's ontological necessity, which he develops only later in *Cur Deus homo*, is to argue that the crucifixion was necessary for the world's salvation, not because God had arbitrarily settled on it, but because humanity's sins had deprived God of the honor he was rightly due, and only Christ's heroic suffering could make appropriate satisfaction.[36] So God allows Christ to make restitution on behalf of humanity through his death but does not will Christ's death; he wills only that restitution be made to his honor.[37]

[35] *CDH* I.10, 259. [36] See especially *CDH* I.11–15, 22; II.18.

[37] The practice of sacramental confession, and especially the obligation of making restitution for stolen property, may have influenced Anselm's thinking about God's honor. In traditional sacramental theology, of the sort that Anselm would have been familiar with, auricular confession involves both penitential works and, potentially, acts of restitution. Penitential works are ascetic practices assigned by the confessor that express repentance, assist interior healing, and lead to growth in virtue. In cases of theft, when reasonably possible, penitents are also asked to make restitution for stolen property, as a way of repairing the damage done by their sins and ensuring that their repentance is sincere. The role of restitution in sacramental confession, even more than the role of penitential works, may lay behind some of Anselm's ideas about the necessity of making satisfaction to God for the honor stolen by sin (see esp. *CDH* I.11). Theologians often make the connection between sacramental confession and Anselm's theory of redemption, but the idea of making satisfaction to God's honor is usually linked to acts of penance rather than the restitution of stolen property. See, for example, Adolf Harnack, *History of Dogma*, trans. Neil Buchanan, vol. 6 (London: Williams and Norgate, 1897), 56n98. The practices of both penance and restitution undoubtedly shaped Anselm's understanding of redemption, but given the centrality of restoration to his account of God's honor, restitution may have played a more significant role.

Among modern scholars, Anselm's appeal to God's honor has received mixed appraisals. Adolf Harnack deconstructs Anselm's account of God's honor as confused and contradictory.[38] He sees it leading to "the worst thing in Anselm's theory: the mythological conception of God as the mighty private man, who is incensed at the injury done to his honor and does not forego his wrath till he has received an at least adequately great equivalent."[39] Others acknowledge that Anselm's ideas about God's honor offend modern ears but nonetheless see them as getting at the deep structure of things, and also as an entirely fitting way of locating the necessity of the crucifixion in the immense debt incurred by our disobedience to God.[40] What can be said about these competing evaluations? Although analyses like Harnack's distort the subtlety and grace of Anselm's argument—whatever the failings of his theory, Anselm does not portray God as "the mighty private man, who is incensed at the injury done to his honor"—they do put their finger on an important difficulty. To explain the necessity of the crucifixion by appealing to this notion of God's honor, we must choose between two unattractive options. Either God is like Harnack's "mighty private person," a stickler who demands restitution for his offended honor before forgiving his creatures, which Anselm cannot have meant to suggest, or else God must defer to the rules governing his honor, as though God's honor has claims on God. Even if we take this notion of God's honor as a proxy for the harmonious ordering of the universe (which, while going beyond the text, is not an unreasonable interpretation), this second option suffers from serious deficiencies. It implicitly suggests that there is some cosmic calculus of honor and dishonor, and that Christ's supererogatory obedience cancels out the dishonor caused by our disobedience. But whatever the salvific efficacy of Christ's obedience, it does not of course erase past sins, and therefore cannot actually cancel out any dishonor. Hence, any balancing of the scales of honor and dishonor requires the subjective evaluation of a judge—and thus reverts back to God's arbitrary will. Consequently, Anselm's appeal to God's honor cannot explain the crucifixion's necessity as anything transcending an arbitrary divine decision.

There is a deeper, more fundamental problem. Even with the buffer of God's honor between God's will and Christ's crucifixion, God still wants the actual crucifying of Christ. Even if God were not responsible for setting Christ's crucifixion as a requirement for the world's salvation, he nonetheless wills the crucifying of Christ as a means of reconciling the world to himself. Suppose, for example, we are threatened with havoc unless we kill an innocent person. Even though we would not want the innocent person's death for its own sake, it would be wrong, regardless of the beneficial consequences, to

[38] Harnack, *History of Dogma*, 72.

[39] Harnack, *History of Dogma*, 76. Translation slightly modified.

[40] Rogers, "A Defense of Anselm," 191–5.

comply, because if we did, we would necessarily intend the innocent person's death, and thus be guilty of murder. Similarly, it is irrelevant whether the salvific efficacy of Christ's crucifixion derives from the ontological implications of God's honor or the arbitrary will of the Father. Either way, if God saves the world through his Son's sheer experience of suffering and death, he necessarily intends his Son's death as the chosen means to his end—and thus wills the actual crucifying of Christ.

The Success and Failure of Anselm's Solution

Anselm's solution to the problem of God's apparent injustice in Book I.8–10 is tortuous, confusing, and maddening. The dialogue format of *Cur Deus homo* heightens the chaos. It allows Anselm to jump around from topic to topic, changing the angle of approach when it suits his purpose, without ever having to pull his argument together into a tight, logically consistent synthesis. At any moment, he can put a question on the lips of his interlocutor that subtly reframes the issues so that he does not have to linger over the weaker points of his solution. Consequently, Anselm is able to maintain a rhetorical illusion of utter transparency—since he answers each of his interlocutor's questions with serene confidence—even while presenting an argument that is profoundly evasive. Reading these three chapters is like being blindfolded and spun around: we end up dizzy and tend to cling to the most stable things in sight. In this case, the most stable things in sight are Anselm's manifest desire to avoid implying that God wills the actual crucifying of his Son and his confidence that his solution successfully avoids this implication. Anselm thus secures a rhetorical success of sorts. But on the more important question, of whether his solution actually works, Anselm falls short. His solution cannot avoid the implication that God intends the death of his Son and thus wills the crucifying of Christ and its associated moral evil.

EVALUATING ANSELM'S INTERPRETATION OF THE CRUCIFIXION

Anselm's theory of redemption harmonizes well with the New Testament evidence considered in earlier chapters. According to Anselm, Jesus both foresees the crucifixion and sees himself advancing his objectives through it. Likewise, the crucifixion is integral to God's plan of salvation and necessary to its accomplishment; Anselm in fact frames *Cur Deus homo* as an inquiry into the necessity of the Incarnation and, implicitly, of Christ's crucifixion. He also attempts to provide an explanation of the crucifixion's salvific efficacy that does not imply God's willing of moral evil. On this point, however, Anselm does not succeed. Whatever its rhetorical success, his argument is unsound and even logically incoherent. Ironically, Anselm's attempts to avoid implying God's willing of moral evil only make things worse. In order to mitigate the problem of God's apparent injustice, he describes the Son as choosing to suffer on his own initiative, but he does not adequately locate this independent willing in the Son's humanity. In this way he inadvertently undermines the unity of the Trinity.

How could Anselm, one of the greatest logicians of his day, and an acknowledged expert on the theology of the Trinity,[41] have gotten himself into these logical muddles? There seem to be many factors. First, the issues surrounding double effect reasoning are subtle and complex, as indicated by the controversy that marks contemporary literature on the subject. There is nothing approaching a consensus about its finer points, and even specialists in the field sometimes apply double effect reasoning in ways that are highly tendentious. So the deficiencies of Anselm's double effect reasoning and the problematic understanding of intention on which it depends are in keeping with the difficulty of the subject matter. Still, the sheer complexity of the philosophical issues involved does not fully explain the lapses in his logic. His mistakes are not unforced errors; his theological commitments lead him to argue in problematic ways.

Beauty and Redemption

Anselm's aesthetic sensitivity partly explains his convoluted logic. Many have noted the important place he accords to beauty in his theology, often in order to argue that his aesthetic sensitivity belies accusations of theo-legalism.[42] This emphasis on beauty as a controlling theme in Anselm's theology seems right,

[41] In the hopes of facilitating reconciliation with Eastern Orthodox Christians, Pope Urban II asked Anselm to speak about the procession of the Holy Spirit at the Council of Bari in 1098—a clear indication of his reputation as a theologian of the Trinity.

[42] See Southern, *Saint Anselm*, 212–13; Brian Leftow, "Anselm on the Beauty of the Incarnation," *Modern Schoolman* 72 (1995): 109–24; Stephen R. Holmes, "The Upholding of Beauty: A Reading of Anselm's *Cur Deus Homo*," *Scottish Journal of Theology* 54 (2001): 189–203; David Bentley Hart, *The Beauty of the Infinite: The Aesthetics of Christian Truth* (Grand Rapids, MI: Eerdmans, 2003), 369–72. This line of interpretation has been inspired especially by Hans Urs von Balthasar, who seeks to rehabilitate Anselm's theory of redemption by emphasizing the hermeneutic significance of beauty. See Hans Urs von Balthasar, *The Glory of the Lord: A Theological Aesthetics*, ed. John Riches, trans. Andrew Louth, Francis McDonagh, and Brian McNeil, 7 vols., vol. 2 (Edinburgh: T & T Clark, 1984), 211–53. See also Olsen's sympathetic critique, where Olsen argues that, though von Balthasar overstates his case, his essential point is correct: Olsen, "Hans Urs von Balthasar," esp. 56–8.

and it provides a helpful corrective to some of the stronger criticisms leveled against him. Perhaps due to the same sensitivity that made him alert to the problem of God's apparent injustice, Anselm is exceptionally attentive to the aesthetic dimension of Christ's heroism. It is often claimed that the feudalism of his social context is the key to understanding his notion of God's honor, and therefore his entire theory of redemption. But his appreciation for beauty—especially "the indescribable beauty that belongs to our redemption, accomplished in this way"[43]—seems much more important.

Nonetheless, a hermeneutic that privileges Anselm's attention to beauty, however appropriate and rehabilitating, cannot overcome the objections of his critics. Anselm's theory cannot avoid implying that God wills Christ's actual experience of crucifixion and thus the moral evil of those crucifying him. For all his appreciation for beauty, Anselm is too ready to isolate the moral beauty of self-sacrifice from its narrative context. He reifies the moral beauty of Christ's sacrifice as though it is a bartering chip of value in and of itself which can be used to compensate God for the reified ugliness of sin. For Anselm, the historical particulars that constitute the concrete reality of Christ's crucifixion are not important; what is important is the sheer act of self-sacrifice. In this way, while Anselm's theological method is marked by great confidence in the power of human reason, it is also marked by disregard of history and narrative. Christ's entrance into a culture and religion that started before him is irrelevant, as are the historical particulars of Christ's actions before and after his crucifixion. For Anselm, what matters is the idea of self-sacrifice; historical background and immediate context are immaterial. But acts of self-sacrifice cannot be evaluated apart from the intentions informing them, and intentions cannot be reconstructed apart from their narrative context.

Anselm's attention to moral beauty, and also his sense of its power to reconcile, may have its origins in the catharsis often caused by hearing the story of Christ's passion. It is easy to see how Anselm could have made this leap. Christ's actions in the Gospel narratives are heroic and transcendently beautiful. In the unfolding of events, there is a sense of dramatic fulfillment and completion, of the tragedy of his rejection being overcome precisely by his patient acceptance of evil. The sins of those crucifying Christ are dramatically reversed and overcome by Christ's goodness and Christ's resurrection. Consequently, the Gospel narratives can have a tremendous cathartic effect. But Anselm seems to reify the catharsis of dramatic reversal, taking it as the core of the redemptive significance of the crucifixion, rather than the overflow from some deeper mystery.

[43] *CDH* I.3, 248.

From the Devil's Ransom to the Father's Ransom

Another structural flaw in Anselm's theory of redemption is its failure to account for the evil on display in the passion narratives. After categorically rejecting the devil's ransom interpretation, Anselm does not assign any alternative theological significance to the evil actors in the story of Christ's crucifixion; he simply ignores them. This omission creates a narrative vacuum. The passion narratives involve evil as well as divine goodness, and so any adequate theory of redemption must give a theological account for that evil. Anselm, however, gives short shrift to the role of evil in the drama of salvation. By doing so, he makes it difficult to secure the salvific significance of the crucifixion without implicitly attributing injustice to God. He eliminates the theological problem of how the devil could have rights over and against God, but he replaces it with the theological problem of how the Father could want or need the death of his Son. The devil's ransom interpretation had given a plausible account of who wants the crucifixion. It made perfect sense that the devil would want to see Christ crucified. But after Anselm takes the devil out of the narrative, without giving his part to anyone else, saying who wants the crucifixion becomes problematic; the only actors left in the drama are divine.

Despite their differences, Anselm's account of redemption shares an important structural feature with the one he criticizes in Book I.6–7 of *Cur Deus homo*: each interprets the crucifixion as a transaction. Every transaction involves someone who gives and someone who receives. When the crucifixion is interpreted as a transaction, the Son, in his humanity, is obviously the one who gives. But who receives? In the interpretation Anselm criticizes in Book I.6–7, the recipient is both unambiguous and plausible. In Anselm's theory, however, the recipient's identity is neither unambiguous nor plausible. Is the recipient the Triune God, God the Father, or God's honor? It is not clear, and none of the alternatives are very plausible. Anselm's ambiguity provides rhetorical cover for his argument (since he does not clearly settle on a recipient, it is more difficult to criticize his choice), but his theory nonetheless fails to suggest a plausible recipient. More importantly, he does not alter the transactional structure of the narrative he is attempting to replace.

In the end, Anselm trades the devil's ransom for the Father's ransom. In place of a dramatic tension between God and the devil, he sets up a dramatic tension between God the Father and God the Son. Although Anselm rejects the idea that redemption is a transaction between God and the devil, he affirms the more basic premise that redemption is, in fact, a kind of transaction. Some unfortunate consequences follow. As the recipient of the transaction, the Father inevitably becomes the one who wants the crucifying of Christ. Furthermore, the inner unity of the Trinity is shattered. The Son still obeys the

Father, but Father and Son no longer share one will. In Anselm's interpretation of the crucifixion, the Son's human aversion to the Father's will in the garden of Gethsemane has slipped into the inner life of the Trinity. Anselm does not want to affirm this implication, but once he empties the drama of all actors except Father and Son, his logic and rhetoric cannot hold it off. After Christ's crucifixion, the Father is the last one standing. By process of elimination, no one else remains who could be responsible for the Son's death, and thus *want* the Son's death. The tension is no longer between God's will and Christ's human will; the tension is now between God the Father and God the Son.

Anselm's interpretation of the crucifixion suffers from another related problem. It cannot give any explanation for why God chose to bring about humanity's redemption through morally evil actions. The devil's rights interpretation has a ready explanation: the devil had to be tricked into overreaching, and hence, in order to accomplish his purposes, God had to tolerate the moral evil of Christ's crucifixion. Anselm's theory, however, cannot explain why Christ endured a death brought about by morally evil actions. Even granting that there might be something uniquely heroic and reparative about sacrificing one's life for others,[44] his theory cannot explain—nor does it try to explain—why death by leprosy, after spending many years working in a leper colony, or death by drowning, in the process of rescuing someone, could not have been equally redemptive. Granted, Anselm could concede the validity of this objection and maintain that the circumstances of Christ's death were in fact irrelevant, and that it would have sufficed if Christ had given his life for others without being killed. It seems unlikely, however, that he would want to do so. In any case, such a theory would sit uneasily with the Gospel narratives, which implicitly assign theological significance to the mode of Christ's death and the fact that he suffers at the hands of unjust men.

CONCLUSION

For Anselm, the crucifixion is a transaction between God the Father and God the Son, where the beauty of Christ's heroism makes the restitution required

[44] Bracketing other questions about his theory of redemption, Anselm makes a good case in *CDH* II.18 that Christ's acceptance of death made satisfaction for our sins in a uniquely efficacious manner. He argues that, since Christ was sinless, he was exempt from the punishment of death, and he owed God only justice and virtue. Consequently, when Christ accepted death, his self-sacrifice was supererogatory, and it was able to make satisfaction for the honor lost by our disobedience. Anselm's argument is not invulnerable to criticism; nonetheless, considered within the context of his theological presuppositions, it has a strong inner logic.

by God the Father for the ugliness of sin. Consequently, no matter how much he fights it, Anselm cannot avoid implying that God wills the actual crucifying of Christ, nor thus imputing injustice to God. He replaces the devil's ransom with the Father's ransom: a theory of redemption that solves some problems, but creates others, and ultimately is much less flattering to God.

9

Abelard's Response to Anselm

Peter Abelard (1079–1142) was a near contemporary of Anselm, and like Anselm, he is known today especially for his interpretation of Christ's crucifixion. Although Abelard does not cite *Cur Deus homo*, he formulates his theory of redemption in direct response to Anselm.[1] Abelard's disagreement with Anselm about redemption ranks high among historic theological controversies, as does his subsequent and highly politicized clash on the same topic with Bernard of Clairvaux (1090–1153). According to the standard typology, Anselm and Abelard represent two diametrically opposed interpretations of the crucifixion: Anselm proposes an objectivist theory, in which the crucifixion is primarily about making satisfaction for sin and repaying a debt, while Abelard proposes a subjectivist theory, in which the crucifixion is primarily about revealing God's love and inspiring charity.[2] For all the contrast between their theories, however, and for all the pedagogical usefulness of emphasizing this contrast, their theories of redemption share profound structural similarities. Like Anselm, Abelard constructs his theory as an alternative to the devil's ransom interpretation, and like Anselm, he frames his theory as a solution to the problem of God's apparent injustice—and also like Anselm, Abelard falls short. This chapter evaluates Abelard's theological interpretation of the crucifixion, focusing on his *Commentary on Romans*. It concludes that Abelard avoids implying that God wills moral evil but cannot give a plausible account of the crucifixion's necessity.

[1] Anselm and Abelard were contemporaries, but Anselm was older, and he had been dead for some years when Abelard laid out his theory of redemption in his *Commentary on Romans*. Given Anselm's fame, the novelty of Anselm's theory of redemption, and Abelard's evident awareness of the sort of argument that Anselm makes in *Cur Deus homo*—not to mention the structural similarities in their presentation of their respective theories—Abelard must have either read *Cur Deus homo*, or otherwise received a detailed report of Anselm's theory. For a discussion of the evidence that Abelard was acquainted with *Cur Deus homo*, see Richard E. Weingart, *The Logic of Divine Love: A Critical Analysis of the Soteriology of Peter Abailard* (Oxford: Clarendon Press, 1970), 89. For a discussion of Abelard's reception of *Cur Deus homo*, see Southern, *Saint Anselm*, 210–11.

[2] Aulén, *Christus Victor*, 81–100.

THE PROBLEM OF OUR JUSTIFICATION BY CHRIST'S BLOOD

Abelard gives the most complete account of his theory of redemption in his *Commentary on Romans.*[3] When he comes to the verse in Romans about God justifying us by Christ's blood (Rom 3:25), Abelard steps back from a close reading of the text to discuss the meaning of redemption:

> A most pressing problem obtrudes itself at this point, as to what that redemption of ours through the death of Christ may be, and in what way the apostle declares that we are justified by his blood—we who appear to be worthy of still greater punishment, seeing that we are the wicked servants who have committed the very things for which our innocent Lord was slain. And so it seems that we must first investigate why it was necessary for God to take human nature upon him so that he might redeem us by dying in the flesh; and from what person holding us captive, either justly or by fraud, he has redeemed us; and by what standard of justice he has liberated us from the dominion of that person who has given commands to which he willingly submitted in order to set us free.[4]

In this passage, Abelard defines the problem of God's apparent injustice and the parameters of his inquiry in ways similar to Anselm in *Cur Deus homo*. Like Anselm, Abelard explains that his goal is to explain the necessity of the Incarnation, and especially Christ's death on the cross.[5] There are subtle differences though. Abelard stays closer to the language of scripture, framing the problem of God's apparent injustice in terms of justification by Christ's blood; he also gives more attention to the themes of captivity and freedom.

Immediately after defining the problem, Abelard, like Anselm, turns to the devil's ransom interpretation and argues against it.[6] Abelard rejects, not only the idea that the devil had any legal rights over humanity or that God needed to pay the devil a ransom, but also the idea that the devil had complete power over humanity. To make his point, he relies on the parable about the rich man and Lazarus (Luke 16:19–31). When Lazarus died, he was carried by angels to Abraham's bosom. Consequently, Abelard argues, Lazarus must have been beyond the power of the devil, and since this parable is told before Christ's passion, the righteous dead of the Old Testament must also have been beyond the devil's power. And since the devil did not have power over the righteous

[3] References to Abelard's *Commentary on Romans* will cite the book number and then the verse from Romans that he is commenting on. For the Latin critical edition, see Peter Abelard, *Opera Theologica*, ed. Eligii M. Buytaert, 6 vols., vol. 1 (Brepols: Turnholt, 1969).

[4] *CR* II (3:26), in Eugene R. Fairweather, ed. *A Scholastic Miscellany: Anselm to Ockham* (London: S.C.M. Press, 1956), 280.

[5] Compare this passage from Abelard with *CDH* I.1.

[6] As mentioned in the previous chapter, Abelard and his disciples are the only ones among their contemporaries in the schools of theology to accept Anselm's argument against the devil's ransom interpretation. See Southern, *Saint Anselm*, 210.

dead before Christ's passion, his authority evidently did not extend over the whole of humanity. Abelard does not deny that the devil had *some* power over humanity before Christ's passion, but he explains that any such power was granted by God as punishment for human sinfulness, not because the devil had any legal claim to it.

After making his case against the idea that the devil's power once extended over the whole of humanity, Abelard sets his sights on the idea that the devil ever had any legal rights over humanity. He writes:

> And what right to possess mankind could the devil possibly have unless perhaps he had received man for purposes of torture through the express permission, or even the assignment, of the Lord?[7]

Taking the devil's ransom interpretation as a legal theory, Abelard proceeds to reject it on legal terms. He makes a series of common sense observations about the master-slave relationship in order to demonstrate that slaves never gain legal authority over their fellow slaves when they lead them to disobey their common master. Then, applying these observations to the devil, he argues that the same holds true for the devil: just as a slave would never gain authority over his fellow slaves for coaxing them into disobeying their common master, the devil could never have gained legal rights over us by tempting us to disobey God, our common master.[8]

Up to this point, Abelard has approached the problem of God's apparent injustice in a way similar to Anselm. Then he makes a move that Anselm does not. He argues that our sins are against God and, therefore, God could have forgiven us whenever he wanted. Consequently, Jesus did not need to endure crucifixion for our sins to be forgiven. In support of his argument, Abelard notes that Christ forgave sins before his crucifixion, as when he forgave the paralytic (Mark 2:1–12; Matt 9:1–8; Luke 5:17–26) or Mary Magdalene (Luke 7:36–50).[9] God took flesh for our salvation before Christ suffered for us, Abelard argues; surely God could have granted the lesser gift of forgiveness as well. At first, Abelard makes these claims about God's forgiveness of sins in order to attack the devil's ransom interpretation. Since God could forgive sins before the crucifixion, it could not be true that the devil had rights over humanity, or that Jesus had to be crucified in order to reclaim us from the devil. Then, Abelard turns this argument against the idea that God required Christ's crucifixion as expiation for sin. If the sin of Adam was so great that it

[7] *CR* II (3:26), in Fairweather, 281.

[8] Abelard seems to be drawing on Anselm for his line of argument, as Anselm proposes a similar legal analogy in *CDH* I.7; however, Abelard's analogy is more developed.

[9] Anselm does not consider the instances of Christ forgiving sins before his passion in *Cur Deus homo*.

required the death of Christ in expiation, he asks, what could possibly expiate the crime of Christ's crucifixion?[10]

After raising this question and others like it, Abelard observes that ransoms are paid to masters, not to torturers. Since God is our master, only God could have demanded a ransom for our liberation; the devil is merely a torturer who punishes us for our sins. Yet it is absurd to think that God would demand the death of his Son. It would mean, first, that God set the price of the ransom and then paid it to himself, and, second, that God (in some sense) found the death of his Son agreeable. Abelard writes:

> Again, how did he release these captives for a price if he himself exacted or settled the price for release of the same? Indeed, how cruel and wicked it seems that anyone should demand the blood of an innocent person as the price for anything, or that it should in any way please him that an innocent man should be slain—still less that God should consider the death of his Son so agreeable that by it he should be reconciled to the whole world![11]

Abelard's argument is clearly directed against Anselm's theory of redemption, even though Abelard does not name it as his target. Abelard's reasoning is simple and straightforward. It is absurd to think that God would set a price of any kind for the ransom of humanity only to give it right back to himself, or that God would ever be pleased by the death of his Son. Significantly, he does not engage the subtleties of Anselm's argument. He does not discuss the distinction between God being pleased by Christ's heroism rather than his actual death, or the notion that God's stolen honor had to be restored. His lack of specifics may mean that he knew Anselm's theory only secondhand; but if he did have access to *Cur Deus homo*, as is likely, it may mean instead that he regarded the subtleties of Anselm's argument as more rhetorical than substantive—which, as we have seen, would not be an unreasonable judgment.

ABELARD'S SOLUTION

After surveying the devil's ransom interpretation and then Anselm's theory and finding both wanting, Abelard presents his own theory of redemption:

[10] Anselm had anticipated this objection to his theory, and he argues that those who crucified Christ did not know what they were doing and so the gravity of their sin was lessened (*CDH* II.15). If Abelard was aware of Anselm's preemptive response he does not show it. Then again, Anselm's argument is admittedly weak, and so, even if Abelard were aware of it, he might not have felt the need to respond.

[11] *CR* II (3:26), in Fairweather, 283.

> Now it seems to us that we have been justified by the blood of Christ and reconciled to God in this way: through this unique act of grace manifested to us—in that his Son has taken upon himself our nature and persevered therein in teaching us by word and example even unto death—he has more fully bound us to himself by love; with the result that our hearts should be enkindled by such a gift of divine grace, and true charity should not now shrink from enduring anything for him.[12]

Christ's death is redemptive because it reveals God's love and because this revelation of God's love inspires charity in us. We are justified by the blood of Christ, but it is not Christ's death or even his heroic embrace of death that justifies us. We are justified by *witnessing* Christ's death, because this witnessing inspires "that deeper affection in us which not only frees us from slavery to sin, but also wins for us the true liberty of sons of God, so that we do all things out of love rather than fear."[13] According to Abelard, Christ "came for the express purpose of spreading this true liberty of love amongst men,"[14] and he spreads this true liberty of love most of all by laying down his life.

Abelard notes that knowledge of Christ's passion is not strictly necessary for redemption. Since charity is what redeems us, and since hopeful expectation can inspire gratitude and charity, the righteous of the Old Testament did not need the crucifixion to have actually taken place before they could be redeemed. Their hope for the coming of the Messiah was enough. Abelard maintains that, on account of their hope for Christ's coming, the ancient Fathers "were aroused to very great love of God in the same way as men of this dispensation of grace," and that the ancient Fathers were redeemed precisely through this love of God.[15] They were not filled with God's grace to the same extent as Christians, "since a realized gift inspires greater love than one which is only hoped for,"[16] but the difference between the old and new dispensations of grace is a difference of degree, not of kind.

Original Sin, Charity, and Redemption

Abelard's theory of original sin lays the groundwork for his theory of redemption. Abelard maintains that Adam and Eve transmitted the punitive consequences of their sin to their descendants, but he denies that their guilt was transmitted as well.[17] We do not inherit their guilt because "one who does not yet perceive by reason what he ought to do does not have any fault because of

[12] *CR* II (3:26), in Fairweather, 283.
[13] *CR* II (3:26), in Fairweather, 284.
[14] *CR* II (3:26), in Fairweather, 284.
[15] *CR* II (3:26), in Fairweather, 283.
[16] *CR* II (3:26), in Fairweather, 284.
[17] *CR* II (5:19). For a discussion of Abelard's account of original sin, see Weingart, *Logic of Divine Love*, 42–50.

scorn for God"; nonetheless, "he is not immune to the stain of his earlier parents' sin, from which he already incurs punishment even if not fault."[18] Abelard does not deny that original sin has many harmful effects. He holds that it leads to loss of communion with God, physical and spiritual death, weakness of will, the darkening of reason, disorder in the passions, and upheaval in the natural world.[19] Nonetheless, his claim that we do not inherit the guilt of Adam and Eve has significant implications for his interpretation of Christ's crucifixion. There is no guilt from original sin that needs to be wiped out and no legal debt that needs to be repaid; there are only harmful effects that require a remedy.

Abelard's views on charity are also crucial to his theory of redemption.[20] Abelard writes a great deal about charity over the course of his career, especially later in his life. Various aspects of his views about charity are novel, or at least unusual, compared to his contemporaries. (Many scholars now attribute Abelard's increasing attention to charity, as well as certain features of his account, to the influence of Heloise, his onetime lover and lifelong friend, and her ideas about charity.)[21] For Abelard, charity must be disinterested and selfless, without concern for any sort of reward.[22] He writes:

> It should not even be called "charity" if we love him for our own sakes, that is, for our own advantage and for the happiness of his kingdom which we look for from him, rather than for his own sake, establishing the end of our own intention in ourselves, and not in him.[23]

According to Abelard, the selfless love of charity is what justifies us. The elect are justified by "the affection of sincere charity," loving God for himself rather

[18] *Ethics* I.45, in Peter Abelard, *Ethical Writings*, trans. Paul Vincent Spade (Indianapolis: Hackett, 1995), 10.

[19] On Abelard's views on the consequences of original sin, see Weingart, *Logic of Divine Love*, 44–6.

[20] For a discussion of Abelard's *Commentary on Romans*, with particular attention to the topics of justification, charity, grace, and redemption, see Jean Doutre, "Romans as Read in School and Cloister in the Twelfth Century: The Commentaries of Peter Abelard and William of St. Thierry," in *Medieval Readings of Romans*, ed. William S. Campbell, Peter S. Hawkins, and Brenda Deen Schildgen (London: T & T Clark, 2007), 33–57.

[21] Despite the relative paucity of Heloise's extant writings, Constant Mews declines to consider Abelard's thought in isolation from hers. For Mews' discussion of their accounts of love and charity, see Constant J. Mews, *Abelard and Heloise* (Oxford: Oxford University Press, 2005), 58–80, 204–25. Regarding Heloise's influence on Abelard in his account of charity as selfless love, see John Marenbon, *The Philosophy of Peter Abelard* (Cambridge: Cambridge University Press, 1997), 298–303.

[22] On Abelard's account of charity and its selfless character, see Weingart, *Logic of Divine Love*, 169–76; Marenbon, *Philosophy of Peter Abelard*, 287–92; Mews, *Abelard and Heloise*, 206–7.

[23] CR III (7:13), in Peter Abelard, *Commentary on the Epistle to the Romans*, trans. Steven R. Cartwright (Washington, DC: The Catholic Univeristy of America, 2011), 255.

than his gifts.[24] Charity destroys our guilt[25] and "merits eternal life."[26] It is through charity that we receive adoption by God as sons.[27] In his *Commentary on Romans*, Abelard sometimes speaks almost interchangeably of charity, grace, life, and the Holy Spirit, as though they are different facets of the same reality.[28]

Abelard's views on original sin and charity are crucial to understanding his theory of redemption and why he thinks that Christ's death accomplishes our redemption simply by inspiring charity in us. According to Abelard, the guilt of Adam and Eve does not need to be expiated for God to forgive us, and the sheer possession of charity suffices to destroy personal guilt and obtain eternal life. Consequently, the power of the crucifixion to inspire charity in believers fully explains its redemptive significance.

The Necessity of the Crucifixion

In his *Commentary on Romans*, Abelard introduces his theory of redemption as an inquiry into the salvific necessity of Christ's crucifixion.[29] He assumes that Christ's crucifixion is necessary; his theory of redemption simply seeks to explain why. On one occasion, Abelard accuses his contemporary, Alberic of Reims, of heresy, for holding that some of those living before Christ were saved without prophetic knowledge of him—thus indicating that Abelard thinks that it is not only wrong, but heretical, to deny the salvific necessity of Christ's crucifixion.[30] Abelard acknowledges that God could have redeemed us in another way,[31] but, he argues, while God could have redeemed us in many ways, no other way would have been as fitting (*conveniens*).[32]

Abelard's theory, however, cannot give a plausible explanation for the necessity of crucifixion. If charity is what redeems us, it would seem that any divine intervention that inspired charity could have accomplished our redemption. Other interventions might not have inspired charity as effectively, but they would still have redeemed us as long as they inspired *some* charity. Arguably, some divine interventions might have inspired charity even more effectively

[24] *CR* III (8:30). [25] *CR* III (8:4).

[26] *CR* III (8:18), in Cartwright, 274. [27] *CR* III (8:15).

[28] For an example of Abelard's blurring of these realities, see *CR* III (8:2).

[29] *CR* II (3:26). For a discussion of Abelard's views on the necessity of the crucifixion, see Weingart, *Logic of Divine Love*, 90–3.

[30] *Theologia Scholarium*, II.64; Mews, *Abelard and Heloise*, 211. Abelard does not identify the target of his criticisms; he mentions only a teacher in France. According to Mews, however, Abelard is talking about Alberic of Reims. Mews notes that the accuracy of Abelard's reporting is suspect, as Abelard makes a number of exaggerated claims about his opponents in this section of the *Theologia Scholarium* to make them look ridiculous.

[31] *Theologia Christiania* V.38. [32] *Sententie magistri Petri Abelardi* (PL178:1731A).

than Christ's crucifixion. It is not beyond imagining that the instantaneous elimination of all forms of poverty and disease, for instance, or a divine epiphany experienced by everyone on earth, would not have equaled or surpassed the inspirational effect of Christ's passion.

For the sake of argument, let us suppose that it was indeed necessary for God to take flesh—say, because only in this way could God reveal his personal love effectively. Even so, it would not follow that Christ had to die. Christian doctrine and Christian experience suggest that we can manifest the highest degrees of charity, and inspire the same in others, without actually giving our lives. So even assuming that only an Incarnate God could adequately inspire charity, there is no reason to suppose that he would have to die for us. For example, the Son could have inspired charity in us by taking flesh and spending his life taking care of lepers. And even if Jesus had to die in order to inspire charity in us, it still does not follow that he had to be killed or crucified. He could have given his life for others in a way that did not involve his execution. It is true that, by loving those who hated him, even while they put him to death, Jesus gave a peculiarly powerful witness to God's love. Nonetheless, it is difficult to argue that this sort of witness is *uniquely* powerful, or that other forms of self-sacrifice could not also have efficaciously inspired charity.

Abelard's views on the fate of baptized and unbaptized infants present another problem for his theory of redemption. Abelard maintains that baptized infants go to heaven when they die while unbaptized infants do not.[33] Since baptized infants have no capacity for rational thought, they cannot be said to have been inspired to charity by reflecting on Christ's crucifixion. Still, according to Abelard, baptized infants enter into eternal life on their death. His views on the power of baptism conflict with his theory of redemption. His theory of redemption holds that the crucifixion saves us by inspiring charity, but here Abelard implicitly assigns more redemptive significance to the crucifixion than simply the power to inspire charity: through baptism, it gives eternal life to infants. Contemporary theological reflection about the salvation of non-Christians presents similar difficulties for Abelard's theory of redemption. If there is any possibility of salvation for non-Christians, as many Christians affirm and have affirmed,[34] then Abelard's explanation of the crucifixion's salvific necessity cannot be regarded as adequate. Since many non-Christians die without ever hearing the message of the Gospel, they

[33] *CR* II (5:19). For a discussion of Abelard's views on unbaptized infants, see Weingart, *Logic of Divine Love*, 48; Marenbon, *Philosophy of Peter Abelard*, 325.

[34] For a contemporary example, see *Lumen Gentium*, 16, of the Second Vatican Council. For a historical overview of theologians who have argued for possibility of salvation for non-Christians, going back to Justin Martyr and Clement of Alexandria, see Avery Dulles, *The Assurance of Things Hoped For: A Theology of Christian Faith* (New York: Oxford University Press, 1997), 58–60.

likewise die without ever being inspired by the story of Christ's self-sacrifice on the cross. Consequently, to affirm the possibility of salvation for non-Christians, one must either affirm that the crucifixion does something more than inspire charity in believers, or else deny that the crucifixion is indeed necessary for salvation. Neither option is available to Abelard.

Abelard's Use of Traditional Theological Categories

In recent years, many scholars have argued that Abelard's theory of redemption has been misunderstood, and that, contrary to the standard subjectivist interpretation, Abelard thinks that satisfaction for sin—in an expiatory, objectivist sense—plays an important role in the salvific efficacy of Christ's crucifixion.[35] Abelard makes statements that support this interpretation. For example, in his *Commentary on Romans*, he writes that Christ "swept away the penalty for sins by the price of his death."[36] Abelard's use of traditional language about redemption, however, is highly idiosyncratic. He tells Heloise that Christ has purchased and redeemed her by his blood; he states that Christ's cross has freed us from the dominion of the devil; and he affirms that, in order to accept the punishment due for our sins, Christ was cursed by God in his crucifixion.[37] Yet from his comments about the devil's ransom and Anselm's theory, Abelard clearly does not think that Christ's blood literally purchases anything from anyone, or that the devil ever had any rights over humanity, or that the death of Christ was necessary to expiate a debt owed to God. Abelard may use traditional language about redemption, but what he says must be interpreted according to his own theories. So when he writes that Christ "swept away the penalty for sins by the price of his death," this affirmation should be interpreted in the light of his other

[35] For revisionist interpretations of Abelard's theory of redemption, see Weingart, *Logic of Divine Love*, 120–50; Philip L. Quinn, "Abelard on Atonement: 'Nothing Unintelligible, Arbitrary, Illogical, or Immoral about It'," in *Reasoned Faith: Essays in Philosophical Theology in Honor of Norman Kretzmann* (Ithaca, NY: Cornell University Press, 1993), 281–300; Marenbon, *Philosophy of Peter Abelard*, 322–3; Thomas Williams, "Sin, Grace, and Redemption," in *The Cambridge Companion to Abelard*, ed. Jeffrey E. Brower and Kevin Guilfoy (Cambridge: Cambridge University Press, 2004), 258–78; H. Lawrence Bond, "Another Look at Abelard's Commentary on Romans 3:26," in *Medieval Readings of Romans*, ed. William S. Campbell, Peter S. Hawkins, and Brenda Deen Schildgen (London: T & T Clark, 2007), 11–32.

[36] *CR* II (4:25) in Cartwright, 204. Williams cites this passage as evidence that Abelard's theory of redemption has an objectivist dimension. See Williams, "Sin, Grace, and Redemption," 266.

[37] These examples are found in *Letter 5* (PL 178:209–10); *Confession* (PL 178:105–6) and *Sermon 12* (PL 179:481, 484), respectively. They are taken from Jaroslav Pelikan, *The Growth of Medieval Theology (600–1300)*, 5 vols., vol. 3 (Chicago: University of Chicago Press, 1978), 128–9.

comments: namely, that Christ removes our punishment by inspiring charity in us, not by making satisfaction in an expiatory, objectivist sense.

Abelard sought to be an orthodox theologian out of personal conviction, and he also sought to be perceived as such out of political expediency. Consequently, he could not simply walk away from traditional claims about the redemption, especially when so many are taken directly from scripture. To abandon them would have signaled a departure from theological orthodoxy. So there is every reason to suppose that Abelard would want to retain traditional formulae, even when his theories subvert their traditional meaning. For this reason, Abelard's use of traditional formulae should not be taken to mean that he interprets them in the same way as his contemporaries and immediate predecessors. It indicates, rather, that Abelard thinks that these traditional formulae can be interpreted in ways compatible with his theory of redemption.

God's Will and Christ's Crucifixion

Abelard emphatically rejects the idea that God was pleased by Christ's death, or that God required his crucifixion as an expiatory sacrifice for sin. So he obviously *wants* to deny that God wills the actual crucifying of Christ. However he does not explain how his theory can sustain this denial, nor does he directly address the problem of God's will and Christ's crucifixion. Moreover, he is sketchy about God's precise intentions in sending his Son, which makes it difficult to reconstruct the sense in which he thinks that Gods wills Christ's crucifixion.

With that said, Abelard does seem to avoid implying that God wills the moral evil of the crucifixion. He states that Christ "came for the express purpose of spreading this true liberty of love amongst men."[38] He also maintains that Christ accomplished this purpose by taking upon himself our nature, teaching us by word and example, and then persevering in his teaching even to his death.[39] These affirmations do not specify exactly what God intends in sending his Son, with respect to his Son's death. Nonetheless, from what Abelard does say, it seems clear that, for Abelard, God sends his Son, not to die, but to reveal God's love and to teach us how to live. God wants his Son to endure his inevitable violent rejection, knowing that his patient endurance of the cross will reveal God's love even more effectively, but God does not want or intend Christ's death for its own sake. Therefore, he does not will the actual crucifying of Christ and its associated moral evil. God wills only

[38] *CR* II (3:26), in Fairweather, 284.

[39] *CR* II (3:26).

for Christ to reveal the depths of God's love, by persevering in his teaching even to his death and, by doing so, to inspire the same sort of love in us.

EVALUATING ABELARD'S INTERPRETATION OF THE CRUCIFIXION

In his theological reflections on Christ's crucifixion, Abelard shows particular sensitivity to ethical questions. He objects to the devil's ransom interpretation and Anselm's theory because, according to Abelard, each implies a violation of the moral order. Then, in his own theory of redemption, he focuses especially on the ethical implications of Christ's crucifixion, namely, its power to inspire charity. Given Abelard's sensitivity to these ethical issues, it is not surprising that he avoids implying that God wills moral evil in his theological interpretation of the crucifixion. Abelard has often been viewed as a theological gadfly, more interested in being provocative and upsetting apple carts than system building.[40] It has been argued more recently, though, that he does seek to construct his own theological system, and that ethical concerns are at the core of it.[41] This reading of Abelard seems plausible, and his interpretation of the crucifixion bears it out.

Despite its strengths, Abelard's interpretation of the crucifixion fails to cohere adequately with the New Testament evidence. On the one hand, he maintains that Jesus saw his death as advancing his mission, which accords with his historical intentions, and he also maintains that Christ's crucifixion was necessary for our redemption, which likewise accords with the testimony of sacred scripture. On the other hand, for the reasons discussed above, Abelard's theory of redemption cannot give a plausible account of the necessity of the crucifixion. He wants to affirm the crucifixion's necessity but his theory cannot sustain it. On this point, Anselm's theory ranks superior to Abelard's. Whatever its limitations, Anselm's theory can give a very plausible account of why the crucifixion was necessary: because God willed it so. This explanation of the crucifixion's necessity may be thin and unsatisfying, but it works; it can explain why the crucifixion was necessary. For all the advantages of his theory, Abelard cannot match Anselm in this regard. Consequently, while Abelard's theory cannot be ruled out for implying that God wills moral evil, it must be ruled out for disharmony with sacred scripture. It cannot give a plausible rationale for New Testament affirmations about the salvific necessity of the crucifixion.

[40] For a historical study of how this image of Abelard developed, see Marenbon, *Philosophy of Peter Abelard*, 340–9.

[41] Marenbon, *Philosophy of Peter Abelard*, 324–39.

From Ransom to Prophetic Spectacle

For all their differences, Anselm and Abelard interpret Christ's crucifixion in similar ways. Each of them rejects the devil's ransom interpretation and each of them is exceptionally sensitive to the problem of God's apparent injustice to his Son. Furthermore, each of them explains the salvific value of the crucifixion with respect to a spectator. For Anselm, the spectator is God the Father, and the spectacle is the beauty of Christ's heroism, which restores God's stolen honor. For Abelard, the spectator is fallen humanity, and the spectacle is Christ's selfless love, which inspires charity. Anselm and Abelard are often understood as proposing objective and subjective theories of redemption, respectively. In actuality, both theories are subjective: Anselm's being concerned with the subjectivity of God the Father, and Abelard's with the subjectivity of fallen humanity. Neither theory is objective, because neither theory maintains that the crucifixion event accomplishes any objective, ontological transformation. The crucifixion event does not change God, it does not change the nature of human nature, and it does not change the rest of the created order. For both Anselm and Abelard, the salvific value of Christ's crucifixion consists entirely in its subjective effect on a spectator.

The differences between Anselm and Abelard can be traced to the different ways they make up for the devil's absence from their theories. They both exclude the devil from the dramatis personae of the redemption, but they employ different strategies to compensate for this exclusion. It is helpful to pause and consider the newness of the challenge that confronted them. By casting out the devil from the drama of salvation, they were also casting out the theological narrative around which centuries of Christian reflection had been structured. Consequently, their task was not just to develop a new theory; it was to rewrite the drama of salvation without any models of what that drama might look like with one of its central characters missing. Since there were no examples to guide them in their task, and since they were both highly creative thinkers, each with a streak of theological rebelliousness (Anselm, too; not only Abelard), it is not surprising that they rewrote the drama of salvation in different ways. Anselm traded the devil's ransom for the Father's ransom, while Abelard did away with the concept of ransom entirely, replacing it with a prophetic spectacle. Neither theological narrative quite works, but then, constructing plausible narratives is difficult for playwrights, let alone theologians.

CONCLUSION

Abelard follows Anselm in rejecting the devil's ransom interpretation, but he is not satisfied with Anselm's alternative proposal, and he proposes a theory of his own instead. In Abelard's theory, Christ endures crucifixion to impart the final lesson of his teaching mission. Through his crucifixion, he reveals God's love and inspires charity in believers, and in so doing redeems humanity from sin. Abelard's theory avoids implying that God wills moral evil; it is also consistent with the Gospel portrayals of Jesus embracing his death as something that will advance his mission. It cannot, however, adequately explain New Testament claims about the crucifixion's salvific necessity.

10

The Devil's Ransom Revisited

For the first thousand years of Christianity, the metaphor of ransom supplied the dominant interpretative category for making sense of Christ's crucifixion.[1] By allowing himself to be crucified, it was understood, Christ offered a ransom (in Latin, a *redemptio*), and this ransom liberated humanity from the devil and the powers of sin and death. The category of ransom has long lost its relevance to Western soteriology, having been displaced by the dialectic between satisfaction and prophetic spectacle set in motion by Anselm and Abelard. It is not at all evident, however, that the eclipse of ransom constitutes theological progress. Once the original patristic formulation is recovered from underneath centuries of distortion, the devil's ransom interpretation of the crucifixion exhibits considerable theological advantages. It would never have been so widely endorsed for so long otherwise.

This chapter considers the devil's ransom interpretation in its historical origins and essential logical structure, with special attention to Gregory of Nyssa (335–394) and his *Catechetical Oration*. Then it analyzes its implicit solution to the problem of God's will and Christ's crucifixion. It argues that this interpretation of the crucifixion falls squarely within the parameters identified earlier in this study, in the course of its *via negativa* and *via positiva*, and that the devil's ransom interpretation offers many promising resources for contemporary theology.

NEW TESTAMENT ORIGINS

The conflict between Jesus and the devil is central to the narrative of the New Testament. The devil is Christ's chief opponent, and Christ recognizes him as

[1] While it focuses on the category of ransom, this chapter does not mean to imply that patristic authors did not also use other theological categories to interpret the crucifixion, as they in fact did. Nonetheless, for reasons that cannot be discussed here, the category of ransom seems to have played a controlling role in their interpretation of the crucifixion and to have ordered their use of other metaphors, images, and concepts. Much of the secondary literature seems to agree, insofar as it implicitly treats ransom as the most important category for understanding patristic interpretations of the crucifixion.

such. The devil's antagonism toward God and his status as leader of the opposition are his most defining characteristics. Hence his principal title: Satan, the Adversary (in Greek, ὁ σατανᾶς). In the Gospels, it is the devil, not any human agent, who orchestrates Christ's crucifixion and bears the greatest responsibility. Accordingly, Jesus describes his passion as the hour of the power of darkness (Luke 22:53), thus classifying it as a demonic work. Even Judas, the iconic figure of sin and betrayal, is presented as a tool that the devil uses and then discards, and Judas' eventual suicide indicates a weakness of resolve alien to the devil's persona. Judas may set the passion in motion, but he does so only after Satan has entered him (Luke 22:3; John 13:2, 13:27).

The devil is a powerful opponent. The rule of Satan extends over the whole world (1 John 5:19).[2] Christ calls him "the ruler of this world" (John 12:31, 14:30, 16:11).[3] In the temptation in the desert, the devil offers Christ all the kingdoms of the world (Luke 4:5–8; Mat 4:8–10) because they are his to offer. Paul refers to the devil as "the god of this world" (2 Cor 4:4). Paul uses similar expressions as collective terms for all of the demons taken together. They are "the rulers of this age" (1 Cor 2:6–8); "the world rulers of this present darkness" (Eph 6:12); "rulers" (Rom 8:38; Eph 3:10, 6:12; Col 1:16, 2:15); "powers" (Rom 8:38; Eph 3:10, 6:12; Col 2:15); and "the elemental spirits of the universe" (Gal 4:3; Col 2:8, 2:20). The rule of Satan extends over the other demons. Paul calls him "the ruler of the power of the air" (Eph 2:2), a seeming reference to his headship over the other demons. Similarly, the Pharisees describe Beezelbul as "the ruler of demons" (Mark 3:22; Matt 9:34, 12:24; Luke 11:15), and Jesus implicitly endorses this designation (Matt 12:25–32; Mark 3:23–30; Luke 11:17–26). Although Jesus rejects the connection between personal sin and physical suffering (see Luke 13:2–5; John 9:2–3), a connection often made by his contemporaries, he affirms that physical suffering can in some instances have its origins in the devil, as when he speaks about a stricken woman having been bound by Satan for eighteen years (Luke 13:11–16).[4]

From the beginning, Jesus' public ministry is punctuated by encounters with demons. He prepares for his public ministry by facing the devil in the wilderness (Mark 1:12–13; Matt 4:1–11; Luke 4:1–13). In Matthew's version, when he goes out to the wilderness, he goes for the explicit purpose of

[2] My attention to the rule of Satan in the New Testament, as well as this overview of it, is indebted to Gerard Lukken. See Gerard M. Lukken, *Original Sin in the Roman Liturgy: Research into the Theology of Original Sin in the Roman Sacramentaria and the Early Baptismal Liturgy* (Leiden: Brill, 1973), 157–66.

[3] On the conflict between Jesus and the devil in John's Gospel, see Judith L. Kovacs, "'Now Shall the Ruler of This World Be Driven Out': Jesus' Death as Cosmic Battle in John 12:20–36," *Journal of Biblical Literature* 114 (1995): 227–47.

[4] Lukken, *Original Sin*, 158.

subjecting himself to the devil's temptations (Matt 4:1). During his public ministry Jesus performs numerous exorcisms, many of which are described in detail, and he often interprets his mission in terms of overcoming the devil's reign and establishing God's kingdom in its place. He compares the devil to a strong man guarding a palace and hints that he has come to despoil him (Luke 11:21–22; cf. Mark 3:27; Matt 12:29). Jesus connects the ministry of the seventy disciples to a vision of Satan falling like lightning from heaven (Luke 10:18), and he speaks about his approaching crucifixion as "the judgment of this world," when "the ruler of this world" will be cast out (John 12:31–32). In a vision to Paul, Jesus speaks of leading the Gentiles "from darkness to light and from the power of Satan to God" (Acts 26:18).

The epistles and the book of Revelation also place the conflict between Jesus and the devil at the center of their theological narratives. John writes, "The reason the Son of God appeared was to destroy the works of the devil" (1 John 3:8). The letter to the Hebrews states that the Son took flesh in order that "through death he might destroy him who has the power of death, that is, the devil" (Heb 2:14). In Galatians, Paul speaks of God sending his Son to redeem us from bondage to "the elemental spirits of the universe" (Gal 4:3–9). In Revelation, "the accuser of our brothers" is conquered by the blood of the Lamb (Rev 12:11).

Under the rule of Satan, humanity is enslaved to sin. The devil leads us to sin, and by sinning we become slaves to sin. In John, Jesus says that "every one who commits sin is a slave to sin" (John 8:34). Likewise, in Romans, Paul contrasts those who are slaves to sin with those who are slaves to righteousness and God (Rom 6:16–22). The rule of Satan is marked especially by the sin of idol worship. Baruch had linked the worship of idols to the worship of demons (Bar 4:7), and Paul develops this Jewish idea in the context of faith in Christ (1 Cor 10:19–21; Col 2:8–23).[5] Sin does not only lead to slavery; it also establishes a relationship with the devil. Sinners are children of the devil (1 John 3:8–10), and they have the devil for their father (John 8:44), because "he who commits sin is of the devil" (1 John 3:8).

The devil's centrality to the Gospel narratives explains one half of the story of how the New Testament gave rise to the devil's ransom interpretation of the crucifixion; the other half is explained by New Testament allusions to Christ giving himself as a ransom (in Greek, a *λύτρον*). In the ancient world, ransoms were associated with the practice of liberating slaves and captives by a payment of some sort. Drawing on this cultural context, the New Testament often describes Christ (or Christ's blood) as a ransom, insofar as Christ's death obtains the freedom and salvation of those who had been slaves to sin (Mark 10:45; Matt 20:28; Luke 24:21; Rom 3:24; 1 Cor 1:30; Eph 1:7; Col 1:14; Tim

[5] Lukken, *Original Sin*, 160.

2:6; Titus 2:14; Heb 9:12; 1 Pet 1:18–19; Rev 5:9). It also describes God purchasing a people for himself through the blood of his Son (Acts 20:28; cf. 1 Pet 2:9). These New Testament descriptions do not signify a transaction between two parties, but rather Christ's liberation of humanity at great personal cost; they are metaphorical, not literal. Their metaphorical character is especially evident from the fact that they never name the ransom's recipient. Christ himself (or his blood) is the ransom, and both God and Christ are the ones offering the ransom, but the ransom's recipient is never named—which is not what we would expect if these descriptions referred to an actual transaction between two parties.

While its ransom language does not imply an actual transaction, the New Testament, especially when considered in its Jewish and Hellenistic context, does suggest that Christ's ransoming of humanity involves a change of ownership. In the Old Testament, there are many references to the Lord ransoming Israel from Egyptian slavery through his servant Moses, and afterward claiming Israel as his own possession (Exod 19:5, Deut 26:18, Isa 43:21, Mal 3:17, Ps 134:4, Ps 73:2).[6] Furthermore, considered in itself, the Hebrew word for redeemer (*go'el*) has connotations of belonging and kinship; it suggests that the redeemer acts for the redeemed because they are kin. So when Isaiah prophesies that "your redeemer is the Holy One of Israel" (Isa 41:14), or when Job refers to the Lord as his redeemer (Job 19:25), overtones of belonging and kinship are implicit.[7] The New Testament draws on this Jewish cultural context in its own construction of redemption. For example, 1 Pet 2:9, which speaks of Christians as "a purchased people" (λαὸς εἰς περιποίησιν), alludes to both Exod 19:5 and Mal 3:17.[8]

The New Testament's Hellenistic context also sheds light on its ransom language. In Greek society, when buying their freedom, slaves would often make a pretense of presenting the ransom payment on behalf of a god.[9] The slave's master would receive the payment as though coming from the god, and the slave would become the god's property. Through this ritual ransoming, the slave would receive freedom and, without accruing any cultic obligations, that god's special protection. This religious custom finds echoes in Greek military conventions.[10] In times of war, Greeks would often take prisoners

[6] Stanislas Lyonnet and Léopold Sabourin, *Sin, Redemption, and Sacrifice: A Biblical and Patristic Study* (Rome: Biblical Institute Press, 1970), 110–12; Lukken, *Original Sin*, 166, esp. n14.

[7] Tryggve N. D. Mettinger, *In Search of God: The Meaning and Message of the Everlasting Names*, trans. Frederick H. Cryer (Philadelphia: Fortress Press, 1988), 162–7.

[8] Lyonnet and Sabourin, *Sin, Redemption, and Sacrifice*, 112–19.

[9] Adolf Deissmann, *Light from the Ancient East: The New Testament Illustrated by Recently Discovered Texts of the Graeco-Roman World*, trans. Lionel R. M. Strachan, Rev. ed. (London: Hodder & Stoughton, 1927), 318–30; Lyonnet and Sabourin, *Sin, Redemption, and Sacrifice*, 105–10; Lukken, *Original Sin*, 164–5.

[10] The summary of Greek customs given here derives from W. Kendrick Pritchett, *The Greek State at War*, vol. 5 (Berkeley: University of California Press, 1991), 284–8.

and hold them for ransom. The practice was standard and widespread, and it was governed by well-established conventions. Usually the ransom was paid by family members, but sometimes prisoners would be ransomed by wealthy citizens from their home city. After returning home, they were expected to repay their benefactors, either by raising the money themselves, or by submitting themselves to a period of indentured servitude. Until their debts were repaid, ransomed prisoners were held to be in a state of legal obligation. For example, according to the law code of Gortyn, if someone should be ransomed from captivity, "he shall be in the power of the one who ransomed him until he pay what is due."[11] Even prisoners ransomed by their relatives apparently incurred this legal obligation.[12] Similar conventions prevailed in Athens. According to Demosthenes, "The laws enact that a person ransomed from the enemy shall be the property of the ransomer, if he fail to pay the redemption money."[13] These laws stop short of declaring that, from the sheer fact of being ransomed, ransomed prisoners became the property of those who ransomed them. Nonetheless, they strongly suggest that the payment of a ransom was seen to establish new ties of belonging. In the Greek imagination, in both religious and profane contexts, notions of ransom were closely associated with notions of belonging.

Consequently, when Paul makes use of ransom language, it is likely that he has in mind both the Old Testament idea of the Lord liberating and taking possession of Israel, and also the Greek custom of slaves buying their freedom as though on behalf of a god. Sensitivity to this aspect of Paul's conceptual milieu sheds light on his teachings about redemption. When Paul speaks about a Christian through faith becoming simultaneously "a freedman of the Lord" and "a slave of Christ" (1 Cor 7:22), the apparent paradox is illuminated by the Old Testament understanding of redemption and the Hellenistic practice of slaves buying back their freedom under the pretense of being purchased by a god. For Paul, we are liberated from slavery by becoming the property of Christ. Just as God claims a people for himself by ransoming the Israelites from slavery in Egypt, and just as a slave is free because he is the property of a god, so, too, Christians are free because they are the property of Christ.

In his letters, Paul often connects freedom from bondage with belonging to Christ. In Galatians, Paul sees our liberation from "the elemental spirits of the universe" coming about through our adoption by God (Gal 4:3–9). In Colossians, he maintains that our liberation comes through being joined to Christ, especially by Christ's death and resurrection, and becoming part of his body

[11] *The Law Code of Gortyn*, Col. 6.50–52, in Ronald F. Willetts, *The Law Code of Gortyn* (Berlin: Walter de Gruyter, 1967), 44.

[12] Willetts, *The Law Code of Gortyn*, 69.

[13] Demosthenes, *Against Nikostratos*, 11, in Pritchett, *The Greek State at War*, 286.

(Col 2:8–20). Paul speaks about God making us alive with Christ and, through Christ's crucifixion, canceling our debts to the law (Col 2:14). He also speaks about God triumphing over the demons, seemingly because God has dispossessed the demons of those they once held in bondage, and now claimed humanity for his own (Col 2:15). Paul's language remains in the realm of metaphor; there is no indication that he means to imply any sort of legal transfer of ownership.[14] In light of his Jewish and Hellenistic context, however, Paul's understanding of ransom clearly involves something more than a generic liberation from moral and physical evil. It also involves belonging. Paul is particularly concerned with the contrast between slavery to "the elemental spirits of the universe," and the freedom obtained by being joined to Christ, especially in his passion and resurrection.[15]

The amount of attention given by the New Testament to the devil made it inevitable that early Christians would wonder about the devil's role in God's plan of salvation. Despite their brevity and ambiguity (or perhaps because of their brevity and ambiguity), certain New Testament passages encouraged this sort of speculation. Those passages that describe humanity as being ransomed by the blood of Christ, or liberated from a state of diabolic slavery, seem to have been particularly influential. Gradually, early Christian speculation began to coalesce into the idea that Christ's crucifixion had ransomed us from the devil.

THE DEVIL'S RANSOM IN THE EARLY CHURCH

In the early Church, the devil's ransom interpretation of Christ's crucifixion takes many forms.[16] It is not a single, monolithic interpretation, but rather a

[14] Lyonnet and Sabourin, *Sin, Redemption, and Sacrifice*, 79–119; Lukken, *Original Sin*, 161–6.

[15] The theological centrality of ransom had a very practical implication in early Christianity: it encouraged Christians to work for the liberation of prisoners. Early Christian literature, building on a well-established Jewish tradition, exhorted Christians to care for the imprisoned, especially those who had been imprisoned for their faith. Some Christians sacrificed their own freedom to win the release of captives. See Carolyn Osiek, "The Ransom of Captives: Evolution of a Tradition," *Harvard Theological Review* 74 (1981): 365–86.

[16] For historical studies of the devil's ransom in the early Church, see Adolf Harnack, *History of Dogma*, trans. James Millar, vol. 3 (London: Williams and Norgate, 1897), 305–10; Jean Rivière, *The Doctrine of the Atonement: A Historical Essay*, trans. Luigi Cappadelta, vol. 2 (London: Kegan Paul, Trench, Trübner, 1909); Hastings Rashdall, *The Idea of Atonement in Christian Theology* (London: MacMillan, 1919); Aulén, *Christus Victor*, 16–60; H. E. W. Turner, *The Patristic Doctrine of Redemption: A Study of the Development of Doctrine during the First Five Centuries* (London: A. R. Mowbray, 1952), 53–61; Louis Richard, *The Mystery of the Redemption*, trans. Joseph Horn (Dublin: Cahill, 1965), 149–56; Frederick William Dillistone,

family of interpretations. Nonetheless, despite the wide range of variations, all versions of the devil's ransom interpretation share certain common features. Christ allows the powers of evil to crucify him, but their malice backfires in this supreme act of overreaching, so that, through his acceptance of death, Christ ends up conquering the devil and liberating humanity from sin and death. The ransom, then, consists in Jesus handing himself over to be crucified. Some authors speak of God offering this ransom to the devil as the price of humanity's salvation. Others do not describe the crucifixion as a transaction in any sense, but simply as the way in which Christ ransoms humanity from a condition of suffering and slavery. Still others connect the devil's ransom to a divine deception in which God prevents the devil from realizing that Jesus is God, thus tricking the devil into attacking Jesus and thereby undermining his own interests.

The devil's ransom interpretation takes shape as the early Church works to clarify the logic behind the New Testament narrative. It draws inspiration especially from those scripture passages that speak of Christ giving his life as a ransom, or that emphasize the devil's opposition to God and Christ. The ecclesial experience of baptism, and especially infant baptism, also plays a significant role in the development of the devil's ransom interpretation. In the early Church, baptism liturgies are linked, not only to the forgiveness of sins, but also to the exorcism of demonic power. Baptism is seen as releasing, and thus ransoming, the baptized from bondage to the devil—a view that naturally fosters the devil's ransom interpretation. By the early third century, baptisms typically took place only after a separate exorcism ritual; some early patristic texts also attribute an exorcizing power to the baptisms themselves.[17] The practice of infant baptism had a special role in reinforcing this theology

The Christian Understanding of Atonement (Philadelphia: Westminster Press, 1968), 93–8; Jaroslav Pelikan, *The Emergence of the Catholic Tradition (100–600)*, 5 vols., vol. 1 (Chicago: University of Chicago Press, 1971), 148–52; J. N. D. Kelly, *Early Christian Doctrines*, 5th ed. (London: Adam & Charles Black, 1977), 163–88, 375–400, passim; Michael Slusser, "Primitive Christian Soteriological Themes," *Theological Studies* 44 (1983): 558–60; Neil Forsyth, *The Old Enemy: Satan and the Combat Myth* (Princeton: Princeton Univesity Press, 1987), 334–42, 363–7; Basil Studer, *Trinty and Incarnation: The Faith of the Early Church* (Edinburgh: T & T Clark, 1993), 48–50; C. W. Marx, *The Devil's Rights and the Redemption in the Literature of Medieval England* (Cambridge: D. S. Brewer, 1995), 7–46; Eugene Teselle, "The Cross as Ransom," *Journal of Early Christian Studies* 4 (1996): 147–70; Nicholas Constas, "The Last Temptation of Satan: Divine Deception in Greek Patristic Interpretations of the Passion Narrative," *Harvard Theological Review* 97 (2004): 139–63; Brian Daley, "'He Himself is Our Peace' (Eph 2:14): Early Christian Views of Redemption in Christ" in *The Redemption: An Interdisciplinary Symposium on Christ as Redeemer*, ed. Stephen T. Davis, Daniel Jendall, and Gerald O'Collins (Oxford: Oxford University Press, 2004), 158–65; Anderson, *Sin: A History*, 111–32.

For a historical study of Augustine that goes into great detail about the role of the devil in his theology of redemption, see Jean Rivière, *Le dogme de la rédemption chez Saint Augustin* (Paris: J. Gabalda, 1933).

[17] Lukken, *Original Sin*, 185–7.

of baptism.[18] Early Christians struggled to explain the established practice of infant baptism.[19] If baptism forgave sins, what was the point of baptizing infants who could not have committed any personal sins? In wrestling with this question, patristic authors increasingly suggest that baptism frees infants from the power of the devil.[20] This understanding of infant baptism naturally influenced their views on the devil's influence over humanity more generally, and thereby helped pave the way for the devil's ransom interpretation.

Important elements of the devil's ransom interpretation can be found very early in the writings of patristic authors. In the early second century, for example, Ignatius of Antioch writes that the devil was ignorant of Christ's divinity at the time of his crucifixion.[21] Fuller expositions come slightly later. From some brief passages of his *Adversus haereses* (c. 180–199),[22] Irenaeus is usually cited as the earliest writer to propose the devil's ransom interpretation in a coherent form. Origen and Tertullian take it up in the third century; it also appears in Gregory Thaumaturgus.[23] In the fourth century it is employed by numerous authors, including Eusebius of Caesarea, Basil, Gregory of Nyssa, Cyril of Jerusalem, John Chrysostom, Jerome, Ambrose, and Augustine.

Scholarship on the devil's ransom interpretation has focused on theological writings, but the acts of martyrs also witness to its early and widespread influence.[24] Early Christians saw martyrs as privileged imitators of Jesus, even as other Christs, whose suffering conformed them to Christ in a special

[18] Controversy surrounds the historical origins of infant baptism, and not the least because Christians remain divided about its theological and scriptural legitimacy. Nonetheless, it is hard to dispute that infant baptism had become a widespread practice by the beginning of the third century, and there are strong grounds for thinking that its origins are apostolic. Notable among them is this passage from Origen: "It has to be believed, therefore, that concerning this David also said what we recorded above, 'in sins my mother conceived me.' For according to the historical narrative no sin of his mother is declared. It is on this account as well that the Church has received the tradition from the apostles to give baptism even to little children." See his *Commentary on Romans*, 5.9.11, in Origen, *Commentary on Romans*, trans. Thomas B. Scheck (Washington, DC: The Catholic University of America Press, 2001), Vol. 1, 367.

[19] For example, Origen notes that his fellow Christians often asked why infants were baptized. See his *Homilies on Luke*, 14.5.

[20] Lukken, *Original Sin*, 187–200. Eventually, infant baptism came to be explained as a remedy for the corrupting effects of Adam's sin, and this emphasis on the liberating effects of baptism was displaced. Yet it never disappeared, and it remains an essential part of baptism liturgies in both Eastern and Western Christianity.

[21] Ignatius of Antioch, *Letter to the Ephesians*, 19.

[22] Irenaeus, *Adversus haereses*, 3.18.7, 5.1.1, 5.21.1–3.

[23] Origen, *Homilies on Joshua*, 8.3; *Commentary on Romans*, 2.13.29, 3.7.14, 4.11.4, 5.3.7, 5.10.9–12; *Commentary on Matthew*, 8.8, 12.28, 13.8–9, 16.8; *Homilies on Exodus*, 6.9; *Homilies on Luke*, 23; *Exhortation to Martyrdom*, 12; *Contra Ceslum*, 1.31, 7.17; *Commentary on John*, 6.35, 37; 8.59; 28.19; Tertullian, *De fuga in persecutione* 2, 12; *De carne Christi* 17; *De idololatria*, 5; Gregory Thaumaturgus, *Homily on All Saints*.

[24] Candida R. Moss, *The Other Christs: Imitating Jesus in Ancient Christian Ideologies of Martyrdom* (New York: Oxford University Press, 2010), 87–102.

way.[25] Consequently, when describing the acts of martyrs, they often present a martyr's death as mirroring Christ's death, and, strikingly, some draw on the devil's ransom interpretation in their narration.[26] For example, *The Letter of the Churches of Lyons and Vienne*, one of the earliest martyrdom accounts, describes the devil swallowing the martyrs, only to vomit them later—an image often used to describe Christ's death and resurrection in the devil's ransom interpretation.[27] Since the letter dates from the third century, and possibly even the late second century, early Christians must have been using this sort of imagery to describe Christ's crucifixion from very early on.[28]

From its organic connection to the New Testament narrative and Christian baptismal practice, and from its widespread attestation in both East and West, the devil's ransom interpretation seems to have developed spontaneously, rather than in deference to any particular theologian, or even any particular cluster of theologians. Even so, it remains on the sidelines of Christological and soteriological reflection. Patristic authors often describe Christ's work of salvation as a kind of ransom or liberation, but they do not give much attention to the idea of Christ ransoming humanity specifically from the devil. In the early Church, there are no treatises on the devil's ransom and few sustained discussions of it. There are only scattered references to it in works of scriptural exegesis or treatises on other topics. It is always considered in a larger context, and it always plays a limited role. Early Christians rarely consider the salvific efficacy of the crucifixion in isolation from the resurrection and the sacramental life of the Church, and so the precise mechanics of how the cross contributes to the economy of salvation also receives minimal attention.

The Devil's Rights

In some versions of the devil's ransom, the devil has legal rights over humanity, acquired through the sin of Adam. Rather than reclaiming us by the sheer exercise of his power, God hands over his Son, the New Adam, to be crucified. By orchestrating Christ's crucifixion, however, the devil forfeits his rights over humanity, and God reclaims us as his own.

Patristic authors give different explanations for how the devil comes to forfeit his rights. Although their explanations tend to be cursory, and rarely delve into the matter with any depth or systematic tenacity, two explanations seem especially prominent. One holds that the devil demands Christ in exchange for his rights, as the price of our redemption. After

[25] Moss, *The Other Christs*. [26] Moss, *The Other Christs*, 87–102.
[27] The letter is preserved by Eusebius in his *Ecclesiastical History*, 5.1–2.
[28] Moss, *The Other Christs*, 93–4.

having Christ crucified, though, he cannot hold him in death and so loses Christ along with the rest of humanity.[29] The other explanation, which seems more common, accounts for how the devil loses his rights without referring to a prior agreement between God and the devil.[30] In this explanation, since Christ is sinless, and thus outside the devil's jurisdiction, the devil oversteps his authority when he orchestrates Christ's crucifixion. As a result, he loses his legal rights over humanity and must surrender us back to God. But whatever the precise forensic explanation, the devil loses his jurisdiction over humanity and God reclaims us once again as his own. In choosing to redeem us in this way, proponents of this interpretation argue, God puts his justice and wisdom, and not just his power, on triumphant display.

The idea of the devil having rights seems to develop, in large part, from patristic reflection on a suggestive passage in Colossians. In this passage, Paul states that God nailed to the cross "our *chirographum*" (ἡμῶν χειρόγραφον), that is, the record of our debts to the law, and, in doing so, God triumphed over the rulers of this world (Col 2:14–15).[31] In their scripture commentaries and theological works, patristic authors maintain that this *chirographum* is a record of our sins, drawn up either by God or by Satan, which Satan uses to claim dominion over us.[32] As a result, many authors infer from this passage that the devil acquired rights over humanity on account of our sins. The idea of the *chirographum* takes on a life of its own and patristic authors make use of it in a variety of ways. For example, Origen explains that the devil purchases us with sin, the coin proceeding from his treasury and bearing his image and inscription (cf. Matt 22:20). The devil can reclaim Christians with this coin, "and again write for them documents of slavery and bond sureties of sin (*chirographa*) and mingle those whom he made his slaves for the price of sin

[29] For an example of this explanation, see Origen, *Commentary on Matthew*, 16.8. Some variations of this explanation talk about the devil receiving Christ as a ransom, without saying what happens afterward. For example, in his *Commentary on Romans*, 2.13.29, Origen talks about the devil demanding the blood of Christ as the price of our redemption, but does not say what happens after he receives it. Likewise, in his *Homily on Psalm 48*, 3–4, Basil talks about God persuading the devil to accept Christ as a ransom for our freedom, but also neglects to discuss what happens afterward.

[30] For an example of this explanation, see Augustine, *De Trinitate*, 4.17–18, 13.16–23.

[31] For discussions of the precise meaning of *chirographum*, Deissmann, *Light from the Ancient East*, 330–4; Eugene Best, *An Historical Study of the Exegesis of Colossians 2:14* (Rome: Pontificia Universitas Gregorian, 1956); Markus Barth and Helmut Blanke, *Colossians: A New Translation with Introduction and Commentary* (New York: Doubleday, 1994), 369–72; Margaret Y. MacDonald, *Colossians and Ephesians*, vol. 17 (Collegeville: Liturgical Press, 2000), 102–3; Anderson, *Sin: A History*, 113–21. Gary Anderson comments, "This text [Col 2:14] was central to early Christianity and may be the most cited New Testament passage on the subject of the atonement" (114).

[32] Lukken, *Original Sin*, 176–81. For a sampling of patristic commentary on the *chirographum*, see Peter Gorday, ed. *Colossians, 1–2 Thessalonians, 1–2 Timothy, Titus, Philemon*, vol. 9 (Chicago: Fitzroy Dearborn, 2000), 33–5.

with the servants of God."[33] Other patristic authors make use of the idea of the *chirographum* in similar ways. Eucherius of Lyons (d. 449) describes it as a document written by sinners "with the hand of iniquity," that is, their sins.[34] Leo the Great speaks of a *chirographum* by which we were sold to Satan and made his captives.[35]

Speculation about the devil's rights also stems from patristic sensitivity to questions of divine justice, and especially to the question of how Christ's crucifixion manifests God's justice. Many patristic authors argue that God chose to redeem us through Christ's crucifixion because it better manifested his justice. Augustine, for example, argues that God wanted to overcome the devil through his justice, not his power.[36] God chose the cross as the means to defeat the devil because it saved humanity without relying on his omnipotence, and thus manifested his justice as well as his power. Leo the Great writes that since the devil persuaded Adam to sin of his own free will, without forcing him, sin had to be destroyed in the same way, "so that the norm of justice did not prevent the gift of grace."[37] In a similar vein, Irenaeus talks about how God overcame the devil by relying on "persuasion" (*suadela*), rather than force (*vis*), "so that justice should not be violated, nor God's earlier handiwork utterly ruined."[38] Like other patristic authors, Irenaeus also draws attention to how God reverses the devil's injustice. Christ's obedience reverses Adam's disobedience, and by resisting the devil's temptation, he undoes Adam's capitulation.[39] Mary's obedience reverses Eve's disobedience, and Christ dying on a tree reverses Adam sinning by eating the fruit of a tree.[40] According to Irenaeus, Christ even dies on the same day of the week when Adam ate the forbidden fruit and became subject to death.[41]

This line of reasoning about God's justice and Christ's crucifixion naturally fosters interest in the devil's rights. Unsurprisingly, in the writings of many patristic authors, their discussion of God's justice is inseparable from their discussion of the devil's rights. The one flows naturally into the other. Nonetheless it should be noted that the concept of justice found in these discussions is richer and more holistic than legal justice; it is more akin to poetic justice. It is striking how often patristic authors slip into poetry in their descriptions of how the crucifixion brought about the devil's defeat. For example, Origen writes that "visibly Christ is crucified in the flesh, but invisibly, the devil is fixed to the cross, along with his principalities and powers."[42] Origen's

[33] Origen, *Homilies on Exodus*, 6.9, in Origen, *Homilies on Genesis and Exodus*, trans. Ronald E. Heine (Washington, DC: The Catholic University of America Press, 1982), 296.

[34] Eucherius, *Formulae spiritalis intellegentiae*, 9.

[35] Leo the Great, *Sermons*, 61.4.

[36] Augustine, *De Trinitate*, 13.17.

[37] Leo the Great, *Sermons*, 28.3.

[38] Irenaeus, *Adversus haereses*, 5.1.1.

[39] Irenaeus, *Adversus haereses*, 3.18.1, 5.21.2.

[40] Irenaeus, *Adversus haereses*, 5.19.1.

[41] Irenaeus, *Adversus haereses*, 5.23.2.

[42] Origen, *Homilies on Joshua*, 8.3.

wordplay expresses contemplative satisfaction at the poetic justice of the devil being hoisted by his own petard, crucified by his crucifixion of Christ.

This broad overview of the devil's rights allows us to consider a much more complex and difficult question. In what sense, exactly, do patristic authors mean to attribute rights to the devil? That is, do the devil's rights have any ontological or legal status, or are they simply a metaphor for something else? Many scholars assume that most patristic authors thought that, up until Christ's crucifixion, the devil had legally binding rights of ownership over humanity, which even God had to respect.[43] It is not at all clear, however, that they actually did think so.[44] First, no patristic author ever states explicitly that these rights have true legal status, and patristic comments about the devil's rights are too brief and too vague to draw any such conclusion from their writings. The devil's rights appear only rarely in patristic literature, and when the topic comes up, patristic authors spend little time on them. Typically, they mention them in the course of treating some other subject, and after a brief

[43] Harnack, *History of Dogma*, 307; Rivière, *The Doctrine of the Atonement*, 111–35; Rashdall, *The Idea of Atonement*, 364–5; J. A. MacCulloch, *The Harrowing of Hell: A Comparative Study of Early Christian Doctrine* (Edinburgh: T & T Clark, 1930), 205–6; Marx, *The Devil's Rights*, 13–15; Gerald O'Collins, *Christology: A Biblical, Historical, and Systematic Study of Jesus* (Oxford: Oxford University Press, 1995), 198–9.

[44] Gustaf Aulén was the first to offer a significant challenge to the conventional reading of the devil's rights. In *Christus Victor*, Aulén acknowledges that patristic authors often attribute rights to the devil, but he argues that their underlying soteriology should not be characterized as legalistic, and that "there is no intention of comprehending the Divine action within a legal scheme" (47–55).

But although Aulén unequivocally repudiates the legalistic interpretation of earlier scholars, he leaves the positive content of his own interpretation ambiguous. For example, he opposes Gregory of Nyssa with Gregory of Nazianzus, on the grounds that Nyssa attributes rights to the devil while Nazianzus rejects the idea of God paying an actual ransom the devil (48–50). By this rhetorical opposition, Aulén implies that Gregory of Nyssa holds for a more literal notion of the devil's ransom than Gregory of Nazianzus. Elsewhere, he softens this opposition. He notes again and again that the rights language should be read, not in the service of rationalistic theories, but as graphic illustrations of God's triumph over the powers of evil and death. He also argues that Gregory of Nazianzus' repudiation of literalistic understandings of the devil's ransom is hardly noteworthy, since, in his opinion, no patristic author should be read as endorsing such a crude idea (55). Nonetheless, despite this softening, the rhetorical opposition between Nyssa and Nazianzus gives the impression that he thinks that the notions of *some* patristic authors require purification. He heightens this impression by critiquing the way patristic authors theologize about God deceiving the devil (55).

The brevity and ambiguity of Aulén's discussion of the devil's rights (and the devil's ransom more generally) helps to explain a curious feature of the reception of *Christus Victor*. On the one hand, Aulén succeeded in generating renewed appreciation for patristic approaches to the crucifixion; on the other hand, he was not able to overturn conventional reconstructions of the devil's ransom. Everywhere, his book is rightly regarded as a milestone in the recovery of patristic soteriology, and yet, even among those sympathetic to his argument, caricature understandings of the devil's ransom continue to persist. Because Aulén never provides a close textual analysis of what patristic authors mean when they talk about the devil having rights, or of how the idea functions in their theology, it is difficult for his readers to see just how radically conventional interpretations misread the sources.

comment they return to their primary interest. So we have little to evaluate. Moreover, their comments about the devil's rights—usually found in biblical commentaries or homilies, or in the course of discussing some aspect of the Gospel narratives—make great use of narrative and metaphor, and thus are difficult to translate into doctrinal statements. Consequently, due to their ambiguity, brevity, and context, patristic comments about the devil's rights cannot be taken as attributing to them any true status, whether ontological or legal. In fact, the opposite conclusion seems warranted.

Second, patristic authors sometimes say things that qualify the status of the devil's rights. For example, in his *Commentary on Romans*, Origen explains that, when a soul sins, it hands over to death "something like the *chirographa* of its immorality" (*velut chirographa immortalitatis suae*).[45] By modifying *chirographa* with *velut*, Origen indicates that he does not want to be taken literally when he talks death acquiring *chirographa*. Although Origen is talking about death, not the devil, patristic authors often associate death with the devil. It is reasonable to infer, therefore, that Origen should also not be taken literally when he talks about the devil acquiring *chirographa* (which, as mentioned above, he does elsewhere).[46]

In *De Trinitate*, which probably gives the devil's rights more sustained attention than any other theological treatise in the patristic period, Augustine also makes some important qualifications about the status of the devil's rights.[47] In one passage in Book 4, he twice indicates that the devil's rights are not rights in the fullest sense. He writes:

> So by a death of the flesh the devil lost man, who had yielded to his seduction, and whom he had thus as it were (*tanquam*) acquired full property rights over.... Yet in [Christ's] being slain in his innocence by the wicked one, who was acting against us as it were (*velut*) with just rights, he won the case against him with the justest of all rights...[48]

In this passage, Augustine twice qualifies the status of the devil's rights, but he does not explain why they are not rights in the fullest sense. His use of two different modifiers (*tamquam* and *velut*) may suggest that he is straining to articulate something that he has not fully worked out in his own mind. But whatever exactly he means, it is clear he thinks that they fall short of being rights in the fullest sense. He underscores this point by contrasting the devil's pseudo-rights with the rights by which Christ triumphs over the devil, rights

[45] Origen, *Commentary on Romans*, 5.3.3 (PG 14:1026C). In his English translation, Thomas Scheck renders this difficult passage as follows: "What seems to be made known in this is that since a soul created by God is itself free, it leads itself into slavery by means of transgression and hands over to death, so to speak, the IOU of its own immortality which it had received from its own Creator" (Vol. 1, 336).

[46] See Origen, *Homilies on Exodus*, 6.9.

[47] *De Trinitate*, 4.17–18, 13.16–23.

[48] Augustine, *De Trinitate*, 4.17, 165.

that Augustine describes, without any sort of qualification, as "the justest of all rights."

Later in *De Trinitate*, in Book 13, Augustine again qualifies the status of the devil's rights. First, rather than qualifying the devil's rights directly, he qualifies the divine justice by which humanity was handed over to the devil. He writes:

> By a kind of divine justice (*quadam justitia Dei*) the human race was handed over to the jurisdiction (*potestatem*) of the devil for the sin of the first man, which passes by origin to all who are born of the intercourse of the two sexes, and involves all the descendants of the first parents in its debt.[49]

The divine justice operative in granting the devil power over humanity is not justice without qualification; it is justice only by analogy. With this nuance, Augustine likewise implies that the devil's rights over humanity are not a typical sort of rights; they are rights only by analogy. Shortly after this passage, Augustine describes in more detail God's interactions with the devil. He explains that God conquered the devil by Christ's crucifixion, not because he could not have conquered the devil by sheer power, but in order to give a good example to humanity. In the course of making his argument, he explicitly denies that God ever lost humanity from his jurisdiction:

> Nor did he lose man from the jurisdiction (*potestatis*) of his own law when he let him be under the devil's jurisdiction (*potestate*), because not even the devil is cut off from the jurisdiction (*potestate*) of the Almighty or from his goodness either for that matter.[50]

For Augustine, the devil never had any absolute rights over humanity. God could have chosen "countless other ways" to set us free.[51] He was under no obligation to hand his Son over to the devil. Nonetheless, Augustine finds it useful to talk about the devil having rights, as a way to explain how Christ's crucifixion manifests God's justice.

Augustine's insistence about the qualified status of the devil's rights becomes all the more striking when we consider the amount of time elapsed between the writing of Book 4 and Book 13 of *De Trinitate*.[52] As many as sixteen years may separate the two books, yet he makes a point of qualifying the status of the devil rights in each of them, and his emphasis on their qualified status only increases. Book 13 is much more forceful and articulate than Book 4. Augustine's consistency suggests that he had a settled intuition

[49] Augustine, *De Trinitate*, 13.16, 355. Translation slightly modified.

[50] Augustine, *De Trinitate*, 13.16, 356.

[51] Augustine, *De Trinitate*, 13.21, 359–60.

[52] For the dating of the various parts of the *De Trinitate*, see Lewis Ayres, *Augustine and the Trinity* (Cambridge: Cambridge University Press, 2010), 118–20. According to Ayres, Book 4 was written between 411 and 414, and Book 13 was written between 419 and 427.

on this point of doctrine, and his increasing precision over time suggests that, the more he thought about the matter, the more he wanted to make sure that the devil's rights were not mistaken as having any sort of absolute jurisdiction, or any binding authority over God. Augustine's other comments about the devil's rights should be read in the context of these qualifications. Otherwise, they are easy to misinterpret. For example, he writes:

> The devil was holding on to our sins, and using them to keep us deservedly fixed in death. He who had none of his own discharged them, and was undeservedly led away by the other to death. Such was the value of that blood, that he who killed Christ even with a momentary death he did not owe would no longer have the right to hold anyone who had put on Christ in an eternal death he did owe.[53]

When read out of context, this passage can seem to imply that the devil has rights that bind even God. In the light of his earlier qualifications, however, it is clear that Augustine's intentions are otherwise. He is using legal imagery to express the fittingness of the means God chose to redeem us.[54]

Perhaps following the example of Augustine, Gregory the Great also qualifies the legal status of the devil's jurisdiction over humanity. He writes, "When the devil sought the death of Christ unjustly, he lost us whom he was holding quasi-justly [*quasi juste*]."[55] Gregory does not discuss the precise ontological status of the devil's rights, but by qualifying *juste* with *quasi*, he shows awareness that his words are susceptible to misunderstanding. His word choice also suggests that, like Augustine, he does not think that the devil's rights carry any true legal authority; they are rights only by analogy.

These sorts of nuances are easy to miss, because patristic and medieval understandings of the devils' rights are often conflated. Western scholars tend to read patristic texts through the lens of medieval interpretation, and medieval theologians have a more reified notion of the devil's rights than their patristic predecessors. Medieval theologians see themselves in seamless continuity with the patristic theological tradition, but they approach the question of the devil's rights differently. While the medieval approach cannot be identified with any single interpretation—medieval theology is far too fluid and pluralistic—a new literalistic tendency seems to emerge during the Middle Ages. Metaphorical language becomes reified, at least to some degree, and medieval theologians start to read patristic texts as though the devil's rights have ontological substance. It is not clear exactly when this tendency first

53 Augustine, *De Trinitate*, 13.21, 360.

54 For a study of redemption in Augustine that complements the account given here, see J. Patout Burns, "How Christ Saves: Augustine's Multiple Explanations," in *Tradition and the Rule of Faith in the Early Church*, ed. Ronnie. J. Rombs and Alexander Y. Hwang (Washington, DC: The Catholic University of America Press, 2010), 193–210.

55 Gregory the Great, *Moralia in Job*, 33.7.14.

emerged, but it can be no later than Anselm, since his hostile reconstruction of the devil's ransom interpretation in *Cur Deus homo* and his *Meditation on Human Redemption* already exhibits this literalistic reading of the devil's rights. By the twelfth century, the very idea of interpreting the devil's rights metaphorically seems to have become less accessible to both proponents and detractors of the devil's ransom interpretation of the crucifixion. The terminology is the same, but the words have started to mean something different.

How did this shift in meaning come about? By the time of Anselm, two unrelated theological trends had created an atmosphere favorable to a literalistic reading of the devil's rights. First, it is well established that, sometime early in the second millennium, medieval culture and theology started to focus on the salvific effects of the crucifixion in isolation from the salvific effects of the resurrection. With this new focus on the crucifixion, theologians would have naturally started paying more attention to patristic remarks about the devil's rights, perhaps taking them more seriously than their authors ever had. This trend could easily have encouraged a more literalistic reading of the devil's rights. Second, in the eleventh century, legal theory was undergoing tremendous renewal.[56] This renewal could also have contributed to a metaphysical hardening of the devil's rights. Without realizing it, theologians could have started reading patristic texts in a way that assigned the devil's rights more metaphysical weight than their authors had intended.

Another possibility is that, whatever the influence of these two trends, the literalistic reading of the devil's rights gained currency only after Anselm's *Cur Deus homo*. Anselm's hostile reconstruction of the devil's ransom interpretation is almost universally assumed to represent accurately the views of his theological opponents.[57] In polemical contests, however, no one should be presumed to represent an opposing position accurately. Granted, we have grounds to trust Anselm's reconstruction and think that it accurately reflects a reifying tendency among his contemporaries. We know that the devil's rights featured prominently in the soteriological reflection of many theologians of this period, including Gilbert Crispin, Anselm's friend, and another Anselm, the master of the cathedral school of Laon.[58] Their interpretations may have given Anselm cause for concern and prompted his critique.

[56] The period 1000–1140 is an age of reform in canon law, and many commentaries on canon law are written during this period. Then Gratian's writes his *Decretum* around 1140, and the period which follows immediately afterward (1140–1234) is sometimes called the classical period of canon law. See Constant van de Wiel, *History of Canon Law* (Louvain: Peeters, 1991); Wilfried Hartmann and Kenneth Pennington, eds., *The History of Medieval Canon Law in the Classical Period, 1140–1234: From Gratian to the Decretals of Pope Gregory IX* (Washington, DC: The Catholic University of America Press, 2008).

[57] The secondary literature on *Cur Deus homo* shows a remarkable lack of interest in whether Anselm accurately depicts what his theological opponents thought about the devil's rights. The question is never raised; it is simply assumed that he does.

[58] Southern, *Saint Anselm*, 197–211; Marx, *The Devil's Rights*, 17–46.

Nevertheless, it is also possible that Anselm does not accurately depict what his theological opponents thought, or that he accurately depicts only what some of them thought. Anselm may not even have any particular theologians in mind; he may be ruling out possible misconceptions about the devil's rights as a kind of theological exercise.[59] Given that it took some time before his argument succeeded in discrediting the notion of the devil's rights, we have good reason to think that the views of its advocates were more sophisticated than Anselm's reconstruction would suggest. The schools of theology initially tended to ignore *Cur Deus homo*—only Abelard and his disciples took it seriously—and even those who appreciated his argument, mostly monks, tended to retain elements of the devil's ransom interpretation.[60] This lack of traction suggests that Anselm's theological opponents (assuming he had any) did not think he had accurately described their views and therefore saw his criticisms as falling short. Although Anselm's hostile reconstruction of the devil's rights eventually became normative, his triumph may not follow any decisive intellectual battle but rather a war of attrition. Anselm was one of the theological superstars of the Middle Ages. Copies of *Cur Deus homo* spread quickly throughout Europe; manuscripts were distributed even before he had finished the final version.[61] After a few generations, the devil's ransom interpretation might well have been better known from Anselm's hostile reconstruction than the writings of its proponents, and as time went on, there would have been fewer and fewer people capable of offering a sophisticated defense.

The writings of Bernard of Clairvaux provide some evidence in favor of this historical thesis. After reading Abelard's *Commentary on Romans*, Bernard dedicated himself to refuting his theories. In a letter he wrote to the pope denouncing Abelard's theological errors, he accuses Abelard of denying that Christ took flesh to free us from the yoke of the devil.[62] In laying out his own position, though, Bernard stops short of talking about the devil's rights; he talks instead about the devil's power and the justice of God's plan of salvation.[63] In this way, he evades the force of Abelard's objections to the devil's ransom interpretation, which focus especially on the idea of the devil having rights over humanity. Bernard's response to Abelard demonstrates a resilience that one might not have expected from Anselm's and Abelard's descriptions of the devil's ransom interpretation. Perhaps Bernard developed his position in

[59] Schmitt's critical edition identifies numerous patristic sources for Book I.6–7 of *Cur Deus homo*. See Anselm, *Opera Omnia*, II.53–59. It is an open question whether Anselm means to ascribe the views he rejects to weighty authorities such as Ambrose, Augustine, and Leo the Great.

[60] Southern, *Saint Anselm*, 210.

[61] Anselm, *CDH*, pref.

[62] See Bernard of Clairvaux, *Epistula de erroribus Petri Abaelardi*, Letter 190, CCCM 8:39.6.

[63] Jean Rivière, *Le dogme de la rédemption au dèbut du moyen-age* (Paris: J. Vrin, 1934), 206–13.

the course of responding to Abelard; perhaps this sort of position was already being articulated in some circles. Either way, Bernard's silence about the devil's rights does not represent a substantive concession to the critique of Anselm and Abelard. Bernard does not show any discomfort with the idea of assigning the devil an important role in the drama of salvation, and his theology of redemption incorporates many other elements of the devil's ransom interpretation. Rather than a substantive concession, his avoidance of rights language seems more like an implicit acknowledgement that rights language, when applied to the devil, had become reified and theologically toxic.

God's Deception of the Devil

In their accounts of the devil's ransom, many patristic authors maintain that God overcomes the devil by deception.[64] God lures the devil to crucify Jesus, and then uses the devil's own actions to defeat him. In some narratives, the devil does not recognize Christ's true identity, either because God disguises Christ's divinity from the devil, or because it is beyond the devil's power to recognize who Christ truly is. In other narratives, the devil knows Christ's true identity, but he does not realize how the crucifixion will undermine his own interests. In all narratives, God provokes the devil deliberately. The devil is lured into attacking Christ and in doing so falls into a trap.

The theme of deception is fueled by speculation on a passage from First Corinthians. In this passage, Paul implies that the devil did not understand the divine plan of salvation when he crucified Christ. He writes:

> Yet among the mature we do impart wisdom, although it is not a wisdom of this age or of the rulers of this age, who are doomed to pass away. But we impart a secret and hidden wisdom of God, which God decreed before the ages for our glorification. None of the rulers of this age understood this; for if they had, they would not have crucified the Lord of glory. (1 Cor 2:6–8)

Who are "the rulers of this age"? It is not clear. Paul could be talking about demons, or the human rulers who put Christ to death, or both.[65] Nonetheless, based on comparison with parallel Pauline passages, "the rulers of this age"

[64] For an excellent overview of patristic conjecture about God's deception of the devil, see Constas, "The Last Temptation of Satan." See also Rivière, *The Doctrine of the Atonement*, 158–93; MacCulloch, *The Harrowing of Hell*, 199–216; Aulén, *Christus Victor*, 47–55; Darby Kathleen Ray, *Deceiving the Devil: Atonement, Abuse, and Ransom* (Cleveland, OH: Pilgrim Press, 1998), 118–25.

[65] Modern scholarship is divided about the identity of "the rulers of this age," and each possibility is favored by many scholars. For a summary of how different scholars come down on this question, see Joseph A. Fitzmyer, *First Corinthians: A New Translation with Introduction and Commentary* (New York: Yale University Press, 2008), 175–6.

seem to be demons, or at least to include demons among their number. In any case, this passage led many patristic authors to conclude that the devil, one of the "rulers of this age," did not recognize Christ's divine identity, or at least did not know that Christ's crucifixion would lead to God's victory (since the passage does not speak of "the rulers of this age" being ignorant of Christ's divinity, only of God's "secret and hidden wisdom").[66]

The motif of the devil's ignorance extends beyond the crucifixion. For example, in one of the earliest references to the devil's ignorance, Ignatius of Antioch writes:

> The Prince of this world was in ignorance of the virginity of Mary and her childbearing and also of the death of the Lord—three mysteries loudly proclaimed to the world, though accomplished in the stillness of God![67]

Other patristic authors make similar claims. Commenting on Luke's Gospel, Ambrose speaks of Mary and Joseph concealing the miraculous nature of Christ's birth in order to keep his true identity from the devil.[68] Origen, Ambrose, and Leo the Great each maintain that the devil tempts Christ to see whether or not he is divine, because he does not know.[69] Nonetheless, while patristic authors make claims about the devil being ignorant of Christ's divinity at many different moments in the economy of salvation, those who make such claims focus especially on the devil's ignorance at the time of Christ's crucifixion.

Although God's deception of the devil often features a disguise of some sort, more essential to patristic narratives of the divine deception is the idea of a stratagem that tricks the devil into bringing about his own downfall. First, since patristic authors would have been well aware that the demons identify Jesus as the Holy One of God in Mark 1:24 and Luke 4:34, we might question whether any of them mean it literally when they talk about the devil being ignorant of Christ's true identity, or at least without significance qualification. Second, some patristic authors explicitly affirm that God led the devil into a trap without concealing Christ's divinity.[70] For example, Gregory the Great says that the devil knew Christ's identity, but did not realize that

[66] Patristic authors do not universally interpret "the rulers of this age" as demons. For example, see Ambrose, *Commentary on Luke*, 2.3.

[67] Ignatius of Antioch, *Letter to the Ephesians*, 19, in Clement of Rome and Ignatius of Antioch, *The Epistles of St. Clement of Rome and St. Ignatius of Antioch*, trans. James A. Kleist (New York: Paulist Press, 1946), 67.

[68] Ambrose, *Commentary on Luke*, 4.71.

[69] Origen, *Homilies on Luke*, 6; Ambrose, *Commentary on Luke*, 4.18–19; Leo the Great, *Sermons*, 42.3.

[70] Jerome, Augustine, John Chrysostom, Gregory the Great, and Bede each maintain that the devil recognized or suspected Christ's divinity, at least by the time of the crucifixion. Daniel J. Saunders, "The Devil and the Divinity of Christ," *Theological Studies* 9 (1948): 537–44.

the crucifixion was a trap.[71] Similarly, Bede affirms that the devil knew that Christ was the Son of God, but did not foresee that he would be condemned by crucifying Christ.[72]

While patristic authors voice different opinions about the devil's knowledge, every version of the divine deception involves deliberate provocation. God tempts the devil with the opportunity to crucify Christ, and when the devil takes the bait, God uses the devil's injustice against him. The element of provocation is especially clear in a passage from Macarius Magnes (fourth to fifth cen.), where Macarius suggests that Christ pretends to be afraid in the Garden of Gethsemane in order to provoke the devil:

> Now man had met his fall through two things, a tree, and the food from that tree. In the case of the latter, Christ had already won back the victory by fasting from food; but it was only when he pretended to be hungry that the devil attacked him as he had the first Adam, and was beaten. Just in the same way Christ now provokes him to a second conflict, by pretending to be afraid, so that by means of a tree he may counteract the deceit once caused through a tree, and when his tree is planted, he may slay from it him who himself shows his enmity in a tree.[73]

Similarly, in his *Commentary on John*, Cyril of Alexandria says that Christ's words to Judas at the Last Supper—"what you are going to do, do quickly" (John 13:27)—were really spoken to the devil, to provoke him to act and thus hasten his own downfall.[74]

The divine deception is typically described in narrative form, with frequent deployment of metaphoric imagery and poetic language. Pseudo-Athanasius (4th cen.) compares Christ to a general who "assumes the appearance of one staggering under Satan's power, so that when the enemy draws near he might completely subdue him."[75] Augustine describes a mousetrap baited with Christ's blood, an image which is picked up by many later Latin theologians.[76] Other authors, inspired by John the Baptist's identification of Jesus as the

[71] See Gregory the Great, *Moralia in Job*, 33.7.14; and Saunders, "The Devil and Divinity of Christ," 541–2.

[72] Bede, *Commentary on Mark*, 1.1.

[73] Macarius Magnes, *Apocriticus*, 3.9, in Macarius Magnes, *The Apocriticus*, trans. T. W. Crafer (London: S.P.C.K., 1919), 59. Translation slightly modified.

[74] Cyril of Alexandria, *Commentary on John*, 9.

[75] Pseudo-Athanasius, *Homily on the Passion and the Cross* (PG 28:228) in Constas, "The Last Temptation of Satan," 151. Pseudo-Athanasius also compares Christ to Odysseus, who returns home in disguise and tricks one of his wife's more obnoxious suitors into a wrestling match by pretending to be weak. Origen makes use of military imagery in a slightly different context. He compares Christ to a king who disguises himself in the uniform of his enemy's soldiers, in order to persuade them to desert and return with him to his kingdom (Origen, *Commentary on Romans*, 5.10.11).

[76] Augustine, *Sermons*, 130.2, 134.6, 263.1. See also Jean Rivière, "Muscipula Diaboli. Origène et le sens d'une image augustinienne," *Recherches de théologie ancienne et médiévale* 1 (1929): 484–96.

Lamb of God (John 1:29, 36) and Jesus' self-identification as the good shepherd who lays down his life for his sheep (John 10:11), talk about Christ putting on a sheepskin to trick the wolf, that is, the devil, into attacking. Proclus of Constantinople writes, "He required a lamb's fleece to attract the wolf who was devouring men."[77] Much later, in the *Acts of Saint Eustratius*, an eleventh century work, Symeon Metaphrastes uses the same image.[78] Just as Augustine's mousetrap became a stock metaphor in the West, Christ's sheepskin disguise seems to have become a stock metaphor in the East.

By far, however, the most famous image associated with the divine deception is the fishhook. God baits a fishhook baited with Christ's humanity, and the devil swallows it whole, bringing about his own downfall. Today, the fishhook is associated almost exclusively with Gregory of Nyssa, but in fact many other patristic authors used the image of the fishhook as a metaphor for God's victory over the devil, including Pseudo-Athanasius, John Chrysostom, Rufinus, Fulgentius Ferrandus, Barsanuphius, Gregory the Great, and John Damascene.[79] Gregory Thaumaturgus, Athanasius, Cyril of Jerusalem, Ambrose, and Proclus of Constantinople used similar metaphors.[80] Gregory of Nyssa is not the first to use the fishhook metaphor, either. Some of these authors are writing earlier than Gregory; others are writing contemporaneously.[81]

The sheer number of different authors who used the fishhook metaphor suggests that they were drawing on a strong oral tradition. But why would this

[77] Proclus of Constantinople, *Orations*, 13.3 (PG 65:793) in Rivière, *The Doctrine of the Atonement*, 169.

[78] Symeon Metaphrastes, *Acts of Saint Eustratius* (PG 116:493), as noted in MacCulloch, *The Harrowing of Hell*, 205.

[79] See Pseudo-Athanasius, *Homily on the Passion and the Cross*; John Chrysostom, *Homilies on Matthew*, 26:39; Rufinus, *Expositio symboli*, 16; Fulgentius Ferrandus, *Epistula 3 ad Anatolium*, 4; Barsanuphius, *Epistles*, 62; Gregory the Great, *Moralia*, 33.7.14; John Damascene, *De orthodoxa fide*, 3.27.

[80] Gregory Thaumaturgus speaks of the devil casting a hook at God, only to be hooked himself, in his *Homily on All Saints*. Athanasius recounts a homily of Antony of the Desert, in which Antony speaks of Christ hooking the devil, although without saying that Christ used his flesh as bait (*Life of Antony*, 24). Cyril of Jerusalem and Ambrose affirm that Christ's body is offered as bait to the devil, but they do not mention a fishhook (Cyril of Jerusalem, *Catechetical Lectures*, 12.15; Ambrose, *Commentary on Luke*, 4:11–12). Proclus of Constantinople talks about Christ using his cross to fish out Adam from Tartarus (*Orations*, 29.24–26).

[81] The *Catechetical Oration* was written between 381 and 387. Gregory of Thaumaturgus died in the late third century, Cyril of Jerusalem wrote his *Catechetical Lectures* in the 340s, Pseudo-Athanasius's *Homily on the Passion and the Cross* dates earlier than 350, and Athanasius wrote his *Life of Antony* in the mid-fourth century. Ambrose, Rufinus, and John Chrysostom are roughly contemporaneous with Gregory of Nyssa. For the dating of the *Homily on the Passion on the Cross* and the *Catechetical Oration*, respectively, see Hubertus R. Drobner, "Eine Pseudo-Athanasianiche Osterpredigt über die Wahrheit Gottes und ihre Erfüllung," in *Christian Faith and Greek Philosophy in Late Antiquity: Essays in Tribute to George Christopher Stead*, ed. Lionel R. Wickham and Caroline P. Bammel (Leiden: Brill, 1993), 43–51; Gregory of Nyssa, *Discours cateícheítique*, trans. Raymond Winling (Paris: Les Éditions du Cerf, 2000), 125–6.

metaphor in particular become so lodged in the Christian imagination? Certainly there are other ways to characterize the cross as a divine stratagem. Augustine's mousetrap is proof of it, as is Pseudo-Athanasius' military ruse, or Proclus' sheepskin disguise. The reason seems clear. Apart from the theological genius of the metaphor, its origins are profoundly scriptural, and so naturally it resonated with patristic authors who were thoroughly immersed in scripture. Although we are barely aware of it now, the fishhook metaphor synthesizes and juxtaposes a number of key scripture texts.[82] Patristic authors associate the fishhook with God's words to Job, when he asks him whether he can "draw out Leviathan with a fishhook" (Job 41:1), and with other references to Leviathan (cf. Ps 104:26; Is 27:1). They also connect the worm that baits the fishhook with scriptural references to worms (Ps 22:6; Is 41:14), and, of course, patristic authors relate the devil fish that swallows the worm to the whale that swallows Jonah (Jon 2:11) and Christ's saying about the sign of Jonah in Matthew (Mt 12:39–40). Sometimes patristic authors refer to these texts explicitly; most of the time they do not. But even when the texts are not cited, the associations that the metaphor calls up would have bestowed on it certain authoritative status; they would also have made it difficult to forget.

The connections between these different texts must have been made very early. In the mid-third century, in his *Homily on All Saints*, Gregory Thaumaturgos speaks of the devil casting a hook at God, only to hook himself instead. In the course of his description, Gregory alludes to the dragon and hook of Job 41:1, and he explicitly refers to Jonah and the whale. Even earlier, at the end of the second century, Irenaeus identifies Jonah's whale with the devil in *Adversus haereses*.[83] Likewise, around the same time, the *Letter of the Church of Lyons and Vienne* makes use of Jonah imagery to describe the deaths of martyrs, and thus, implicitly, the death of Christ. From the third century on, extant allusions to the fishhook metaphor multiply considerably in patristic writings, and because these allusions come from sources that span the geographical confines of the Roman Empire, the metaphor cannot be seen as the exclusive property of any particular region. It seems rather to have developed spontaneously throughout the Christian community, and not just in the Eastern reaches of the empire.

The fishhook imagery probably originates from Jewish commentary on Jonah. According to the *Midrash Jonah*, Jonah did not die, but like Elijah was taken up bodily to heaven,[84] and in the Messianic age he will bind Leviathan, the sea creature of Ps 104:26, and then lead him to paradise so

[82] Constas, "The Last Temptation of Satan," 147–9.

[83] Irenaeus, *Adversus haereses*, 3.20.1.

[84] Salomon Buber, ed. *Midrasch Tehillim* (Wilna: Wittwe & Gebrüder Romm, 1891), 26, as cited in Bezalel Narkiss, "The Sign of Jonah," *Gesta* 18 (1978): 64.

that the righteous can feast on him at the Messianic banquet.[85] This idea seems to have grown out of Jewish reflection on Job 40:25–30, where the Lord asks Job, "Can you draw out Leviathan with a fishhook . . . or will you put him on a leash for your maidens?"[86] Although the four extant versions of the *Midrash Jonah* were compiled in the ninth to thirteenth centuries, their contents were already well established much earlier, perhaps as early as the first century, and it is likely that Jesus and the earliest Christians were aware of these interpretative traditions.[87] We know that many early Christians certainly were, because early Christian art shows the unmistakable influence of Jewish midrash in its depictions of Jonah.[88] Consequently, with Jewish midrash prophesying that Jonah would use a fishhook to snare Leviathan, and with Jonah such an obvious Christ figure (Matt 12:39–40), it would have been natural, almost inevitable, for early Christians, and especially early Jewish Christians, to describe Christ's victory over the devil with fishhook imagery. The early and widespread adoption of the imagery becomes even more understandable when we consider that Leviathan is easily taken as a symbol for the devil—since Leviathan is translated as dragon (*δράκων*) in the Septuagint (Ps 104:26; Isa 27:1; Job 40:25), the same word used in Revelation for the devil (Rev 12:9, 20:2)—and that Isaiah had prophesied that the Lord would slay Leviathan on the day of messianic judgment (Isa 27:1; cf. Job 3:8). But whatever its historical origins, the fishhook motif presents a magnificent distillation of biblical themes and imagery. God places Christ, the worm of Ps 22,[89] on the hook of Job 41:1, in order to lure the dragon of Rev 12:9, so that Christ can fulfill the saying about the sign of Jonah of Mt 12:39–40, and thus fulfill God's promise to slay the dragon in Is 27:1.

Christ's Descent to the Dead and the Harrowing of Hell

Christ's descent to the dead—and especially its associated ransoming of captives—figures prominently in the theological reflection of the early Church.[90] Multiple passages in the New Testament refer to Christ's descent

[85] Adolph Jellinek, *Bet ha-midrash*, vol. 1 (Jerusalem: Bamberger et Vahrman, 1938), 98–9. as cited in Narkiss, "The Sign of Jonah," 64.

[86] Narkiss, "The Sign of Jonah," 65n28.

[87] Narkiss, "The Sign of Jonah," 63.

[88] Narkiss, "The Sign of Jonah," 69.

[89] Constas shows that some patristic authors explicitly identify Christ with the worm that baits the fishhook. See Pseudo-Chrysostom, *In illud, simile est regnum coelorum grano sinapis* (Matt 13:31) (PG 64:23) and Barsanuphius, *Epistle 62*. See also Macarius Magnes, *Apocriticus*, 3.9; Constas, "The Last Temptation of Satan," 147–9.

[90] See MacCulloch, *The Harrowing of Hell*; Jean Daniélou, *The Theology of Jewish Christianity*, trans. John A. Baker, vol. 1 (London: Darton, Longman & Todd, 1964), 233–48; Alois Grillmeier, "Der Gottessohn im Totenreich," in *Mit Ihm und in Ihm* (Freiburg: Herder, 1975),

to the dead, either implicitly or explicitly. The most important are two passages from First Peter, which speak of Christ bringing the Gospel to the dead, preaching to "the spirits in prison," so that "though judged in the flesh like men, they might live in the spirit like God" (1 Pet 3:18–22, 4:6). Passages in other New Testament epistles also refer to Christ's descent to the dead (Rom 10:6–7, 14:9; Eph 4:8–10, 5:14; Phil 2:9–11; Heb 13:20–21).[91] Patristic authors often read about plundering the strong man's palace (Luke 11:21–22; cf. Mark 3:27; Matt 12:29) as referring to Christ's descent to the underworld and his rescue of the dead.[92] They also interpret the raising of "many bodies of the saints" after Christ's death (Matt 27:52–53) as the direct result of Christ's descent to the underworld.[93]

Many of the earliest patristic authors mention Christ's descent to the dead in their writings, including Ignatius, Polycarp, Justin Martyr, Melito of Sardis, Marcion, Irenaeus, Tertullian, Cyprian, Hippolytus, Clement of Alexandria, Origen, and Gregory Thaumaturgus.[94] Although the Nicene Creed does not mention it, many early creeds, including the Apostles' Creed, feature a clause about the descent.[95] Greek creeds profess a descent to Hades, while Latin creeds profess a descent either to the lower places (*ad inferos*), or to hell (*ad inferna*). The descent is also mentioned in numerous apocryphal and pseudonymous writings, most notably the *Gospel of Nicodemus* (c. 425), whose descent material may originate from as early as the second or third century.[96] Patristic authors often describe the descent in narrative form. For example, a fourth century homily for Holy Saturday describes Christ meeting Adam in

76–174; Markwart Herzog, *Descensus ad inferos* (Frankfurt am Main: J. Knecht, 1997); Jeffrey A. Trumbower, *Rescue for the Dead: The Posthumous Salvation of Non-Christians in Early Christianity* (Oxford: Oxford University Press, 2001); Jared Wicks, "Christ's Saving Descent to the Dead: Early Witnesses from Ignatius of Antioch to Origen," *Pro Ecclesia* 17 (2008): 281–309; Hilarion Alfeyev, *Christ the Conqueror of Hell: The Descent into Hades from an Orthodox Perspective* (Crestwood, NY: St. Vladimir's Seminary Press, 2009), 43–154. Belief in Christ's descent to the dead is well attested from very early on. The belief was central enough to early Christianity that even a non-Christian such as Celsus was aware of it (Origen, *Contra Celsum*, 2.43). For a concise summary of the evidence, see the survey of early Christian literature given by Wicks.

[91] Harold Attridge argues that Heb 2:10–18 has been missed as one of the earliest attestations of Christ's descent to the dead. Similarly, MacCulloch finds allusions to the descent in many passages from Hebrews. Harold W. Attridge, "Liberating Death's Captives: Reconsideration of an Early Christian Myth," in *Gnosticism & the Early Christian World*, ed. James E. Goehring et al. (Sonoma: Polebridge Press, 1990), 103–15; MacCulloch, *The Harrowing of Hell*, 48–9.

[92] Wicks, "Christ's Saving Descent," 307. See, for example, Origen, *Commentary on Romans*, 5.10.11–12.

[93] See, for example, Ignatius of Antioch, *Letter to the Magnesians*, 9.2, and Clement of Alexandria, *Stromateis*, 6.6, 47.1.

[94] For more details, see MacCulloch, *The Harrowing of Hell*, 83–108; Wicks, "Christ's Saving Descent; Alfeyev, *Christ the Conqueror of Hell*, 43–101.

[95] MacCulloch, *The Harrowing of Hell*, 67–82; J. N. D. Kelly, *Early Christian Creeds* (London: Longmans, Green, and Co., 1950), 378–83.

[96] MacCulloch, *The Harrowing of Hell*, 131–73; Wicks, "Christ's Saving Descent."

the netherworld, and then grasping Adam's hand, raising him up, and leading him out.[97]

Most early Christian literature about the descent affirms certain core tenets. According to the consensus, Christ descends to the dead in his human soul, preaches the Gospel, defeats the guardians of the underworld, and then ushers the souls of the righteous from "the bosom of Abraham" (cf. Luke 16:22–23) to heaven.[98] Beyond these core tenets, there is much disagreement. Some patristic authors think that Christ rescues only the righteous figures of the Old Testament; others think that he also rescues the righteous Gentiles.[99] Although their views are unusual and frequently rejected as heterodox, some early Christians also affirm that Christ rescued all or most of the dead, or at least speculate that he might have.[100]

For patristic authors, the devil's ransom and the descent to the dead are closely linked to each other. It is not hard to see why. Jesus speaks of giving his life as a ransom for many, and his descent to the dead brings about the release—the ransom—of those held captive in the underworld. And if Christ himself is the ransom, the devil must be the one receiving the ransom, since the crucifixion is orchestrated by the devil. The connection is smooth and logical. In fact, it seems likely that Christian beliefs about the descent to the dead played a role in the historical development of the devil's ransom interpretation. By reflecting on the descent and the idea of Christ liberating the righteous dead, early Christians seem to have found it more and more fitting to describe Christ's saving work as a ransom. Certainly the descent is far better attested in early Christian literature than the notion of either the devil's ransom or the devil's rights, suggesting that Christian beliefs about the descent settled into stable form before the devil's ransom interpretation.

Among patristic authors, the saying about the sign of Jonah in Matt 12:39–40 serves as an important bridge between the devil's ransom and the descent to the dead. It leads them to interpret Christ's descent as the prophetic fulfillment of Jonah's three days and three nights in the belly of the whale. (Jewish midrash, which sees the belly of the whale symbolic of the netherworld, may also lie behind this interpretative tradition.)[101] It also leads them to interpret

[97] *Ancient Homily for Holy Saturday* (PG 43:439–64). For a discussion of this homily, once wrongly attributed to Epiphanius, see MacCulloch, *The Harrowing of Hell*, 192–8.

[98] Wicks, "Christ's Saving Descent," 308–9.

[99] Wicks, "Christ's Saving Descent," 308–9; MacCulloch, *The Harrowing of Hell*, 253–87. Tertullian has a different view. According to Tertullian, only martyrs go to heaven before the Last Judgment, and even righteous Old Testament figures remain in the underworld, although their condition improved after Christ's visit on Holy Saturday. See Tertullian, *De anima*, 55; and Wicks, "Christ's Saving Descent," 298–9.

[100] See MacCulloch, *The Harrowing of Hell*, 253–99; Trumbower, *Rescue for the Dead*, 91–140.

[101] Tertullian, *Against Marcion*, 34; DeJellinek, *Bet ha-midrash*, 104; Narkiss, "The Sign of Jonah," 65.

Christ coming out from the netherworld, with the righteous dead in tow, as the prophetic fulfillment of Jonah coming out from the whale. For example, in a passage from his *Commentary on Romans*, Origen uses Jonah imagery to reflect on the themes of ransom and descent simultaneously. He writes:

> Christ, like Jonah in the belly of the sea monster, entered into this death, namely to that place which the Savior himself called the heart of the earth, where he says the Son of Man was going to spend three days and three nights, following the precedent of Jonah (Matt 12:40), in order to release those who were being held there by death. For it was on this account that he also took up the form of a slave (Phil 2:7), that he might be able to enter that place where death was holding dominion, in accordance with what the prophet says under the *persona* of Christ, "And I was reckoned with those who go down to the pit" (Ps 28:1), and again, "What profit was there in my blood when I go down to corruption?" (Ps 30:9).[102]

Similarly, Cyril of Jerusalem speaks of the devil vomiting the souls of the dead. He writes, "[Christ's] body thus served as a bait for death so that the serpent, instead of swallowing it as he hoped, might be forced to disgorge those whom he had already swallowed."[103] John Damascene also takes up the Jonah imagery to describe the descent and the ransom of captives. He combines it with the image of the fishhook:

> Death approaches, gulps down the bait of the body, and is pierced by the hook of the divinity. Then, having tasted of the sinless and life-giving body, it is destroyed and gives up all those whom it had swallowed down of old.[104]

In all of these quotations, Jonah imagery figures conspicuously. Its prominence suggests that the saying about the sign of Jonah played an important, formative role in early Christian reflection on the descent to the dead, and that this reflection, in turn, helped foster the devil's ransom interpretation of the crucifixion.

Internal Critique

Some patristic authors explicitly repudiate the idea that Christ was given as a ransom to the devil. In a famous passage in one of his orations, Gregory of

[102] Origen, *Commentary on Romans*, 5.10.10, Vol. 1, 371–3.

[103] Cyril of Jerusalem, *Catechetical Lectures*, 12.15, in Edward Yarnold, *Cyril of Jerusalem* (London: Routledge, 2000), 146. Similarly, Proclus of Constantinople writes: "Death vomiting forth the one whom he swallowed in his ignorance; a tomb becoming the treasure-house of life and resurrection; captivity becoming the source of freedom." *Orations*, 13.3, in Proclus of Constantinople, *Homilies on the Life of Christ*, trans. Jan Harm Barkhuizen (Brisbane: Centre for Early Christian Studies, Australian Catholic University, 2001), 172.

[104] John Damascene, *De orthodoxa fide*, 3.27, in *Writings*, trans. Frederic H. Chase Jr. (Washington, DC: The Catholic University of America Press, 1958), 332.

Nazianzus forcefully rejects the idea that Christ's blood was poured out as a ransom to the devil, calling the idea outrageous.[105] Less famously, but earlier, probably between 290 and 300, Adamantius also rejects the idea that God paid a ransom to the devil.[106] Gregory's oration is often cited as proof that the devil's ransom interpretation never found universal acceptance in the early Church. Yet the evidence is not so straightforward. Gregory of Nazianzus does indeed reject literalistic accounts of the devil's ransom interpretation (though it is not clear to what extent any of his contemporaries actually endorsed them, as will be discussed below), but he retains other elements, such as the divine deception and the devil's defeat by trickery, and he still frames redemption as a contest between God and the devil. For example, in another oration, he writes:

> "The light shines in the darkness" of this life and the flesh, and it is persecuted by the darkness but not overcome, I mean by the adverse power, who out of shamelessness leapt upon the visible Adam but encountered God and was defeated, so that we, putting aside the darkness, may draw near to the light, and thus become perfect light, children of perfect light.[107]

Likewise, although John Damascene rejects the idea that Christ's blood was given to the devil,[108] he makes use of other elements of the devil's ransom interpretation, including the fishhook imagery, only with the hook catching death rather than the devil.[109] The criticism of Gregory of Nazianzus and John Damascene, then, is not a wholesale rejection of the devil's ransom interpretation; it is an internal critique. They are not trying to demolish the devil's ransom interpretation, but rather to police its boundaries. Their criticisms, then, should bolster—not diminish—estimations of its influence in the early Church.

[105] Gregory of Nazianzus, *Orations*, 45.22.

[106] Adamantius, *De recta in Deum fide*, 1.27. For its date of composition, see Adamantius, *Dialogue on the True Faith in God*, ed. Garry W. Trompf, trans. Robert A. Pretty (Leuven: Peeters, 1997), 16–17.

[107] Gregory of Nazianzus, *Orations*, 39.2, in *Festal Orations*, trans. Nonna Verna Harrison (Crestwood, NY: St. Vladimir's Seminary Press, 2008), 79–80. Later in the same oration, he continues with this theme: "For since the deceptive advocate of evil thought he was unconquerable as he ensnared us with the hope of divinity, he was ensnared by the obstacle of flesh. Just as when he meant to attack Adam he encountered God, so also by the new Adam the old was saved and the condemnation of the flesh was abolished, since death was put to death by flesh" (*Orations*, 39.13, 89). Richard Winslow notes these passages, but he minimizes their significance for interpreting Gregory on the devil's ransom; he argues that the excerpt from Oration 45 is much more important. See Donald F. Winslow, *Dynamics of Salvation: A Study in Gregory of Nazianzus* (Philadelphia: Philadelphia Patristic Foundation, 1979), 107–14. Jean Rivière comments on these passages to similar effect. See Rivière, *The Doctrine of the Atonement*, 164–5.

[108] John Damascene, *De orthodoxa fide*, 3.27.

[109] John Damascene, *De orthodoxa fide*, 3.1, 3.27. Jean Rivière notes the contrast between these two aspects of John's theology, but rather than seeing them as compatible, he suggests that John's synthesis is "somewhat incoherent." See Rivière, *The Doctrine of the Atonement*, 169.

With these considerations in mind, let us return to Gregory's famous repudiation of the devil's ransom interpretation and give it a closer look. He writes:

> Now then, we will examine an issue and doctrine overlooked by many but in my view very much to be examined. To whom was the blood poured out for us, and why was it poured out, that great and renowned blood of God, who is both high priest and victim? For we were held in bondage by the Evil One, sold under sin, and received pleasure in exchange for evil. But if the ransom is not given to anyone except the one holding us in bondage, I ask to whom this was paid, and for what cause? If to the Evil One, what an outrage! For the robber would receive not only a ransom from God, but God himself as a ransom, and a reward so greatly surpassing his own tyranny that for its sake he would rightly have spared us altogether. But if it was given to the Father, in the first place how? For we were not conquered by him. And secondly, on what principle would the blood of the Only-begotten delight the Father, who would not receive Isaac when he was offered by his father but switched the sacrifice, giving a ram in place of the reason-endowed victim? It is clear that the Father accepts him, though he neither asked for this nor needed it, because of the divine plan, and because the human being must be sanctified by the humanity of God, that God might himself set us free and conquer the tyrant by force and lead us back to himself by the mediation of the Son, who also planned this to the honor of the Father, to whom it is manifest that he yields all things.[110]

In this passage, Gregory forcefully rejects the idea of a commercial transaction between God and the devil. But immediately before doing so, he speaks about our being "held in bondage by the Evil One," and immediately after doing so, he talks about God "conquering the tyrant by force." These phrases show that, despite rejecting a literalistic account of the devil's ransom, he still sees the devil having power over humanity, and he still characterizes redemption as a struggle between God and the devil. It is also notable that Gregory begins the passage by saying, "Now then, we will examine an issue and doctrine overlooked by many but in my view very much to be examined." In this introduction, Gregory implies that other Christians (presumably previous theologians and his contemporaries) talked about Christ's blood being poured out for us, and used this expression with some frequency, but had not given much thought to its theological implications. Consequently, his views on the devil's ransom should not be taken as contradicting prevalent opinion; rather, he is self-consciously exploring new theological territory. While this theological territory may not have been as unexplored as he suggests, he gives no indication that he sees himself as challenging established theological opinion. As a result we should not conclude that Gregory of Nazianzus was an exception among his contemporaries, or that he represented another school of

[110] Gregory of Nazianzus, *Orations*, 45.22, in *Festal Orations*, 182.

soteriology. While he stands out for the critical attention he gives to literalistic understandings of the devil's ransom, he does not repudiate the tradition that gave rise to them indeed, his writings incorporate many of its tropes.

Metaphor, Death, and the Devil

Such things as Gregory's internal critique and Augustine's habit of qualifying the status of the devil's rights draw our attention to the role of metaphor and symbolic language in the devil's ransom interpretation.[111] Patristic authors usually discuss the devil's ransom in homilies and sermons, literary forms in which the use of metaphor is natural and expected, or while commenting on sacred scripture, which itself is replete with metaphor and symbolic language. Consequently, patristic descriptions of the devil's ransom should be taken in a fluid, metaphorical sense, and not as straightforward theological assertions. One telling clue about their theological grammar lies in the way that they often talk about the devil and death interchangeably. In some instances, patristic authors weave back and forth between the devil and death as they describe the enemy who receives the ransom, or who is overcome by Christ. For example, a passage from Origen's *Commentary on Matthew* describes the devil receiving the soul of Christ as a ransom and then not being able to hold him. Immediately afterward, Origen starts talking about death as not being able to hold either Christ or those Christ came to rescue.[112] In his *Adversus haereses*, Irenaeus moves between the devil and death in a similar way, as does Eusebius of Caesarea throughout the course of an entire book of the *De theophania*.[113] This movement between the devil and death is also found in acts of the martyrs. *The Martyrdom of Montanus and Lucius*, for example, speaks of the martyrs conquering the devil in two places and death in another.[114]

In other instances, patristic authors apply to death the same metaphors and imagery elsewhere used with the devil. In an oration on the Lord's passion, Proclus of Constantinople describes Christ battling death, but what he says could easily be applied to the devil. Proclus lauds Christ's victory over "the ancient tyrant," apparently meaning death, and then he applies the deception theme to death, with death receiving Christ as an ordinary mortal, only to be

[111] On the importance of social and theological context for the proper interpretation of religious metaphors, see Janet Martin Soskice, *Metaphor and Religious Language* (Oxford: Clarendon Press, 1985), 142–61.

[112] Origen, *Commentary on Matthew*, 16.8. This book of the *Commentary on Matthew* has not been translated into English; Hastings Rashdall, however, translates this particular passage in *The Idea of Atonement*, 259.

[113] Irenaeus, *Adversus haereses*, 3.18.7; Eusebius of Caesarea, *De theophania*, 3.

[114] Martyrdom of Montanus and Lucius, 6.4, 10.2, 19.6; Moss, *The Other Christs*, 100.

emptied of its treasure.[115] In his *Commentary on Romans*, Origen describes death holding the same *chirographa* that elsewhere he assigns to the devil.[116] Eusebius describes death attacking Jesus like "a terrible beast," only to be overcome by the power of the Word of God.[117] This description evokes demonic imagery, especially since the word he uses for beast (θήρ), in another form equivalent in meaning, can also be used to describe demonic creatures (see, for example, Rev 11:7).[118] Although he does not speak about Jesus giving himself as a ransom to the devil,[119] Athanasius does talk about Christ giving himself as a ransom to death.[120] John Damascene applies the fishhook imagery to death, so that the hook baited with Christ's body catches death instead of the devil.[121]

This interplay between death and the devil in patristic writings has strong scriptural warrant. The New Testament connects death and the devil explicitly, most notably when the devil is described as "him who has the power of death" (Heb 2:14). Perhaps more importantly, while the Old Testament, taken as a whole, lacks a clearly defined notion of the devil, it frequently personifies death, and it often portrays death as humanity's principal enemy.[122] Given that, in early Christianity, the devil usurps death's role and becomes the new leader of the opposition, it would have been natural for patristic authors to describe the devil with the Old Testament's reservoir of death imagery, or to symbolize the devil with death, and vice versa.

Origen shows particular sensitivity to the role of metaphor and symbolic language in theological discourse. We have already noted how Origen qualifies the legal status of the *chirographa*, and thus implicitly the devil's rights, and how he talks about the devil and death interchangeably in his interpretation of

[115] Proclus of Constantinople, *Orations*, 11.1, 158–9. See also *Orations*, 13.

[116] Origen, *Commentary on Romans*, 5.3.3; cf. *Homilies on Exodus*, 6.9.

[117] Eusebius of Caesarea, *De theophania*, 3.61.

[118] Barbara Friberg, Timothy Friberg, and Neva F. Miller, eds., *Analytical Lexicon of the Greek New Testament* (Grand Rapids, MI: Baker, 2000).

[119] George Dion Dragas, "St Athanasius on Christ's Sacrifice," in *Sacrifice and Redemption: Durham Essays in Theology*, ed. S. W. Sykes (Cambridge: Cambridge University Press, 1991), 73–100 95. According to Dragas, Athanasius does not explicitly say that Christ's self-sacrifice was offered to the devil, but he implies as much in *Contra Arianos* 2.55 and in the short treatise *In illud Omnia mihi tradita sunt*. The texts that Dragas cites, however, do not seem sufficient to make his case.

[120] Athanasius writes, "How then has he given himself for us, if he had not put on flesh? For having offered it, he gave himself for us, in order that taking death upon him in it, he might bring to nought the devil who had the power of death. Hence we always offer the eucharist in the name of Jesus Christ and we do not disregard the grace which came to us through him. For the Saviour's incarnate presence has been ransom for death and salvation for all Creation." *Ad Adelphium*, 6, in Dragas, "St Athanasius on Christ's Sacrifice."

[121] *De orthodoxa fide*, 3.27.

[122] I am grateful to Michael Legaspi for sharing with me an unpublished manuscript that establishes this point in detail. As examples of such portrayals of death in the Old Testament, he cites the following texts: Isa 5:14, 14:9, 28:15–18; Prov 1:12–13; Hos 13:14; Song 8:6.

the devil's ransom. These instances alone would give us reason to interpret Origen's theological claims about the devil's ransom in metaphoric terms. What is more striking, though, is that Origen reflects explicitly on the symbolic potential of death and the devil. Two lengthy excerpts from his *Commentary on Romans* are worth quoting in full:

> For just as Christ is indeed one in essence but may be designated in many ways according to his virtues and operations (for example he is understood to be grace itself, as well as righteousness, peace, life, truth, the Word) so perhaps also the devil can himself be understood by various designations. For he should be thought of as the sin which is said to exercise dominion. Also one has to believe that he is that death of which it is said, "For the last enemy, death, will be destroyed." Moreover he is understood to be a desolation according to what has been spoken by the prophet, "You have become a desolation and you will not exist in eternal time." Furthermore I think that what the Apostle says, "Therefore, do not let sin reign in your mortal bodies," could be said even more about the devil. For he is the author of sin and death and desolation, and the author of an invention is logically named after the things he has invented.[123]

> In the Scriptures "death" is a single term, but signifies many things. For the separation of the body from the soul is called death. But this cannot be said to be either good or bad; it is neutral, what is termed "indifferent." And again the separation of the soul from God is called the death that comes through sin. This kind is plainly bad and is named "the wage of sin." This death "God did not make, nor does he delight in the destruction of the living"; "but through the devil's envy this death entered the world." Further, the very author of this death, the devil, is called death; and he is also said to be Christ's last enemy, who will be destroyed. Moreover, the place below in the underworld, where souls were being held by death, is also named death. There is even a praiseworthy kind of death, namely, that by which someone dies to sin and is buried together with Christ, through which correction comes to the soul and eternal life is attained.[124]

In these passages, Origen displays great sensitivity to the way that scripture talks about death and the devil as symbolic of larger realities, and thus implicitly suggests that his own references to death and the devil should not always be taken in a strictly literal sense.

In patristic texts, comments about the devil's ransom or the devil's rights are few and far between, and usually brief. Consequently it is difficult to generalize about what patristic authors mean by them. Simply because certain patristic authors talk about the devil having rights it should not be assumed that they think that the devil truly has cosmic legal claims over humanity. Barring clear evidence to the contrary, the opposite should be assumed. In patristic writings, talk about the devil's rights generally serves as a metaphor for the devil's *de*

[123] Origen, *Commentary on Romans*, 5.6.7, Vol. 1, 348–9.
[124] Origen, *Commentary on Romans*, 6.6.5, Vol. 2, 18.

facto power to harm humanity. There is no sense that the devil has legitimate *de jure* power over humanity which legally obliges even God. Likewise, when patristic authors talk about the devil's ransom their comments also need to be interpreted metaphorically. They should not be read as asserting that a commercial transaction actually takes place between God and the devil. Patristic authors do not declare themselves to be speaking metaphorically, but what they mean to assert can be discerned by looking at the full context of their writings. It is not surprising that they do not clarify exactly what they mean by talking about the devil's rights or a ransom paid to the devil. Judging from the paucity of references, the devil's rights and the devil's ransom played little role in patristic thinking about the economy of salvation; consequently, they would not have felt the need to clarify what they meant. Furthermore, a "right" is not an actual thing; it is an abstract concept. As such, it is close kin to metaphor, since, to adapt Nietzsche's phrase, a concept is nothing other than a worn-out metaphor.[125] To clarify the status of the devil's rights, patristic authors would first have had to clarify the status of legal rights more generally—a challenging task in any age, and one which they could hardly be expected to attempt before talking about the devil having rights.

The Sign of Jonah as Hermeneutical Key

The devil's ransom interpretation of the crucifixion is typically characterized as a theory. As we have seen, however, it stops short of the systematic coherence that we usually associate with theories. Nor do patristic authors offer this interpretation of the crucifixion as a theory; they present themselves as simply clarifying the latent meaning of sacred scripture.[126] While not without its usefulness, the custom of describing this interpretation as a theory can therefore be misleading. It is better understood as a loose exegetical

[125] Nietzsche identifies truths with worn-out metaphors. See Friedrich Nietzsche, "On Truth and Falsity in their Ultramoral Sense," in *Collected Words*, ed. Oscar Levy (London: T. N. Foulis, 1911), 180.

The relationship of concepts to metaphor is complex and controversial. Nonetheless, many contemporary philosophers have maintained that they are intimately connected, as discussed in Soskice, *Metaphor and Religious Language*, 74–83. The work of earlier thinkers can also be used to argue for a close connection between metaphor and concept. Aquinas maintains that the human intellect can only understand things through imaginative phantasms, which in turn ultimately derive from sense perception (*ST* I 84.7)—a position that easily leads to the conclusion that concepts are intrinsically metaphorical. In any case, whatever the precise relationship of concepts to metaphor, it must be acknowledged that the concept of legal rights depends on a complex web of beliefs and customs and language games, and even philosophers of law struggle to explain precisely what legal rights are.

[126] One exception might be Augustine, whose lengthy comments about redemption and the devil's rights in Book 13 of *De Trinitate* have a decidedly experimental feel, as though he is offering a provisional theory without being entirely committed to it.

tradition, a broad approach to making sense of Christ's crucifixion. As such, it draws on the same treasury of images, metaphors, themes, and scripture passages, but it does not set forth a monolithic theory of redemption.

Nevertheless, for all their differences, patristic authors show a remarkable thematic unity in their presentation of the devil's ransom interpretation. Even though they seldom discuss the devil's ransom or the devil's rights in their writings, and thus lack obvious mechanisms for coordinating with each other, they manifest a great deal of unity in the way they read certain scripture passages and exploit certain images and metaphors. So what can explain this thematic unity? What could be the gravitational center holding together this theological approach to the crucifixion? The exegetical tradition that surfaces in Matt 12:40 provides the only plausible answer. The sign of Jonah is the hermeneutical key to the devil's ransom.

Evidence for this proposal comes from a variety of sources. First, we know that Jonah figured prominently in the early Christian imagination. Images of Jonah, especially images relating to the story of the whale, appear with overwhelming frequency in early Christian art.[127] In the earliest period of Christian art, in the second through fourth centuries, Old Testament subjects are four times more popular than New Testament subjects,[128] and among Old Testament subjects, Jonah is the most common, appearing far more frequently than any other Old Testament figure.[129] Catacombs and sarcophagi from the pre-Constantinian era feature almost one hundred images of Jonah, compared to a dozen or less instances of other biblical figures (including Jesus).[130] Early Christian representations of Jonah can convey many layers of religious meaning.[131] They can express hope for the future resurrection of Christians. They can also allude to the death and resurrection of Jesus.[132] Since these images are found mainly in catacombs and objects associated with burial, scholars often

[127] For an excellent study of Jonah in early Christian art, with particular attention to the artistic influence of pagan and Jewish sources, see Narkiss, "The Sign of Jonah." It is worth emphasizing that most images of Jonah relate to the story of the whale. Despite Jonah's preaching being central to the book of Jonah and the sayings of Jesus in the Gospels, depictions of his preaching are very rare in early Christian art. See Narkiss, "The Sign of Jonah," 63–9.

[128] Robin Margaret Jensen, *Understanding Early Christian Art* (Abingdon: Routledge, 2000), 68–9.

[129] "The most popular Old Testament scene depicted by the Early Christian artists was Jonah lying asleep, naked, under a booth covered by a climbing gourd vine, near a sea monster from whose mouth he had emerged" (Narkiss, "The Sign of Jonah," 63–9).

[130] Jensen, *Understanding Early Christian Art*, 69. See also Narkiss, "The Sign of Jonah," 63n2.

[131] For an overview of the symbolic meanings associated with images of Jonah, see Ernest Cadman Colwell, "The Fourth Gospel and Early Christian Art," *The Journal of Religion* 15 (1935): 191–206; 194–5. For a study of the scripture exegesis implicit in early Christian images of Jonah, see Stephen J. Davis, "Jonah in Early Christian Art: Allegorical Exegesis and the Roman Funerary Context," *Australian Religion Studies Review* 13 (2000): 72–83.

[132] Jensen, *Understanding Early Christian Art*, 78.

interpret them as primarily expressing hope for a future resurrection.[133] Yet because the Gospels so strongly identify Jonah as a type of Christ, it is more plausible that these images were meant to allude simultaneously to both the resurrection of Christ and the future resurrection of Christians. In this way, early Christian art testifies to the hermeneutic significance of the sign of Jonah for early Christian reflection on the paschal mystery of Christ's death and resurrection. We would not have been able to guess its hermeneutic importance from the New Testament evidence alone; the New Testament alludes to the story of Jonah only very infrequently.[134]

Jonah's prominence in early Christian art finds an echo in patristic writings. Although patristic authors do not devote the same proportion of their attention to Jonah, they discuss him frequently, often in connection to the death and resurrection of Jesus.[135] Justin Martyr's *Dialogue with Trypho* supplies a good example. In the course of explaining how Christ's death and resurrection were prophesied by the Jewish scriptures,[136] Justin touches on Jonah and Christ's saying about the sign of Jonah.[137] Since Justin cites only a handful of scripture texts in his explanation, his attention to the book of Jonah suggests that it came easily to mind on the topic of the paschal mystery—not only for Justin, but also for early Christians more generally. Likewise, while discussing the economy of salvation, Irenaeus refers to Jonah and the sign of Jonah to illustrate his meaning.[138] Justin and Irenaeus' allusions to Jonah give us some sense of his hermeneutic significance to early Christian theology of

[133] For an example of this prioritization, see Davis, "Jonah in Early Christian Art."

[134] For an extended argument in favor of the historical and theological significance of early Christian art in reconstructing early Christian theology, with attention to the significance of Jonah imagery, see Colwell, "The Fourth Gospel."

In the course of his argument, Colwell notes, "It should always be remembered that the literature and the art are but partial expressions of the much more inclusive religious movement which produced them. The whole of early Christianity is not to be found in one of them to the exclusion of the other, nor yet is it all included in both. The main stream is there, but many an eddy and backwash vanished with hardly a trace. Again, it must often have happened that an interest that was widespread in the common faith found a meager reflection in the literature and a fuller expression in the art. For example, the equation of the 'sign' of Jonah with the Passion of Jesus bobs up for only a moment in the stream of gospel tradition, but appears as the most popular of subjects in the subterranean art. The ultimate source of the symbol, however, is not the gospel saying or the painter's brush, but the living faith that had made the identification before the gospels were written or the frescos painted" (198).

[135] For an exhaustive study of patristic reflection on Jonah, see Yves-Marie Duval, *Le livre de Jonas dans la littérature chrétienne grecque et latine. Sources et influence du Commentaire sur Jonas de Saint Jérôme* (Paris: Études Augustiniennes, 1973). For a brief overview in English, see Yvonne Sherwood, *A Biblical Text and Its Afterlives: The Survival of Jonah in Western Culture* (Cambridge: Cambridge University Press, 2000), 11–21. It is noteworthy that Celsus, an early critic of Christianity, was well informed about the story of Jonah. See Origen, *Against Celsus*, 7.53, 57.

[136] Justin Martyr, *Dialogue with Trypho*, 86–108 passim.

[137] Justin Martyr, *Dialogue with Trypho*, 107–8.

[138] Irenaeus, *Adversus haereses*, 3.20.1.

redemption. The strong correspondence between their theology and early Christian artistic expression—for example, four scenes from Jonah's life are commonly depicted in early Christian art, and Justin discusses three of them in the *Dialogue with Trypho*[139]—also points to an early and widespread exegetical tradition.

After Justin and Irenaeus, the two most prominent theologians of the second century, evidence of patristic interest in Jonah multiplies. In the third century, Origen writes a commentary on the book of Jonah, now lost. After Origen, many others write their own commentaries, including Jerome, Theodore of Mopsuestia, Cyril of Alexandria, Theodoret of Cyrus, and Hesychius of Jerusalem. From Justin onwards, when patristic authors want to establish that the resurrection of Jesus was prophesied by the Old Testament, they have a tendency to refer to Jonah and Christ's saying about the sign of Jonah.[140] They also see the story of Jonah as prophetic of Christ's passion. Authors such as Origen, Hilary of Poitiers, Cyril of Jerusalem, Ambrose, Jerome, Theodoret of Cyrus, Heyschius of Jerusalem, and Vercundus of Junca compare Jonah's prayer in the belly of the whale (Jonah 2:2–10) to Christ's prayer on the cross or in the netherworld, and sometimes they suggest that Jonah's prayer is best understood when placed on the lips of Christ.[141] Patristic authors also tend to read the Gospel accounts of the crucifixion with a backward glance to Jonah. For example, in his *Homilies on Matthew*, in his commentary on Matthew's crucifixion narrative, John Chrysostom relates the crucifixion to the sign of Jonah with his first words of commentary, describing it as the fulfillment of Christ's promise for a sign.[142]

The ancient Christian belief that Christ's resurrection had been prophesied to take place three days after his death also points to Jonah's hermeneutic significance. The third day trope appears in many New Testament passages, indicating that it must have featured prominently in the kerygma of the early Church. It appears in the saying about Jesus rebuilding the temple in "three days" (Mark 14:58, 15:29; Matt 26:61, 27:40; John 2:19–20); it also appears in Peter's speech to Cornelius and his household, when Peter specifies that God

[139] Colwell, "The Fourth Gospel," 194–5. For a detailed discussion of the typical scenes in the Jonah cycle, see Narkiss, "The Sign of Jonah," 69–71; Davis, "Jonah in Early Christian Art," 72–83.

[140] This historical judgment is the considered opinion of Duval; his monograph provides an overview of the data that supports it. See Duval, *Le livre de Jonas*, 173.

[141] Origen, *Commentariorum series in Matthaeum*, 136; Hilary of Poitiers, *Commentary on the Psalms*, 68.5; Cyril of Jerusalem, *Catechetical Lectures*, 14.20; Ambrose, *Commentary on the Psalms*, 43.86; Jerome, *Commentary on Jonah*, 2.2; Theodoret of Cyrus, *Commentary on Jonah*, 2.3; Verecundus of Junca, *Commentary on the Canticle of Jonah*, 3. See Duval, *Le livre de Jonas*, 203–5, 217–18, 246–7, 427–32, 552, 602–4. Hesychius of Jerusalem's commentary on Jonah's prayer is found only in fragments. For a discussion of Hesychius' commentary and a careful survey of the extant manuscripts, see Duval, *Le livre de Jonas*, 449–51, 629–45.

[142] John Chrysostom, *Homilies on Matthew*, 88.

raised Jesus "on the third day" (Acts 10:40). In the Gospels, Jesus prophesies on multiple occasions that his resurrection will take place after three days, or on the third day (Mark 8:31, 9:31, 10:34; Matt 16:21–23, 17:22–23, 20:17–19; 27:63; Luke 9:22, 18:31–33). In Luke, the angel at the tomb reminds the women that Jesus had prophesied about rising on the third day (Luke 24:7).

Two passages in the New Testament make an additional claim. They specify that a third day resurrection had been prophesied by the scriptures. Paul writes that "he was raised on the third day in accordance with the scriptures" (1 Cor 15:4). Likewise, in Luke's Gospel, Jesus tells the disciples on the road to Emmaus that "it is written" that the Christ should rise from the dead on the third day (Luke 24:46). But to which scripture passage—or passages—are Paul and Luke referring? Neither gives any indication. Among the passages that Paul and Luke might have had in mind, the two principal contenders are from Jonah and Hosea:

> And the LORD appointed a great fish to swallow up Jonah; and Jonah was in the belly of the fish three days and three nights. (Jonah 2:1)

> After two days he will revive us; on the third day he will raise us up, that we may live before him. (Hos 6:2)

Among contemporary scholars, the consensus is that Paul and Luke did not have Jonah 2:1 in mind when they wrote about the scriptures prophesying Christ's third day resurrection. According to the consensus, the custom of drawing parallels between Jonah's three days in the whale and Christ's death and resurrection, which surfaces only in Matt 12:40, represents a late tradition, and therefore could not have influenced Paul or Luke. Instead, scholars maintain that Paul and Luke are thinking of Hos 6:2,[143] or that their conviction about the third day does not truly originate from scripture,[144] or else that Paul merely meant to say the scriptures prophesied Christ's resurrection, not that they said it would happen specifically on the third day.[145]

Nonetheless, there are good reasons to think that Paul and Luke are referring to Jonah 2:1, at least in part, and that a Christological reading of Jonah lies behind the third day trope that figures so prominently in the kerygma of the early Church. In Mark's Gospel, in the three passion predictions, Jesus predicts that he will rise, not "on the third day," but "after three

[143] Mark Proctor, "'After Three Days' in Mark 8:31; 9:31; 10:34: Subordinating Jesus' Resurrection in the Second Gospel," *Perspectives in Religious Studies* 30 (2003): 399–424; Mark Proctor, "'After Three Days He Will Rise': The (Dis)appropriation of Hosea 6.2 in the Markan Passion Predictions," in *Biblical Interpretation in Early Christian Gospels*: Vol. 1, *The Gospel of Mark*, ed. Thomas R. Hatina (London: T & T Clark, 2006), 131–50.

[144] Selby Vernon McCasland, "The Scripture Basis of 'On the Third Day'," *The Journal of Biblical Literature* 48 (1929): 135.

[145] Bruce M. Metzger, "A Suggestion Concerning the Meaning of I Cor XV.4b," *The Journal of Theological Studies* 8 (1957): 118–23.

days" (Mark 8:31, 9:31, 10:34). Scholars disagree about the significance of Mark's phrasing. While some hold that Mark is deliberately revising an earlier formula,[146] others think that Mark has preserved a primitive tradition.[147] The latter view is more plausible. Since the Gospels have Jesus rising on the third day, "after three days" is the *lectio difficilior*, and therefore this phrasing probably captures a primitive tradition. Precisely because Jesus does not rise after three days, but after only two days, it is difficult to explain why Mark would have revised "on the third day" to "after three days."[148] It is easy, though, to explain why other New Testament authors would have made the opposite revision: namely, because "after three days" conflicts with their narratives of Christ's death and resurrection. Finally, in an episode without parallel in Mark, Matthew also uses the phrasing "after three days" (Matt 27:63). Matthew's independent witness confirms the view that Mark's phrasing represents a primitive tradition. And if it does, then this primitive tradition must trace back to Jonah 2:1. Since the earliest narratives agree that Jesus did not in fact rise after three days, early Christians would not have invented this formula *ex nihilo*, and yet no other scripture passage can be read as prophesying a resurrection "after three days." The patristic evidence supports this genealogy of the third day trope. Patristic authors cite both Jonah and Hosea as prophetic of Christ's resurrection, but they cite Jonah first. Tertullian is the first author to apply Hos 6:2 to Christ's resurrection.[149] But some decades earlier, drawing on Matt 12:40, Justin Martyr had already described Christ's resurrection on the third day as the prophetic fulfillment of Jonah 2:1.[150]

It should also be said that the case for dismissing Matt 12:40 as a late tradition is rather weak. The case rests on two pieces of evidence. First, that Luke's version of the sign of Jonah saying in Luke 11:29–32 shows no awareness of Matt 12:40, and second, that Luke and Matthew are entirely dependent on the same written source for their material on the sign of Jonah. Based on these assumptions, it is natural to conclude that Matthew invented the interpretation that he places on the lips of Jesus in Matt 12:40. But as argued earlier in Chapter 6, Luke's version also hints at Christ's death and

[146] Proctor, "'After Three Days' in Mark"; "'After Three Days He Will Rise.'"

[147] C.S. Mann, *Mark: A New Translation with Introduction and Commentary* (Garden City, NY: Doubleday, 1986), 344; Joel Marcus, *Mark 8–16: A New Translation with Introduction and Commentary* (New Haven: Yale University Press, 2009), 605–6.

[148] For an attempt to explain why Mark would have made this revision, see Proctor, "'After Three Days' in Mark." Others argue that, in calculating the timing of Christ's resurrection from Friday afternoon to Sunday morning, "after three days" and "on the third day" would be regarded as equivalent in Jewish reckoning. See Robert Horton Gundry, *Mark: A Commentary on His Apology for the Cross* (Grand Rapids, MI: Eerdmans, 1993), 447–8.

[149] Tertullian, *Against Marcion*, 4.43; *Against the Jews*, 13. See McCasland, "The Scripture Basis," 132–3.

[150] Justin Martyr, *Dialogue with Trypho*, 107–8.

resurrection, indicating that Luke was aware of the tradition recorded in Matt 12:40, but chose not to emphasize it.[151] As a result, especially when we consider the possibility that Mark's phrasing "after three days" alludes to the same tradition recorded in Matt 12:40, we have good reason to suppose that Matt 12:40 faithfully captures an early Christian tradition. This conclusion finds additional support when we note that Matt 12:40 is the only New Testament text that provides any scriptural explanation for the claim that Christ's resurrection on the third day took place "in accordance with the scriptures."

The saying about the sign of Jonah may also provide the key to unlocking another scriptural puzzle. In Romans, Paul talks about being baptized into Christ's death. He writes:

> Do you not know that all of us who have been baptized into Christ Jesus were baptized into his death? We were buried therefore with him by baptism into death, so that as Christ was raised from the dead by the glory of the Father, we too might walk in newness of life. For if we have been united with him in a death like his, we shall certainly be united with him in a resurrection like his. (Rom 6:3–5)

In this passage, Paul states that baptism symbolizes Christ's death and burial,[152] and his phrasing implies that he expects his audience to be familiar with this symbolic interpretation of baptism. He shows the same expectation elsewhere. In Colossians, he interprets baptism in the same way—this time noting that rising up from the water also symbolizes Christ's resurrection—and again seems to expect his audience to be familiar with this symbolism (Col 2:12).[153] But why would he assume such familiarity? Baptism involves bathing, and so it naturally calls to mind notions of spiritual cleansing and the washing away of sins (see, for example, Acts 2:38). It does not, however, naturally call to mind notions of burial and death. Once we set about interpreting baptism in terms of death and resurrection, the symbolism falls into place neatly.

[151] Luke's knowledge of this tradition may have come directly from Matthew. Some scholars maintain Marcan priority but argue that Luke had access to Matthew. See, for example, Mark Goodacre, *The Case Against Q: Studies in Markan Priority and the Synoptic Problem* (Harrisburg: Trinity, 2002).

[152] Literally translated, Paul writes that "if we have become united to a likeness (*ὁμοίωμα*) of his death, certainly we shall be united to a likeness of his resurrection" (Rom 6:5). His choice of words draws attention to the symbolic nature of baptism. It also suggests that his theology of baptism derives, at least to some extent, from what he perceives as the symbolic meaning of the physical actions associated with baptism.

[153] In Romans, Paul explains that baptism confers a sharing in Christ's death—a notion that clearly presumes the resurrection symbolism of baptism—but he does not refer explicitly to the resurrection symbolism of baptism. In Colossians, however, Paul states explicitly that baptism symbolizes Christ's resurrection, and not merely his death. For an analysis of what these passages imply about baptism in the early Christian community, see Everett Ferguson, *Baptism in the Early Church: History, Theology, and Liturgy in the First Five Centuries* (Grand Rapids, MI: Eerdmans, 2009), 155–60.

Immersion represents death and burial, and rising represents resurrection. Nonetheless, one must be taught to interpret baptism in this way; the physical action of baptism does not naturally lend itself to this interpretation.[154] So the question remains: why would Paul assume familiarity with this symbolic interpretation? It does not seem plausible that Paul had invented it himself and was referring back to his own earlier teachings (especially since Paul had not yet visited the Christian community in Rome when he wrote Romans). It seems, rather, that this teaching was widespread among early Christians, and Paul knew he could expect his audience to be familiar with it.[155]

There are two main possibilities. In the ancient near east, water was often taken as a symbol of chaos (as in Gen 1:1–3). Consequently, it would have been natural for early Jewish Christians to see the waters of baptism representing the forces of destruction and death, and afterwards they might have made connections between baptism and Christ's overcoming of death through his resurrection. Yet the passages in Romans and Colossians each emphasize baptism as a sharing, not only in Christ's death and resurrection, but also in his burial. While this hypothesis can explain why early Christians might have seen baptism as symbolizing a passage through death to new life, and thus a sharing in Christ's death and resurrection, it stumbles when it comes to explaining why they also saw it as a sharing in Christ's burial.

The other possibility is that Jonah typology lies behind this symbolic interpretation of baptism. If the story of Jonah and the whale was one of the primary lenses through which early Christians interpreted Christ's death and resurrection, then it would have been natural for them to interpret baptism with Jonah imagery. They would have seen immersion as a symbolic burial in the whale's belly, and thus a symbolic sharing in Christ's three days in the tomb. Given that baptism is the most basic of Christian rituals, and given that it originally involved immersion in water, it would be hard to imagine them *not* making the connection. This theory finds support in patristic theology. Numerous patristic authors interpret the triple immersion of baptism as

[154] Although the physical actions of baptism do not naturally evoke notions of death and burial, Hellenistic culture associated Greek words from the *Bapt-* root with ideas of drowning, ships going down, and being overwhelmed with the troubles of life. See Ferguson, *Baptism in the Early Church: History, Theology, and Liturgy in the First Five Centuries*, 38–59. Consequently, there are some grounds for imagining how early Greek-speaking Christians might have come to interpret baptism as symbolic of Christ's death and burial without being "taught" to do so. On balance, however, the linguistic connotations of the Greek word for baptism, taken in themselves, do not seem sufficient to explain why this symbolic interpretation of baptism was so widespread and universal.

[155] Joseph Fitzmyer comes to the same conclusion. See Joseph A. Fitzmyer, *Romans: A New Translation with Introduction and Commentary* (New Haven, CT: Yale University Press, 1993), 431.

symbolic of Christ's three days in the tomb.[156] Cyril of Jerusalem draws on Matt 12:40, explaining the triple immersion in terms of "the three days and three nights that Jesus spent in the belly of the earth," and thus, implicitly, the story of Jonah.[157] This patristic interpretative tradition does not prove that Christians before Paul were using the story of Jonah to interpret baptism. Patristic authors might have started commenting on Paul's notion of being baptized into Christ's death, and then only later started seeing connections with Jonah 2:1 and Matt 12:40. Nonetheless, the fact that many patristic authors make this connection might also testify to a very early tradition about baptism—and thus to the theology of baptism present in Paul's letters deriving from an early Christian reading of Jonah. It is not inconceivable that this tradition about baptism goes back to Jesus himself.[158] If it does, then Jesus' descriptions of his death as a "baptism" in Mark 10:38–39 and Luke 12:50 might also allude to the story of Jonah.

The evidence indicates that Jonah loomed large in the early Christian theological imagination, much larger than we would have guessed from the New Testament evidence alone. Early Christian art represents Jonah more frequently than any other figure, including Jesus; patristic authors frequently interpret Christ's death and resurrection in light of Jonah; and even the ancient and universal belief that Christ's resurrection on the third day had been prophesied by the scriptures likely traces back to Jonah. Jonah's significance to early Christianity explains many otherwise puzzling aspects of early Christian theology. The whale simultaneously symbolizes both death and the devil; likewise, Christ's principal opponent is simultaneously both death and the devil. The sign of Jonah saying emphasizes the time Jesus spent among the dead, buried in the heart of the earth; likewise, in striking contrast to modern and contemporary Christianity, early Christianity emphasizes the redemptive significance of Christ's descent to the dead. Jonah also explains why the fishhook metaphor and its associated images are so widely attested among early Christians.[159]

[156] See, for example, Gregory of Nyssa, *Catechetical Oration*, 35, *On the Baptism of Christ*; Leo the Great, *Letters*, 16.4; John Damascene, *De orthodoxa fide*, 4.9. See also Lukken, *Original Sin*, 143.

[157] Cyril of Jerusalem, *Catechetical Lectures*, 20.4 (PG 33:180C–181A). Note that Cyril's quotation slightly alters Matt 12:40, reversing the saying's descriptions of Jonah and Christ. Matt 12:40 refers to being in the belly of the whale and Christ being in the heart of the earth, but Cyril talks about Christ being in the belly of the earth. This slight reversal suggests that Cyril has Jesus' saying about the sign of Jonah consciously in mind.

[158] In a similar vein, Fitzmyer argues that the baptismal tradition to which Paul refers ultimately traces back to Jesus' own teaching, and particularly his descriptions of his imminent death as a baptism. See Fitzmyer, *Romans*, 431.

[159] Contemporary Christian theology does not give comparable attention to Jonah, but the early Christian emphasis makes considerable sense. After all, the sign of Jonah is the only sign that Jesus promises in the synoptic Gospels (for the parallels with John 2:19, see Chapter 6 n36), and Matt 12:40 is one of the few occasions when Jesus explains the meaning of his death. The

The devil's ransom interpretation of the crucifixion does not lead to the fishhook metaphor; it derives from the fishhook metaphor and the wider Christian culture that gave rise to it. Origen provides a striking illustration of this point in his *Commentary on Romans*. In a section often cited as an early witness to the devil's ransom interpretation, Origen begins discussing the sign of Jonah, and then, by way of elaboration, proposes a parable in which Christ disguises himself in order to overcome the devil and liberate his captives.[160] The flow of his thinking suggests that his reflections on the devil's ransom are driven by his reflections on the sign of Jonah, and not vice versa. In light of this rhetorical progression, which is typical of patristic exegesis, it is striking that Matthew's first pericope about the sign of Jonah (Matt 12:38–42) is sandwiched between two other pericopes about unclean spirits (Matt 12:22–32, 12:43–45). The placement suggests that the patristic tendency to associate the sign of Jonah with the devil's ransom may trace back to a much earlier thought pattern. The conventional history of Christian doctrine sees Gregory of Nyssa's fishhook metaphor as an idiosyncratic approach to redemption and the *reductio ad absurdum* of the devil's ransom interpretation. In fact, the theological culture of early Christianity had long taken the sign of Jonah as the hermeneutic key to the death and resurrection of Jesus, and Gregory has simply adapted one of its stock images to his own purposes.[161]

GREGORY OF NYSSA AND THE *CATECHETICAL ORATION*

Gregory of Nyssa's *Catechetical Oration* contains one of the earliest and most influential examples of the devil's ransom interpretation of the crucifixion.[162]

saying about the sign of Jonah is also a riddle, not a parable. Since riddles naturally awaken curiosity, the saying's originator likely wanted Christians to give it special attention. Whether or not the saying about the sign of Jonah traces back to Jesus, the fact that it is enshrined in the Gospels provides Christians with a powerful reason to let it guide their reflections on the paschal mystery.

[160] Origen, *Commentary on Romans*, 5.10.10–12.

[161] The Eastern Orthodox keep alive the memory of Jonah's hermeneutic primacy by reading the entire book of Jonah during the divine liturgy every Holy Saturday.

[162] Studies of Gregory of Nyssa on the *Catechetical Oration* and the devil's ransom interpretation of the crucifixion include the following: Rivière, *The Doctrine of the Atonement*, 111–35; Rashdall, *The Idea of Atonement*, 303–8; Aulén, *Christus Victor*, 47–55; E. V. McClear, "The Fall of Man and Original Sin in the Theology of Gregory of Nyssa," *Theological Studies* 9 (1948): 175–212; A. S. Dunstone, *The Atonement in Gregory of Nyssa* (London: Tyndale Press, 1964); Richard Jakob Kees, *Die Lehre von der Oikonomia Gottes in der Oratio Catechetica Gregors von Nyssa* (Leiden: Brill, 1995); Ray, *Deceiving the Devil*, 121–5; Nyssa, *Discours Catéchétique*, Introduction and notes; Morwenna Ludlow, *Gregorgy of Nyssa, Ancient and (Post)modern* (Oxford: Oxford University Press, 2007), 108–24.

It is a short work, written in the late fourth century and modeled on Athanasius' *De Incarnatione*.[163] Drawing on ordinary human experience, Greek metaphysics, and sacred scripture, it sets out an elegant synthesis of core Christian beliefs for a philosophically sophisticated audience. Gregory seems to have written it especially for catechists and evangelists, to help them understand the faith better and communicate it more effectively. The work, therefore, is suffused with an apologetic tone; Gregory is working hard throughout to make the inner coherence of Christian doctrine more evident so that it can be more easily understood and believed. The synthetic and apologetic aims of the *Catechetical Oration*, combined with its brevity, make it an ideal case study of the devil's ransom interpretation in its full theological context.

Gregory begins the *Catechetical Oration* by discussing God's existence, the divine attributes, and the Trinity. Afterward, he moves on to creation and the nature of evil and argues that the moral evil of sin necessarily led to the ontological evils of suffering and death. Then, in the greater part of the treatise, he explains how God redeems us from our fallen condition through the Incarnation, the paschal mystery, and the sacraments; a small section of this explanation touches on the devil's ransom. It is thus within the context of a comprehensive summary of Christian doctrine, and in a very small section of it, that Gregory lays out his version of the devil's ransom. With this overview of the *Catechetical Oration*, let us consider in detail its argument and its approach to the devil's ransom.

As mentioned above, Gregory begins by discussing God and the Trinity. Then he turns to creation, and he explains that, at our creation, we enjoyed face-to-face communion with God, immortality, and freedom from suffering.[164] Prompted by the devil's temptation, however, we withdrew from goodness and chose evil. This free choice of evil corrupted both soul and body, and, as a result of our sin, we deprived ourselves, not only of our communion with God, but also our immortality and freedom from suffering.[165] Gregory explains:

> Now in the case of a lamp, when the flame has caught the wick too much and one is unable to blow it out, one mixes water with the oil, and by this means dims the flame. In just such a way the adversary deceitfully mingled evil with man's free will and thus in some measure quenched and obscured God's blessing. When this failed, the opposite necessarily entered in. Now the opposite of life is death; of power, weakness; of blessing, cursing; of candor, shame; and of every good thing,

[163] "It seems undeniable that this treatise of Athanasius [the *De Incarnatione*] served as a model for Gregory of Nyssa's *Catechetical Discourse*, even though Gregory takes a very different approach to many issues." Daley, "'He Himself is Our Peace,'" 163n35.

[164] *Catechetical Oration*, 6, in Gregory of Nyssa, "Address on Religious Instruction," in *Christology of the Later Fathers* (Louisville: Westminster John Knox Press, 2006), 280.

[165] *Catechetical Oration*, 6–8.

> its contrary. That is why humanity is in its present plight; for that beginning provided the occasion for such a conclusion.[166]

For Gregory, moral evil leads to suffering and death by metaphysical necessity. Evil is the privation of goodness,[167] and moral evil, the privation of moral goodness, inevitably leads to other evils, that is, to other privations. The suffering endured by humanity after sin is not an extrinsic punishment inflicted by God: it is the natural consequence of turning away from moral goodness.

For Gregory, then, the problem that Christ comes to solve is not merely sin; it also encompasses the collective reality of suffering, death, and the rule of evil. Accordingly, since this collective reality is the problem, the solution is not merely forgiveness; the solution is an integral human nature, with body and soul fully healed, and our immortality restored. He explains:

> Why, then, they ask, did the divine stoop to such humiliation? . . . If, then, the love of man is a proper mark of the divine nature, here is the explanation you are looking for, here is the reason for God's presence among men. Our nature was sick and needed a doctor. Man had fallen and needed someone to raise him up. He who had lost life needed someone to restore it. He who had ceased to participate in the good needed someone to bring him back to it. He who was shut up in darkness needed the presence of light. The prisoner was looking for someone to ransom him, the captive for someone to take his part. He who was under the yoke of slavery was looking for someone to set him free. Were these trifling and unworthy reasons to impel God to come down and visit human nature, seeing humanity was in such a pitiful and wretched state?[168]

Christ comes to rescue humanity from its miserable situation. He is not sent to win God's forgiveness; God's forgiveness is presupposed. Gregory does not puzzle about how Jesus could forgive sins before his crucifixion, but he does not need to puzzle: in his understanding, God's forgiveness does not require Christ's crucifixion.

Since our problem is more ontological than epistemological, it follows that the solution must likewise be more ontological than epistemological. Accordingly, for Gregory, our salvation is obtained more through the life and actions of the Word made flesh than his teaching and instruction.[169] Among the various moments of Christ's life, the most pivotal, with respect to the economy of salvation, is his resurrection.[170] Through the resurrection, Gregory explains, Christ overcame the power of death:

[166] *Catechetical Oration*, 6, 280–1. [167] *Catechetical Oration*, 5.

[168] *Catechetical Oration*, 14, 290; 15, 290–1. [169] *Catechetical Oration*, 35.

[170] Raymond Winling argues that the resurrection of Christ plays a key role in the structure and message of the *Catechetical Oration*. See Raymond Winling, "La résurrection du Christ comme principe explicatif et comme élèment structurant dans le *Discours catéchétique* de Grégoire de Nysse," *Studia Patristica* 22 (1989): 74–80.

> He united himself with our nature, in order that by its union with the Divine it might become divine, being rescued from death and freed from the tyranny of the adversary. For with *his* return from death, our mortal race begins *its* return to immortal life.[171]

Our death has its origins in Adam, and our resurrection its origins in Christ.[172] By his divine power, Christ reunited his soul to his body after they had been separated in death. Then, due to his ontological solidarity with the rest of humanity, the possibility of reuniting body and soul passed to us, and his resurrected human nature became the principle of our resurrection.[173]

Gregory explains that, in order to restore fallen humanity, it was necessary for God to join himself to every aspect of the human condition, so that every aspect could be healed. The divine power "had to touch the beginning and to extend to the end, covering all that lies between."[174] Nonetheless, although God became man to join himself to every aspect of the human condition, he came especially to join himself to our death so that he could join our death to his life. The Word became flesh to face death and overcome it in his resurrection:

> The birth was accepted by him for the sake of the death. For he who eternally exists did not submit to being born in a body because *he* was in need of life. Rather was it to recall *us* from death to life. Our whole nature had to be brought back from death. In consequence he stooped down to our dead body and stretched out a hand, as it were, to one who was prostrate. He approached so near death as to come into contact with it, and by means of his own body to grant our nature the principle of the resurrection, by raising our total humanity along with him by his power.[175]

For Gregory, the sending of the Son is ordered to the resurrection. It is not just one phase in Christ's life, or the inevitable sequel to the crucifixion: the resurrection is the goal (*σκοπός*) of the Incarnation.[176]

The power of the resurrection is communicated to humanity through the sacraments. Baptism communicates spiritual regeneration, and "[God's] grace is present in those who are born again through this sacramental act."[177] The triple submersion in water symbolizes Christ's three days in the tomb, and rising out of the water symbolizes his resurrection. By this symbolic imitation of Christ's death and resurrection, and by the believer's faith and repentance, God purifies the soul from sin and prepares it for resurrection.[178] Baptism,

171 *Catechetical Oration*, 25, 302.

172 "Now just as the principle of death had its origin in a single person and passed to the whole of human nature, similarly the principle of the resurrection originated in one Man and extends to all humanity" (*Catechetical Oration*, 16, 293–4).

173 *Catechetical Oration*, 16.

174 *Catechetical Oration*, 27, 304.

175 *Catechetical Oration*, 32, 310. See also 15, 291.

176 *Catechetical Oration*, 15.

177 *Catechetical Oration*, 34, 314.

178 *Catechetical Oration*, 35. See *Rom* 6:4.

however, is not sufficient to communicate salvation and immortality. Baptism joins us spiritually to Christ, but we are composed of body and soul and so our bodies, as well as our souls, must be joined to Christ. Therefore, something else is needed: the Eucharist. The soul is joined to Christ through faith and baptism, and the body is joined to Christ through reception of the Eucharist.[179] By our union with Christ's incorruptible body, our bodies also become immortal.

After explaining that God restores humanity through Christ's resurrection—and only after doing so—Gregory turns to the devil's ransom. He acknowledges that his explanation of the resurrection's salvific efficacy may not satisfy those wondering why God did not choose to redeem humanity by divine fiat. In response, Gregory argues that it was necessary for our restoration to manifest God's justice and wisdom and not simply his goodness.[180] His sheer desire to save us manifested his goodness, but his way of saving us, in order to manifest his justice and goodness, had also to be just and wise. From these opening remarks, Gregory proceeds to explain why God's chosen means of restoration were both just and wise.

For Gregory, the justice of God's plan emerges particularly in its reversal of the devil's injustice. Earlier in the *Catechetical Oration* Gregory had explained that, in the state of innocence, Adam had been invulnerable to direct assaults from the devil, and so the devil had been forced to approach him with guile and deception.[181] As he explains the justice of God's chosen means of restoration, Gregory returns to the devil's temptation of Adam, but this time he gives a more detailed description of the devil's deceit:

> By the deceit of the advocate and contriver of wickedness, [the mind] was convinced that good was its opposite. Nor would this deception have succeeded, had not the fishhook of evil been furnished with an outward appearance of good,

[179] "Owing to man's twofold nature, composed as it is of soul and body, those who come to salvation must be united with the Author of their life by means of both. In consequence, the soul, which has union with him by faith derives from this the means of salvation; for being united with life implies having a share in it. But it is in a different way that the body comes into intimate union with its Saviour . . . And what is this remedy? Nothing else than the body which proved itself superior to death and became the source of our life. For, as the apostle observes (cf. 1 Cor 5:6), a little yeast makes a whole lump of dough like itself. In the same way, when the body which God made immortal enters ours, it entirely transforms it into itself" (*Catechetical Oration*, 37, 318).

Gregory does not say explicitly that baptism is the cause of the soul's union with Christ; he mentions only faith. However, this comment follows immediately after a lengthy discussion of baptism, in which he describes baptism as purifying from sin and communicating a share in God's life through the combination of faith and water. Consequently, from the context, it is clear that Gregory means for the two sacraments of baptism and Eucharist to correspond to the salvation of soul and body, respectively.

[180] *Catechetical Oration*, 20–4. [181] *Catechetical Oration*, 6.

> as with a bait. Of his own free will man fell into this misfortune, and through pleasure became subject to the enemy of life.[182]

Since we can be attracted only by what seems good, the devil covered the fishhook of evil with the bait of pleasure, thus giving it the outward appearance of good. We swallowed it whole, and in this way made ourselves subject to the power of evil and death. (It is here that Gregory first uses the metaphor of the fishhook in the *Catechetical Oration*, but it is the first man, not the devil, who swallows it.)

In order to manifest his justice, Gregory argues, God could not simply reclaim humanity by sheer force; he had to best the devil on his own terms. It would be unjust to free slaves by force who had sold their freedom; likewise, it would be unjust for God to free us from the devil by force. Instead, God buys us back:

> When once we had voluntarily sold ourselves, he who undertook out of goodness to restore our freedom had to contrive a just and not a dictatorial method to do so. And some such method is this: to give the master the chance to take whatever he wants to as the price of the slave.[183]

In Gregory's telling, God allowed the devil to take whatever he wanted in exchange for the humanity he held captive, and the devil chose Christ because "he recognized in Christ a bargain which offered him more than he held."[184] By giving the devil a ransom for his captives, and by declining to use force, God liberated humanity in a way that manifested his justice and reversed the devil's injustice.

Gregory makes God's reversal of the devil's injustice more explicit in his telling of the divine deception. "Justice is evident," he writes, "in the rendering of due recompense, by which the deceiver was in turn deceived."[185] He explains that God deceived the devil by concealing Christ's divinity underneath the veil of his flesh. In this way, God reverses the devil's temptation. Just as the devil had tricked us into selling ourselves into slavery, God tricks the devil into bringing about his own downfall.[186]

[182] *Catechetical Oration*, 21, 298.
[183] *Catechetical Oration*, 22, 299.
[184] *Catechetical Oration*, 23, 300.
[185] *Catechetical Oration*, 26, 303.
[186] To fend off the charge that his narrative ascribes unfitting behavior to God, Gregory makes use of something that we could classify as double effect reasoning. First, drawing on ordinary moral intuitions, he notes that we judge acts of deception according to the intentions informing them. He writes: "The conspirator and the one who cures the victim both mix a drug with a man's food. In the one case it is poison; in the other it is an antidote for poison. But the mode of healing in no way vitiates the kindly intention. In both instances a drug is mixed with the food; but when we catch sight of the aim, we applaud the one and are incensed at the other" (*Catechetical Oration*, 26, 303). Then, on the basis of this distinction, Gregory argues that the intention informing God's deception of the devil made it consonant with God's justice, goodness, and wisdom: "For he who first deceived man by the bait of pleasure is himself deceived by the camouflage of human nature. But the purpose of the action changes it into something good. For

> The opposing power could not, by its nature, come into immediate contact with God's presence and endure the unveiled sight of him. Hence it was that God, in order to make himself easily accessible to him who sought the ransom from us, veiled himself in our nature. In that way, as it is with greedy fish, he might swallow the Godhead like a fishhook along with the flesh, which was the bait. Thus, when life came to dwell with death and light shone upon the darkness, their contraries might vanish away. For it is not in the nature of darkness to endure the presence of light, nor can death exist where life is active.[187]

In his telling of the story, Gregory uses the image of the fishhook to show how God's intervention reverses the devil's injustice. The devil had caught man on a fishhook baited with pleasure; God catches the devil on a fishhook baited with the Word made flesh. The passage is rich in metaphor and imagery and incorporates many of the themes and motifs found in other patristic descriptions of the devil's ransom: the devil's inability to recognize Christ's divinity; the divine deception; the descent to the dead; the ransom of captives from the devil; the metaphoric blurring of death and the devil; and the allusions to Jonah. Gregory does not explicitly ascribe rights to the devil, but he does suggest that the devil's authority over humanity had some legitimacy to it.

As a mythical story, Gregory's telling of the devil's downfall succeeds admirably with its smooth prose and colorful images. As a coherent narrative, however, it falls short. The central conceit of the story is that the devil claims Christ as the ransom price for his captives without realizing his true identity. But Gregory does not explain how the devil was planning to release his other captives after claiming his ransom; there is no dialogue between God and the devil, laying out the terms of the exchange. In fact, although he does not say as much, Gregory's metaphysical principles suggest that the devil would not be able to release his captives even if he wanted to honor his agreement (which he surely would not). By the time Gregory turns to the story of the devil's downfall, he has already established that Christ's resurrection is the principle of our resurrection and, therefore, our liberation from death. So it is not as though the devil could open up the gates of hell and release his prisoners whenever he wanted. They are as stuck as he is. The devil communicates death; he does not and cannot communicate life. Still, Gregory's skillful storytelling

the one practiced deceit to ruin our nature; but the other, being at once just and good and wise, made use of a deceitful device to save the one who had been ruined" (26, 303).

Whatever we make of Gregory's argument, crucial elements of double effect reasoning are evident: namely, a distinction between action and intention, and the justification of a seemingly problematic action by the intention informing it. The commonality with Anselm is striking. At crucial moments in their theological narratives, Gregory and Anselm each turn to double effect reasoning to advance their argument. Gregory applies double effect reasoning to God's deception of the devil, while Anselm applies it to God's willing of Christ's crucifixion, but each employs double effect reasoning to preserve God from the appearance of injustice.

[187] *Catechetical Oration*, 24, 301.

makes it easy for the reader to suspend disbelief and follow him to the final scene without worrying about the details.

The plot holes in Gregory's theological narrative do not indicate that Gregory was guilty of oversight; it indicates, rather, that he was not interested in constructing a coherent narrative. He had told his readers at the outset that his purpose in telling his story was to explain how God's chosen means of redemption manifested his goodness, justice, and wisdom, and that is what his story does. It is not coincidental, therefore, that after describing God's method for overcoming the devil, Gregory pauses and reflects on how it shows forth God's goodness, justice, and wisdom:

> All God's attributes are at once displayed in this—his goodness, his wisdom, and his justice. That he decided to save us is proof of his goodness. That he struck a bargain to redeem the captive indicates his justice. And it is evidence of his transcendent wisdom that he contrived to make accessible to the enemy what was [otherwise] inaccessible.[188]

By the time Gregory comes to the story of the devil's downfall, he had already laid out the central principle of salvation: namely, that we are restored through Christ's resurrection. The story of the devil's downfall simply fills in the gaps. It gives a loose, colorful explanation of why God's chosen means of redemption were fitting—especially by emphasizing how God's justice reverses the devil's injustice—but it is not meant to be an explanation of the mechanics of redemption; that explanation had already been provided in his discussion of the resurrection.

For Gregory, God does not offer the devil a ransom in a literalistic sense, as is especially evident from the plot holes in his narrative. The devil's ransom is a metaphor to illustrate how God's plan of salvation manifests his wisdom and justice; it does not refer to an actual commercial transaction. Moreover, in the theological narrative of the *Catechetical Oration*, the devil does not even play the role of God's primary adversary; it is rather death and all the attendant miseries of fallen human condition that God is striving to overcome. Notably, outside his discussions of Adam's fall and the devil's ransom, Gregory shows little interest in the figure of the devil, but he returns again and again, in every part of his treatise, to the corruption of human nature and its restoration through Christ's resurrection. These priorities reflect his larger theological commitments. In Gregory's soteriology, the emphasis is on the resurrection and the communication of its power through the sacraments, not the crucifixion. The crucifixion is the price of salvation, but it is not what does the saving. Accordingly, the devil's ransom is far less central to Gregory's soteriology than the resurrection.

[188] *Catechetical Oration*, 23, 300.

RECONSTRUCTING THE DEVIL'S RANSOM

The received reconstruction of the devil's ransom runs something like this: through sin, the devil obtains legal authority over humanity, and God can only redeem humanity if the devil crucifies Christ, someone over whom he does not have any legal rights. So God allows the devil to crucify Christ, and as a result humanity is set free from the power of sin and death. Anselm offers the earliest extant version of this reconstruction in Book I.7 of *Cur Deus homo*, and despite many challenges over the past century, it endures to the present day, far overshadowing every other alternative reconstruction of the devil's ransom. As we have seen, however, this reconstruction seriously distorts what patristic authors thought about the crucifixion. A more accurate reconstruction would run something like this: through sin, humanity becomes subject to evil, suffering, and death. In order to restore humanity, God becomes man, so that he can draw out the power of evil in all its various manifestations and take it upon himself. Then, after absorbing the full force of evil in his crucifixion, Christ overcomes death by his resurrection and makes it possible for us to share in his victory by being joined to his Person through the sacraments. The devil does not have any true rights over humanity, nor is any literal ransom paid to him. The language of rights and ransom serves only as a way of praising God's wisdom and justice in bringing about our salvation through Christ's crucifixion; it does not ascribe any true legal authority to the devil.

Many reconstructions of the devil's ransom emphasize God's deception of the devil. God, however, does not deceive the devil in every version of the devil's ransom, nor is divine deception essential to its narrative. The divine stratagem works, and therefore the narrative works, because the devil cannot resist an opportunity to strike at his Creator, whatever the consequences. God's appearance in the flesh tempts the tempter with an offer he cannot refuse; knowledge of the eventual outcome is irrelevant. The crucifixion cannot satisfy the devil's malicious desires, but evil is not rational. And so, no matter what knowledge patristic authors attribute to the devil, the results are the same: as Origen writes, "Christ's blood did not quench his thirst, but it broke his might."[189]

Throughout its many variations, the defining feature of the devil's ransom is not deception, not trickery, and not even the devil (its essential structure would hold together just as well if Christ's crucifixion were caused entirely by human agents), but *God's deliberate provocation of evil.* In each version, God intervenes in human history to call out evil and draw it to himself. Evil takes the bait and overreaches, and God reclaims humanity from the

[189] Origen, *Commentary on Romans*, 4.11.4, in Rivière, *The Doctrine of the Atonement*, 118.

dominion of evil and death. In this way the redemption of humanity is brought about by God's deliberate provocation of evil. God turns evil against itself and it swallows its own tail. We are saved, in the words of Cyril of Jerusalem, "by the very weapons the devil was using to defeat us."[190]

Once we consider the writings of patristic authors in their full context, Anselm's reconstruction of the devil's ransom interpretation cannot stand. It does not come close to doing justice to patristic conceptualizations of the devil's ransom. Yet, despite the advances made by Gustaf Aulén and others, and despite controversies surrounding Anselm's own approach to redemption, Anselm's reconstruction still reigns as the default paradigm for understanding the devil's ransom. How did this come to pass?

Since Anselm, soteriological reflection in the West has focused on the crucifixion, and when that same narrow focus is brought anachronistically to the writings of the patristic era, distortion necessarily results, because patristic authors do not focus on the cross in the same way. For patristic authors, salvation comes through the resurrection and the sacraments. The crucifixion is necessary and crucial, but it is not the locus of salvation; it is only the ransom, the price of salvation. Patristic authors give little attention to the devil's ransom in their writings, because it is Christ's resurrection, not his crucifixion, that brings about our resurrection. Contrary to Anselm, for patristic authors redemption is not about making forgiveness possible; it is about making possible the purification and restoration of human nature. There is no sense in which God could not, or would not, forgive humanity unless Christ died on the cross—which is why, unlike many theologians after Anselm, patristic authors are completely untroubled by stories of Jesus forgiving sins before his crucifixion.

When it is assumed that salvation comes only through the crucifixion, and not the entire paschal mystery and the sacraments, it is difficult to grasp the metaphorical character of the devil's ransom. A legal story of redemption, where Christ's crucifixion cancels some legal debt, is the only kind of story that can enable the cross to bear the entire weight of salvation. Consequently, those who assume that salvation comes only through the crucifixion inevitably drift toward legalistic reconstructions of the devil's ransom. They cannot help presuming that patristic authors share their sense of the crucifixion's role in the mechanics of redemption, and thus intend for the cross to bear the entire weight of salvation. Legalistic reconstructions of the devil's ransom are theologically unattractive and even ridiculous, but they make sense and they work logically, so it is easy to think that they accurately represent the patristic consensus. But patristic authors are not telling a legal story of redemption.

[190] Cyril of Jerusalem, *Catechetical Lectures*, 12.15, in Yarnold, *Cyril of Jerusalem*, 146.

They are telling an ontological story, and they think the pivotal moment of salvation is the resurrection, not the crucifixion.

The wrong questions have been brought to the evidence. When questions are asked about how patristic authors interpret the crucifixion, the answer is that they interpret the crucifixion as Christ giving himself as a ransom to the devil and death. But other questions are more helpful. When questions are asked about how God rescues us from sin, suffering, and death, the answer is that they think that we are restored through the descent to the dead and the resurrection, and then by being joined to Christ through the Holy Spirit and the sacraments. We are redeemed by Christ's cross and thus "bought with a price" (1 Cor 6:20, 7:23), but we are rescued from our fallen condition by Christ's bodily resurrection.

EVALUATING THE DEVIL'S RANSOM INTERPRETATION OF THE CRUCIFIXION

In the devil's ransom interpretation, God does not send his Son to be crucified for the sake of being crucified. He does not even send his Son to be crucified for the sake of enduring crucifixion with patience and charity. Rather, God sends his Son to absorb the malicious fury of evil and then conquer death through his resurrection. In this narrative, God intends his Son's overcoming of evil and death, but he does not intend his Son's death. God wills that Christ provoke evil to overstep its limits, but he does not will the crucifying of Christ. Consequently, the devil's ransom interpretation of the crucifixion neither implies that God wills moral evil nor impugns God's goodness. In this way, it falls squarely within the parameters identified by the *via negativa*. And since it maintains that Jesus saw his death as advancing his mission, and that the crucifixion is integral and necessary to God's plan of salvation, it also fits neatly with the scriptural evidence identified in the *via positiva*. Therefore, according to the criteria identified in this study, the devil's ransom interpretation constitutes an adequate solution to the problem of God's will and Christ's crucifixion.

Two Objections to the Devil's Ransom Interpretation

Two objections might be raised against the devil's ransom interpretation. First, if Anselm's theory of redemption implies that God wills moral evil, then it seems that the devil's ransom interpretation must as well. Like Anselm's theory, the devil's ransom interpretation maintains that God sends his Son to accomplish our redemption through his crucifixion. The crucifixion is not extrinsic to God's plan; it is a crucial moment in its accomplishment. Therefore, God must intend the crucifixion as a means to an end, just as he does in Anselm's theory, and thus will moral evil. Either that or Anselm's theory does not truly imply that God wills moral evil.

Here is where the earlier work on intention and moral value pays off. To respond to this objection, we need to recall the important distinction between what our intentions imply logically and what our intentions imply ontologically. We necessarily intend whatever our intentions imply logically, but we do not necessarily intend what our intentions imply ontologically. That is, we can intend something without intending everything ontologically bound up with it. In the devil's ransom interpretation, God's intentions in handing over his Son do not logically imply the intending of his death; they merely imply it ontologically. God intends to provoke evil so that it overreaches, and then to overcome death through Christ's resurrection. Yet neither the idea of provoking evil to weaken it, nor the idea of overcoming death, includes the idea of Christ's death. God does not intend his Son's crucifixion as a means to an end; it is the nonintended side effect of what he does intend. God wants evil to overreach, and God wants to overcome death, but he does not want the actual crucifying of his Son.

In Anselm's theory, however, God's intentions in handing over his Son logically imply the intending of his death, and thus the willing of moral evil. God wills the heroic self-sacrifice of Christ for its own sake, as the chosen means to the end of making satisfaction. But because it is not possible to will heroic self-sacrifice for its own sake without also willing the occasion of that self-sacrifice, Anselm cannot avoid implying that God wills Christ's crucifixion—and thus moral evil. It is the difference between the soldier who jumps on a grenade to protect others and the police officer who gets himself killed in the line of duty so that his family can pay off its debts. In the devil's ransom interpretation, Jesus is like the soldier who jumps on a grenade. He causes his own death, but he does not intend it. In Anselm's theory, Jesus is like the police officer who gets himself killed in the line of duty. He not only causes his own death; he also intends it. Consequently, God wills moral evil twice: first, in God the Son's act of suicide, performed in his human nature, and second, in the Triune God's willing of this act of suicide and, implicitly, the actual crucifying of Christ.

The devil's ransom interpretation is able to safeguard God's goodness because it takes the narrative context of the crucifixion seriously. It does not consider the crucifixion in isolation from what comes before or what comes afterward. Nor does it portray the crucifixion as an elaborate Trinitarian spectacle with God's creatures supplying only local color and spectators for the performance. Instead, salvation occurs through a sacred economy that fully involves created freedom. In Jesus of Nazareth, God acts on the same plane as his creatures, and through their free response to his saving initiative, God brings about humanity's redemption. Some respond positively to Jesus, welcoming the kingdom of God and helping to build it up; others reject Jesus and advance God's purposes in spite of themselves. Either way, God's creatures freely cooperate with God's plan of salvation and help bring it to completion.

The dramatic structure of the devil's ransom interpretation is well suited to Judeo-Christian revelation. Christian faith is not about abstract theological principles; it is about God's intervention in human history, especially in the person of Jesus Christ. Consequently, the dramatic structure of the devil's ransom interpretation parallels the structure of revelation. Moreover, with its emphasis on narrative, the devil's ransom interpretation is refreshingly unconcerned with abstract concepts such as satisfaction and atonement. It does not repudiate the hermeneutic value of abstract concepts, but it privileges the narrative from which these abstractions are abstracted. It puts them in their proper context—and in their proper place. In this way of looking at things redemption is not divine accounting, with God settling humanity's debt to himself or making up for our sins. It is a gripping story of good triumphing over evil through a maneuver that is clever, transcendently beautiful, and dramatically satisfying.

The genius of the devil's ransom interpretation is that God incorporates evil choices into the economy of salvation without condoning them. God deliberately provokes the devil by sending his Son, but the devil is the one who chooses to attack Christ. Similarly, Jesus provokes a violent reaction from his contemporaries by his preaching and his ministry, but those who respond with violence are fully responsible for their violence. God redeems us through the crucifixion without wanting or willing the actual crucifying. With the devil's ransom interpretation, making sense of God's plan of salvation does not require any mental gymnastics about free will, divine foreknowledge, and the nature of time and eternity. The drama of salvation can be understood in an intuitive way as the story of a clever trap. God allows his creatures to misuse their freedom, and then he uses their evil choices to overcome evil and death. By granting evil a genuine role in the drama of salvation, the devil's ransom interpretation avoids any implication that God secretly orchestrates Christ's crucifixion behind the scenes, or somehow secretly condones it.

In this way of looking at things, the problem of Judas evaporates. In the devil's ransom interpretation, God sends his Son to draw the malice of human society to himself, but he does not want the actual malice; he wants to protect us from ourselves and give evil a chance to undermine itself. Consequently, the necessity of Judas' betrayal rests not in divine ordination but in our fallen condition. It was Judas, not God, who imposed necessity on his betrayal. God knew that it is inevitable that *someone* would betray Jesus, and from all eternity he knew that it would be this man Judas; still, he did not ordain

Judas' betrayal. This crucial distinction harmonizes with Jesus' words at the last supper: "For the Son of Man goes as it is written of him, but woe to that man by whom the Son of Man is betrayed! It would have been better for that man if he had not been born" (Mark 14:21; cf. Matt 26:25, Luke 22:23). In this saying, Jesus affirms the necessity of his betrayal, but, strikingly, he says only that it was necessary for him to be betrayed, and that it would be better for his betrayer not to have been born; he does not say that it was necessary for Judas to betray him.

Some contemporary theologians, most notably Gustaf Aulén, are attracted to the devil's ransom interpretation precisely because it gives a much stronger account of God's goodness. The feminist theologian Darby Kathleen Ray particularly appreciates the way that evil ends up causing its own downfall.[191] Although she finds the devil's ransom interpretation problematic in many respects, especially inasmuch as it posits a personified spirit of evil, she thinks that it brings out God's absolute opposition to evil and violence. She also sees useful applications for theological ethics. She thinks that, just as penal substitution theories of redemption can encourage passivity in the face of evil, the devil's ransom interpretation can encourage us to confront evil and overcome it through nonviolent strategies.

René Girard's scapegoat theory of redemption could be classified as a variation of the devil's ransom interpretation.[192] As with patristic authors, for Girard, Christ's mission is deliberately provocative. Christ draws out the evil in human society, and by accepting his crucifixion he reveals the sociological mechanism that had preserved social harmony by scapegoating outsiders. In this way, Christ breaks the cycle of violence that had dominated human civilization from the beginning. Not coincidentally, Girard writes approvingly about the patristic idea of God triumphing over the devil through some kind of stratagem:

> The Greek Fathers, in treating Satan as the victim of a kind of divine ruse, suggest aspects of revelation now obscured because the anthropology of the Cross remains obscure.... The idea of Satan duped by the Cross is therefore not magical at all and in no way offends the dignity of God. The trick that traps Satan does not include the least bit of either violence or dishonesty on God's part. It is not really a ruse or trick; it is rather the inability of the prince of this world to understand the divine love.[193]

Like Abelard, Girard has a hard time explaining why Christ's crucifixion offers anything more than a good example, or how it could have been necessary for

[191] Ray, *Deceiving the Devil*, esp. 118–45.

[192] While he does not suggest that Girard's theory could be classified as a variation of the devil's ransom interpretation, Michael Kirwan also notes the similarities between them. See Michael Kirwan, *Girard and Theology* (London: T & T Clark, 2009), 70–3.

[193] Girard, *I See Satan Fall*, 152.

our salvation. But what is appealing about his theory is that, just like in patristic theories, God opposes evil with his own goodness and simply allows evil to bring about its own downfall.

The second objection to the devil's ransom interpretation concerns the status it assigns to the devil. According to this objection, it is inconceivable that an all-powerful God would find it necessary to pay a ransom—metaphorical or otherwise—to anyone or anything, let alone an evil being. By suggesting that God pays a ransom to the devil and death, even if only in metaphorical terms, the devil's ransom interpretation seems to elevate the status of the devil beyond due limits, and thus verge into something approaching Manichaeism.

Against the caricature reconstructions offered by Anselm and others, this objection would indeed have great merit. Against what patristic authors actually propose in their writings, however, it does not. In its essential logical structure, the devil's ransom interpretation does not imply an evil principle with powers rivaling God's; it does not even require the existence of a malevolent spiritual being. Its narrative works as long as there is evil at work in human society. According to the devil's ransom interpretation, Jesus calls out the malice of his contemporaries, absorbs it in his own flesh, and then overcomes it by his resurrection. Whether this malice is demonic as well as human is irrelevant: either way, the narrative works. Patristic authors affirm that the devil is somehow involved in Christ's crucifixion, but the logic of their interpretation holds together just as well if Christ's crucifixion instead had purely human causes. In any case, as we have seen, patristic authors often speak about the devil in ways that encompass a wide range of cosmic, social, and personal evils. For patristic authors, evil in a global sense, and not merely the devil, is the author of Christ's crucifixion, the tyrant forced to release his captives and the opponent trampled by Christ's resurrection. Consequently, regardless of whether or not the devil's ransom interpretation provides an adequate account of redemption, accusations of Manichaeism are misplaced. Unless the sheer affirmation of the devil's existence renders someone dualist—in which case even Jesus himself would have to be considered Manichean—patristic authors are innocent of the charge. It also bears emphasizing that patristic authors never defined their understanding of redemption by reference to the devil; classifying it according to the place it assigns the devil is a later innovation.

The New Testament in Light of the Devil's Ransom

The devil's ransom interpretation is not only compatible with Christ's historical attitude toward his death and New Testament affirmations about the necessity of the crucifixion; it also harmonizes well with other elements of the Gospel narratives, even those aspects that have been perennially problematic for other interpretations. Christ's forgiveness of sins before his crucifixion does not raise any problems because redemption is about more than the forgiveness of sins; it is about overcoming evil and death through Christ's bodily resurrection. Likewise, the episodes where Jesus seems to be deliberately provocative can be taken at face value without questioning either his sanity or their historicity.[194]

The language of ransom connects with scripture in a way that the language of satisfaction and even atonement does not.[195] The word "redemption" has its etymological origins in *redemptio*, the Latin word for ransom, and thus traces back to the ransom saying of Mark 10:45. Nonetheless, the concept of redemption has become so unhooked from its original scriptural and theological context that the connection between redemption and ransom is no longer immediately perceived. Redemption has lost its association with the practice of liberating captives and slaves by the payment of a price. Instead, redemption has become a vague theological category, often used synonymously with salvation or atonement, whose content depends entirely on the theology of the person using it. Because the language of ransom relies more directly on the theological categories of scripture, it ensures easier access to the lifeblood of Christian theology.

By following the categories of scripture more closely, the devil's ransom interpretation of the crucifixion also allows for a precise distinction between redemption and salvation. Currently, these two categories are used almost interchangeably, but arguably it more closely follows New Testament usage to make a firm distinction between them. According to the devil's ransom interpretation, we can say that our redemption was achieved once and for all by Christ through his cross, but our salvation comes by being joined to the resurrected Christ though the Holy Spirit and the sacraments. And while there are no degrees of redemption, since we are all equally redeemed, we can say that there are degrees of salvation: the more we are healed from the wounds of sin and death, the more we are saved, that is, the more we are rescued from our predicament.

The devil's ransom interpretation also unlocks the full meaning of Christ's saying about the good shepherd. In John's Gospel, Jesus declares, "I am the good shepherd. The good shepherd lays down his life for the sheep" (John

[194] For example, E. P. Sanders argues that it is historically implausible that Jesus knowingly brought about his own death, because it would mean that Jesus was "weird." See Sanders, *Jesus and Judaism*, 332–3.

[195] The word "atonement" was coined by William Tyndale to translate the participle of καταλλάσσω, a Greek word meaning "to reconcile," in 2 Cor 5:19. So atonement language is grounded in scripture. Yet atonement language is not used exclusively to describe our reconciliation with God (for example, 1 Cor 7:11 talks about a wife reconciling with her husband). Moreover, unlike ransom language, it does not refer to the specific event of the crucifixion, but rather to Christ's work of salvation considered in its entirety.

10:11). But in what context does the good shepherd lay down his life? He hints at the answer in the next verse. He says, "He who is a hireling and not a shepherd, whose own the sheep are not, sees the wolf coming and leaves the sheep and flees; and the wolf snatches them and scatters them" (John 10:12). So the good shepherd does not lay down his life by searching out lost sheep at great risk to his own life. He lays down his life by staying around and confronting the wolf. Jesus does not say how the good shepherd confronts the wolf, but his words give us some clues. The repeated formula about laying down his life (John 10:11, 10:15, 10:17–18; cf. John 15:13) suggests that the good shepherd confronts the wolf in a nonviolent way, not by fighting it physically. And there is only one way the shepherd could spare his sheep in a nonviolent way: by attracting the wolf to himself so that the wolf attacks him instead. The good shepherd lays down his life by allowing the wolf to satisfy its hunger with his own flesh.

The good shepherd, however, does not only lay down his life. He also takes it up again. Jesus says, "For this reason the Father loves me, because I lay down my life, that I may take it again" (John 10:17). This verse presents a puzzle. Jesus lays down his life in order that he can take it up again. But he has just been saying that he lays down his life for his sheep, hinting that he lays it down in the process of staying around to confront the wolf. So which is it: does he lay down his life for his sheep, or does he lay it down in order to take it up again? The devil's ransom interpretation solves this puzzle. The good shepherd lays down his life with both intentions in mind. He lays down his life to protect his sheep from the wolf's aggression, but he also lays down his life to conquer death by taking it up again, so that "they may have life, and have it abundantly" (John 10:10). And just as the good shepherd does not intend to cause his own death, but only to protect his sheep, so too, when Jesus draws the world's malice to himself, he does not intend to cause his own death, but only to protect the world from its own malice.

The good shepherd imagery brings out an important aspect of the devil's ransom interpretation. It works only because it supposes the presence of preexisting malice. Jesus is not coming into the world to rouse a peaceful world to violence against himself; not only would such a world not need redemption, to do so would imply intending his own death, and thus suicide. He is coming into a world already full of sin and malice and drawing the world's evil to himself—and thus away from others. In other words, the devil's ransom interpretation works only because it contains an element of substitution. Jesus takes on himself the violence that would otherwise have been directed toward others, knowing that while his opponents are occupied with him they cannot be tormenting others, and knowing that, unlike anyone else, he can overcome death—not just for himself, but for everyone and for all time.

The Crucifixion and Divine Unity

Unlike Anselm's theory of redemption and those theories bearing the marks of its influence, the devil's ransom interpretation of the crucifixion allows for a strong account of divine unity. In the narrative of the devil's ransom, the individual divine Persons have distinct roles in the economy of salvation, but the Trinity functions as a glorious unity. The Son faces his passion with the Father and the Holy Spirit, as the Trinity's emissary to a fallen world. He does not face his passion alone, in order to offer his suffering to the Father as part of an intra-Trinitarian exchange, because he faces his passion on the Father's behalf. The Son is the Father's ambassador to humanity; the Son is not humanity's ambassador to the Father. The Son also represents humanity to the Father, mediating on our behalf, but he brings this secondary role to perfection only after he has returned to the Father and taken his seat, on his throne, at the Father's right hand. Jesus says to Philip at the Last Supper: "Whoever has seen me, has seen the Father" (John 14:9). The devil's ransom interpretation of the crucifixion makes it easier to see the Father in the Son, even on the cross, because the Son is more clearly the Father's ambassador.

Because it gives evil an authentic role in the drama of salvation, the devil's ransom interpretation avoids dividing the Persons of the Trinity against themselves. There is dramatic tension between Christ's human will and the divine will, but there is no dramatic tension between Father and Son. The dramatic tension is between God and evil, and between God and death, but not between God and Christ, or between God's justice and God's mercy. It is not an accident that patristic soteriology is notably devoid of the tension between Father and Son that pervades Anselm's theory of redemption. Because the devil's ransom interpretation can account for the dramatic tension evident in the crucifixion without appealing to any intra-Trinitarian explanation, it prevents conflict from seeping into conceptions of the Trinity.

In the Dominican Church of Santa Maria Novella in Florence, a side wall displays one of the few paintings by Massacio, a fresco called *The Holy Trinity*. This painting captures the Trinitarian implications of the devil's ransom interpretation. It shows Christ crucified with God the Father standing behind the cross, with his arms also stretched out, gripping the crossbeam, as though God the Father is holding up the cross on which Christ is being crucified. The Holy Spirit, depicted as a dove, descends from the Father to the Son, visually and symbolically uniting them to each other. Christ's eyes are closed, perhaps he has already died, but the eyes of God the Father are open and he looks out at us with a sober expression. From the way he is supporting the cross, with his arms stretched out, it is as though he is helping his Son suffer and showing us his Son at the same time. It is as if he is saying with his eyes, "Look at my Son." There is no sense in which God the Father wants the crucifying of his Son.

In Massacio's *Holy Trinity* and the devil's ransom interpretation, the crucifixion is a revelation of the Father's mercy just as much as it is a revelation of the Son's mercy. The Father sends his Son so that we can be united to him through his humanity, and in this way come to share his place in the life of the Trinity. The Father does not come himself because we are to share the Son's place in the Trinity, not the Father's place, and not the Spirit's place, and so it must be the Son who comes. The Son suffers for our sins, not because this suffering wins God's forgiveness, but because this suffering is ontologically necessary for our restoration and sanctification. Consequently, although the divine Persons have different roles in the economy of salvation, there is no opposition between God the Father and God the Son. The Trinity functions as a unity, executing together the decisions of a single undivided will.

CONCLUSION

For the first thousand years of Christianity, Christian theology and culture were deeply informed by the devil's ransom interpretation of the crucifixion. This approach to redemption has been eclipsed since then, but it offers considerable resources for contemporary theology, and it deserves a warm welcome back into the fold of mainstream theological reflection. By giving a role to evil in the drama of salvation and emphasizing the resurrection, the devil's ransom interpretation makes it possible to affirm the redemptive character of Christ's crucifixion, without implying that the Father wills the crucifying of anyone, let alone his own beloved Son.

Epilogue

In the garden of Gethsemane, when Jesus prays to his Father, we hear only one side of the conversation. We hear Jesus asking for this cup to pass from him, and then we hear him saying, "Not my will, but yours be done," but we do not hear the Father's response. The Father does not say anything we can hear, and he may not say anything Jesus can hear, either. Afterward, Jesus returns to his disciples, ready for his passion, and Judas arrives with the temple guard. As they lead him off to trial, we are left with some unanswered questions. What was the Father's will, exactly, and how could it be in keeping with divine goodness for the Father's will to require Christ's crucifixion?

This study has sought to address this theological difficulty and then work toward a solution. The first and second parts were devoted to clarifying the parameters of the problem and considering what the Father has revealed about his will in creation and sacred scripture. Then the third part of this study applied these philosophical and exegetical results to three influential interpretations of the crucifixion. According to these criteria, it concluded that that Anselm and Abelard's theories of redemption have serious flaws, while the devil's ransom interpretation offers an adequate solution to the problem of God's will and Christ's crucifixion.

Looking back, it is easier to understand the attention given in the first part to philosophical concepts such as intention, moral value, and double effect reasoning. Precise theological judgments require precise philosophical tools, and these philosophical discussions were necessary to differentiate between Anselm's theory of redemption and the devil's ransom interpretation in their implications for God's will. Without precise philosophical distinctions, it would not be possible to explain why Anselm's theory of redemption implies divine willing of moral evil and the devil's ransom interpretation does not. Anselm's theory of redemption is routinely dissected and criticized by theologians but, because the criticisms often lack precision, they are easily dismissed by Anselm's defenders. The clarification of intending and willing in this study aimed at making its criticism of Anselm's theory more difficult to deflect. Similarly, the devil's ransom interpretation presumes that provoking violence against oneself can be morally good in certain circumstances, and so this study's accounts of double effect reasoning and the ethics of self-sacrifice were necessary to lay the groundwork for defending this thesis. These tools can be used to evaluate other theories of redemption to see whether or not they imply God's willing of moral evil. Even if the tools themselves are found wanting, by the very fact of providing them, this study has identified some of the philosophical issues surrounding the problem of God's will and Christ's crucifixion and proposed a roadmap for tackling them.

Again looking back, it also easier to appreciate the peculiarly narrow focus of the second part. Typically, exegetical studies focus on areas of interpretative controversy and then take a position one way or the other. This study, however, focused on areas of widespread agreement, and then drew relatively modest conclusions. The attention given to fairly noncontroversial conclusions might have seemed puzzling. These conclusions, however, prove their theological significance when it comes to time to apply them to theological interpretations of the crucifixion. With these exegetical conclusions alone, we can rule out Abelard's theory of redemption, and we can do it without getting into contested areas of New Testament exegesis, thus making our theological verdict that much sturdier. These modest exegetical conclusions can also be used to evaluate other theories of redemption to see whether they fulfill a bare minimum of coherence with the New Testament evidence. The conclusions about Jesus' attitude toward his death are particularly useful, because some theories of redemption maintain that Jesus did not realize that his death would advance his mission until after his resurrection.

The philosophical and exegetical chapters allowed for new critiques of Anselm and Abelard's theories of redemption. That these two theories could be critiqued is not new; both are frequent targets of theological criticism. What is new, though, is the narrow focus of this study's criticisms, which, to the extent that these criticisms are successful, makes them more difficult to refute. These critiques set the stage for a rehabilitation of the theological interpretation of the crucifixion that both Anselm and Abelard were reacting against, namely, the devil's ransom interpretation. The study attempted this rehabilitation by first correcting common misunderstandings, and then, building on the philosophical and exegetical results of the earlier chapters, by showing how the devil's ransom interpretation offers an adequate solution to the problem of God's will and Christ's crucifixion.

It should be emphasized that this study does not mean to draw any conclusions beyond the narrow confines of its stated objectives. Among other things, it should not be taken as a complete repudiation of Anselm and Abelard's theories of redemption. Despite their serious flaws, each has considerable strengths, and this study does not mean to deny those strengths. Likewise, this study does not mean to propose the devil's ransom interpretation offered by patristic authors as an approach to redemption adequate for contemporary Christianity, as though there were no need to incorporate later theological developments; it means, rather, to argue for its rehabilitation as a theological resource.

To put it otherwise: the New Testament uses many metaphors to describe the salvific effects of Christ's death and resurrection. Since Anselm, in Western reading of sacred scripture, legal metaphors have more or less controlled interpretation of the rest. This study does not mean to deny the hermeneutic value of the New Testament's legal metaphors. It does not mean to deny, either, the value of derived metaphors such as satisfaction. It is proposing that we need new controlling metaphors—or rather, that we need to revert to older controlling metaphors. Then the other metaphors will fall into place.

Bibliography

Abelard, Peter. *Opera Theologica*. Edited by Eligii M. Buytaert. 6 vols. Vol. 1, *Corpus Christianorum. Vol. 2, Continuatio Mediaevalis*. Brepols: Turnholt, 1969.

——. *Ethical Writings*. Translated by Paul Vincent Spade. Indianapolis: Hackett, 1995.

——. *Commentary on the Epistle to the Romans*. Translated by Steven R. Cartwright. Washington, DC: The Catholic University of America, 2011.

Adamantius. *Dialogue on the True Faith in God*. Translated by Robert A. Pretty. Edited by Garry W. Trompf. Leuven: Peeters, 1997.

Adams, Frederick. "Intention and Intentional Action: The Simple View." *Mind and Language* 1 (1986): 281–301.

Adams, Marilyn McCord. "Satisfying Mercy: Saint Anselm's *Cur Deus Homo*, Reconsidered." *Modern Schoolman* 72 (1995): 91–107.

Adams, Robert Merrihew. "A Modified Divine Command Theory of Ethical Wrongness." In *Divine Commands and Morality*, 83–108. Oxford: Oxford University Press, 1981.

——. *Finite and Infinite Goods: A Framework for Ethics* Oxford: Oxford University Press, 1999.

Ahearne-Kroll, Stephen P. *The Psalms of Lament in Mark's Passion: Jesus' Davidic Suffering*, Society for New Testament Studies Monograph Series. Cambridge: Cambridge University Press, 2008.

Alfeyev, Hilarion. *Christ the Conqueror of Hell: The Descent into Hades from an Orthodox Perspective*. Crestwood, NY: St. Vladimir's Seminary Press, 2009.

Anderson, Gary A. *Sin: A History*. New Haven: Yale University Press, 2009.

Anderson, Robert. "Boyle and the Principle of Double Effect." *American Journal of Jurisprudence* 52 (2007): 259–72.

Anscombe, G. E. M. "Modern Moral Philosophy." *Philosophy* 33 (1958): 1–19.

——. *Intention*. 2nd ed. Oxford: Blackwell, 1963.

——. "Medalist's Address: Action, Intention and 'Double Effect'." *Proceedings of the American Catholic Philosophical Association* 56 (1982): 12–25.

Anselm. *Opera Omnia*. Edited by F. S. Schmitt. 6 vols. Edinburgh: Thomas Nelson and Sons, 1946–1961.

——. *Basic Writings*. Translated by Thomas Williams. Indianapolis: Hackett, 2007.

Aquinas, Thomas. *Summa theologiae*. Edited by Thomas Gilby. Latin and English ed. 61 vols. New York and London: McGraw-Hill and Eyre and Spottiswoode, 1964–80.

Aristotle. *Nicomachean Ethics*. Translated by Roger Crisp. Cambridge: Cambridge University Press, 2000.

Armstrong, Christopher. "St Anselm and His Critics: Further Reflection on the *Cur Deus Homo*." *Downside Review* 86 (1968): 354–76.

Attridge, Harold W. "Liberating Death's Captives: Reconsideration of an Early Christian Myth." In *Gnosticism & the Early Christian World*. Edited by James E. Goehring et al., 103–15. Sonoma: Polebridge Press, 1990.

Augustine. *The Trinity*. Translated by Edmund Hill. Edited by John E. Rotelle. Hyde Park, NY: New City Press, 1991.

Aulén, Gustaf. *Christus Victor: An Historical Study of the Three Main Types of the Idea of Atonement*. Translated by A. G. Herbert. London: S.P.C.K, 1931.

Aulisio, Mark. "In Defense of the Intention/Foresight Distinction." *American Philosophical Quarterly* 32 (1995): 341–54.

——."On the Importance of the Intention/Foresight Distinction." *American Catholic Philosophical Quarterly* 70 (1996): 189–205.

Austriaco, Nicanor. *Biomedicine and Beatitude: An Introduction to Catholic Bioethics*. Washington, DC: The Catholic University of America (2011).

Ayres, Lewis. *Nicaea and its Legacy: An Approach to Fourth-Century Trinitarian Theology*. Oxford: Oxford University Press, 2004.

——.*Augustine and the Trinity*. Cambridge: Cambridge University Press, 2010.

Bailey, Kenneth E. "Informal Controlled Oral Tradition and the Synoptic Gospels." *Asia Journal of Theology* 5 (1991): 34–54.

——."Informal Controlled Oral Tradition and the Synoptic Gospels." *Themelios* 20 (1995): 4–11.

——."Middle Eastern Oral Tradition and the Synoptic Gospels." *Expository Times* 106 (1995): 363–7.

Baker, Mark D. and Green, Joel B. *Recovering the Scandal of the Cross: Atonement in New Testament and Contemporary Contexts*. Downers Grove, IL: InterVarsity Press, (2011).

Barth, Karl. *Church Dogmatics*. Translated by G. W. Bromiley et al. Vol. II/2. Edinburgh: T & T Clark, 1957.

Barth, Markus, and Helmut Blanke. *Colossians: A New Translation with Introduction and Commentary*, The Anchor Bible. Vol. 34B. New York: Doubleday, 1994.

Bartlett, Anthony W. *Cross Purposes: The Violent Grammar of the Christian Atonement*. Harrisburg: Trinity, 2001.

Bathrellos, Demetrios. *The Byzantine Christ: Person, Nature, and Will in the Christology of Saint Maximus the Confessor*. Oxford: Oxford University Press, 2004.

Battin, M. Pabst, and David J. Mayo, eds. *Suicide: The Philosophical Issues*. London: Peter Owen, 1980.

Bauckham, Richard. *Jesus and the Eyewitnesses: The Gospels as Eyewitness Testimony*. Grand Rapids, MI: Eerdmans, 2006.

——.*The Testimony of the Beloved Disciple: Narrative, History, and Theology in the Gospel of John*. Grand Rapids, MI: Baker Academic, 2007.

Bayer, Hans F. *Jesus' Predictions of Vindication and Resurrection: The Provenance, Meaning, and Correlation of the Synoptic Predictions* Wissenschaftliche Untersuchungen zum Neuen Testament. Vol. 20, Second Series. Tübingen: J.C.B. Mohr, 1986.

Beauchamp, Tom L. "What is Suicide?" In *Ethical Issues in Death and Dying*. Edited by Tom Beauchamp and Seymour Perlin, 97–102. Englewood Cliffs, NJ: Prentice-Hall, 1978.

Bellinger, William H., and William R. Farmer, eds. *Jesus and the Suffering Servant: Isaiah 53 and Christian Origins*. Harrisburg: Trinity, 1998.

Bennett, Jonathan. "Whatever the Consequences." *Analysis* 26 (1966): 83–102.

——. "Foreseen Side Effects versus Intended Consequences." In *The Act Itself*, 194–225. Oxford: Oxford University Press, 1995.

Bergmann, Michael, Michael J. Murray, and Michael C. Rea, eds. *Divine Evil? The Moral Character of the God of Abraham*. Oxford: Oxford University Press, 2011.

Berkman, John. "How Important is the Doctrine of Double Effect for Moral Theology? Contextualizing the Controversy." *Christian Bioethics: Non-Ecumenical Studies in Medical Ethics* 3 (1997): 89–114.

Best, Eugene. *An Historical Study of the Exegesis of Colossians 2:14*. Rome: Pontificia Universitas Gregorian, 1956.

Betz, O. "Jesus and Isaiah 53." In *Jesus and the Suffering Servant: Isaiah 53 and Christian Origins*. Edited by William H. Bellinger and William R. Farmer, 70–87. Harrisburg: Trinity, 1998.

Blackburn, Simon. *Ruling Passions: A Theory of Practical Reasoning*. Oxford: Oxford University Press, 1998.

Bond, H. Lawrence. "Another Look at Abelard's Commentary on Romans 3:26." In *Medieval Readings of Romans*. Edited by William S. Campbell, Peter S. Hawkins, and Brenda Deen Schildgen, 11–32. London: T & T Clark, 2007.

Bond, Helen K. *Pontius Pilate in History and Interpretation*, Society for New Testament Studies Monograph Series. Vol. 100. Cambridge: Cambridge University Press, 1998.

——. *Caiaphas: Friend of Rome and Judge of Jesus?* Louisville: Westminster John Knox Press, 2004.

Boyle, Joseph. "*Praeter intentionem* in Aquinas." *The Thomist* 42 (1978): 649–65.

Bratman, Michael. "Two Faces of Intention." *The Philosophical Review* 93 (1984): 375–405.

Breytenbach, Cilliers. "The Septuagint Version of Isaiah 53 and the Early Christian Formula 'He Was Delivered for Our Trespasses'." *Novum Testamentum* 51 (2009): 339–51.

Brown, Hunter. "Anselm's *Cur Deus Homo* Revisited." *Église et Théologie* 25 (1994): 189–204.

Brown, Joanne Carlson, and Carole R. Bohn, eds. *Christianity, Patriarchy and Abuse: A Feminist Critique*. New York: Pilgrim Press, 1989.

Brown, Joanne Carlson, and Rebecca Parker. "For God So Loved the World?" In *Christianity, Patriarchy and Abuse: A Feminist Critique*. Edited by Joanne Carlson Brown and Carole R. Bohn. New York: Pilgrim Press, 1989.

Brown, Raymond E. *The Death of the Messiah: From Gethsemane to the Grave. ACommentary on the Passion Narratives in the Four Gospels*. 2 vols, Anchor Bible Reference Library. New York: Doubleday, 1994.

Buber, Salomon, ed. *Midrasch Tehillim*. Wilna: Wittwe & Gebrüder Romm, 1891.

Bultmann, Rudolf. *The History of the Synoptic Tradition*. Translated by John Marsh. 2nd ed. Oxford: Blackwell, 1972.

——. *Theology of the New Testament*. Vol. 1. Waco, TX: Baylor University Press, 2007.

Burkett, Delbert R. *The Son of Man Debate: A History and Evaluation*, Society for New Testament Studies Monograph Series. Vol. 107. Cambridge: Cambridge University Press, 1999.

Burns, J. Patout. "How Christ Saves: Augustine's Multiple Explanations." In *Tradition and the Rule of Faith in the Early Church*. Edited by Ronnie. J. Rombs and Alexander Y. Hwang, 193–210. Washington, DC: The Catholic University of America Press, 2010.

Burridge, Richard A. *What Are the Gospels? A Comparison with Graeco-Roman Biography*. Cambridge: Cambridge University Press, 1992.

——. *What Are the Gospels? A Comparison with Graeco-Roman Biography*. 2nd ed. Grand Rapids, MI: Eerdmans, 2004.

——. *Imitating Jesus: An Inclusive Approach to New Testament Ethics*. Grand Rapids, MI: Eerdmans, 2007.

Byrskog, Samuel. *Story as History—History as Story: The Gospel Tradition in the Context of Ancient Oral History*, Wissenschaftliche Untersuchungen zum Neuen Testament. Vol. 123. Tübingen: J.C.B. Mohr, 2002.

Cane, Anthony. *The Place of Judas Iscariot in Christology*. Aldershot: Ashgate, 2005.

Carol, Juniper. *Why Jesus Christ? Thomistic, Scotistic, and Conciliatory Perspectives*. Manassas, VA: Trinity Communications, 1988.

Carroll, John T., and Joel B. Green. *The Death of Jesus in Early Christianity*. Peabody, MA: Hendrickson, 1995.

Casey, Maurice. *The Solution to the "Son of Man" Problem*, Library of New Testament Studies. London: T & T Clark, 2007.

Castañeda, Hector-Neri. "Intentions and the Structure of Intending." *Journal of Philosophy* 68 (1971): 453–66.

Cavanaugh, Thomas. *Double-Effect Reasoning: Doing Good and Avoiding Evil*. Oxford: Oxford University Press, 2006.

Chisholm, Roderick M. "The Structure of Intention." *Journal of Philosophy* 67 (1970): 633–47.

Choquette, Imelda. "*Voluntas*, *Affectio*, and *Potestas* in the *Liber De Voluntate* of St. Anselm." *Mediaeval Studies* 4 (1942): 61–81.

Chow, Simon. *The Sign of Jonah Reconsidered: A Study of Its Meaning in the Gospel Traditions*, Coniectanea Biblica New Testament Series. Vol. 27. Stockholm: Almqvist & Wiksel International, 1995.

Colwell, Ernest Cadman. "The Fourth Gospel and Early Christian Art." *The Journal of Religion* 15 (1935): 191–206.

Constantinople, Proclus of. *Homilies on the Life of Christ* Translated by Jan Harm Barkhuizen. Brisbane: Centre for Early Christian Studies, Australian Catholic University, 2001.

Constas, Nicholas. "The Last Temptation of Satan: Divine Deception in Greek Patristic Interpretations of the Passion Narrative." *Harvard Theological Review* 97 (2004): 139–63.

Daley, Brian. "'He Himself is Our Peace' (Eph. 2:14): Early Christian Views of Redemption in Christ" In *The Redemption: An Interdisciplinary Symposium on Christ as Redeemer*. Edited by Stephen T. Davis, Daniel Jendall and Gerald O'Collins, 149–76. Oxford: Oxford University Press, 2004.

Daly-Denton, Margaret. *David in the Fourth Gospel: The Johannine Reception of the Psalms* Arbeiten zur Geschichte des Antiken Judentums und des Urchristentums. Leiden: Brill, 2000.

Daniélou, Jean. *The Theology of Jewish Christianity*. Translated by John A. Baker. Vol. 1, The Development of Christian Doctrine Before the Council of Nicea. London: Darton, Longman & Todd, 1964.

Danker, Frederick W. *A Greek-English Lexicon of the New Testament and Other Early Christian Literature*. 3rd ed. Chicago: University of Chicago Press, 2000.

Davies, Brian. "The Problem of Evil." In *The Philosophy of Religion: A Guide to the Subject*. Edited by Brian Davies, 163–201. Washington, DC: Georgetown University Press, 1998.

——. *The Reality of God and the Problem of Evil*. London: Continuum, 2006.

Davis, Stephen J. "Jonah in Early Christian Art: Allegorical Exegesis and the Roman Funerary Context." *Australian Religion Studies Review* 13 (2000): 72–83.

Davis, Stephen T., Daniel Kendall, and Gerald O'Collins, eds. *The Redemption: An Interdisciplinary Symposium on Christ the Redeemer*. Oxford: Oxford University Press, 2004.

de Vitoria, Francisco. *Comentarios a la Secunda secundae de santo Tomás*. Edited by Vicente Beltrán de Heredia. Vol. 3, Biblioteca de teólogos espanôles. Vol. 4. Salamanca 1932–35.

DeConick, April D. *The Thirteenth Apostle: What the Gospel of Judas Really Says*. Rev. ed. London: Continuum, 2009.

Deissmann, Adolf. *Light from the Ancient East: The New Testament Illustrated by Recently Discovered Texts of the Graeco-Roman World*. Translated by Lionel R. M. Strachan. Rev. ed. London: Hodder & Stoughton, 1927.

Delaney, Neil. "A Note on Intention and the Doctrine of Double Effect." *Philosophical Studies* 134 (2007): 103–10.

——. "Two Cheers for 'Closeness': Terror, Targeting and Double Effect." *Philosophical Studies* 137 (2008): 335–67.

Delio, Ilia. "Revisiting the Franciscan Doctrine of Christ." *Theological Studies* 64 (2003): 3–23.

Devine, Philip E. "The Principle of Double Effect." *American Journal of Jurisprudence* 19 (1974): 44–60.

Dillistone, Frederick William. *The Christian Understanding of Atonement*. Philadelphia: Westminster Press, 1968.

Donnelly, John, ed. *Suicide: Right or Wrong?* 2nd ed. Amherst, NY: Promotheus Books, 1998.

Doutre, Jean. "Romans as Read in School and Cloister in the Twelfth Century: The Commentaries of Peter Abelard and William of St. Thierry." In *Medieval Readings of Romans*. Edited by William S. Campbell, Peter S. Hawkins, and Brenda Deen Schildgen, 33–57. London: T & T Clark, 2007.

Dragas, George Dion. "St Athanasius on Christ's Sacrifice." In *Sacrifice and Redemption: Durham Essays in Theology*. Edited by S. W. Sykes, 73–100. Cambridge: Cambridge University Press, 1991.

Drobner, Hubertus R. "Eine Pseudo-Athanasianiche Osterpredigt über die Wahrheit Gottes und ihre Erfüllung." In *Christian Faith and Greek Philosophy in Late Antiquity: Essays in Tribute to George Christopher Stead*. Edited by Lionel R. Wickham and Caroline P. Bammel, 43–51. Leiden: Brill, 1993.

Duff, R. A. "Absolute Principles and Double Effect." *Analysis* 36 (1976): 68–80.

Dulles, Avery. *The Assurance of Things Hoped For: A Theology of Christian Faith.* New York: Oxford University Press, 1997.
Dunn, James D. G. *Jesus Remembered,* Christianity in the Making. Vol. 1. Grand Rapids, MI: Eerdmans, 2003.
Dunstone, A. S. *The Atonement in Gregory of Nyssa,* Tyndale Lecture in Historical Theology, 1963. London: Tyndale Press, 1964.
Duval, Yves-Marie. *Le Livre de Jonas dans la littérature chrétienne grecque et latine: Sources et influence du Commentaire sur Jonas de Saint Jérôme.* Paris: Études Augustiniennes, 1973.
Edwards, Richard Alan. *The Sign of Jonah in the Theology of the Evangelists and Q,* Studies in Biblical Theology, 2nd Series. Vol. 18. London: S.C.M. Press, 1971.
Eire, Carlos M. N. "Pontius Pilate Spares Jesus: Christianity without the Crucifixion." In *More What If? Eminent Historians Imagine What Might Have Been.* Edited by Robert Cowley, 48–67. London: MacMillan, 2001.
Evans, C. Stephen. *Kierkegaard's Ethics of Love: Divine Commands and Moral Obligations.* Oxford: Oxford University Press, 2004.
Fairweather, Eugene R., ed. *A Scholastic Miscellany: Anselm to Ockham.* London: S.C.M. Press, 1956.
——."Incarnation and Atonement: An Anselmian Response to Aulén's Christus Victor." *Canadian Journal of Theology* 7 (1961): 167–75.
Ferguson, Everett. *Baptism in the Early Church: History, Theology, and Liturgy in the First Five Centuries.* Grand Rapids, MI: Eerdmans, 2009.
Finlan, Stephen. *Problems with Atonement.* Collegeville, MN: Liturgical Press, 2005.
Finnis, John. "Intention and Side-Effects." In *Liability and Responsibility.* Edited by R. G. Frey and Christopher W. Morris, 32–64. Cambridge: Cambridge University Press, 1991.
——."Object and Intention in Moral Judgments According to Aquinas." *The Thomist* 55 (1991): 1–27.
Finnis, John, Germain Grisez, and Joseph Boyle. "'Direct' and 'Indirect': A Reply to Critics of Our Action Theory." *The Thomist* 65 (2001): 1–44.
Fitzmyer, Joseph A. *The Gospel According to Luke.* 2 vols, Anchor Bible. Vol. 28A. New York: Doubleday, 1985.
——.*Romans: A New Translation with Introduction and Commentary.* New Haven, CT: Yale University Press, 1993.
——.*First Corinthians: A New Translation with Introduction and Commentary,* Anchor Bible. Vol. 32. New York: Yale University Press, 2008.
FitzPatrick, William J. "Acts, Intentions, and Moral Permissibility: In Defence of the Doctrine of Double Effect." *Analysis* 63 (2003): 317–21.
Florovsky, Georges. "Cur Deus Homo? The Motive for the Incarnation." In *Collected Works,* 163–70, 1976.
Foot, Philippa. "The Problem of Abortion and the Doctrine of the Double Effect." *Oxford Review* 5 (1967): 5–15.
——."Morality, Action, and Outcome." In *Morality and Objectivity: A Tribute to J. L. Mackier.* Edited by Ted Honderich, 25–38. London and Boston: Routledge and Kegan Paul, 1985.

Forsyth, Neil. *The Old Enemy: Satan and the Combat Myth*. Princeton: Princeton University Press, 1987.

Frey, R. G. "Some Aspects of the Doctrine of Double Effect." *Canadian Journal of Philosophy* 5 (1975): 259–83.

——. "Suicide and Self-Inflicted Death." *Philosophy* 56 (1981): 193–202.

Friberg, Barbara, Timothy Friberg, and Neva F. Miller, eds. *Analytical Lexicon of the Greek New Testament*. Grand Rapids, MI: Baker, 2000.

Gathercole, Simon. *The Gospel of Judas: Rewriting Early Christianity*. Oxford: Oxford University Press, 2007.

Gerhardsson, Birger. *Memory and Manuscript: Oral Tradition and Written Transmission in Rabbinic Judaism and Early Christianity*, Acta Seminarii Neotestamentici Upsaliensis. Uppsala: Gleerup, 1961.

——. *The Gospel Tradition*. Lund: Gleerup, 1986.

——. "The Secret of the Transmission of the Unwritten Jesus Tradition." *New Testament Studies* 51 (2004): 1–18.

Girard, René. *The Scapegoat*. Baltimore: John Hopkins University Press, 1986.

——. *Things Hidden Since the Foundation of the World*. Stanford: Stanford University Press, 1987.

——. *I See Satan Fall Like Lightning*. Translated by James G. Williams. Maryknoll, NY: Orbis Books, 2001.

Goergen, Donald. "Albert the Great and Thomas Aquinas on the Motive of the Incarnation." *The Thomist* 44 (1980): 523–38.

Goodacre, Mark. *The Case Against Q: Studies in Markan Priority and the Synoptic Problem*. Harrisburg: Trinity, 2002.

Gorday, Peter, ed. *Colossians, 1–2 Thessalonians, 1–2 Timothy, Titus, Philemon*. Vol. 9, *Ancient Christian Commentary on Scripture*. Chicago: Fitzroy Dearborn, 2000.

Green, Joel B. *The Death of Jesus: Tradition and Interpretation in the Passion Narrative*. Vol. 33, Second Series, Wissenschaftliche Untersuchungen zum Neuen Testament. Tübingen: J.C.B. Mohr, 1988.

Gregory of Nazianzus. *Festal Orations*. Translated by Nonna Verna Harrison. Crestwood, NY: St. Vladimir's Seminary Press, 2008.

Gregory of Nyssa. *Discours cateícheítique*. Translated by Raymond Winling, Sources Chrétiennes. Vol. 453. Paris: Les Éditions du Cerf, 2000.

——. "Address on Religious Instruction." In *Christology of the Later Fathers*, 268–325. Louisville: Westminster John Knox Press, 2006.

Grey, Mary. *Redeeming the Dream: Feminism, Redemption and Christian Tradition* London: S.P.C.K., 1990.

Grillmeier, Alois. "Der Gottessohn im Totenreich." In *Mit Ihm und in Ihm*, 76–174. Freiburg: Herder, 1975.

Gudmundsdottir, Arnfridur. *Meeting God on the Cross: Feminist Christologies and the Theology of the Cross*. New York: Oxford, 2010.

Gundry, Robert Horton *Mark: A Commentary on His Apology for the Cross*. Grand Rapids, MI: Eerdmans, 1993.

Hanink, James G. "Some Light on Double Effect." *Analysis* 35 (1975): 147–51.

Hannah, John D. "Anselm on the Doctrine of Atonement." *Bibliotheca Sacra* 135 (1978): 333–44.

Harman, Gilbert. "Practical Reasoning." *Review of Metaphysics* 29 (1976): 431–63.

Harnack, Adolf. *History of Dogma*. Translated by James Millar. Vol. 3. London: Williams and Norgate, 1897.

——. *History of Dogma*. Translated by Neil Buchanan. Vol. 6. London: Williams and Norgate, 1897.

Hart, David Bentley. "A Gift Exceeding Every Debt: An Eastern Orthodox Appreciation of Anselm's Cur Deus Homo." *Pro Ecclesia* 7 (1998): 333–49.

——. *The Beauty of the Infinite: The Aesthetics of Christian Truth*. Grand Rapids, MI: Eerdmans, 2003.

Hartmann, Wilfried, and Kenneth Pennington, eds. *The History of Medieval Canon Law in the Classical Period, 1140–1234: From Gratian to the Decretals of Pope Gregory IX*. Washington, DC: The Catholic University of America Press, 2008.

Hays, Richard B. *Echoes of Scripture in the Letters of Paul*. New Haven: Yale University Press, 1989.

——. *Moral Vision of the New Testament: Community, Cross, New Creation*. San Francisco: Harper, 1996.

Hengel, Martin. *The Atonement: The Origins of the Doctrine in the New Testament*. Translated by J. Bowden. Philadelphia: Fortress Press, 1981.

——. *The Johannine Question*. Translated by J. Bowden. London: S.C.M. Press, 1989.

Henry, Desmond Paul. *The Logic of Saint Anselm*. Oxford: Oxford University Press, 1967.

Herzog, Markwart *Descensus ad inferos*, Frankfurter theologische Studien. Vol. 53. Frankfurt am Main: J. Knecht, 1997.

Hills, Alison. "Defending Double Effect." *Philosophical Studies* 116 (2003): 133–52.

——. "Intentions, Foreseen Consequences and the Doctrine of Double Effect." *Philosophical Studies* 133 (2007): 257–83.

Holmes, Stephen R. "The Upholding of Beauty: A Reading of Anselm's *Cur Deus Homo*." *Scottish Journal of Theology* 54 (2001): 189–203.

Hooker, Morna. *Jesus and the Servant: The Influence of the Servant Concept of Deutero-Isaiah in the New Testament*. London: S.P.C.K., 1959.

——. "Did the Use of Isaiah 53 to Interpret His Mission Begin with Jesus?" In *Jesus and the Suffering Servant: Isaiah 53 and Christian Origins*. Edited by William H. Bellinger and William R. Farmer. Harrisburg: Trinity, 1998.

Horan, Daniel P. "How Original Was Scotus on the Incarnation? Reconsidering the History of the Absolute Predestination of Christ in Light of Robert Grosseteste" *The Heythrop Journal* 52 (2011): 374–91.

Hull, Richard. "Deconstructing the Doctrine of Double Effect." *Ethical Theory and Moral Practice* 3 (2000): 195–207.

Hume, David. *A Treatise of Human Nature*. Edited by David F. Norton and Mary J. Norton. Oxford: Clarendon Press, 2007.

Idziak, Janine Marie. *Divine Command Morality: Historical and Contemporary Readings*. New York: Edwin Mellen Press, 1979.

Ingham, Mary Elizabeth. "John Duns Scotus: An Integrated Vision." In *The History of Fransciscan Theology*. Edited by Kenan B. Osborne, 185–230. St. Bonaventure, NY: The Franciscan Institute, 1994.

Janowski, Bernd, and Peter Stuhlmacher, eds. *The Suffering Servant: Isaiah 53 in Jewish and Christian Sources*. Grand Rapids, MI: Eerdmans, 2004.

Jeffrey, Steve, Mike Ovey, and Andrew Sach. *Pierced for Our Transgressions: Rediscovering the Glory of Penal Subsitution*. Nottingham: InterVarsity Press, 2007.

Jellinek, Adolph. *Bet ha-midrash*. Vol. 1. Jerusalem: Bamberger et Vahrman, 1938.

Jensen, Robin Margaret. *Understanding Early Christian Art*. Abingdon: Routledge, 2000.

Jeremias, Joachim. "*Ἰωνᾶς*." In *Theological Dictionary of the New Testament*. Edited by Gerhard Kittel and Gerhard Freidrich, 406–10. Grand Rapids, MI: Eerdmans, 1965.

——. *The Eucharistic Words of Jesus*. Translated by Norman Perrin. 3rd ed. London: S.C.M. Press 1966.

John of Damascus. *Writings*. Translated by Frederic H. Chase Jr. Washington, DC: The Catholic University of America Press, 1958.

John Paul II. *Fides et Ratio: On the Relationship between Faith and Reason*. Boston: Pauline Books & Media, 1998.

Kaczor, Christopher. "Double-Effect Reasoning from Jean Pierre Gury to Peter Knauer." *Theological Studies* 59 (1998): 297–316.

Kamm, Frances M. "The Doctrine of Double Effect: Reflections on Theoretical and Practical Issues." *Journal of Medicine and Philosophy* 16 (1991): 571–85.

Kant, Immanuel. *The Conflict of the Faculties*. Translated by Mary J. Gregor. New York: Abaris, 1979.

Kasser, Rodolphe, and Gregor Wurst, eds. *The Gospel of Judas, Critical Edition*. Washington, DC: National Geographic Society, 2007.

Kees, Richard Jakob. *Die Lehre von der Oikonomia Gottes in der Oratio Catechetica Gregors von Nyssa*. Leiden: Brill, 1995.

Kelly, J. N. D. *Early Christian Creeds*. London: Longmans, Green, and Co., 1950.

——. *Early Christian Doctrines*. 5th ed. London: Adam & Charles Black, 1977.

Kenny, Anthony. "Philippa Foot on Double Effect." In *Virtues and Reasons: Philippa Foot and Moral Theory: Essays in Honour of Philippa Foot*. Edited by Rosalind Hursthouse, Gavin Lawrence and Warren Quinn, 77–87. Oxford Clarendon Press, 1995.

Kertlege, Karl, ed. *Der Tod Jesu: Deutungen im Neuen Testament*, Quaestiones disputatae. Freiburg: Herder, 1976.

Keshgegian, Flora A. "The Scandal of the Cross: Revisiting Anselm and His Feminist Critics." *Anglican Theological Review* 82 (2000): 475–92.

Kessler, Edward. *Bound by the Bible: Jews, Christians and the Sacrifice of Isaac*. Cambridge: Cambridge University Press, 2004.

Khatchadourian, Haig. "Is the Principle of Double Effect Morally Acceptable?" *International Philosophical Quarterly* 28 (1988): 21–30.

Kierkegaard, Soren. *Fear and Trembling*. Translated by Sylvia Walsh. Cambridge: Cambridge University Press, 2006.

Kirwan, Michael. *Girard and Theology*. London: T & T Clark, 2009.

Koester, Craig R. "Why Was the Messiah Crucified? A Study of God, Jesus, Satan, and Human Agency in Johannine Theology." In *The Death of Jesus in the Fourth Gospel*. Edited by Gilbert Van Belle, 163–80. Leuven: Leuven University Press, 2007.

Kovacs, Judith L. "'Now Shall the Ruler of This World Be Driven Out': Jesus' Death as Cosmic Battle in John 12:20–36." *Journal of Biblical Literature* 114 (1995): 227–47.

Kupfer, Joseph. "Suicide: Its Nature and Moral Evaluation." *Journal of Value Inquiry* 24 (1990): 67–81.

Lee, Steven. "Double Effect, Double Intention, and Asymmetric Warfare." *Journal of Military Ethics* 3 (2004): 233–51.

Leftow, Brian. "Anselm on the Beauty of the Incarnation." *Modern Schoolman* 72 (1995): 109–24.

Levenson, Jon D. *The Death and Resurrection of the Beloved Son: The Transformation of Child Sacrifice in Judaism and Christianity*. New Haven: Yale University Press, 1993.

Levering, Matthew. "Natural Law and Natural Inclinations: Rhonheimer, Pinckaers, McAleer." *The Thomist* 70 (2006): 155–201.

——."God and Natural Law: Reflections on Genesis 22." *Modern Theology* 24 (2008): 151–77.

Levy, Sanford S. "Paul Ramsey and the Rule of Double Effect." *Journal of Religious Ethics* 15 (1987): 59–71.

Lichtenberg, Judith. "War, Innocence, and the Doctrine of Double Effect." *Philosophical Studies* 74 (1994): 347–68.

Litwa, M. David. "Self-Sacrifice to Save the Life of Another in Jewish and Christian Traditions." *The Heythrop Journal* 50 (2009): 912–22.

Lombardo, Nicholas E. *The Logic of Desire: Aquinas on Emotion*. Washington, DC: The Catholic University of America Press, 2011.

Long, Stephen A. "A Brief Disquisition Regarding the Nature of the Object of the Moral Act According to St. Thomas Aquinas." *The Thomist* 67 (2003): 45–71.

——.*The Teleological Grammar of the Moral Act*. Naples, FL: Sapientia Press, 2007.

Louth, Andrew. *Maximus the Confessor*. London: Routledge, 1996.

Ludlow, Morwenna. *Gregory of Nyssa, Ancient and (Post)modern*. Oxford: Oxford University Press, 2007.

Lukken, Gerard M. *Original Sin in the Roman Liturgy: Research into the Theology of Original Sin in the Roman Sacramentaria and the Early Baptismal Liturgy*. Leiden: Brill, 1973.

Lyonnet, Stanislas, and Léopold Sabourin. *Sin, Redemption, and Sacrifice: A Biblical and Patristic Study*, Analecta Biblica. Vol. 48. Rome: Biblical Institute Press, 1970.

MacCulloch, J. A. *The Harrowing of Hell: A Comparative Study of Early Christian Doctrine*. Edinburgh: T & T Clark, 1930.

MacDonald, Margaret Y. *Colossians and Ephesians*. Vol. 17, Sacra Pagina. Collegeville: Liturgical Press, 2000.

MacIntyre, Alasdair. "Hume on 'Is' and 'Ought'." *The Philosophical Review* 68 (1959): 451–68.

——.*After Virtue*. 2nd ed. Notre Dame: University of Notre Dame Press, 1984.

Madden, John D. "The Authenticity of Early Definitions of Will (*Thelesis*)." In *Maximus Confessor*. Edited by Felix Heinzer and Christoph Schonborn, 61–79. Fribourg: Éditions Universitaires Fribourg Suisse, 1982.

Magnes, Macarius. *The Apocriticus*. Translated by T. W. Crafer. London: S.P.C.K., 1919.

Mangan, Joseph T. "An Historical Analysis of the Principle of Double Effect." *Theological Studies* 10 (1949): 41–61.

Mann, C. S. *Mark: A New Translation with Introduction and Commentary*. Garden City, NY: Doubleday, 1986.

Mapel, D. R. "Revising the Doctrine of Double Effect." *Journal of Applied Philosophy* 18 (2001): 257–72.

Marcus, Joel. *Mark 8–16: A New Translation with Introduction and Commentary*. The Anchor Bible. New Haven: Yale University Press, 2009.

Marenbon, John. *The Philosophy of Peter Abelard*. Cambridge: Cambridge University Press, 1997.

Marquis, Donald B. "Some Difficulties with Double Effect." *Southwestern Journal of Philosophy* 9 (1978): 27–34.

——. "Four Versions of Double Effect." *Journal of Medicine and Philosophy* 16 (1991): 515–44.

Martin, Robert M. *Suicide: The Philosophical Issues*. Edited by M. Pabst Battin and David J. Mayo, 48–68. London: Peter Owen, 1980.

Martinez, Ernest R. *Gospel Accounts of the Death Of Jesus: A Study of the Death Accounts Made in the Light of the New Testament Traditions, the Redaction, and the Theology of the Four Evangelists*, Analecta Gregoriana. Vol. 303. Rome: Editrice Pontificia Università Gregoriana, 2008.

Marx, C. W. *The Devil's Rights and the Redemption in the Literature of Medieval England*. Cambridge: D. S. Brewer, 1995.

Matthews, Gareth B. "Saint Thomas and the Principle of Double Effect." In *Aquinas' Moral Theory: Essays in Honor of Norman Kreztmann*. Edited by Scott MacDonald and Eleonore Stump, 63–78. Ithaca, NY: Cornell University Press, 1999.

Maximus the Confessor. *On the Cosmic Mystery of Jesus Christ*. Translated by Paul M. Blowers and Robert Louis Wilken. Crestwood, NY: St. Vladimir's Press, 2003.

May, William E. "Contemporary Perspectives on Thomistic Natural Law." In *St. Thomas Aquinas and the Natural Law Tradition: Contemporary Perspectives*. Edited by John Goyette, Mark S. Latkovic, and Richard S. Myers, 113–56. Washington, DC: The Catholic University of America Press, 1994.

McCasland, Selby Vernon. "The Scripture Basis of 'On the Third Day'." *The Journal of Biblical Literature* 48 (1929): 124–37.

McClear, E. V. "The Fall of Man and Original Sin in the Theology of Gregory of Nyssa." *Theological Studies* 9 (1948): 175–212.

McGray, James W. "Bobby Sands, Suicide, and Self-Starvation." *Journal of Value Inquiry* 17 (1983): 65–75.

McIntyre, Alison. "Doing Away with Double Effect." *Ethics* 111 (2001): 219–55.

McIntyre, John. *St Anselm and His Critics: A Reinterpretation of the Cur Deus Homo*. London: Oliver, 1954.

McKnight, Scot. *Jesus and His Death: Historiography, the Historical Jesus, and Atonement Theory*. Waco, TX: Baylor University Press, 2005.

Meier, John P. "The Eucharist and the Last Supper: Did It Happen?" *Theology Digest* 42 (1995): 335–51.

Mettinger, Tryggve N. D. *In Search of God: The Meaning and Message of the Everlasting Names*. Translated by Frederick H. Cryer. Philadelphia: Fortress Press, 1988.

Metzger, Bruce M. "A Suggestion Concerning the Meaning of I Cor XV.4b." *The Journal of Theological Studies* 8 (1957): 118–23.

Mews, Constant J. *Abelard and Heloise*. Oxford: Oxford University Press, 2005.

Meyer, B. F. *The Aims of Jesus*. London: S.C.M. Press, 1979.

Möhle, Hannes. "Scotus's Theory of Natural Law." In *The Cambridge Companion to Duns Scotus*. Edited by Thomas Williams. Cambridge: Cambridge University Press, 2003.

Montaldi, Daniel F. "A Defense of St Thomas and the Principle of Double Effect." *Journal of Religious Ethics* 14 (1986): 296–332.

Morriston, Wes. "What If God Commanded Something Terrible? A Worry for Divine-Command Meta-Ethics." *Religious Studies* 45 (2009): 249–67.

Moss, Candida R. *The Other Christs: Imitating Jesus in Ancient Christian Ideologies of Martyrdom*. New York: Oxford University Press, 2010.

Narkiss, Bezalel. "The Sign of Jonah." *Gesta* 18 (1978): 63–76.

Nelson, William N. "Conceptions of Morality and the Doctrine of Double Effect." *Journal of Medicine and Philosophy* 16 (1991): 545–64.

Nietzsche, Friedrich. "On Truth and Falsity in their Ultramoral Sense." In *Complete Works*. Edited by Oscar Levy. London: T. N. Foulis, 1911.

——. *The Anti-Christ*. Translated by R. J. Hollingdale. Harmondsworth: Penguin Books, 1968.

O'Collins, Gerald. *Christology: A Biblical, Historical, and Systematic Study of Jesus*. Oxford: Oxford University Press, 1995.

O'Keeffe, Terence M. "Suicide and Self-Starvation." *Philosophy* 59 (1984): 349–64.

Odozor, Paulinus Ikechukwu. "Proportionalists and the Principle of Double Effect: A Review Discussion." *Christian Bioethics: Non-Ecumenical Studies in Medical Ethics* 3 (1997): 115–30.

Olsen, Glenn W. "Hans Urs von Balthasar and the Rehabilitation of St Anselm's Doctrine of the Atonement." *Scottish Journal of Theology* 34 (1981): 49–61.

Origen. *Homilies on Genesis and Exodus*. Translated by Ronald E. Heine. Washington, DC: The Catholic University of America Press, 1982.

——. *Commentary on Romans*. Translated by Thomas B. Scheck. 2 vols. Washington, DC: The Catholic University of America Press, 2001.

Osiek, Carolyn. "The Ransom of Captives: Evolution of a Tradition." *Harvard Theological Review* 74 (1981): 365–86.

Oyen, Geert Van, and Tom Shepherd, eds. *The Trial and Death of Jesus: Essays on the Passion Narrative in Mark*. Leuven: Peeters, 2006.

Page, Sydney. "The Suffering Servant between the Testaments." *New Testament Studies* 31 (1985): 481–97.

Pelikan, Jaroslav. *The Emergence of the Catholic Tradition (100–600)*. 5 vols. Vol. 1, *The Christian Tradition: A History of the Development of Doctrine*. Chicago: University of Chicago Press, 1971.

——. *The Growth of Medieval Theology (600–1300)*. 5 vols. Vol. 3, *The Christian Tradition: A History of the Development of Doctrine*. Chicago: University of Chicago Press, 1978.

Pesch, R. *Das Abendmahl und Jesu Todesverständnis*, Quaestiones disputatae. Freiburg: Herder, 1978.

Peters, Ted. "Atonement in Anselm and Luther, Second Thoughts about Gustaf Aulén's *Christus Victor*." *Lutheran Quarterly* 24 (1972): 301–14.

Pilsner, Joseph. *The Specification of Human Actions in St Thomas Aquinas*. Oxford: Oxford University Press, 2006.

Pinckaers, Servais. *The Sources of Christian Ethics*. Translated by Mary Thomas Noble. Washington, DC: The Catholic University of America Press, 1995.

Piper, Ronald A. "The Characterisation of Pilate and the Death of Jesus in the Fourth Gospel." In *The Death of Jesus in the Fourth Gospel*. Edited by Gilbert Van Belle, 121–62. Leuven: Leuven University Press, 2007.

Pitcher, George. "'In Intending' and Side Effects." *Journal of Philosophy* 67 (1970): 659–68.

Pitre, Brant J. *Jesus, the Tribulation, and the End of the Exile: Restoration Eschatology and the Origin of the Atonement*, Wissenschaftliche Untersuchungen zum Neuen Testament. Tübingen: J.C.B. Mohr, 2005.

Popkes, Wiard. *Christus Traditus: eine Untersuchung zum Begriff der Dahingabe im Neuen Testament*, Abhandlungen zur Theologie des Alten und Neuen Testaments. Vol. 49. Zurich: Zwingli Verlag, 1967.

Predelli, Stefano. "Bombers: Some Comments on Double Effect and Harmful Involvement." *Journal of Military Ethics* 3 (2004): 16–26.

Pritchett, W. Kendrick. *The Greek State at War*. Vol. 5. Berkeley: University of California Press, 1991.

Proctor, Mark. "'After Three Days' in Mark 8:31; 9:31; 10:34: Subordinating Jesus' Resurrection in the Second Gospel." *Perspectives in Religious Studies* 30 (2003): 399–424.

——."'After Three Days He Will Rise': The (Dis)appropriation of Hosea 6.2 in the Markan Passion Predictions." In *Biblical Interpretation in Early Christian Gospels: Vol. 1, The Gospel of Mark*. Edited by Thomas R. Hatina, 131–50. London: T & T Clark, 2006.

Quinn, Philip L. "Abelard on Atonement: 'Nothing Unintelligible, Arbitrary, Illogical, or Immoral about It.'" In *Reasoned Faith: Essays in Philosophical Theology in Honor of Norman Kretzmann*, 281–300. Ithaca, NY: Cornell University Press, 1993.

Quinn, Warren S. "Actions, Intentions, and Consequences: The Doctrine of Double Effect." *Philosophy and Public Affairs* 18 (1989): 334–51.

Radde-Gallwitz, Andrew. *Basil of Caesarea, Gregory of Nyssa, and the Transformation of Divine Simplicity*. Oxford: Oxford University Press, 2009.

Rashdall, Hastings. *The Idea of Atonement in Christian Theology*. London: MacMillan, 1919.

Ray, Darby Kathleen. *Deceiving the Devil: Atonement, Abuse, and Ransom*. Cleveland, OH: Pilgrim Press, 1998.

Redpath, Peter A. "Why Double Effect and Proportionality Are Not Moral Principles for St. Thomas." *Vera Lex* 5 (2004): 25–42.

Reginster, Bernard. *The Affirmation of Life: Nietzsche on Overcoming Nihilism*. Cambridge: Harvard University Press, 2006.

Reibetanz, Sophia. "A Problem for the Doctrine of Double Effect." *Proceedings of the Aristotelian Society* 98 (1998): 217–23.

Reichberg, Gregory M. "Aquinas on Defensive Killing: A Case of Double Effect?" *The Thomist* 69 (2005): 341–70.

Renick, Timothy M. "Charity Lost: The Secularization of the Principle of Double Effect in the Just-War Tradition." *The Thomist* 58 (1994): 441–62.

Rhonheimer, Martin. *Vital Conflicts in Medical Ethics: A Virtue Approach to Craniotomy and Tubal Pregnancies*. Washington, DC: The Catholic University of America Press, 2009.

Richard, Louis. *The Mystery of the Redemption*. Translated by Joseph Horn. Dublin: Cahill, 1965.

Richter, Duncan. "The Ethics of Suicide." *Ethics After Anscombe: Post "Modern Moral Philosophy,"* 76–93. Dordrecht, The Netherlands: Kluwer Academic Publishers, 2000.

Riesenfeld, Harald. *The Gospel Tradition: Essays*. Translated by E. Margaret Rowley and Robert A. Kraft. Oxford: Blackwell, 1970.

Rivière, Jean. *The Doctrine of the Atonement: A Historical Essay*. Translated by Luigi Cappadelta. Vol. 2. London: Kegan Paul, Trench, Trübner, 1909.

——."Muscipula Diaboli. Origène et le sens d'une image augustinienne." *Recherches de théologie ancienne et médiévale* 1 (1929): 484–96.

——.*Le dogme de la rédemption chez Saint Augustin*. Paris: J. Gabalda, 1933.

——.*Le dogme de la rédemption au dèbut du moyen-age*, Bibliothéque Thomiste. Vol. 19. Paris: J. Vrin, 1934.

Rodger, Symeon. "The Soteriology of Anselm of Canterbury, An Orthodox Perspective." *Greek Orthodox Theological Review* 34 (1989): 19–43.

Rogers, Katherin A. "A Defense of Anselm's *Cur Deus Homo* Argument." *Proceedings of the American Catholic Philosophical Association* 74 (2000): 187–200.

Rome, Clement of, and Ignatius of Antioch. *The Epistles of St. Clement of Rome and St. Ignatius of Antioch*. Translated by James A. Kleist. New York: Paulist Press, 1946.

Rooney, Paul. *Divine Command Morality*. Aldershot: Avebury, 1996.

Roth, Cecil. "The Cleansing of the Temple and Zechariah XIV 21." *Novum Testamentum* 4 (1960): 174–81.

Sanders, E. P. *Jesus and Judaism*. Philadelphia: Fortress Press, 1985.

Saunders, Daniel J. "The Devil and the Divinity of Christ." *Theological Studies* 9 (1948): 536–53.

Schillebeeckx, Edward. *Christ*. Translated by John Bowden. New York: Crossroad Publishing Company, 1980.

Schmitt, F. S. *Ein neues unvollendetes Werk des hl. Anselm von Canterbury*. Münster: Aschendorff, 1936.

Schnabel, E. "The Silence of Jesus." In *Authenticating the Words of Jesus*. Edited by Bruce D. Chilton and C. A. Evans, 203–57. Leiden: Brill, 1999.

Schürmann, Heinz. *Jesu ureigener Tod. Exegetische Besinnungen und Ausblick*. Freiburg: Herder, 1975.

Schwager, Raymund. *Must There Be Scapegoats? Violence and Redemption in the Bible*. Translated by Maria L. Assad. San Francisco: Harper and Row, 1987.

——.*Jesus in the Drama of Salvation: Toward a Biblical Doctrine of Redemption*. Translated by James G. Williams and Paul Haddon. New York: Crossroad, 1999.

Schweitzer, Albert. *The Quest of the Historical Jesus: A Critical Study of Its Progress from Reimarus to Wrede*. Translated by William Montgomery. London: A. & C. Black, 1911.

Scotus, John Duns. *Duns Scotus on the Will and Morality*. Translated by Allan B. Wolter. Edited by Allan B. Wolter. Washington, DC: The Catholic University of America Press, 1986.

Sherwood, Yvonne. *A Biblical Text and Its Afterlives: The Survival of Jonah in Western Culture*. Cambridge: Cambridge University Press, 2000.

Shuler, P. L. *A Genre for the Gospels: The Biographical Character of Matthew*. Philadelphia: Fortress Press, 1982.

Sidgwick, Henry. *The Methods of Ethics*. 7th ed. Indianapolis: Hackett, 1981.

Siegert, F., ed. *Drei Hellenistisch-Jüdische Predigten*, Wissenschaftliche Untersuchungen zum Neuen Testament. Tübingen: J.C.B. Mohr, 1980.

Slusser, Michael. "Primitive Christian Soteriological Themes." *Theological Studies* 44 (1983): 555–69.

Smith, Ian A. "A New Defense of Quinn's Principle of Double Effect." *Journal of Social Philosophy* 38 (2007): 349–64.

Soskice, Janet Martin. *Metaphor and Religious Language*. Oxford: Clarendon Press, 1985.

Southern, R. W. *Saint Anselm: A Portrait in a Landscape*. Cambridge: Cambridge University Press, 1990.

Squires, John T. *The Plan of God in Luke-Acts*. Cambridge: Cambridge University Press, 1993.

Stempsey, William E. "Laying Down One's Life for Oneself." *Christian Bioethics: Non-Ecumenical Studies in Medical Ethics* 4 (1998): 202–24.

Stern-Gillet, Suzanne. "The Rhetoric of Suicide." *Philosophy and Rhetoric* 20 (1987): 160–70.

Stocker, Michael. "Desiring the Bad: An Essay in Moral Psychology." *The Journal of Philosophy* 76 (1979): 738–53.

Studer, Basil. *Trinty and Incarnation: The Faith of the Early Church*. Edinburgh: T & T Clark, 1993.

Sullivan, Denis. "The Doctrine of Double Effect and the Domains of Moral Responsibility." *The Thomist* 64 (2000): 423–48.

Sulmasy, Daniel P. "Commentary: Double Effect—Intention is the Solution, Not the Problem." *Journal of Law, Medicine and Ethics* 28 (2000): 26–9.

Talbert, C. H. *What is a Gospel? The Genre of the Canonical Gospels*. Philadelphia: Fortress Press, 1977.

Tanner, Norman P., ed. *Decrees of the Ecumenical Councils*. 2 vols. Washington, DC: Georgetown University Press, 1990.

Teselle, Eugene "The Cross as Ransom." *Journal of Early Christian Studies* 4 (1996): 147–70.

Thomasma, David C. "Assisted Death and Martyrdom." *Christian Bioethics: Non-Ecumenical Studies in Medical Ethics* 4 (1998): 122–42.

Tidball, Derek, David Hilborn, and Justin Thacker, eds. *The Atonement Debate: Papers from the London Symposium on the Theology of Atonement*. Grand Rapids, MI: Zondervan, 2008.

Trumbower, Jeffrey A. *Rescue for the Dead: The Posthumous Salvation of Non-Christians in Early Christianity*. Oxford: Oxford University Press, 2001.

Turner, H. E. W. *The Patristic Doctrine of Redemption: A Study of the Development of Doctrine during the First Five Centuries*. London: A. R. Mowbray, 1952.

Ugorji, L. I. *The Principle of Double Effect: A Critical Appraisal of Its Traditional Understanding and Its Modern Reinterpretation*. Frankfurt: Peter Lang, 1985.

Van Belle, Gilbert, ed. *The Death of Jesus in the Fourth Gospel* Leuven: Leuven University Press, 2007.

Velleman, J. David. "The Guise of the Good." *Noûs* 26 (1992): 3–26.

von Balthasar, Hans Urs. *The Glory of the Lord: A Theological Aesthetics*. Translated by Andrew Louth, Francis McDonagh, and Brian McNeil. Edited by John Riches. 7 vols. Vol. 2. Edinburgh: T & T Clark, 1984.

Weingart, Richard E. *The Logic of Divine Love: A Critical Analysis of the Soteriology of Peter Abelard*. Oxford: Clarendon Press, 1970.

Weiss, Paul. "Sacrifice and Self-Sacrifice." *Review of Metaphysics* 2 (1949): 76–98.

Wicks, Jared. "Christ's Saving Descent to the Dead: Early Witnesses from Ignatius of Antioch to Origen." *Pro Ecclesia* 17 (2008): 281–309.

Wiel, Constant van de. *History of Canon Law*. Louvain: Peeters, 1991.

Willetts, Ronald F. *The Law Code of Gortyn*. Berlin: Walter de Gruyter, 1967.

Williams, Thomas. "Sin, Grace, and Redemption." In *The Cambridge Companion to Abelard*. Edited by Jeffrey E. Brower and Kevin Guilfoy, 258–78. Cambridge: Cambridge University Press, 2004.

Winling, Raymond. "La résurrection du Christ comme principe explicatif et comme élèment structurant dans le *Discours catéchétique* de Grégoire de Nysse." *Studia Patristica* 22 (1989): 74–80.

Winslow, Donald F. *Dynamics of Salvation: A Study in Gregory of Nazianzus*, Patristic Monograph Series. Vol. 7. Philadelphia: Philadelphia Patristic Foundation, 1979.

Wittgenstein, Ludwig. *Culture and Value*. Translated by Peter Winch. Edited by G. H. von Wright and Heikki Nyman. Oxford: Blackwell, 1980.

——. *Philosophical Investigations*. Translated by G. E. M. Anscombe. 3rd ed. Oxford: Blackwell, 2001.

Woodward, P. A., ed. *The Doctrine of Double Effect: Philosophers Debate a Controversial Moral Principle*. Notre Dame: University of Notre Dame Press, 2001.

——. "Nancy Davis and the Means-End Relation: Toward a Defense of the Doctrine of Double Effect." *American Catholic Philosophical Quarterly* 77 (2003): 437–59.

Wright, N. T. *Jesus and the Victory of God, Christian Origins and the Question of God*. Vol. 2. Minneapolis: Fortress Press, 1996.

Yarnold, Edward. *Cyril of Jerusalem*. London: Routledge, 2000.

Zeis, John. "Killing Innocents and the Doctrine of Double Effect." *Proceedings of the American Catholic Philosophical Association* 78 (2004): 133–44.

Index

Abelard, Peter
  on devil's ransom and devil's rights 167–71, 176–7, 178, 179, 197
  on God's will and Christ's crucifixion 177–8
  interpretations of Christ's crucifixion 9, 12, 13, 15–16, 17, 168–80, 240, 241
    evaluation of 178–9
  on justification through Christ's blood 169–71, 172
  necessity of crucifixion 174–6
  original sin, charity and redemption 172–3
  response to Anselm 168–80, 181
  theological categories used by 176–7
  see also redemption, theories of, Abelard's
Abraham, sacrifice of Isaac by 86–8, 103n11
action(s), human 29n10, 32, 89
  being and 44–5
  desire and 48, 49, 54–5
  evaluation of 14, 22–3
  God's will and 82, 83–8
  intentional 23–4, 25–6, 31, 33–42, 45, 226–7n186
  moral value of 10–11, 50, 51, 54–5, 56, 60, 65, 69
  morally ambiguous 43, 52–3, 64, 72–3
  morally defective 43, 50, 51, 72–3, 75
  morally evil 43, 82–3, 92
  morally good 43, 61, 72–3, 75, 78
  ontology of 24, 25, 35, 43, 51, 57, 67
  see also aspects; consequences; effects; natural inclination(s)
Acts of the Apostles, on Christ's crucifixion 135, 138, 140
Adam
  Christ as New 189, 207n107
  Christ fishing from Tartarus 201n80
  Christ's meeting in netherworld 204–5
  disobedience of 191, 224, 225
  see also original sin
Adamantius 207
Adams, Frederick 36n17
adultery 85
agent(s), human 22, 23
  desire in 27–8, 46
  intending by 24, 38, 41
  intentions of 30, 34–8, 64–5
  rational 32–3, 48, 49n7
  see also action(s), human; natural inclination(s)
Akedah, *see* Isaac, Abraham's sacrifice of
Alberic of Reims 174
Albert the Great 4–5
Alexander of Hales 16
Ambrose 188, 197n59, 199, 201, 215
animals
  cognition in 31n13, 48, 50, 81
  intentions of 30, 31, 32
Anscombe, Elizabeth 42, 53n10, 56n15, 65n9
  on intention 21–2n1, 25n4, 29–30, 35, 37, 40
Anselm of Canterbury
  beauty and redemption 163–4
  on devil's ransom and devil's rights 165–6, 196–7, 229–30, 235
    rejection of 146–7, 148, 165–6, 167, 169n6, 179
  on God's will and Christ's crucifixion 145–6, 148–62, 226–7n186
  interpretation of Christ's crucifixion 12, 13, 15, 17, 145–67, 179–80, 181, 231–2, 241
    evaluation of 162–7, 179–80, 231–2, 241
  Lambeth fragments 148–9n10
  problem of God's apparent injustice to his Son 145, 147–62, 163, 164, 165, 167–8, 179
  see also Abelard, Peter, response to Anselm; redemption, theories of, Anselm's
Anselm of Laon 196
Antony of the Desert 201n80
apostles 107–8, 113n29, 130, 188n18
  see also John, Gospel of; Luke, Gospel of; Mark, Gospel of; Matthew, Gospel of; Paul; Peter
Apostles' Creed 204
Aquinas, Thomas 43n3, 46n5, 54–5n13, 212n125
  on Abraham's sacrifice of Isaac 86–7
  and double effect reasoning, 61–3, 65–9
  ethics of 42, 44n4
  on God's will and Christ's crucifixion 5, 145–6n2
  on intention 21–2n1, 25n5
  on killing in self-defense 61–3, 65–9
Aristotle 21–2n1, 29n10, 42, 49n7, 57, 89

asceticism 59, 160n37
aspects 77, 82
  effects distinguished from 26n6, 32–3
  foreseen 29, 51
  intending of 26, 27, 37, 38
  nonintended 51n9
  physical 63n6, 67
  see also action(s), human; consequences; effects
Athanasius 201, 210, 222
atonement 190n31, 233
  difference between redemption and 236
Attridge, Harold W. 204n91
Augustine 6, 36n15, 191, 199n70, 202
  on devil's ransom and devil's rights 188, 193–4, 197n59, 209, 212n126
Aulén, Gustaf, *Christus Victor* theory of redemption 12, 192n44, 230, 234

Bailey, Kenneth E. 124n44, 125, 126, 127
baptism 102–3, 219n154
  of infants 175, 187–8
  symbolizing Christ's death 218–20, 224–5
Barsanuphius 201
Barth, Karl 2–3
Baruch, Book of 183
Basil 188, 190n29
Bauckham, Richard 124n44, 126–7
Bayer, Hans F. 105n16
beauty, redemption and 163–4, 166–7, 179
Bede 199n70, 200
being 43–5, 55, 56
  see also human beings
Bennett, Jonathan 63n5
Bernard of Clairvaux 168, 197–8
bioethics 63n6
  see also ethics
Blackburn, Simon 54–5n13
body, human
  movements of 24, 25–6, 40, 71
  soul's union with 211, 224, 225n179
  see also human beings
Bonaventure 5
Bratman, Michael 36n17
Bultmann, Rudolf 96, 120, 124, 127
Burridge, Richard A. 120n41
Byrskog, Samuel 124n44, 126, 127

Caiaphas 138–9
Cajetan, Tommaso de Vio 65
captivity 169, 185, 206n103
  see also slavery
Casey, Maurice 111n25
Castañeda, Hector-Neri 28n8
Cavanaugh, Thomas 29n9, 61n1, 64
Celsus 203–4n90
Chalcedon, Council of 7, 10, 158
charity, inspired by crucifixion 9, 167, 172–80, 231
  see also love
chirographum, humanity's 190–1, 193, 210
  see also sin(s)
Chisholm, Roderick M. 28n8, 36n15
choice
  free 22, 23, 83, 113, 222
  natural inclinations and 44, 47
  see also free will; rational choice
Chow, Simon 105n16
Christ, *see* Jesus Christ
Clement of Alexandria 204
cognition 31n13, 32, 50, 54–5n13, 81
Colossians, epistle 185–6, 190, 218
Colwell, Ernest Cadman 214n134
commanding, God's 84–8, 101, 111, 134, 150–8
common good 54, 75
confession, sacramental 160n37
conscience 57, 58
consequences 118, 229
  of crucifixion 88–9, 131
  foreseen 51–3
  moral value of 10, 85
  of original sin 172–3
  positive outweighing negative 151n15, 161–2, 165
  see also action(s), human; aspects; effects
Constas, Nicholas 203n89
Council of Bari 163n41
Councils of Constantinople, Second and Third 6, 7–8
covenant 110, 134
creation, God's will revealed in 14, 84, 85, 92, 222
crucifixion, Christ's 107–8, 152, 165, 215, 238–9
  Abelard on 12, 13, 15–16, 17, 168–80, 181, 231–2, 241
  Anselm on 12, 13, 15, 17, 145–67, 179–80, 181, 231–2, 241
  aspects willed by God 89–91, 92
  charity inspired by 9, 167, 172–80, 231
  Christ's provocation of 91, 92, 117–19
  deception of the devil regarding 166, 198–203, 207, 226, 229, 234
  devil conquered by 181–3, 187, 193–5, 200, 203, 221, 228
  devil's orchestration of 190, 192, 205, 229, 235
  devil's ransom interpretation of 15–16, 146–7, 148, 165–6, 167–71, 176–7, 178, 179, 181–239, 241
  in God's plan of salvation 162–3

justification through 169–71, 172, 191
necessity of 140–42, 162–3, 168, 179–80, 230
New Testament evidence about 1–3, 14–15, 235–6
ontology of 89, 141–2, 160–2
parables of 98, 103
patristic authors on 9, 12, 181n1, 192n44, 229, 230–1
salvation and 13, 89, 132–42, 145, 149, 153–4, 159–61, 189, 230–1
theological interpretations of 5, 10, 11, 12–13, 15–17, 86
Trinity's ordaining of 152n18, 153–4, 155, 157n27, 232
see also intentions, God's, and Christ's crucifixion; redemption, theories of; salvation; will, God's, and Christ's crucifixion
crucifying, of Christ 198, 200, 232
devil's overreaching by 146, 166, 187
God's will and 23, 88–92, 142, 145–6n2, 152–3, 162, 167, 231, 233, 239
moral evil of perpetrators 10, 132, 138–40, 141, 142, 164, 171n10
not intended or willed by God 88–92, 136–40, 142
see also will, God's, and Christ's crucifixion
Cur Deus homo (Anselm of Canterbury), *see* Anselm of Canterbury, interpretation of Christ's crucifixion
Cyprian 204
Cyril of Alexandria 200, 215
Cyril of Jerusalem 188, 201, 206, 215, 220, 230

Daniel, Book of 111
David 114–15, 116, 140
Davies, Brian 10–11n23
death
Christ's crucifixion liberating mankind from 2, 9, 16, 187, 207n107, 210n120, 219, 223–4, 229, 231–2, 236–7
devil associated with 193, 226, 227–8
evil of 222, 223
God's triumph over 92n4, 192n4, 228
nonintended 29, 50, 67, 69–70, 71, 77, 79
Old Testament portrayals of 210
as separation from God 211, 238
see also self-defense; self-sacrifice; suicide
death, Christ's
baptism symbolizing 218–20, 224–5
God's intentions and 136–40, 162, 231
God's will and 3–4, 148, 151–3, 155, 158–9, 165–6
Jonah story alluding to 104–5, 202, 213–14, 216, 221
necessity of 116–17, 118–19, 128, 169
see also crucifixion, Christ's; crucifying, of Christ; Jesus Christ, attitude toward own death; sin(s), Christ's expiation of; will, God's, and Christ's crucifixion
Demosthenes 185
departure, Christ's references to 102, 109
descent to the dead, Christ's 203–6, 220, 231
desire(s)
actions and 48, 49, 54–5
agents' capacity for 27–8, 46, 49n7
Aquinas on 43n3, 54–5n13
of Christ to die for humanity's salvation 157–8
inner structure of 46–7, 54–5, 58, 59, 85
intention and 27, 30, 31, 81
moral judgments and 55–6, 58
see also natural inclination(s); rational desire
Deutero-Isaiah, *see* Isaiah, Book of
devil, the 211
baptism's exorcism of 187–8
Christ's conquest of 181–3, 187, 193–5, 200, 203, 221, 228
death associated with 193, 226, 227–8
dramatic tension between God and 165–6, 182, 183–4
God's deception of 166, 198–203, 207, 226, 229, 233, 234
God's triumph over 186, 194, 207, 208, 234
injustice of 191, 200, 225, 226–7, 228
orchestration of Christ's crucifixion 190, 192, 205, 229, 235
overreaching by 146, 166, 187
power of 169–70, 182, 187–8, 194, 197, 208, 229
among rulers of this age 198–9
see also evil
devil's ransom interpretation of the crucifixion 181–239
Abelard's rejection of 168, 169–71, 176–7, 178, 179, 197
Anselm on 146–7, 148, 165–6, 167, 169n6, 179, 196–7, 229–30, 235, 241
crucifixion and 15–16, 186, 212–13, 231, 241
divine unity in 238–9
in the early church 9, 12, 186–221
Christ's descent to the dead 203–6, 220, 231
and devil's rights 189–98
God's deception of the devil 166, 198–203, 207, 226, 229, 234
harrowing of hell 203–6
internal critique of 206–9
metaphor's role in 209–12, 228, 230, 235

devil's ransom interpretation of the crucifixion (*cont.*)
 sign of Jonah as key 212–21
 evaluating 231–9, 240
 Gregory of Nyssa and the *Catechetical Oration* 181, 221–8
 as metaphor 209–12, 228, 230, 235
 New Testament origins 181–6, 187, 235–7
 success of 13, 16–17
 see also devil's rights; ransom saying
devil's rights 16, 227
 Abelard on 176–7
 Anselm on 165–6, 196
 in early church 9, 12, 189–98, 205, 209–13, 227
 see also devil's ransom interpretation of the crucifixion
disciples, *see* Apostles
double effect reasoning 14, 61–79
 Anselm's use of 145, 151, 159, 163
 Aquinas and 61–3, 65–9
 and Christ's crucifixion 90–1
 and devil's ransom interpretation 231–2
 ethics and 241
  of self-defense and 65–9
  of self-sacrifice and 74–9, 80, 90–1
 Gregory of Nyssa's use of 226–7n186
 hit-man scenario and 71–2
 hostage scenario and 70
 intention and 21–2n1, 63n6
 military targets and 69–70, 77
 moral analysis and 41, 64–72
 origins of 61–4, 65–6
Dragas, George Dion 210n119
Dunn, James D. G. 125n46

effects
 aspects distinguished from 26n6, 32–3
 foreseen 28–9, 51, 69
 future 56
 ignorance of 29n9
 intended 26, 51, 55, 65, 67, 70, 72–3, 76–7
 means-end formulations and 37
 negative 51, 55, 61, 63–4
 negative outweighing positive 52, 75
 positive outweighing negative 51–2, 54–5, 56, 60, 68–70, 73, 76, 78, 85–6, 151n15
 unintended 29–30, 39, 51n8
 see also action(s), human; aspects; consequences; nonintended effects; side effects, nonintended
Eire, Carlos M. N. 128n59
Elijah 100, 102, 104–5, 202
ends 38–41, 49n7
 see also means-end formulations
Ephrem, on will of the Trinity 6
epistles, *see individual epistles*
ethics 10, 21, 46, 54, 178, 234
 Aquinas on 42, 44n4
 bioethics 63n6
 faith and 87–8
 of self-defense 65–9
 of self-sacrifice 74–9, 80, 90–1, 241
 virtue 42, 59, 63
Eucharist 101, 109–10, 129–30, 210n120, 225
Eucherius of Lyons 191
Eusebius of Caesarea 188, 209, 210
evaluation, *see* action, human, evaluation of; moral evaluation
evangelists
 information conveyed by 97–8, 101n9
 portrayal of Christ 111, 113, 115n32, 118–19
 on prayer in Garden of Gethsemane 133
 pursuit of truth 124, 127–9
 on sign of Jonah 104, 117n36
 sources used by 124–7
 see also John, Gospel of; Luke, Gospel of; Mark, Gospel of; Matthew, Gospel of
Eve 172–4, 191
 see also original sin
evil 223, 226
 Christ's overcoming of 9, 164, 186, 231, 236, 237
 fishhook metaphor of 225–6
 God's triumph over 80, 192n44, 229–30, 232, 234–5, 238
 human 10, 92
 role in salvation 165, 233–4, 238, 239
 see also devil, the; moral evil
existentialism 46
eyewitness testimony 121, 122, 124n44, 126–7
 see also Gospels, historicity of portrayals in

faith 99, 106
 Christian 183, 185, 186n15, 214n134, 222, 224–5, 233
 Jewish 80, 87–8, 183
Father, *see* God the Father
Finnis, John 29n9
First Corinthians, epistle 130, 196
First Peter, epistle 141, 204
fishhook metaphor 201–3, 210, 220
 and devil's ransom interpretation 206, 207, 221
 of evil 225–6, 227
 see also God the Father, devil deceived by
Fitzmyer, Joseph A. 220n158
Foot, Philippa 62n4
forgiveness

Christ's 170, 230, 236
God's 174, 223, 239
of sins 110, 187
free will 22, 191, 222, 226, 233
freedom 58, 169, 183–4, 185, 232–3
human 158, 193n45
true 172, 177–8
see also death, Christ's crucifixion liberating mankind from
Fulgentius Ferrandus 201

Galatians, epistle 133–4, 135–6, 185
Gerhardsson, Birger 125, 126n48
Gethsemane, Christ's prayer in
cup metaphor 1, 101–3, 109, 116, 133, 151, 157, 160, 240
for Father's will 1, 6–8, 133, 151, 166, 240
provoking the devil by 200
Gilbert Crispin 196
Girard, René, scapegoat theory of redemption 3, 4, 9, 91n12, 234–5
God the Father 11, 172, 189, 233
apparent injustice to Son 3–4, 5
Abelard on 168, 169, 170, 179
Anselm on 145, 147–62, 163, 164, 165, 167–8, 179
commanding by 84–8, 101, 111, 134, 150–8
devil deceived by 166, 198–203, 207, 226, 229, 233, 234
devil's conflict with 165–6, 182, 183–4, 186, 208, 209
dramatic tension between Christ and 156, 165–6, 238
forgiveness of 174, 223
honor of restored 160–1, 164, 166n44, 171, 179
intending by 81, 83
justice of 190–1, 194, 197, 225–6, 226–7n186, 228, 238
love from 159, 168, 175, 180
mercy of 238, 239
power of 190, 191
provocation of evil by 229–30, 232, 238
ransom of 165–6, 167, 179, 184
reconciliation with 172, 236n195
will of 5–8, 81
wisdom of 190, 199, 225–6, 226–7n186, 228
see also goodness, God's; intentions, God's, and Christ's crucifixion; salvation, God's plan of; Trinity; will, God's, and Christ's crucifixion
God the Son, *see* Jesus Christ
good, the 48–9, 50–1, 52, 57–9, 60
see also common good
good shepherd, Christ as 109, 114–15, 201, 236–7
goodness 43, 223
Christ's 89–90, 164
God's 10–11, 80, 82, 85, 88–9, 92, 165, 225, 226–7n186, 228, 232–4
Gortyn, law code of 185
Gospel of Nicodemus 204
Gospels
Christ's interpretation of his death in 109–19
on clash of intentions 138
devil's ransom interpretation's origins in 182, 235–6
on Father's will 132–3
historicity of portrayals in 95–7, 111, 119–31
Christ's historical attitude 128–31
evaluating claims of 120–3
eyewitness testimony used in 121, 122, 124n44, 126–7
literary genre of 119–20
reliability of sources 124–7
resurrection prophecies in 216, 217
and story of Jonah 214
see also narratives, theological; synoptic Gospels; *and individual Gospels*
grace 158, 172, 191
from baptism 224–5
through Christ 210n120, 211
Gratian, *Decretum* 196n56
Greece, ancient, slaves buying freedom in 184–5, 185–6
Gregory of Nazianzus 6, 192n44
on devil's ransom 206–7, 208, 209
Gregory of Nyssa 6, 7, 201, 221, 226–7n186
Catechetical Oration 181, 221–8
on devil's ransom and devil's rights 188, 192n44
Gregory Thaumaturgus 188, 201n80, 201n81, 202, 204
Gregory the Great 195, 199–200, 201
guilt 2, 23, 138, 172–4

happiness 54–5, 58, 75, 173
Harman, Gilbert 39n18
Harnack, Adolf 161
Hays, Richard B. 115n32
Hebrews, epistle 134
hell, harrowing of 203–6
see also descent to the dead, Christ's
Heloise 173
Hengel, Martin 127
Heraclitus 126
Hesychius of Jerusalem 215
Hilary of Poitiers 215
Hippolytus 204

historicity, *see* Gospels, historicity of portrayals in
Holy Spirit 109, 140
joining to Christ through 231, 236, 238–9
see also Trinity
Hooker, Morna 112n27
Hosea 216, 217
human beings 31n13, 81, 83
see also body, human
human nature 45–6, 49, 54, 57–8, 224–5
humanity 92, 161, 179
chirographum of 190–1
Christ's 158–9, 172, 183–4, 223, 238
devil's power over 188, 189, 190, 194, 208, 212, 227, 229
God's ownership of 185–6, 192
redemption of 145, 230, 233
restoration of 151–2, 153, 154, 156, 224–5, 227–8, 230, 239
sins of 160–1, 183–4
see also action(s), human; soul, human
Hume, David 54–5n13
is-ought problem 56–7
hunger strikes 79
see also protests, moral value of; self-sacrifice

idol worship 183
Ignatius of Antioch 188, 199, 204
ignorance 22–3, 29n9, 58
Incarnation
Anselm's explanation of 147n6, 147n8
death overcome through 224, 227
necessity of 4–5, 162–3, 169, 175
redemption through 153n20, 154–5, 156, 210n120, 223
inclination(s), *see* natural inclination(s)
injustice, devil's 191, 200, 225, 226–7, 228
see also God the Father, apparent injustice to Son
institution narratives 129–30, 131
see also Eucharist
intellect 48, 50
intending 14, 21, 23, 240
agent's 38, 41
aspects of 26, 27, 37, 38
categories of 81–2n1
divine *vs.* human 81
foreseen effects of 28–9
God's 81, 83
nonrational 32, 81
ontology of 37, 41, 91
rational 32, 41, 80–1
willing and 32–3, 41, 134–35
intention(s)
bodily movements related to 24, 25–6, 33–4, 63n6, 71
of Christ regarding crucifixion 11, 90–1, 92
clash of, in New Testament 137, 138–9
hidden 27, 34
intuitions regarding 23, 27, 61, 72–3
isolated from intentional action 33–41
issues surrounding 6, 21–2n1
judging acts of deception by 226–7n186
knowledge and 27, 30, 31, 34, 80–1
language of 26–7, 28, 30, 40–1, 65
limit cases and 27
logic of 26–30, 37, 232
moral value and 65–72, 72–3, 80
nonrational 30–1
ontology of 22–6, 30, 34–5, 37, 39, 232
rational 30–3
transivity of 28–9, 30
see also action(s), human, intentional
intentions, God's, and Christ's crucifixion 134–40, 151
in giving over his Son 136–40, 189, 232
in sending his Son 135–6, 156n26, 224, 231–2
intuitions
regarding God's will and Christ's crucifixion 1, 82
regarding human actions 23, 85
regarding intentions 23, 27, 61, 72–3
regarding moral value 59, 61, 64–5
regarding redemption theories 9–10
see also moral intuitions
Irenaeus 2, 191, 204
on devil's ransom 188, 209
on sign of Jonah 202, 214, 215
Isaac, Abraham's sacrifice of 86–8, 103n11
Isaiah, Book of, Christ's fulfillment of 113–14, 184, 203
see also servant songs, Christ's fulfillment of
is-ought problem 56–7

Jeremiah, prophecies of 55, 110, 113, 114
Jeremias, Joachim 105n16
Jerome 188, 199n70, 215
Jerusalem, Christ's predictions regarding destruction of 106–7
Jesus Christ
descended from David's line 114–15, 116
descent to the dead 203–6, 220, 231
devil conquered by 181–3, 187, 193–4, 203, 221, 228
divinity hidden from the devil 198, 199, 226
dramatic tension between God and 156, 165–6, 238
forgiveness of sins by 170, 230, 236
God's commands to 84–8, 101, 111, 134, 150–8

goodness of 89–90, 164
as good shepherd 109, 114–15, 201, 236–7
heroism of self-sacrifice 134, 145, 148, 158–60, 164, 166, 171, 176, 179, 232
Jonah as type of 214, 215
as Lamb of God 200–1
love of 172, 179
martyrs as imitators of 188–9
as New Adam 189, 207n107
obedience by 7, 134, 150, 154, 156, 161, 191
provocation by 153, 231, 232, 233, 234, 236
return of 106, 109, 224
transfiguration of 102, 103n11
two natures in 10, 156, 158–9, 162, 172, 223, 238
virtues manifested by 89–90, 152, 166n44, 211
see also Incarnation; Trinity
Jesus Christ, attitude toward own death 95–131
acceptance 101, 150, 153–4, 160, 166n44, 180
advances personal mission 99, 109–11, 119, 128–31, 140–1, 162, 178, 180, 231, 241
desired for world's salvation 157–8
Gospel portrayals of 97–119
historical view of 95–7, 128–31
intentionality of 11, 90–1, 92, 95, 153, 237
as necessity 116–17, 118–19
persevering unto 177–8, 180
provocation of opponents 91, 92, 117–19
violence of expected 95–8, 101–4, 109–10, 128–9, 130, 162
see also crucifixion, Christ's; intentions, God's, and Christ's crucifixion; passion, Christ's; prophecies, Christ's; suffering, Christ's; will, God's, and Christ's crucifixion
Job 184, 202, 203
John the Baptist 99, 100, 200–1
John Chrysostom 188, 201n81, 215
on God's deception of the devil 199n70, 201
John Damascene 201, 206, 207, 210
John, Gospel of 115, 118, 183
on clash of intentions 138–9
Father's will in 132–3
good shepherd theme in 236–7
on necessity of crucifixion 117, 141
passion alluded to 108–9, 116
on rebuilding the Temple 117–18n36
temple cleansing narrative in 113n30, 114
John the Presbyter 127
Jonah
in early Christian art 213–14, 215, 220
in Jewish commentary 105n15, 105n16, 214–15
sign of 104–5, 111, 117–18n36, 202–3, 205–6, 212–21
as type of Christ 214, 215
Josephus 104n13
Judaism 80, 110
on Abraham's sacrifice 86, 88
commentary on Jonah 105n15, 105n16, 214–15
Judas, betrayal by 5, 136–7, 138, 182
Christ's predictions regarding 100–1, 115
Christ's words to 118, 138, 234
necessity of 140, 233–4
role of 1, 2–3
Judas, Gospel of 2
justice
Christ persevering in 150–2, 153, 155, 156n26, 158, 159, 166n44
God's 190–1, 194, 197, 225–6, 226–7n186, 228, 238
poetic 191–2
Justin Martyr 204, 214, 215, 217

Kant, Immanuel 62n4, 87
Kierkegaard, Soren 84, 87
Kirwan, Michael 234n192
knowledge 23, 32, 46, 58, 69, 156, 229
intention and 27, 30, 31, 34, 80–1

language 209, 236
ambiguities in 71–2
of intention 21, 26–7, 28, 30, 40–1, 65
of moral value 57, 65
of ransom 184–6, 236
of willing 21, 32, 81
see also metaphor
Last Supper
Christ's predictions during 100–1, 109–10, 112, 115–16
words to Judas 118, 138, 234
institution of Eucharist at 101, 109–10, 129–30
Legaspi, Michael 210n122
Leo the Great 191, 197n59, 199
Letter of the Church of Lyons and Vienne 189, 202
Leviathan 202–3
life 59
eternal 111, 116, 174, 175, 211
see also self-sacrifice
logic, of intention 26–30, 37, 232
love 177–8, 223
Christ's 172, 179
God's 159, 168, 175, 180
see also charity, inspired by crucifixion

Luke, Gospel of 117, 199
  resurrection prophecies in 115, 216, 218
  on sign of Jonah 104, 111, 117–18n36, 217–18

MacCulloch, J. A. 204n91
MacIntyre, Alasdair 42, 53n10
McIntyre, John 148–9n10
Magnes, Macarius 200
Mangan, Joseph T. 63–4
Manichaeism 235
mankind, *see* humanity
Marcion 204
Mark, Gospel of 115, 126
  ransom saying in 96, 110–11, 117, 236
  resurrection prophecies in 216–17, 218
Martyrdom of Montanus and Lucius, The 209
martyrs 188–9, 202, 205n99, 209
Mary, Virgin 191
Massacio, *The Holy Trinity* 238–9
Matthew, Gospel of 115, 117, 118
  on the sign of Jonah 104, 105, 111, 117–18n36, 202, 217, 220n157, 221
Maximus the Confessor 7–8
means-end formulations
  and Christ's crucifixion 90, 91, 153, 232
  determining intentions based on 36–8, 77
  double effect reasoning and 67, 69–70, 71
Meier, John P. 129n62
Melito of Sardis 204
mercy, divine 238, 239
messianic kingdom, establishment of 113, 114, 116
metaphor 2, 117, 181, 200, 212n125, 242
  of baptism 102–3
  devil's ransom 184, 186, 209–12, 228, 230, 235
  language of 195–6
  see also fishhook metaphor; Gethsemane, Christ's prayer in, cup metaphor
Mews, Constant J. 173n21, 174n30
moral analysis 23, 38, 41
  see also double effect reasoning
moral evil 43, 48–50, 54–5, 70–2, 166, 222
  God's will and 4n7, 9–10, 13, 80–92, 138, 146, 163–4, 168, 177–8, 180, 231–2
moral goodness 54–5, 61, 67, 68, 84, 223
moral intuitions 86, 88
  double effect reasoning and 68–9
  judging acts of deceptions by 226–7n186
  moral value and 52–6, 72
  see also intuitions
moral judgments 42, 49n7, 52–3, 55–6, 57
moral obligation 42, 56–60
moral theory 61–2, 70, 85–6
  see also double effect reasoning
moral value 14, 42–60
  double effect reasoning and 64–72
  God's will and 84, 92
  intention and 65–73, 80
  moral evil and 48–50
  moral intuitions and 52–6, 59–60, 61
  moral obligation and 42, 56–60
  natural inclination as measure of 43–7
  nonintended effects and 50–2
  ontology of 42–3, 82, 92
  of protests 77–8, 79
  see also action(s), human, moral value of
morality 54, 87
Moses 102, 104, 110, 111, 184

narratives, theological
  of the crucifixion 13–14, 15, 73, 74, 79, 80, 95, 164, 165
  and God's willing of moral evil 9–10, 84, 88–90, 92
  institution of the Eucharist 129–30, 131
  of patristic authors 179, 183, 226–7n186, 228
  temple cleansing 113n30, 114
natural inclination(s)
  advancing 46, 49–50, 51n9, 52, 57, 59, 72, 75
  frustrating 45, 49–51, 60, 67, 72, 75, 79, 84–5, 87, 92
  moral value grounded in 43–7, 54–5, 56, 59
  to self-preservation 67, 68, 75
nature, *see* human nature; Jesus Christ, two natures in
necessity, logical 28–9, 38, 232
necessity, ontological 28–9, 38, 92, 142, 160, 232, 239
  see also crucifixion, Christ's, necessity of; salvation, crucifixion necessary for
New Testament 210, 214
  Christ's descent to the dead 203–4
  on crucifixion 1–2, 3, 13, 132–42, 154, 178, 180, 235–6
  devil's ransom interpretation's origins in 181–6, 187, 235–7
  evidence from 11, 14–15, 132–4, 162
  Father's will in 133–40
  redemption in 155, 184, 241–2
  resurrection prophecies in 216, 217, 218
  see also Gospels; *and individual epistles and Gospels*
Nicene Creed 204
Nietzsche, Friedrich 58–9, 212
nonintended effects 27–30
  of evil actions 83
  intended effects and 55, 65, 76
  moral value and 50–2, 69–70

negative 51n9, 60, 61, 75, 151n15
see also side effects, nonintended

Oates, Captain Lawrence 78
Ockham's razor 68, 131
Old Testament
Christ's death as fulfillment of 111–16
portrayals of death in 210
ransom language in 184, 185
on redemption of the righteous 169, 172, 205
see also Abraham, sacrifice of Isaac by; Adam; David; Elijah; Eve; Isaiah, Book of, Christ's fulfillment of; Job; Jonah; Moses; original sin; psalms, Christ's suffering prophesied in
Olsen, Glenn W. 163n42
ontology
of actions 24, 25, 35, 43, 51, 57, 67
of the crucifixion 89, 141–2, 160–2
of intending 37, 41, 91
of intention 22–6, 30, 34–5, 37, 39, 232
moral value grounded in 42–3, 82, 92
and necessity 28–9, 92, 160
oral tradition, scriptural 124–7
Origen
on *chirographa* 190–1, 193, 210
on Christ's descent to the dead 204
on devil's ransom 188, 209, 210–11, 229
on God's deception of the devil 200n75
on God's justice 191–2
on sign of Jonah 206, 215, 221
original sin 86–7, 172–4, 188n20, 194
ownership, biblical concept of 184–6

Page, Sydney 112n27
parables 98, 102–3, 106, 130–1
passion 54–5n13, 89, 182
passion, Christ's 165, 175, 186
Christ's predictions of 96–7, 99–101, 102, 103, 111, 116
God's willing of 145–6n2
Gospel narratives of 108–9, 116, 164
necessity of 152, 160, 172
sign of Jonah related to 214n134, 215
see also crucifixion, Christ's; crucifying, of Christ; Gethsemane, Christ's prayer in
patristic authors
on baptism 187–8, 219–21
on Christ's descent to the dead 204–6
on the crucifixion 9, 12, 181n1, 192n44, 229, 230–1
on devil's ransom 188–9, 206–9, 209–12, 213, 227, 235, 241–2
on devil's rights 189–98, 211–12
on God's deception of the devil 199–200, 201–2, 234
on humanity's *chirographum* 190–1
on Jonah 205–6, 214–15, 221
on resurrection 217, 230
on will of the Trinity 6–8
see also individual authors
Paul
on baptism 218–20, 220
on Christ's crucifixion 140, 186
on death 211
on the devil 182, 198
on the Eucharist 225n179
on faith in Christ 183, 185
on humanity's *chirographum* 190–1
on resurrection prophecies 216
see also First Corinthians, epistle; Galatians, epistle; Romans, epistle
Peter 126
on Christ's crucifixion in Acts and First Peter 135, 140, 141
on resurrection 215–16
see also First Peter, epistle
Philippians, epistle 134
philosophy 21, 59
moral 54–5n13, 65
see also Aristotle
Pilate 136, 137, 138–9
Pitcher, George 28n8
pluralism 54, 56
Polycarp 204
power
of the devil 169–70, 182, 187–8, 194, 197, 208, 229
of God 190, 191
will to 58–9
predestination 135
principle of double effect, *see* double effect reasoning
Proclus of Constantinople
on Christ's descent to the dead 206n103, 209–10
on God's deception of the devil 201, 202
prophecies, Christ's
of death 99–101, 111–16, 179, 217, 220–1n159
of rejection 99, 100, 101, 102n10, 103, 107, 114, 115, 116n35
of the resurrection 97, 99, 102, 109, 215, 216, 217
of suffering 113n29, 113n30, 115–16
protests, moral value of 77–8, 79
provocation 77–8, 240
by Christ 91, 92, 117–19, 153, 231–4, 236
God's deliberate 9, 200, 229–30, 232, 233

psalms, Christ's suffering prophesied in 113n29, 113n30, 115–16
Pseudo-Ambrose 145n1
Pseudo-Athanasius, on God's deception of the devil 200, 201, 202

Quinn, Warren S. 62n4

ransom saying 9, 117, 184–6
  in Mark's Gospel 96, 102, 107, 110–11, 236
  see also devil's ransom interpretation of the crucifixion
rational choice 22, 32, 48–51, 57, 58, 232
  see also choice
rational desire 31, 32, 48–51
  see also desire(s)
rationality 31, 43
Ray, Kathleen Darby 234
reason 48, 50, 54–5n13
  see also double effect reasoning
redemption 155, 185, 220
  beauty and 163–4, 166–7, 179
  crucifixion necessary for 2–3, 135–6, 141, 145–6, 147n8, 172, 174, 178, 224, 230–3, 239
  difference between atonement or salvation and 236
  God's plan of 195, 207, 208, 222, 228, 229, 233
  through Incarnation 5, 156
  mechanics of 3–4, 5, 142, 148, 230–1
  origin of word 184, 236
  theology of 3, 4, 5, 214–15
  as transaction 165–6
redemption, theories of 9–10
  Abelard's 9, 168, 169, 171–8, 240, 241
  Anselm's 4–5, 9, 146–8, 160n37, 162, 164–5, 167, 171, 230–2, 238, 240–1
  Christus Victor 12, 192n44, 230, 234
  Girard's scapegoat 3, 4, 91n12, 234–5
  objectivist 168, 176, 177, 179
  penal substitution 4, 234
  subjectivist 168, 179
  see also crucifixion, Christ's; devil's ransom interpretation of the crucifixion; devil's rights
rejection
  Christ's experience of 164, 177, 233
  Christ's predictions of 99, 100, 101, 102n10, 103, 107, 114, 115, 116n35
restitution, acts of 160n37
resurrection, Christ's 141, 164, 186, 215, 217n148, 223n170, 236
  baptism in terms of 218–20
  Christ's predictions of 97, 99, 102, 109, 215, 216, 217
  death conquered through 219, 232
  devil's ransom and 189, 239
  humanity's restoration through 224–5, 227, 228, 230
  Jonah story alluding to 104–5, 111, 213–14, 216, 221
  salvation through 196, 223–5, 228, 230–1, 236
return, Christ's references to 106, 109, 224
Revelation, Book of 183, 203
rich man and Lazarus, parable of 103–4, 169
Riesenfeld, Harald 125
rights, legal, 196, 212
  see also devil's rights
Rivière, Jean 207n109
Romans, epistle 183, 218n153
Rufinus 201, 201n81
Rupert of Deutz 4–5n11, 155n23

sacraments
  joining with Christ through 229, 231, 236
  resurrection and 189, 224–5, 230
  see also confession, sacramental; Eucharist
sacrifice 74–5, 137
  see also Abraham, sacrifice of Isaac by; self-sacrifice
salvation
  Christ's work as ransom for 205, 210n120, 236n195
  crucifixion necessary for 1–3, 13, 15, 145, 149, 153–4, 158–62, 174–6, 179, 180, 183–4, 196
  devil's role in 186, 239
  difference between redemption and 236
  economy of 189, 199, 212, 214, 223–4, 232–4, 238–9
  evil's role in drama of 165, 239
  God's plan of 15, 89, 132–42, 197, 230, 231, 233
  through resurrection 196, 223–5, 228, 230–1, 236
Sanders, E. P. 129n61, 236n194
Satan, *see* devil, the
Scheck, Thomas 193n45
Schillebeeckx, Edward 3–4
Schmitt, F. S. 148–9n10, 197n59
Schopenhauer, Arthur 58, 59n21
Schwager, Raymond 3
Schweitzer, Albert 91
Scotus, John Duns 4–5, 87, 155
scripture
  divine willing and 148–9n10, 178
  oral tradition in 124–7
  see also New Testament; Old Testament
second coming, *see* return, Christ's references to

self-defense 61–3, 65–9, 71–2
self-sacrifice 11, 86, 129n62, 175
  ethics of 74–9, 80, 90–91, 241
  see also Jesus Christ, heroism of self-sacrifice
servant songs, Christ's fulfillment of 111–13, 116, 119, 136
  see also Isaiah, Book of, Christ's fulfillment of
side effects, nonintended 36n15, 37, 39–40, 50, 67, 70–71, 77–78
  see also effects; nonintended effects
sign of Jonah, *see* Jonah
sin(s) 182, 222
  Christ's expiation of 134–5, 141, 145, 148, 166n44, 168, 170–1, 176–7, 239
    through crucifixion 2, 15–16, 168, 180, 187, 229, 236
  devil's rights resulting from 190, 211
  forgiveness of 170, 187–8, 230, 236
  humanity's 160–1, 183–4
  ugliness of 164, 167
  see also chirographum, humanity's
slavery
  Christ's crucifixion liberating us from 172, 187
  devil's 190, 226
  of human soul 193n45
  Israel's 110, 183–7
  ransom from 184–5, 185–6
  redemption from 223, 236
  see also captivity
Son of God, *see* Jesus Christ
Son of Man, Christ's use of term 111
  see also Jesus Christ
soul, human 193n45, 211, 224–5
suffering 182, 222, 223
suffering, Christ's
  God's will and 89–90, 148, 152, 158–9
  necessity of 116–17, 141
  prophesies of 99–104, 107–8, 111, 113n29, 113n30, 115–16
  salvation through 162, 187
  for sins 135, 136, 239
  voluntary choice of 153–5, 158, 160, 163
suicide 50, 76, 78, 182
  not intended by Christ 10, 91, 153, 232
Symeon Metaphrastes 201
synoptic Gospels 108, 130
  on Christ's expectation of his death 98–108
  on Christ's fulfillment of scriptures 101, 115–16n33
  passion predictions in 99–100, 116–17
  sign of Jonah in 104–5, 220–1n159
  temple cleansing episode in 113n30, 114n31
  see also Luke, Gospel of; Mark, Gospel of; Matthew, Gospel of

teleology 42, 57
temple
  Christ's predictions regarding destruction of 106–7, 114
  cleansing episode in 113–14, 117
  rebuilding of 117–18n36
Tertullian 188, 204, 205n99, 217
Theodore of Mopsuestia 215
Theodoret of Cyrus 215
theologians and theology 5, 110, 160n37
  Ablelard's categories of 176–7
  Christian 7–8, 80, 81–2n1, 92, 236
  of the crucifixion 10, 11, 12–13, 15–17, 86
  medieval 195–8
  see also narratives, theological; patristic authors
Trinity
  Anselm as theologian of 153–4, 155, 156–7, 163n41
  Christ's crucifixion ordained by 152n18, 153–4, 155, 157, 232
  tension within 150, 163, 165–6
  unity of 6–8, 163, 165–6, 238–9
  see also God the Father; Holy Spirit; Jesus Christ
truth 23, 25, 92, 121–2
  Christ persevering in 90, 152, 153, 155
  evangelists' pursuit of 124, 127–9
Tyndale, William 236n195

unity, divine 6–8, 155, 156, 163, 165–6, 238–9

Vercundus of Junca 215
via negativa 13, 80, 181, 231
via positiva 14, 181, 231
vindication, Christ's predictions of 102n10, 103, 105, 108, 111
vineyard owner, parable of 103
violence 234, 240
  Christ's expectation of violent death 95–8, 101–4, 109–10, 128–9, 130, 162
virtue ethics 42, 59, 63
  see also Jesus Christ, virtues manifested by
Vitoria, Francisco de 66
von Balthasar, Hans Urs 163n42

will, God's 5–8, 136, 158, 161–2
  Christ's will differentiated from 5–8, 133, 156, 157
  moral value grounded in 84, 92
  see also moral evil, God's will and
will, God's, and Christ's crucifixion 1–5, 11, 88–91, 132–4
  Abelard on 177–8
  Anselm on 145–6, 148–62, 164
  Aquinas on 145–6n2

will, God's, and Christ's crucifixion (*cont.*)
  devil's ransom interpretation and 16–17, 231–5, 238–9
  moral evil and 80, 88–91
  New Testament evidence regarding 14–15, 132–4
  philosophical considerations of 13–14, 241
  problem of 1–5, 8–13, 15–17, 41
  see also crucifying, of Christ, God's will and; death, Christ's, God's will and; intentions, God's, and Christ's crucifixion
will, human 32, 58–9, 80–1, 158–9
  see also free will
Williams, Thomas 176n36
willing 9, 14, 21, 83, 156, 240
  categories of 81–2n1, 148–9n10
  divine *vs.* human 11, 41, 81–2
  intending and 32–3, 41, 134–5
Winling, Raymond 223n170
Winslow, Richard 207n107
wisdom
  God's 190, 199, 225–6, 226–7n186, 228
  moral judgments and 52
Wittgenstein, Ludwig 21–2n1, 24, 30, 64
Wright, N. T. 91n12, 106n19

Zechariah, prophecies of 110, 113, 114–15, 115n32